U.S.A. NI UMERETE

Born in the USA

Pacific Formations:
Global Relations in Asian
and Pacific Perspectives

Series Editor: Arif Dirlik

After Postcolonialism: Remapping Philippines–United States Confrontation
by E. San Juan, Jr.

Born in the USA: A Story of Japanese America, 1889–1947
edited by Frank Chin

Displacing Natives: The Rhetorical Production of Hawai'i
by Houston Wood

Chinese on the American Frontier
edited by Arif Dirlik with the assistance of Malcolm Yeung

Encounters: People of Asian Descent in the Americas
edited by Roshni Rustomji-Kerns with Rajini Srikanth and
Leny Mendoza Strobel

Inside Out: Literature, Cultural Politics, and Identity in the New Pacific
edited by Vilsoni Hereniko and Rob Wilson

Surviving the City: The Chinese Immigrant Experience in New York, 1890–1970
by Xinyang Wang

Teaching Asian America: Diversity and the Problem of Community
edited by Lane Ryo Hirabayashi

Voyaging through the Contemporary Pacific
edited by David L. Hanlon and Geoffrey M. White

What Is in a Rim? Critical Perspectives on the Pacific Region Idea, 2d edition
edited by Arif Dirlik

U.S.A. NI UMERETE

Born in the USA

A STORY OF
JAPANESE AMERICA,
1889–1947

FRANK CHIN

ROWMAN & LITTLEFIELD PUBLISHERS, INC.

Lanham • Boulder • New York • Oxford

ROWMAN & LITTLEFIELD PUBLISHERS, INC.

Published in the United States of America
by Rowman & Littlefield Publishers, Inc.
A Member of the Rowman & Littlefield Publishing Group
4720 Boston Way, Lanham, Maryland 20706
www.rowmanlittlefield.com

12 Hid's Copse Road
Cumnor Hill, Oxford OX2 9JJ, England

British Library Cataloguing in Publication Information Available

Library of Congress Cataloging-in-Publication Data

Born in the USA: A story of Japanese America, 1889-1947 / Frank Chin.
    p. cm. – (Pacific formations)
    Includes bibliographical references and index.
    ISBN 0-7425-1851-5 (alk. paper) – ISBN 0-7425-1852-3 (pbk. : alk. paper)
    1. Japanese Americans—History—Miscellanea. I. Chin, Frank, 1940- II. Series.

E184.J3 S84 2002
973'.04951—dc21   2002001878

Printed in the United States of America

♾™ The paper used in this publication meets the minimum requirements of
American National Standard for Information Sciences—Permanence of Paper for
Printed Library Materials, ANSI/NISO Z39.48-1992.

JOHN DOS PASSOS
THE "USA" TRILOGY
"THE 42ND PARALLEL"
"1919"
"THE BIG MONEY"

In December 1937
Hemingway and Steinbeck got the news:
It was done.

Contents

Introduction   xv

Part I: THE ISSEI

1. The Issei Are Here   3
   American Bookshelf Presents: BANZAI! by Parabellum (Theodor Weicher)   4

2. Shosuke Sasaki, Issei: Japanese American Conscience   5

3. James Omura, Nisei Newsman   11
   American Songbook Presents: Japanese Love Song   13

4. Sessue Hayakawa: Zen and the Movies   14
   American Bookshelf Presents: A Japanese Nightingale   17
   by Onoto Watanna (Winifred Eaton)
   Storytime for Children: Urashima Taro   19

5. Kentaro Takatsui, Kibei-Nisei: "I Have Pictures"   21
   American Bookshelf Presents: On the Duty of Civil Disobedience   22
   by Henry David Thoreau

6. Kentaro Takatsui, Kibei-Nisei: Japtown   24
   American Songbook Presents: I Want to Go to Tokio   33

7. Shosuke Sasaki, Japanese American Conscience: 34
   Father and the Prostitutes
   American Bookshelf Presents: The Story of the Caliph Stork   38
   by Wilhelm Hauff

8. Kentaro Takatsui, Kibei-Nisei: Paris Hotel, Seattle   40
   American Bookshelf Presents: Ford, The Universal Car   42

9. Kentaro Takatsui, Kibei-Nisei: The First Car   44
   American Songbook Presents: That Tango Tokio   46

10. Kentaro Takatsui, Kibei-Nisei: Picture of the Japanese Navy Visits   47

11. Dr. Clifford Uyeda, Traveler   49

12. Shosuke Sasaki, Japanese American Conscience: Higher Standards   50

13. Nobu Kawai, The Volunteer   53
    Storytime for Children: Momotaro, the Peach Boy   61

14. James Omura, Nisei Newsman: "All Mothers Cook"   63
    American Bookshelf Presents: Seed of the Sun by Wallace Irwin   68
    Issei Poem: A Bright Morning after the Rain by Shisei Tsuneishi   70

15. Paul Tsuneishi: "Dad Was Writing Haiku All His Life"   71

16. Frank Seishi Emi, Leader   72
    American Songbook Presents: Cherry Blossom   75

17. Gordon Hirabayashi, on Civil Disobedience: White Man's Country   76
    American Bookshelf Presents: The Pride of Palomar by Peter B. Kyne   84

18. Uhachi Tamesa: Early Seattle   86

19. Number One Hotel   93

20. Moving to Town   95
    American Songbook Presents: The Japanese Sandman Song   98

Part II: THE NISEI DREAM

21. The Nisei and the News   101
    Hot Off the Press! L.A. Japanese Daily News   102

22. James Omura, Nisei Newsman: Iron Chink   103
    Hot Off the Press! The Nikkei Shimin   105
    American Songbook Presents: Blinky Winky   108
    Shhh! Hush! Hush! Japanese American Courier   109
    Hot Off the Press! Japanese American Courier   111

23. James Sakamoto: JACL 1929-1930   112
    Hot Off the Press! Japanese American Courier   114

24. James Omura, Nisei Newsman: Omura and Sakamoto   115
    Hot Off the Press! Los Angeles Rafu Shimpo   117

25. James Omura, Nisei Newsman: Tajiri Was a Shrewd Poker Player   118
    American Bookshelf Presents: Her Father's Daughter   122
    by Gene Stratton-Porter
    Hot Off the Press! New World Daily   124

26. James Omura, Nisei Newsman: The Great Nisei Novel   125
    Hot Off the Press! New World Daily   126

27. James Omura, Nisei Newsman: "I'm like Popeye"   127
    American Bookshelf Presents: The Great American Novel   129
    by Clyde Brion Davis

28. James Omura, Nisei Newsman: Explotation—Betrayal—I Attacked It   131
    Hot Off the Press! Japanese American Courier.   132

29. Gordon Hirabayashi, on Civil Disobedience: "I Knew about   134
    James Sakamoto of Seattle"
    Hot Off the Press! New World Daily   135

30. Dr. Clifford Uyeda, Traveler   136
    American Bookshelf Presents: Honorable Spy Exposing Japanese   137
    Military Intrigue in the United States by John Spival
    Hot Off the Press! Rafu Shimpo   140
    Japanese American Citizens League Northwest Conference   149

31. Dr. Clifford Uyeda, Traveler: "There Was a JACL Convention"   150

32. Nobu Kawai, The Volunteer: Courting, Dating, and Radio   151

33. Gordon Hirabayashi, on Civil Disobedience: Golden   154

34. Frank Emi, Leader: Brothers and Sisters   163
    American Bookshelf Presents: Ford Manual Model T   167

35. Frank Emi, Leader: "Frank Showed Her How to Make Pumpkin Pie"   168
    Japanese American Citizens League Articles of Incorporation   172

36. Dr. Clifford Uyeda, Traveler: "I Really Didn't Have Any Ambition"   173

37. Tom Oki, Fair Play Committee: Cosmopolitan   174
    Hot Off the Press! Enter: "The Magazine for the American Born Japanese"   176
    Shhh! Hush! Hush! JACL Convention in Monterey   188
    Hot Off the Press! Current Life   189

Part III: DECEMBER 7, 1941—THE CLOSING PAPERS

38. Pearl Harbor Time   195
    American Bookshelf Presents: Artillary at the Golden Gate   196

39. Tom Oki, Fair Play Committee: December 7, 1941   199
    JACL Statement: by Joe Masaoka   202

40. Frank Emi, Leader: "Around Pearl Harbor Time"   203

41. Ike Matsumoto, Fair Play Committee: "Hey, Pearl Harbor's   204
    Getting Bombed!"
    Telegram   205

42. Ben Kuroki, Boy from Nebraska   206
    Hot Off the Press! Japanese American Courier   207
    American Songbook Presents: Remember Pearl Harbor   208
    Ameriocan Bijou Presents: Air Force   209

43. Ben Kuroki, Boy from Nebraska: "I Felt Guilty Because I   212
    Was of Japanese Ancestry"

44. Dave Kawamoto, Fair Play Committee   213

45. Gloria Kubota: Nisei and the Zen Man   214
    Hot Off the Press! Current Life   216

46. James Omura, Nisei Newsman: "The Age of the Nisei"   218
    Shhh! Hush! Hush! Mike Masaru Masaoka: "Mr. JACL"   219

47. Nobu Kawai, The Volunteer: "I Always Admired Mike Masaoka"   239

48. James Omura, Nisei Newsman: "I Pinned 'Sold Down the River'   242
    on the JACL"
    Hot Off the Press! Seattle Post-Intelligentser   246

49. Nobu Kawai, The Volunteer: "I Was President of the JACL Chapter"   247
    The JACL Anti-Axis Committee   251
    Hot Off the Press! Pasadena Star-News   253
    Shhh! Hush! Hush! The Japanese Question in the United States   255
    by Lt. Com. K. D. Ringle
    Hot Off the Press! Seattle Times   257
    "The Tolan Committee"   259

50. George Townsend, Project Director: "I Was Born and Raised   261
    in the Town Where John Dillinger Ended Up"
    Hot Off the Press! Japanese American Courier   269

51. Gordon Hirabayashi, on Civil Disobedience: 271
    "I Could Take a Stand"

52. James Omura, Nisei Newsman: "Tokie Slocum Was   277
    Rough and Gruff"
    "The Tolan Committee"   278
    Hot Off the Press! Rafu Shimpo   282

53. James Omura, Nisei Newsman: "Voluntary Evacuation"   283
    Hot Off the Press! Japanese American Courier/Seattle Times   286

54. Shosuke Sasaki, Japanese American Conscience: 288
    From His Diary

55. Shosuke Sasaki, Japanese American Conscience: 292
    Plot against Sakamoto's Life
    Hot Off the Press! Independence Day, 1942   294

56. Ike Matsumoto, Fair Play Committee   297

57. Yosh Kuromiya, Fair Play Committee   299
    Hot Off the Press!   300
    American Songbook Presents: Shhh! It's a Military Secret   302
    The WRA All-JACL Meeting   303

58. Nobu Kawai, The Volunteer: "We Attended the Convention"   305
    Shhh! Hush! Hush! War Department Military Intelligence Division   307
    American Bookshelf Presents: If He Hollers Let Him Go   309
    by Chester Himes
    Shhh! Hush! Hush! From the Files of the Project Director   310

59. Nobu Kawai, The Volunteer: Return to Gila   312
    The First Christmas in Camp: 1942:   314
    Manzanar, California
    Christmas at Heart Mountain by Floyd Schmoe   316

Part IV: US AND THEM

Shhh! Hush! Hush! Mike Masaoka: The JACL vs. Japanese America   321

60. Gordon Hirabayashi, on Civil Disobedience: 324
    "To Whom It May Concern"
    Shhh! Hush! Hush! Japanese Located in Strategic Areas   332

61. Kentaro Takatsui, Kibei-Nisei: Will You Volunteer for the Army?   337
    Will You Renounce Japan?

62. Joe Kurihara, Veteran from Hawaii   343
    War Relocation Authority: Application for Leave Clearance   349
    Statement of United States Citizen of Japanese Ancestry   354

63. Frank Emi and Frank Inouye   358

64. Nobu Kawai, The Volunteer: "Without a War Record I   365
    Wouldn't Have a Leg to Stand On"

65. Min Yasui, Resister or Turncoat?   367

66. Assimilation: Another Word for Racial Extinction?   368
    Hot Off the Press! The Pacific Citizen   369

67. Ben Kuroki, Boy from Nebraska: Mission over Ploesti   370

68. Dr. Clifford Uyeda, Traveler   372

69. James Wong Howe, American Cinematographer   374

70. Frank Emi, Leader: "Say, This Guy Knows What   378
    He's Talking About"

71. Shisei Tsuneishi: Block Head   380
    Restoration of the Draft: 1944   382

72. Frank Emi, Leader: "That's When I Took Over"   383
    Hot Off the Press! Rocky Shimpo   385

73. Gloria Kubota, Nisei and the Zen Man   387
    Fair Play Committee: February 24, 1944   388

74. Hajiime "Jim" Akutsu, "No-No Boy"   389

75. James Omura, Nisei Newsman: At the Denver *Rocky Shimpo*   391
    Hot Off the Press! Rocky Shimpo   392

76. Err-Rocky Shimpo!   396
    Fair Play Committee: March 4, 1944   397

77. Gloria Kubota, Nisei and the Zen Man   398
    Hot Off the Press! The Pacific Citizen   400

78. Mits Koshiyama, Fair Play Committee   401

79. Frank Emi, Leader: "You Got a Pass?"   402
    Hearing Board for Leave Clearance   403

80. Fair Play Frank Emi vs. JACL Nobu Kawai   415
    Letter to Kiyoshi Okamoto   423
    Hot Off the Press! Heart Mountain Sentinel   424

81. Gordon Hirabayashi, On Civil Disobedience: "I Got Off at Spokane" 425
   Hot Off the Press! Wedding Bells and Jail Cells 426
   Letter from Kiyoshi Okamoto 427

82. Frank Emi, Leader: Letter to a "No-No Boy" 428

83. Ben Kuroki, Boy from Nebraska: A Visit to Heart Mountain 433
   Song of Cheyenne, from a County Jail 436

84. Min Yasui, Resister or Turncoat? 438

85. Yosh Kuromiya, Fair Play Committee 439

86. Ike Matsumoto, Fair Play Committee 440

87. James Omura, Nisei Newsman: "Mr. Yasui Isn't In Yet" 441

88. Yosh Kuromiya, Fair Play Committee 443

89. Mits Koshiyana, Fair Play Committee 444

90. The Sixty-Three Men from Heart Mountain 445

91. Kozie Sakai: Letter to Frank Emi 446

92. Gloria Kubota, Nisei and the Zen Man 449

93. Arthur Emi, Little Brother 450

94. Frank Emi, Leader 451
   Hot Off the Press! Wyoming Tribune 452

95. Nobu Kawai, The Volunteer: "Am I In, or Am I Out?" 453
   Hot Off the Press! The Pacific Citizen 455

96. Frank Emi, Leader: A Surprise Witness 456
   Hot Off the Press: Wyoming Eagle 457

97. Frank Emi, Leader: "Why Was He Up There?" 458
   Hot Off the Press! Wyoming Tribune 459

98. Frank Emi, Leader: "We Lost Our Case" 460

99. James Omura, Nisei Newsman: "Vindicated as a Person, 461
   Vindicated in My Profession"
   Hot Off the Press! Wyoming Eagle 462

100. James Omura, Nisei Newsman: "It Was No Fun" 463

101. White Bigot, Where Are You? 464

102. Heart Mountain Fair Play Committee 466

103. Grace Kubota Ybarra, Daughter of Zen Man 468
   Hot Off the Press! Stars and Stripes 469

104. Frank Emi, Leader: "The Proudest Thing I Ever Did"   470
     Draft Resisters Pardoned, Convictions of Leaders Reversed   471

105. Hajiime "Jim" Akutsu, "No-No Boy"   472

106. James Wong Howe, American Cinematographer: "I Have a Story.   474
     It's a Beautiful Story."

Appendixes

     Numbers   479

     From Proclamation 2762   481

     After the War, What Happened to the JACL?   486

     To the Issei?   489

     To the Kibei-Nisei?   490

     To the Draft Resisters?   490

     To the Heart Mountain Fair Play Committee?   492

Index   495

About the Author   501

Introduction

On December 7, 1941, the world changed for Japanese America. The sneak attack on Pearl Harbor by the Imperial Japanese Navy gave the Nisei, second-generation Japanese in America, of the Japanese American Citizens League (JACL) the opportunity—or compelled them—to choose between Japan and the United States. For most of the Japanese Americans the choice had been made at their birth. A majority of Nisei saw the war as a difference in politics: Japanese politics against American politics. Politically, they favored America. Culturally, they were, in varying degrees, Japanese. But the Nisei were born in the United States. They were citizens from birth under the constitution. Some Nisei felt they owed this status to their parents, who had been barred from citizenship, for their forebearance of the laws arrayed against them. Others looked on their parents as a handicap to white acceptance.

This book looks at the war years of the late nineteenth century and the first half of the twentieth century through the words and lives of Nisei who saw their knowledge of Japanese as no threat to their legal status as American citizens. Shosuke Sasaki, an Issei, first-generation intellectual; James Omura, a Nisei journalist; Kentaro Takatsui, a Kibei-Nisei, a Nisei who had spent part of childhood in Japan, educated in Japan; Uhachi Tamesa, an Issei who made his fortune in America; and Frank Emi, a grocer and judo man, were all over the country blissfully and wistfully leading their separate lives until President Franklin Roosevelt imposed Executive Order 9066 on "all persons of Japanese ancestry," and they all individually responded to the order, the evacuation, and the camps as acts of racial discrimination, with what they saw as American revulsion.

Organized against the Issei and the Japanese characteristics of the Japanese Americans are the "100% Americans" of the Japanese American Citizens League (JACL): James Sakamoto, founder of the JACL and newspaper editor; Nobu Kawai, who organized the only chapter of the JACL founded in a camp; Larry Tajiri, editor of the JACL newspaper and code-named confidential informant to the FBI; and Mike M. Masaoka, leader of the JACL, and also code-named confidential informant to the FBI, as well as an informant to the FBI under another code name.

Part I of this book, entitled "The Issei," opens with a quote from an 1881 anti-Japanese novel, depicting a war between Japan and the United States starting in 1941 while the Japanese settle in America and learn, work, and adapt in this country. The Issei, the first generation of Japanese Americans to land in America, had been barred from United States citizenship by the same racist laws that barred Chinese; but the Nisei, the second generation, by virtue of having been born in the United States, were U.S. citizens, with all the rights that came with citizenship, from birth.

The Issei set up newspapers, hotels, Japanese American and Chinese restaurants, and entertainment halls while the whites applied pressure in popular songs and novels to deny the Japanese Americans their civil rights and the right to own or lease land. The Nisei grew up on these songs and novels.

In Part II, "The Nisei Dream," the Nisei, the first generation of Japanese Americans born and raised on the mainland, are out of high school, some are out of college, some out of medical and law school; some are venturing into publishing Japanese American—as opposed to purely Japanese—newspapers. The Nisei are of an age where they are ready to be tested and proved as Americans. While some dreamed of becoming the great American leaders of their people, others dreamed of writing great literature.

This was a time when literature—the Hemingway novel, the William Saroyan short story, the poetry of Emily Dickinson—was the dominant form of entertainment. Americans dreamed of writing the Great American Novel, and Japanese Americans dreamed of writing the Great Japanese American Novel. Two candidates for the author of the Great Japanese American Novel were friends James Omura and Larry Tajiri. Omura was the publisher of a Nisei magazine, *Current Life*, critical of the JACL; Tajiri was an editor and writer allied with the JACL. Yet, according to Omura, they were friends. The variety of points of view, interests, and writing on display in Omura's magazine, from annoying to brilliant, gives some indication of what Japanese America might have become if not for World War II.

"December 7, 1941: The Closing Papers," Part III, tells of the consequences of the war and the sociological/anthropological theory of "assimilation" on the

Japanese Americans. The Japanese American Citizens League was organized with the name, and illusion, of being a civil rights organization. The JACL believed the Nisei should shed their Japanese characteristics and be assimilated by the dominant whites. Publicly, they went through the motions of representing Japanese America and claimed to be the only nationally organized group capable of representing Japanese America. Covertly, they worked against Japanese American civil rights as "confidential informants to the FBI." They were also covert informants to Army intelligence and the Office of Naval Intelligence.

It was the JACL's self-appointed mission to prevent or discredit all test cases seeking to prove that the selective military orders and concentration camps violated Japanese American civil rights. Their aim was the absorption and assimilation of Japanese America into the white population, thereby rendering civil rights irrelevant.

Part IV, "Us and Them," tells the story of the conflict for the soul of Japanese America, between the JACL and individual Japanese Americans, around military service and the draft.

Japanese American individuals and one organization inside a concentration camp, the Heart Mountain Fair Play Committee, fought for individual Japanese American civil rights and found themselves locked tooth and nail against the JACL's policy against test cases. There were draft resisters from all but two of the nine camps, but their resistance was, in the words of James Omura, "too unorganized and basically unsound in their viewpoints"; they were acting on their own, acting emotionally and without legal advice. The forty-four from Minidoka, Idaho, for instance, didn't know of each other's existence until they had been tried and convicted and were on a bus together. Heart Mountain was the only camp where money was collected for lawyers, and the leaders waged a publicity campaign to recruit members and win sympathy for their stand. They briefly had the ear of Japanese America, but unfortunately not the ear of those who made American movies. These movies were well made by the best directors, actors, and cameramen in Hollywood and consequently are still seen on TV, examples of film art. The war challenged Japanese Americans to justify themselves before an America more interested in revenge against the Japanese enemy than in an emerging minority just entering its second generation. The question is, Did it emerge?

This book could not have been written without the help of Michi Weglyn, author of *Years of Infamy*, who provided reams of documents and years of her time, encouraging me, a Chinese, not Japanese American, to write this book. Aiko Herzig-Yoshinaga, former researcher to the Joan Bernstein Commission on the Wartime Relocation and Internment of Civilians, and her husband, Col. Jack Herzig-Yoshinaga, have been generous with the fruits of their research, to me and all others studying the Evacuation and Internment, as has Art Hansen of the University of California, Fullerton. The help of Stephan Sumida and Tamiko Nimura, and Special Collections at the University of Washington Library has been invaluable; Paul Tsuneishi and Lawson Inada, my fellow interviewers; Frank Abe, producer of *Conscience and the Constitution*; and Martha Nakagawa, Rita Takahashi, Brian Tatsuno and Glenn Hayashi, Gary Maehara, and Jack Chin have provided raw research, help, and encouragement. Thanks also to Violet di Cristoforo and Mako for their translations of *Song of Cheyenne*. Special thanks to my daughter Betsy Chin Gardner and Sam Chin for their help typing. Acknowledgment is given to the Civil Liberties Public Education Fund for money and the Bancroft Library at University of California, Berkeley, and the Special Collections Library at the University of Washington, in Seattle, for materials used in this book. Copies of all the tapes I made for this book are scattered between the CARP Collection, at Bancroft Library Oral History Collection, at Berkeley; the Holland Library, at Western Washington State University, at Pullman; and the Japanese American National Museum, Los Angeles. And a special thank you to Karen Seriguchi.

PART I

The Issei

The Issei Are Here

They keep shops, they clear the land of rocks and boulders, and they farm; they labor in milltowns in Washington, mines in Colorado, railroads all over the west. The Issei, the first generation of Japanese in America, men and women, are here. They are in the towns where they can be seen in numbers, in districts of their own next to the railroad. They are in the country and wilderness, with their crops and their solitude—the Issei are all over America in the 1800s. And they are staying. It doesn't matter what their government or our government says. They're here, and they're staying. Some people are bothered by their presence. Some people are delighted.

Banzai!

by

PARABELLUM

(Theodor Weicher)

Charles Scribner's Sons
New York

1881

... So it was after the terrible night of Port Arthur and so it was now.

It was of course as yet impossible to figure out in detail how the Japanese had managed to take possession of the Pacific States within twenty-four hours. But from the dispatches received from all parts of the country during the next few days and weeks the following picture could be drawn.

The number of Japanese on American soil was in round numbers one hundred thousand. The Japanese had not only established themselves as small tradesmen and shopkeepers in the towns, but had also settled elsewhere as farmers and fruit growers; Japanese coolies and Mongolian workmen were to be found whenever new buildings were going up as well as on all the railways. The Japanese element never attracted undue attention in any one particular spot. Nevertheless they were to be found everywhere.

We never for a moment realized that this whole immigration scheme was regulated by a perfect system, and that every Japanese immigrant had received his military orders and was in constant touch with the secret military centers at San Francisco. ... The Japanese invasion, which our politicians dismissed as possible only in the dim and distant future, was actually completed at the beginning of the year 1908.

A hundred thousand Japanese had established the line of an eastern advance-guard long before the Pacific States had any idea of what was up. During Sunday after the capture of San Francisco, the occupation of Seattle, San Diego and the other fortified towns on the coast, the landing of the second detachment of the Japanese army began, and by Monday evening the Pacific States were in the grip of no less than one hundred and seventy thousand men.

Shosuke Sasaki, Issei

JAPANESE AMERICAN CONSCIENCE

Shosuke Sasaki gulps his words low, swallows them into his chest. He is an Issei, an immigrant-generation Japanese American. He shows me albums of photographs from 1919. "Now this man is a friend, at whose home I used to go play. He and his wife had no children. And they welcomed my coming in the house to play. And when I left Japan he wanted a farewell picture. And he took me to a photographer and we had that taken.

"This is coming across to this country. This is on the *Arabia Maru*. That's me sitting there with some of the ship's officers.

"When we came to this country, my father had been here many years. My brother Mokichi, my mother Mot (Tsuda was her family name), my sister Meiko, and I. We all came at the same time together in 1919. The old *Arabia Maru*. Ten-thousand ton ship. We came first class.

"Of course, my brother, being quite a bit older, ten years old, he was running around all over the ship. My mother and sister, they ate their first meal on board ship. They had meals served in the cabin. And I had Japanese food brought in.

"I was eager to test Western food. So I walked into the dining saloon by myself. And one of the waiters was quite amused to see a kid walking in there by himself and asked what did I want. I said, 'I want American food.' And he said, 'All right,' and brought out a plate of soup. I remember it was beef soup,

5

because it had diced carrots in it. I thought it tasted good. Then there was bread set beside me, and he said, 'Now you're supposed to put this butter on the bread,' and he buttered the bread for me.

"Well, when I picked it up to try to eat it, I found the smell of the butter unpleasant. And as a result couldn't eat that piece of bread. I don't remember the rest of the meal, but I do remember that. That night one of the worst typhoons in recent years struck the coast. And the ship was on its way from Kobe to Yokohama, and it was just bobbing up and down like a cork. As a result, I just heaved up everything I had eaten that day.

"I remember it took a little over two weeks to get across. The first Western city I saw was Victoria, British Columbia. I remember getting up very early that morning so we could go on deck and see the town.

"And it was a beautiful spring day. There wasn't a cloud in the sky. It was absolutely blue! I looked out over the railing of the ship, and when I saw the city of Victoria from the ship, I thought, My! What a beautiful place this Western world must be!

"This is after we came to this country. This is the first summer, 1919. We arrived on May 8, 1919. And some people just asked us if we wanted to go for a ride. And in those days we were perfectly innocent and just accepted any ride. They took us out in the country, I remember, and took this picture.

"Pomeroy was the county seat of Garfield County, Washington. Farm town. A mill there, where the farmers brought their wheat. It was also the terminal point for a railroad branch line. I saw so many wagon trains of wheat that I didn't think it was anything unusual. Wheat! Just sacks of wheat piled up. You get used to whole wagon trains coming down the main street of that town with bells jingling, you know. I still remember the sound of those bells on the horses.

"I can't say that I was a mischievous guy. I always asked permission before I hitched a ride on 'em.

"There's an old Buddhist saying: 'All accumulation ends in dispersion. All building ends in destruction. All meetings end in separation. All birth in death.' That is a view certainly shared by most Japanese with any philosophical or religious sensibility.

"I can't say that I know what the average Issei family told their Nisei offspring. That I don't know. What was told to me comes from—most of it—from my mother, who was from an old samurai family, and very proud of her heritage."

One of the stories his mother told, and one of the Japanese movies he's seen, is *Chushingura*. A lot of people tell me of *Chushingura*'s influence and importance and universality, but no one has been able to tell me the story. If it's a story his mother told him, can he tell me the story?

CHUSHINGURA

"This Lord was young. He had just been newly raised to the head of that feudatory, a clan, a feudal government unit. He was making his first trip to Edo, what is now known as Tokyo. Edo, the seat of the Tokugawa government to spend a year there in attendance at the court of the Tokugawa family. The Tokugawa Shogun. That attendance was required on alternate years. Spend a year in Edo and then you come back and he was allowed a year in his own territory. And then he had to go back to Edo again.

"Meantime his family had to remain in their mansion in Edo. In effect, they're almost like hostages, not quite, but the Tokugawa government insisted on that as surety for proper behavior on the part of their feudal lords, to prevent any overt attempts at rebellion.

"Well, this young lord went there. He presented himself to the various household authorities of the Tokugawa Shogunate, among whom was this lord who was in charge of the ceremonies at the court of the Tokugawa family.

"This man was a powerful feudal lord in his own right. Any new lord that went there had to depend on him for instruction in the ceremonies, in particular the proper clothing that one should wear at different functions. According to tradition, this man, this elderly master of ceremonies, was offended by the smallness of the gift that this young lord had brought with him. He was accustomed of receiving much greater and more valuable gifts, and so he regarded the young lord as a country bumpkin who did not know any better, and did not instruct him with the care that he did the others. And on one occasion when there was to be, I think it was an emissary from the imperial court in Kyoto, a man representing the Emperor was making a formal call at the Tokugawa court in Edo. To receive this emissary with proper courtesy required a big turnout of all the feudal lords there and so forth, properly dressed.

"He found he was not dressed properly. All the other lords were dressed up one way, and he was dressed in a manner suitable for some other occasion. He was very much embarrassed and mortified. And when he saw this master of ceremonies, he berated him for not having instructed him properly. The master of ceremonies regarded him with scorn and contempt and told him he was a fool, ignorant, a country bumpkin, which angered the young lord and caused him to draw his sword and attack the old man.

"Of course, he was immediately grasped from behind by his attendants who wanted to prevent him from committing a murder there, and he succeeded in only inflicting a small wound on this old man's head. And he was immediately arrested.

"And then he was questioned by the magistrates who tried to be as lenient as they could. They put leading questions to him, to make it easy for him to say that he had no intention of killing the old man or something of that sort.

"But the young lord, true to samurai training, was totally honest in all the answers. He said, 'Sure I wanted to kill him! I regret I didn't kill him!' That sealed his fate.

"There was an absolute prohibition against unsheathing a sword in either the presence of the Shogun or in the presence of an emissary of the Emperor. That was an absolute prohibition, which the young lord violated. So it was on that basis that they ordered him to die.

"He was condemned to commit *seppuku*. Also his domains were taken away from him. So that all the samurai who had been loyal to him would become *ronin*. And back in his domain, the head of the samurai called all the samurai together and told them what had happened, that they would have to give up their castle. That the *gorojim* was sending a group over to take the castle over. And some of the samurai said, 'Hell with it! We're not going to stand for this! Let's fight 'em! And keep the castle by force!'

"And the leader Oishi Yoshionita, or Oishi Yuranosuke [or Oishi Kuranosuke], said, 'No, if we do that, we may make it impossible for us to gain for our lord the justice which he deserves.' He told them, 'There will be a time when we can strike. But as far as our being able to hold this castle against the overwhelming forces of the Tokugawa government, we don't have a chance. So it's better to give it up peacefully. The real fault is not the Tokugawa government. It is this old man who treated our lord unfairly.' And so the others agreed to peacefully turn over the castle to the Tokugawa forces.

"I have forgotten the exact number—two or three hundred samurai, the retainers of that family of the lord, swore that they would dedicate their lives eventually to gaining justice for their lord."

Samurai are hot.

Samurai have been hot in America since Kurosawa's *Rashomon*, and *Seven Samurai*, unleashed Toshiro Mifune on American art house audiences in college towns from coast to coast. The hottest samurai are, hands down, the samurai in Lord Asano's service, who become the forty-seven Loyal Ronin of *Chushingura*. At the time of the camps, before Toshiro Mifune, *samurai* in Japanese America meant *Chushingura*.

"After they turned over the castle to the Tokugawa, they themselves became ronin, men without a master, without an income. And they had to make a living some way.

"Some became farmers. Some became small merchants. Whatever they could subsist on.

"Others took humble jobs as fishmongers, almost anything. Some of them became small tradesmen, carpenters, so forth. By becoming small tradesmen, repairmen, carpenters, and things, they were able to gain entrance to the mansion. They mapped the insides in detail—where everything was.

"The men were closely watched. Especially their leader was closely watched by the spies of this old man, the master of ceremonies. In order to throw them off the track, Oishi used to become a prominent frequenter of brothels and drinking establishments. He would pretend that he was drunk. He'd be lying apparently dead drunk in the streets." Shosuke Sasaki allows himself a panting laugh at the great samurai Oishi Yuranosuke acting drunk and stupid.

"There's one occasion in the dramatization of that thing that Oishi is lying on the side of the road drunk, and some passerby looks at him he knows who he was, originally, and to see how low the guy's sunk! I think he spits on him with contempt. Oishi doesn't move. So he draws his sword out, and the sword is rusty!

"The sword is the symbol of a samurai's soul. And to allow the sword to be rusted is considered an almost perfect condition of the samurai's soul.

"Then after about almost three years, in the winter, their leader sent out word that they should assemble on such and such a day, on such and such a night and come prepared to make the attack. Some, of course, in the meantime, had died. Some were ill, couldn't make it. For a variety of reasons only forty-seven showed up.

"One of those forty-seven, came in, I think late. I think he did everything that was possible early, and he wasn't in the attack. Because he had obviously made a genuine, wholehearted sincere effort to join them, and he was prevented from being there only because of some development, for which he was not responsible. They include him in the forty-seven.

"Out of the two or three hundred that took that oath, only forty-six showed up.

"And, as they put on their armor, their leader gave them a little bag of coins, gold and silver coins, told each to carry it with them. The purpose of that was, so that if they were killed, the authorities couldn't say that these men entered that mansion to rob it.

"The first thing they did, they posted archers on the roof of the main gate of the mansion. And the purpose of putting archers up there was to shoot down any men the mansion might send out to ask for aid from others. And they went in, and finally located the old man. He was hiding in a pile of laundry somewhere, behind a stove or something like that. Anyway, he was cowering with fear.

"And the men said, 'Well you're a samurai of quite a high rank. You know what we're here for. We can't let you live. But, just out of deference to your rank, we will permit you to take your own life.' Seppuku. But the old guy, he was just shaking. He couldn't do anything. So they killed him. Then they cut his head off, and took it to the grave of their lord of Senga Kuji, a temple, and placed it before the gravestone. . . .

"Then they marched directly to the offices of the police and gave themselves up. Allowed the authorities to hand down their decision as to what should be done with them. As I understand, the Shogun himself! was in favor of letting them go. But his advisors said, 'If you do, you will weaken the laws of your regime. These men have committed a violation of our laws, and therefore must pay the price. Furthermore, according to one advisor, these men have lived up to the highest of samurai traditions. No matter how long they live, they can never equal in glory, in purity what they have just done. If we allow them to continue to live, they may do something later on, which will tarnish the fame and reputation which they have hereby now gained. Wouldn't it be a favor for them to leave this earth now?' And apparently that was the argument that prevailed.

"So the forty-seven wound up committing seppuku.

"I have been to their graves. I guess it was on my trip there in 1975. I asked one of my cousins to take me there. It was raining. At the entrance to the grave plot where the ashes of those men are buried, there's a place where they sold incense.

"Had it been a clear day, I would have bought incense to burn before each of the graves. As it was, it was raining heavily. So, I thought, well, geewhiz, what can I do with incense in the rain?

"The temple charges an entrance fee, if I'm not mistaken. We had to get a ticket or something and present it.

"Anyway we went in. And I stopped at the first tombstone there, as you enter. And I remember it was the tombstone of the lord, Asano Naganori. Then next to it was the leader of the group, Oishi Kuranosuke.

"And from then they had just a whole line of tombstones of the forty-seven, all uniformly lined up. And then I regretted very much my failure to buy that incense. Because, when I went in, here, on each of the these incense burners on each grave were just mounds of unburned incense that people had just left there as an offering. If I ever go back to Japan again, I'll have to go there and make good my failure, and leave some token of my respect."

James Omura, Nisei Newsman

HATO POPPO
Poppoppo hato poppo
Mame ga hoshii ka
Sora yaru zo
Minna de nakayoku
Tabeni koi

"I don't know where I learned that song. It could only have been my mother. She recited it to all of us kids. *Hato poppo! Poppoppo hato poppo!* I remember it clearly.

Poppoppo doves *poppo*
You want some beans?
There, you go.
All together
In harmony now,
Come and eat.

"There were six children in our family. Before I started school at six years old, I was never beyond the confines of our ten-acre property," Jimmie Omura says. A Japanese children's song, a lullaby, his childhood on Bainbridge Island, an island in Puget Sound, his father. "My father was a carpenter. We were never farmers."

I thought he was dead. Everybody thought he was dead. But here he was. Alive.

Paul Jacobs, Frank Chuman, Michi Weglyn, hundreds of mom-and-pop slide show authors, trying to explain why America interned Japanese Americans, during WWII. Everybody writing about the 1942 internment of Japanese Americans in camps quotes Jimmie Omura. He appeared before a congressional committee chaired by California congressman John Tolan, which held hearings in San Francisco on national readiness to rid the West Coast of all Japanese Americans. Omura was the only Japanese American to ask the obvious: "Has the Gestapo come to America?" But we're getting ahead of the story.

This is a story of Japanese America, from the beginning.

James Omura was born on Bainbridge Island, a large, sparsely populated bit of country, a forty-five-minute ferry-boat ride from Seattle.

"I recall no Japanese visitors in those years," Omura says, talking of his childhood, "but we did have *hakujin* visitors. My two sisters and baby brother and me played with the visiting hakujin children. We knew no other Japanese children but ourselves. Ten acres is a lot of area to play in. And mother sang "Hato Poppo" to all the kids. It seems to me the lullaby was about a dragonfly or a butterfly or small bird. It was very soothing. I liked it."

Poppoppo hato poppo
Mame ga hoshii ka
Sora yaru zo
Minna de nakayoku
Tabeni koi

"Mother kept us kids in line with *Obake* stories of Japan. She would really frighten us with these ghost stories. Most of these stories were about unkempt women with long tresses, witch-like features, and bony hands. But she told us one obake story that had to do with our property.

"Our two-story frame house sat on a bluff overlooking Eagle Harbor. The front of the property sloped down to the water's edge. On the left corner at the water's edge, there stood a golden weeping willow tree.

"She told us about the obake that came out of that golden weeping willow tree at night. To us kids, it had branches like the trees that sprouted witch-women in the obake stories my mother told us. We made sure we weren't outside after dark and never went closer than fifty feet to that tree.

"One moonlit night when we were locked out of the house by our guardian, we did see an obake. The three of us. You probably won't believe it though."

Japanese Love Song

words by ANON.

music by CLAYTON THOMAS

She was a maid of Japan
He was the son Choo Lee.
She had a comb and a fan.
And he had two chests of tea.
She wore a gown picturesque,—
While he had a wonderful queue.—
Her features were statuesque,—
Which matter'd but little to Choo,—
Which matter'd but little to Choo.
He smiled at her over the way.
She coquetted at him with her fan;
"I mally you, see?" he would say
To this queer little maid of Japan.—
And day after day she would pose…
To attract him, her Little Choo Lee….
All daintily tip'd on her toes,
This love of a heathen Chinee, Chinee
This love of a heathen Chinee
When she is maid on a fan,
And he's on a package of tea,
of Tea,
And he's on a package of tea.

Sessue Hayakawa

ZEN AND THE MOVIES

A failed naval cadet and failed suicide from Japan, twenty-seven-year-old Kintaro Hayakawa was struck with ambition—to present the first English-language Japanese American theater in Little Tokyo, Los Angeles. And change his name to Sessue, "Snow."

Sessue Hayakawa writes in his autobiography, *Zen Showed Me the Way*,

> During my last weeks at college I had gone again and again to see a play called *Typhoon*. Most of the characters in it were Japanese. They had been played by Americans—Occidentals in Oriental guise—whose stage voices reflected little of the Japanese nuance and inflection when speaking English—save artificial mispronunciation and poor grammar—neither of which was authentic. For all of this though, the play had captivated me with its sheer dramatic appeal.

Interesting that this actor born of a samurai family in Japan had ambitions in the English language, in Japanese American theater. Interesting he was ready to make a stand on English and the authenticity of Japanese accents and characterizations, in 1914. The Americans didn't care. The Japanese didn't care. Only Sessue Hayakawa cared.

In Little Tokyo, he had acted in Japanese-language theater productions and been successful. But he was struck with an idea:

"Now what? I know that look." I had returned to work at the Japanese Theatre and was bearding Toyo Fujita in his office. "Out with it. What have you in mind now?" he pressed.

Being a success only among the Japanese had come to dissatisfy me. I wanted to be better known outside Little Tokyo. If I am going to act in America, I should act for Americans, I thought.

"I find our Japanese plays and Japanese audiences confining," I told Fujita. "I want an English speaking audience to see and hear what I have to offer. I want to act for Americans. And in something they can understand, something that will reach them. A Japanese play won't do, even in translation."

"You are ambitious, aren't you?"

"Why not?"

"It will have to be something with popular appeal, of course," Fujita observed. "Have you a play in mind? Can you do it? And most of all, do you think they'll accept you?"

Thomas Ince, an independent producer-director with his own studio, "Inceville," discovered Sessue Hayakawa in the in Li'l Tokyo production of *Typhoon*. Ince bought *Typhoon*, and in a change of pace from his westerns, his company made a film of it with Sessue Hayakawa in the lead. Reginald Barker directed. The film made Hayakawa a star, the first Japanese star, in 1914. He made one more movie with Thomas Ince then signed with Lasky Famous Players for a salary Thomas Ince could not match: a thousand dollars a week.

Hayakawa's first film at Lasky's Famous Players was *The Cheat*, directed by Cecil B. DeMille. Sessue Hayakawa played a rich and handsome Japanese, who loans a beautiful white girl money. She tries repaying her debt in cash rather than flesh and ends up maddening Hayakawa, in his silk smoking jacket, tie, and perfectly pomaded hair. He bares her shoulder and brands it. Crying, she takes a pistol and shoots him dead. The legend of Sessue Hayakawa—the Hollywood movie star, the gigolo you love to shoot—was born. In the age of the silent screen, he played Mexicans, Chinese, Indians, Latins, Burmese, and Japanese who broke the hearts of wide-eyed white girls.

No one remembers any building owned by Toyo Fujita with a theater in it, or Sessue Hayakawa's theater productions, in Japanese or English. The *Rafu Shimpo* of that year was little more than a bulletin board and a mass of small advertisements. No theater announcements. No theater ads. Every Nisei, old and young at the time of WWII and the camps, is a historian and recites the facts of their life from the immigration of their parents to prevent things like the invention of Japanese American English-language theater from disappearing from memory. But Sessue Hayakawa and *Typhoon* in Li'l Tokyo were before their time. The Nisei remember his Oscar nomination for Best Supporting Actor, in 1958, for his role as the Japanese prison camp commandant in David Lean's *The Bridge on the River Kwai*. But Sessue Hayakawa's career in Li'l Tokyo and Toyo Fujita's theater are forgotten, or they never were.

A Japanese Nightingale

by

ONOTO WATANNA

Ilustrated by

Genjiro Yeto

Taro Burton denounced both the foreigners who took to themselves and deserted Japanese wives, and the native Japanese, who made such a practice possible. He himself was a half-caste, being the product of a marriage between an Englishman and Japanese woman. In this case, however, the husband had proved faithful to his wife and children up to death; but then he had married a daughter of the nobility, a descendant of the proud Jokichi family, and the ceremony had been performed by an English missionary.

Despite the happiness of this marriage, Taro held that the Eurasian was born to a sorrowful lot, and was bitterly opposed to the union of the women of his country with men of other lands, particularly as he was Westernized enough to appreciate how lightly such marriages were held by the foreigners. It was true, of course, that after the desertion the wife was divorced, according to the law, but that, in Taro's mind, only made the matter more detestable.

It was unfortunate that Taro could not have accompanied his friend, for while the latter was not a weak character, he was easy-going, good-natured, and easily manipulated through his feelings.

The young Japanese, had done nothing else, at least would have kept the *nakodas* and their offerings of matrimonial happiness on the other side of the American's doors. As it was, one of them in particular was so picturesque in appearance....

It was this nakoda (Ido was his name, so he told Jack) who brought an applicant for a husband to his house, one day, and besought him at least to hold a look-at meeting with her.

"She is beautiful like unto the sun-goddess," he declared, with the extravagance of his class.

"The last was like the moon," said the young man, laughing. "Have you any stars to trot out?"

"Stars!" echoed the other, for a moment puzzled, and then, beaming with delighted enlightenment, "Ah, yes—her eyes, her feet, hair, hands, twinkling like unto them same stars! She prays for just a look-at meeting with your excellency."

"Well, for the fun of the thing, then," said the other, laughing. "I'm sure I don't mind having a look-at meeting with a pretty girl. Show her into the zashishi (guest-room) and I'll be along in a moment. But, look here," he continued, "You'd better understand that I'm only going through this ceremony for the fun of the thing, mind you. I don't intend to marry any one—at all events, not a girl of that class."

"Nod for a leetle whicheven?" persuaded the nakoda.

"Nod for a leetle while whicheven," echoed the young man, but the agent had disappeared.

When Jack, curious to know what she was like, she who was seeking him for a husband, entered the zashishi, he found the blinds high up and the sunshine pouring into the room. His eyes fell upon her at once, for the shoji at the back of the room was parted, and she stood in the opening, her head drooping bewitchingly. He could not see her face. She was quite small, though not so small as the average Japanese woman, and the two little hands, clasped before her, were the whitest, most irresistible and perfect hands he had ever seen. He had heard of the beauty of the hands of the Japanese women, and was not surprised to find even a girl of this class—she was geisha, of course, he told himself—with such exquisite, delicate hands. He knew she was holding them so that they could be seen to advantage, and her little affected pose amused and pleased him.

After he had looked at her a moment, she subsided to the mats and made her prostration. She was dressed very gaily in a red crepe kimono, tied about with a purple obi. Her hair was dressed after the fashion of the geisha, with a flower ornament at the top and long pointed daggers at either side; but as she bowed her head to the mats, some pin in her hair escaped and slipped, and then a tawny rebellious mass of hair, which was never meant to be worn smoothly, had fallen all about her, tumbled into her eyes and over her ears, and literally covered her little crouching form. She shivered in shame at the mishap, and then knelt very still at his feet.

Winifred Eaton was the sister of Edith Eaton, who wrote under the Chinese name Sui Sin Far. Winifred Eaton claimed to be a Japanese princess named Onoto Watanna. Onoto Watanna is not a Japanese name nor does it have a meaning in Japanese. Many of her Japanese words are nonsense syllables in Japanese. Likewise her Japanese customs are not known to have existed in Japan. She wrote many successful plays, Broadway shows, films, and books about the Japanese. They were sympathetic portrayals but not authentic, unlike her sister's books and stories of the Chinese.

Urashima Taro

Mukashi Mukashi Urashima wa
Tasuketa kame ni tsurerarete
Ryugujoe kitenire ba
E ni mo kakenai utsukushesa

Urashima rescued a turtle
And rode the turtle into the gurgle
Under the sea to the Dragon King's palace
What a beautiful place it was.

Otohime sama no gochiso ni
Tai ya hirame no mai odori
Tada mezurashiku omoshiroku
Tsukihi no tatsu no mo yume no uchi

Princess Otohime spread a feast of goodies
All kinds of fish dashed and danced the wriggle wriggly.
He'd never seen anything like this in his life.
Days passed into months as easily as dreaming.

Asobi ni akite ki ga tsuite
Oitomagoi mo sokosoko ni
Kaeru tochu no tanoshimi wa
Miyage ni moratta tamatebako

Everyday he was happier than the day before
Yet he became homesick and wanted to visit,
The Princess told him he could come back
Only if he did not open the jewel box she gave him.

Kaete mireba ko wa ikani
Moto ita ie mo mura mo naku
Michi ni yukikau hitobito wa
Kao mo shiranai mono bakari

Back where he started from
Everything, even his own home is strange.
Everyone in and out of his house is a stranger.
He wandered down to the beach.

Kokorobosa ni futa toreba
Akete kuyashiki tamatebako
Naka Kara patto shirokemuri
Tachimachi Taro was ojisan

The Princess' words slipped his memory
As he opened the box with her on his mind,
White smoke fanned out from the box
And Urashima Taro was a very old man.

Kentaro Takatsui,
Kibei-Nisei

"I HAVE PICTURES"

"Oh, yes, I remember. I remember."

Kentaro Takatsui was born in 1915, the year of the wood rabbit, in the Washington milltown of Mukilteo.

"Japanese in those days, they always celebrate a hundred days after a baby is born. They celebrate hundred days. Usually in Japan, everybody dresses up and they go to a shrine. A Shinto shrine. But in Mukilteo, there were no Shinto shrines, so they went to a Shinto church in Seattle. Took a photograph in Seattle with everybody dressed up, you know. I have pictures of that when I was a hundred days old."

"That reminds me," Kentaro Takatsui says. "My Japanese teaching was to obey the law. Obey your father and mother. Don't rock the boat. And this is just the opposite of my American teaching. This reminds of what you just said. My American teacher and I want to pass this on to the third and fourth and fifth generation of this country here. In order to fight for your civil rights, see, my bible was Henry David Thoreau. His work 'On Civil Disobedience.'"

"That's my bible," Kentaro Takatsui says. "It's just the opposite. It me. . . . It was my American teaching to revolt. And my Japanese teaching was just the opposite of what JACL was trying to tell us. This is ironic! See?"

On the Duty of Civil Disobedience

by

HENRY DAVID THOREAU

(July 12, 1817–May 6, 1862)

How does it become a man to behave toward this American government to-day? I answer, that he cannot without disgrace be associated with it. I cannot for an instant recognize that political organization as my government which is slave's government also.

All men recognize the right of revolution; that is the right to refuse allegiance to, and to resist, the government, when its tyranny or its insufficiency are great and unendurable. But almost all say that such is not the case now. But such was the case, they think, in the Revolution of '75. If one were to tell me that this was a bad government because it taxed certain foreign commodities brought to its ports, it is most probable that I should not make an ado about it, for I can do without them. All machines have their friction; and possibly this does enough good to counterbalance the evil. At any rate, it is a great evil to make a stir about it. But when the friction comes to have its machine, and oppression and robbery are organized, I say, let us not have such a machine any longer. In other words, when a sixth of the population of a nation which has undertaken to be the refuge of liberty are slaves, and a whole country is unjustly overrun and conquered by a foreign army, and subjected to military law, I think that it is not too soon for honest men to rebel and revolutionize. What makes this duty the more urgent is the fact that the country so overrun is not our own, but ours is the invading army.

Paley, a common authority with many on moral questions, in his chapter on the "Duty of Submission to Civil Government," resolves all civil obligation into expediency; and he proceeds to say, "that so long as the interest of the whole society requires it, that is, so long as the established government cannot be resisted or changed without public inconveniency, it is the will of God that the established government be obeyed, and no longer. . . . This principle being admitted, the justice of every particular case of resistance is reduced to a computation of the quantity of the danger and grievance on the side, and of the probability and expense of redressing it on the other." Of this, he says, every man shall judge for himself. But Paley appears never to have contemplated those cases to which the rule of expediency does not apply, in which a people, as well as an individual, must do justice, cost what it may. If I have unjustly wrested a plank from a drowning man, I must restore it to him, though I drown myself. This, according to Paley would be inconvenient. But he that would save his life, in such a case, shall lose it. This people must cease to hold slaves, and to make war on Mexico, though it cost them their existence as a people.

Kentaro Takatsui,
Kibei-Nisei

JAPTOWN

Kentaro Takatsui is one of three children born to the Takatsui family, in a millcamp in Mukilteo, Washington. They called it "Japtown."

"One was born there in Mukilteo, and died when she was a baby. I was born there. My kid brother was born in Mukilteo. That's about it.

"The sawmill town was by the ocean and about twenty-seven miles north of Seattle. Mukilteo. The sawmill was on the seashore and here is the Caucasian town over here by the railroad track, and the walk towards Everett about half a mile. And there was a little 'Japtown' there on the east side of the highway that runs to Everett.

"There was a small river ran through Japtown. And there was a small reservoir way up there inside of the woods. We used to go up there to fish when we were kids. And sometimes, when a thing like too much rain happens, we'd get water way up to here. The floor of the house flooded. Flooded! Every time it rains.

"When I was about six years old. I had a bad habit of stealing money that mother and father had put away in the piggy bank.

"And he knew I stole it. I think it was big money. Silver dollars was a lot of money. The big ones. You know the big silver dollars? Worth a lot of money! Candy bars only used to cost one cent or two cents. I took my childhood friends out. We went to that little white man's town where the Crown Lumber Company store was. And bought hot dogs, candy, chocolates.

"One day he took me to . . . my father used to have a little garden in the woods, far away from J-Town. They used to have a little shack there where I was born, but they moved to where all the Japanese houses were built close together. This house was a little bit further away from the rest of the houses, and the Caucasians took it over. The lumber mill people gave it to them, so my father used to have a little garden there where he raised vegetables. He took me way into the woods beyond that garden. He took a branch, a stick he found on the ground, and he whacked the hell out of me. I remember I cried. It was day-time. I guess he wanted to take me away from the neighborhood, because the houses were too close together, and he didn't want the people to hear me cry-ing. As I grew up, I see he did me a favor.

"I never stole again."

His family celebrated birthdays, "Japanese style. They make *sekihan*. That's red bean, rice and *omochi*. All kinds of Japanese *gochiso*, you know. It's fine cooking. Fine cuisine."

"There weren't any Santa Claus in Japtown. But we knew about it. We knew who Santa Claus was."

What did a kid do in Mukilteo for fun?

"Oh, we'd go fishing. In those days it was just a few minutes walk from the ocean. And we'd dig up worms in the green grass. We'd dig up all kinds of worms from the ground and put them in a can. We had some homemade fish-ing poles. Go out there, make our own rafts and play around out there. Catch any kind of fish around there. We'd bring it home, and that's our supper.

"There was no TV, no radio, so father and mother all the time, all kinds of fairy tales. Children's fairy tales."

Did he have a favorite?

"Oh, yes. Ushiwakamaru. He's famous. There's this great big samurai called 'Benkei' in this village, Gojyo-no-hashi, in Kyoto. And this big Benkei had this big spear. He would challenge anybody there crossing that bridge and after he defeated them, he would take their swords away. He was famous for that. One day Ushiwakamaru came long, and he tried to do the same to Ushiwakamaru. But Ushiwakamaru was so sharp and jumped around like a hummingbird, you know. Too fast. Benkei couldn't even touch him. He is famous, even in song, a children's song. There is a song about that:

> "*Kyoto no Go-jo o no hashi no ue*
> *Dai no otoko no Benkei iwa.*
> *Nagai naginata furi agete*

"Ushiwaka megakakete kirikakaru
Ushiwakamaru wa tobi noite
Motta ogi o nagetsukete . . . koi, koi, koi
Rankan no ue ni agatte te o taku.

"On the Gojo Bridge in Kyoto
A giant man called Benkei
Raised his long-handled spear up high

"Aiming at Ushiwaka to thrash him
Ushiwakamaru jumped aside
Threw a fart at him. 'Come, come, come'
Jumping on the railing, hands clapping."

"See, Ushiwakamaru was so fast, he jumps up on the *rankan* of the bridge and Benkei can't even touch him. So finally this Benkei, he surrenders. Surrenders to Ushiwakamaru. So that's the story when he's a child. He was famous. When he grows up he's Minamoto no Yoshitsune. That's the younger brother of Yoritomo.

"See, Yoritomo is jealous because Yoshitsune has won too many battles, so Yoritomo, a shogun at the time, wants to kill his kid brother. It's a famous story. Yoshitsune just wanders all over Japan. Hiding. A famous story in history. That song . . . my mother taught me that song when I was six years old. I still remember. I'm eighty-one now."

PICTURE OF MY FATHER

"Oh, I have a picture of my father. He was a handsome man. They called him 'Tom' because Kunimuro was four syllables. He wore a suit and tie on special occasions. But other times, when he works at the sawmill he wore the overalls that they used to wear. Bib comes up to here, you know. A strap here to way down here.

"He worked eight to ten hours, six days a week, you see. He worked as a watchman for the sawmill, and he went around different posts with a watchman's time clock, you know, and went to different posts and punched the time. He worked as a watchman on Sundays. That's how much he worked. I have his book. It shows what day it was, what date, and how many hours he worked. He wrote it down in Japanese."

PICTURE OF THE HOUSE

The house Kentaro Takatsui lived in was "Just rough. It was just a plain wooden country shack. Nothing elaborate. Because, you see, lumber they got for free from the mill. One wall, wooden wall. That's about it. They were using a wood stove. They got all this scrap lumber from the sawmill free," and they built an "Outhouse."

In the teens of the century the "Issei never thought about settling there. They always thought about saving money to go back to Japan, you see calendars! Japanese calendars with Japanese girls on it. I remember that. But no framed pictures or anything like that.

"We had a community hall there in Japtown. Wooden building. Japanese built everything around J-Town. No kitchen, but they had a stage. Once a month, at the hall, the little community hall: silent movies. They had *benshi*, a narrator, I remember. It was only nickel for us.

"You brought your own food. You made your own popcorn in those days. It was after supper, around 6 P.M. or so. Silent movies. Always a didactic theme to it. Loyalty to your country, or *oya koko*, and even the Yakuza movies of those days taught loyalty to your *oyabun*, you know, your boss. Once a month."

EVERY NISEI IS A HISTORIAN

"During the Nishi-jihen, before World War II, there was always propaganda against China. All the young people today judge things from the present perspective. This is wrong. You have to go back to that time, and remember the history of that time, you see. The Americans had what they called Manifest Destiny in America. You know about it in American history. It taught that it was the white man's right to rule the colored races. From the time that Columbus landed in America in 1492, you remember that picture . . . famous picture of Columbus landing. You see it in the American history books. You got a sword in one hand and a cross in the other. You remember that picture?

"This was the kind of atmosphere it was in those days which the average American of today doesn't remember. And the Americans had just lied and lied to the American Indians. Took their land away. And they advanced to the Pacific. They conquered, they lied to the American Indians. Fooled them, and when they were developing the southern part of the United States, the white man would go to Africa and used to bring the black man over here, as animals, slaves, by the millions to develop the South. The Chinese brought over here from China to build the railways and so forth, because you work for nothing practically compared to the white man. And the American Indian wars had just finished, when Commodore Perry came to Japan to force open Japan in 1853. You have to go back to the period to understand this.

"You also have to look at a map of the world at that time. All of Africa was conquered by European countries. The Philippines were occupied by the Spaniards for three hundred years. French Indo-China was occupied by France for three hundred years. India was occupied by the British for a couple of hundred years. The English and European, even the American traders doped the Chinese people, see. You remember the Opium Wars? You must remember the Opium Wars. Dutch were in the East Indies. China was cut up into spheres of influence by the European powers and the American capitalistic power. The reason why Japan had to shut itself up from the rest of the world for 265 years from the rest of the world, they realized that if they let the Europeans in, Japan would also be conquered.

"Nobody ever mentions this today. Everybody says, 'Oh, Japan shut itself off for 265 years from the rest of the world.' They never tell you why they had to do that.

"See, in the Tokugawa era, Tokugawa *bakufu* era began, they found out from these Western traders that came to Japan that they first sent in the Christian missionaries to soften up the natives, and get all kinds of information about that country to send back to the pope in Rome. Then the people in Rome gave that information to the conquering leaders of that nation, and then they'd go in and after the missionaries had softened up the country, they'd conquer that country. Colored people. Orientals, blacks and browns, and so forth. The United States itself took over the Philippines after the Spanish American War. And when the Filipinos tried to revolt against the United States not long after the Spanish American War, they crushed that rebellion. Bad as any other country, you know, Japan was right next door to the Philippines, and they see all this, you see. They pictured America like Hawaii, then taking the Philippines, getting closer to Japan, you see.

"Now the Tokugawa bakufu realized that if they let the Europeans do this, Japan would also be conquered. So they closed up the country and kicked everybody out, except the Dutch in Dejima, in Nagasaki. The Dutch were allowed to trade with Japan in a little island of Dejima in Nagasaki. They got the information from the Dutch about the outside world for a couple of hundred years.

"When Commodore Perry of America came to Japan, forced the doors of Japan open, Japanese found that they were 265 years behind the Europeans. The Industrial Revolution had been finished a century before, and the machine age had come on, and mass production of everything was going on, and they were far behind. Eventually they were at the same stage.

"They never showed any scenes where soldiers slaughtered Chinese as you see in American newspaper pictures. They never showed that. They always showed Japanese soldiers advancing and firing guns, and winning the war. 'Banzai!' and all this stuff.

"My father's older brother did military service during the Nichiro Senso, the Russo-Japan War of 1904 and 1905.

"He was a *gunso,* a sergeant in the Japanese Army. He fought on the mainland of China against Russia. And he was famous as the *'oni-shogun,'* a crack 'devil sergeant.'"

MUKILTEO JAPTOWN CUISINE

"Oh, they economized, those Issei, by golly. The only thing they bought for food was white rice. Or Japanese green tea. Oh, meat, once in a while. Sansei today eat meat every day, but Issei had meat maybe once a month.

"They grew their own vegetables. All kinds of vegetables. Seeds from the Japanese store in Seattle. The salesman from Seattle, the Japanese grocery store salesman from Seattle come down to our place maybe once a month, you know, and sold all kinds of things that he could sell to them. He had some kind of a small truck, because he'd go to the bachelors that had a large mess hall. And on that table he spread out his wares.

"The rest of the time the kids would go fishing out on the dock out there, or catch trout in the river. You'd catch trout that long in the little river where we lived. Take it home and that's our supper. And vegetables. And then when wild blackberries grew, we used to go out and gather wild blackberries. Mother would make jam. Jam would last the whole year for our sandwiches. We all did that.

"Wild watercress. We used to gather them at the river. That is a healthful plant, you know. Lots of minerals in there. "Oh, yeah! *Matsutake* (pine mushroom) too. Also we went out to gather *fuki.* Japanese call it *yuki* and *warabi.* These are greens. Wild vegetables. One is called bracken, and the other is called coltsfoot in English. It's kind of curved on the top. They'd take it home and that's their vegetable. Cook it for vegetable. With the fish from the ocean or river, only thing that cost them was white rice, because they couldn't raise white rice. They had to buy it.

"They had this big brown sack. I think it was about a hundred pounds. Big brown sack. Big, you know. White rice in it. All the families used to get that white rice from some Japanese Seattle store. Sometimes they'd bring it on a truck. Most of the time shipped it on the train. Train is right there. The train station was right there. Stops there from Seattle.

"We didn't have chickens. We had rabbits. We had rabbits in a little caged box, and we ate those rabbits. Those rabbits multiply!

"In those days we didn't have hamburger. We didn't know what hamburger was in those days. Mukilteo, I think steak once a month. The meat man would come with his truck. 'Gong, gong, gong!' you know. Right in the middle of J-town, and all the housewives would come and buy their meat. About once a month Caucasian meat man. Sell meat off a truck."

PICTURE OF A LITTLE KID

"I have pictures when I was a little kid starting school in Mukilteo. We packed a lunch. Just jam on two slices of bread. One apple. The friends from J-Town, they show you the way, you know. The older students. It was about a mile, maybe.

"All mixed. Mostly Caucasian. Ninety-eight percent Caucasian. Just a few of us Japanese in each class. I remember the first grade. And second, third. It was very nice. I enjoyed it.

"We used to go to this Christian church in Mukilteo. Caucasian church towards our grade school. About three-fourths of the way towards the grade school from Japtown. We used to go there, too, when we were small. I used to bring pennies, you know, to put in the collection. And then one day, maybe when I was about eight years old. Somewhere around there. They told us not to come there anymore, so all the Japanese kids you know, never went back to that Caucasian white church.

"And they were talking about some ugly hakujins from the South. I never could understand it, at the time, that they meant people from the southern part of the United States. From Dixieland. They must have come there and told the people that we were colored so, 'We shouldn't be mixing with colored people,' or something like that.

"Later on, I came to understand, but at the time, I couldn't understand. I still remember, you see, because it was such a shock. And one of the Christian Caucasian people, he and his wife used to come down to our little Japtown little hall. He used to come down every Sunday and teach us Sunday School. Reverend Yuji Murphy, famous in Seattle. Ever hear of him? It's Yuji. Not Eugene. Yuji. Japanese name. Yuji. He's famous. He spoke Japanese fluently. He heard about how we were discriminated against, so he used to come to our J-Town about once a month and held Christian services for us. I remember that. And he was our friend, the rest of our lives. Yeah."

BACK TO JAPAN

"My father got seriously ill because I think, as I look back at it now, I think he worked too much. Six days a week, ten hours a day. Then on Sundays, he was working as a watchman. A watchman with a time clock. Every Sunday. Ten years. That's why he got sick. He got seriously ill and had kidney problems, and had to go to Seattle and have a kidney operation. I remember that. That was when I was about ten years old. He was gone about a month. It wasn't too hard on the family. My father had an operation on his kidney. That's why he came to Seattle. He was in the hospital for a couple of months and had an operation on his kidney. When he got well, he wanted to go back to Japan to recuperate for awhile. They saved money. Oh, yes!

"The whole family went in 1925 on the Japanese Nippon Yusen Giasha line. The ship was 12,000 ton and the name of the ship was *Hie Maru*."

"Everybody liked Japan. You see, the exchange rate was just the opposite at that time, as it is now. In Japan, for example, 'Horse's Mouth' said in the *Rafu Shimpo* a couple of weeks ago, 'One cup of coffee in Japan costs $15.00 now in American money.' It's just the opposite of what it was when I was a kid. So, you get on a Japanese ship in those days, and third class looked like first class on an American ship.

"I went with some of my Chinese friends on what they call the American President Line in those days. They went to China, and I went to see them off. I saw the third class that they went on, and it was terrible. American ship. Terrible. But third class we went on a Japanese ship looked like first class on an American ship.

"Wonderful Japanese food. American food sometimes. Maybe lunch. But breakfast and supper always Japanese food.

"We got excited because it took eleven days. Eleven days from Seattle to Yokohama. We could go up on the deck to get fresh air. So the kids on the ship, we all got excited when we saw land, way off there. Way off on the horizon. We ran up and down."

SCHOOL IN JAPAN

"I was somewhere around ten years old and I was put in, I think, second grade or third grade. They were all small kids. You used to see Japanese students come from Japan, to study over here.

"We used to see high school kids that tall sit in the back in the American school, third grade or fourth grade. Same thing happened when I went over there. I fell in love with Japanese art because I was an artist even when I was a kid. I was just enchanted by Japanese art. Water color. Wood block prints. And so was my wife. She loved wood block prints.

"Hiroshige is my favorite wood block artist. Not only that, we loved *Takarazuka*. *Takarazuka* was an all-girl operetta. Oh, they used to put on a huge stage. It was enchanting in those days compared to what you'd see in America. The way they put it on was very colorful. Paintings on the stage. Kabuki was the same thing. We fell in love with Kabuki. Even though we didn't understand what they were saying, we appreciated the art, the music, the atmosphere. Beautiful art on the stage. And the elaborate kimonos they wore. Exaggerated, you know. And the dance movements were beautiful."

Born in America and partly raised and educated in Japan—for two years in Kentaro Takatsui's case—defines Takatsui as a Kibei. He balks at being called Kibei, however. For him, the word *Kibei* carries a nasty connotation. The "pro-Japan" militants of WWII are Kibei, the militaristic *Hoshi-dan,* Black Dragon Society members, are Kibei. Takatsui is not that kind of Kibei, but he is, technically—because of his years in Japan—Kibei.

"Even in that village I went to as a child. I used to do watercolor there in that little village. In Japan, because I was just a kid, was the first time I worked with a *fude,* a Chinese brush. Even the Japanese farmers there appreciated art. To them it is art, and it is beautiful the way they write those *kanji,* you know. Beautiful art, so even in Japanese school, art is something. In fact the whole life is art, you know. Even Japanese farmers. I remember that."

I Want to Go to Tokio
Words by JOE MCCARTHY
Music by FRED FISCHER

There's a little sad eyed Japanese,—
Tenderly he sings to me—
Oh his little sweet-heart 'cross the sea
Who's waiting patiently,
Ev'ry night he'd light a little lantern for
her,
And Dream of Old Japan,
In that oriental light,
All his love tales he would write,
On a silken Fan Yo-san.
CHORUS
I sing a high a-lee sing a-low,
That means I want to go to Tokio.
I got a sweet-heart who's waiting for me,
That's why I want to be beneath the Bamboo Tree
When the lanterns are a glowing,
I can feel my love a-growing,
Ho,Yo-Osan,
Hear your man,
Soon you're goin' to be
Sitting on my Jap-a (k)nee
I see a-high sing a-lee sing a-low
That means I want to go to Tokio.

Shosuke Sasaki, Japanese American Conscience

FATHER AND THE PROSTITUTES

"**M**y father was a rather outspoken person. But since he was bilingual, in the real sense of the word, particularly when he was in Spokane, he was called upon to be one of the Japanese community leaders of that day. My father, when the Russo-Japanese War broke out, was asked to head the committee for a drive for funds for the Japanese war effort. He agreed to do that. Well, they got the money.

"And then! In those days, along with the Japanese laborers they brought here, they used to bring in groups of Japanese prostitutes to take care of these men's needs. So, when word got around that this fund drive was going on, why the prostitutes sent one of their friends over to tell my father that they wanted to make a donation. My father is said to have replied, 'Japan is fighting a holy war for the sake of her existence.' He said, 'For such a holy cause, I cannot accept money earned in such a dirty way!'" Shosuke Sasaki laughs and tries to gulp it down at the same time.

"And I understand this caused great resentment among the girls, the prostitutes, and I don't blame 'em. And so they got their boyfriends to agree to retaliate against my father. My father didn't know this, and he was invited to a dinner or something one night. He had no suspicion of what was going on. He said, yes, he'll go."

When faced with a problem, Shosuke Sasaki responds by going inside and slamming the door behind him, grabbing an armload of books on the vexing subject, then popping out of his cage knowing more about it than anyone in the five western states. The books today are his photo albums telling the story of his migration, his childhood, what he knows of his father and mother.

"That night he got word that one of his friends had suddenly had an accident or something and was in the hospital. So he cancelled this dinner engagement and went to see his friend. Well, the next morning, one of his friends came running over to his place out of breath, and when he saw my father, he said, 'You're alive! I'm glad to see you're alive!'

"My father said, 'What's this about?'"

"He said, 'Don't you know?'"

"'No!'

"He said, 'Last night, those fellas were planning to murder you! When you stepped into that room, they were going to drop a sack over you and beat the life out of you.'"

Shosuke Sasaki laughs and tries not to laugh, and looks like a naughty Tweety Bird. He thumbs through stacks of black photograph albums bound with black twine. Inside are little photographs of different sizes, different finishes, different edges. This is photography from the first age of mass-produced cameras, when cameras were so new people had their pictures taken with them. Box cameras. Cameras with foldout platforms and lenses at the end of bellows. Bayonet lenses. Different lenses. Under the pictures mounted artistically on the black page are captions printed in white ink.

"Right after his marriage and his entry into the Sasaki family, he had left the family there in Japan, and used to come back and visit once in awhile," Shosuke Sasaki says. "My father had some kind of business here, in America." What business Shosuke Sasaki never says and points to another little photograph.

"This is me taken in the yard of my home. And these are my two friends that I used to play with. This is my mother and sister. And this is me dressed up for grade school. I went the first year of grade school there. That hat doesn't fit, because my head was so big. That was the largest regulation size hat for students that they had. All the kids at my school had to wear a hat like that.

"I don't know how my father got into the business. But when we were there, he was running a restaurant of his own, in the middle of Prohibition.

"This was a large wooden building. In the old days, apparently it was a large saloon, and we lived in the back. In the front was the restaurant, and in the back there were several rooms. We used those for living quarters. We ate in the kitchen.

"On busy days, I used to help wash the dishes. My daily task was to bring up two buckets of coal from the coalbin downstairs, which would serve as fuel in the cooking stove.

"Storytelling hour would usually be in the evening, after the restaurant was closed and both of us would be home from school. In that little town, we were the only Japanese family there. My sister and I were the only Japanese children the people there had ever seen. And in many ways, the people there treated us better than they treated their own children—with the exception of one family, who went out of their way to be nasty.

"Now this is a picture of a family, where we used to go and play. This was taken in the autumn of that year. Now this was a boy I got to know when I went to Sunday school. And I remember, he used to bring me things every Sunday. Things he had clipped out, paper dolls and things like that. I don't know what's happened to him. I've lost touch with all these people.

"This was a boy and his sister. That's my sister there. These kids lived across the alley from where we lived. This boy's now dead. He died fighting a wheat-field fire in Pomeroy.

"Her full name was Mathilda Gibson. You can see from this photograph, she was a typical woman of the Victorian period. Very straitlaced and a woman of a very very firm character. Both my sister and I remember her with much gratitude and fondness, because she was kind. To us, she was just like our grandmother, really! Our real grandparents were mostly dead by the time we grew up. And we weren't in Japan anyway! By the time we left Japan, that's right! All our grandparents were gone!

"She was the mother of Ed Gibson, who was my father's best friend in that town. She was a pioneer. Came across on the old Oregon Trail. He told me that her wagon party had been attacked by Indians. Men in her party killed by Indian arrows. And the only elderly person who took us under her wing and treated us as if we were her grandchildren.

"She wasn't that vigorous. Yes, she would tell us stories, and my sister in particular. She taught my sister how to keep house and so forth. My Job! The job she gave me was to sweep the dirt off their sidewalk, in front of their picket fence. She used to give me a nickel for sweeping the dirt off," he says. It's a fond memory.

He points to another picture.

"Now this is her son. Ed Gibson. Edwin. She's there again. He was a volunteer during the Spanish American War. He was a first lieutenant. And I remember, one day they were opening trunks upstairs. And she took out his uniform and said, 'That's Ed's uniform.' He had his officer's sword and so forth. I was quite impressed! Full officer's uniform and sword! But he was a real scholar! Because of the place where he lived, he never received a formal education beyond high school. But to this day, I have never met a man who surpassed him in learning! And I know at least eight or nine people who are Ph.D.s. And I don't know a single one among them who I would rate above him in overall education and knowledge.

"He was in the real estate business. And he was also county auditor. He used to come over to chat with my father, practically every day. They used to exchange books, or loan each other books and magazines. They got along very well.

"Every Christmas, why we used to exchange gifts. And he used to bring his mother over some evenings to eat at our place. We used to go over there. We were invited there for dinner. So we were very close. He was just like an uncle to me.

"I should really have called him 'Uncle Ed.' But I didn't know any better, and since his mother always called him 'Ed' and my father called him 'Ed,' why I just called him 'Ed.' Every Christmas, every birthday he would remember my sister and me by sending us books.

"One of them was—My niece has it now, is *Lodengro* (?) by George Barrow. He's not too well known. But he's a good English writer. He's one of the first who wrote from firsthand experience, on the life of Gypsies. This man was interested in languages. And so when he traveled with this Gypsy group, he made it a point to study their language. I enjoyed the book. Oh, yes.

"His home was practically a library. His living room: he had books on at least three of the walls. Just solid bookcases on the walls. And upstairs. The 'Children's Room,' where he and his brother grew up as children, he had quite a large collection of children's books there. And after awhile he gave us access to all the books in his place.

"He gave us all kinds of fairy tale books, and among the fairy tale books that we enjoyed most were the books by the German fairy tale writer Hauff. And I liked them better than I did Hans Christian Andersen or Grimm, because in most of the fairy tales written by them, the good guy or good person finally won out and they lived happily ever after. Well, I know that life wasn't like that. And the reason I liked Hauff was that in Hauff's fairy tales, the good guy often died and the bad guy triumphed. But usually it turned out that the bad guy's triumph really didn't do him any good anyway."

PRESENTS

The Story of the Caliph Stork

by

WILHELM HAUFF

…They turned towards the east and kept on bowing continually till their beaks nearly touched the ground. But, alas! the magic word had escaped them, and as often as the Caliph bowed, and however eagerly his Vizier added Mu—Mu-Mu, yet every recollection of it had gone, and the poor Chasid and his Vizier were and remained storks.

During the first days they remarked great uneasiness and grief in the streets. But on the fourth day of their enchantment, while sitting on the roof of the Caliph's palace, they saw down below in the street a splendid array. The drums and fifes played; a man dressed in a gold-embroidered scarlet mantle rode a richly caparisoned horse, surrounded by a gaudy train of servants. Half Bagdad rushed about him, and everybody shouted: "Hail, Mizra! the ruler of Bagdad!"

Then the two storks upon the roof of the palace looked at each other, and the Caliph Chasid said: "Do you guess now why I am enchanted, Grand Vizier? This Mizra is the son of my mortal enemy, the mighty Magician Kashnur, who in an evil hour swore revenge on me. But still I do not despair. Come with me, thou faithful companion of my misery; we will betake ourselves to the grave of the Prophet; perhaps at that sacred shrine the magic may be dispelled."

They rose from the roof of the palace and flew towards Medina….

 In the ruined chamber, which was only dimly lighted by a little iron-barred window, he saw a great night-owl sitting on the ground. Heavy tears rolled out of its large round eyes, and with a hoarse voice it uttered its moans from its hooked beak. But when it saw the Caliph and his Vizier, who had also come up in the meantime, it gave a loud cry of joy. Elegantly it wiped the tears from its eye with its brown-flecked wings, and to the great amazement of both, it cried in good human Arabic: "Welcome, ye storks; you are a good omen to me of my deliverance, for through storks I am to be lucky as it was once foretold me."

The Caliph, by the story of the Princess, was plunged into deep thought. "If I am not mistaken," said he, "there is between our misfortunes a secret connection; but where can I find the key to this riddle?" The owl answered him: "O Master! Such is also my belief; for once in my infancy a wise woman foretold of me that a stork should bring me a great fortune, and I know one way by which perhaps we may free ourselves." The Caliph was very much surprised, and asked what way she meant. "The enchanter who has made us both unhappy," said she, "comes once every month to these ruins. Not far from here is a hill where he holds orgies with numerous companions. Often have I spied them there. They then relate to one another their vile deeds. Perhaps he may pronounce the magic word which you have forgotten."

"Speak out, speak out," cried Chasid. "Command all, everything of me."

"It is this, that I may also become free, which can only be if one of you offer me his hand."

The Caliph … resolved to fulfil the condition himself. The owl was immensely pleased.

In the centre of the hall was a round table, covered with many and choicest meats. Round this table was a couch, on which sat eight men. In one of these men the stork recognized the pedlar who had sold them the magic powder. His neighbour asked him to relate his latest deeds. Amongst others he also related the story of the Caliph and his Vizier.

"What sort of word hast thou given them?" asked another enchanter. "A very difficult Latin one, namely, 'Mutabor.'"

Thrice the storks bowed their long necks to the sun, which just then was rising behind the mountains. "Mutabor!" they exclaimed; and straightaway they were changed, and in the great joy of their new-sent life master and servant fell into each other's arms laughing and crying. But who can describe their astonishment on turning round? A lovely lady, grandly dressed, stood before them. Smiling, she gave her hand to the Caliph. "Do you no longer recognize your night-owl?" she said. It was she. The Caliph was so charmed with her beauty and grace, that he exclaimed: "My greatest fortune was that of having been a stork."

Kentaro Takatsui,
Kibei-Nisei

PARIS HOTEL, SEATTLE

"After we came back from Japan, when I was about twelve years old, we set-
tled in Seattle, and we got this Paris Hotel. There was a big hotel on Sixth
Avenue on Weller Street. Right on the corner. Two-story building. Big one. Sixth and
Weller. Close to Chinatown. There was Bailey Gatzert, a grade school, right on Weller
and Twelfth Avenue. Right on the corner there. Red brick building, you know.
The Nippon-Kan, way up on the hill there. Yesler Way and Sixth Avenue South."

Hotels were big business for Issei in Seattle. In 1925, the year Kentaro Takatsui
and his family went to Japan, Issei managed 127 hotels, with a total of 8,575 rooms.

"When a Japanese family ran a hotel, everybody pitched in and helped. My
father had to wake up all hours of the night because customers come in. They
ring the bell. They want to rent a room maybe one o'clock in the morning, midnight, three o'clock in the morning, you know. Usually I didn't do that. But my
father did that. Usually I get up at the usual hour because I had to go to school.

"After we finished American school, we would walk from Bailey Gatzert
grade school, three or four blocks, and we'd go to Japanese school. Japanese language school. It was in a building by itself. It was a big Japanese school. We went
for three hours every evening after American grade school to just study the
Japanese language. College graduates from Japan teaching there. Issei women.
A few young girls who came from Japan and were attending the University of
Washington, took the job there, to teach Japanese.

"We'd go home and help a couple of hours in the hotel, clean up the hallways, clean the steps, because mother and father had finished making the bed in each room in the morning.

"But during summer vacations, weekends, we all helped make beds, you know. That was a seventy-room hotel, by the way. Seventy is a lot of rooms.

"There was a sink down the hall, and a toilet down the hall. And there was a small two-burner gas stove in some of the rooms. And some of the rooms had a sink.

"And I could tell by the signs on the door . . . like for example, that one there would be sealed up and this one would be single, and the other room would be a single. On that door they used to have a sign that said 'Dixie Lee.'

"At the time when I was young, I didn't know, but as I grew a little older, I started to realize that this used to be a whorehouse.

"In that little office, one room there, there were places with a window, and rows of books by the window. Customers used to ring a bell, a small bell there. And then there was a small room next door where father and mother lived by themselves. In one room, my two sisters lived, and one room for my brother and myself.

"Mother spoke very little English. Father spoke very little. Very little. Customers understood. All the Issei were like that. All the Issei. The great majority of the customers were Caucasian. Yeah, working men. Warehouse . . . they worked on the docks. They called them longshoremen, in those days. And people used to work on the ships that go up to Alaska and come back. They rented a room, and when they shipped on a ship to Alaska, nobody was in that room, but they wanted that room kept. When they came back they lived there, you know, because we were a few blocks from the docks.

"In those days it was fifty-five cents a night and up. And up means sixty cents, seventy-five cents, you see. Weekly, rates a little cheaper. Monthly, the rates a little cheaper.

"King Street. King and Maynard. Jackson Street, one street over, used to be Chinatown. There used to be a meat market, right there on the corner of King and Maynard. Russell's Meats. Right on the corner of King and Maynard.

"There was a Welcome Hotel there on Jackson Street and Sixth Avenue. All on that corner. Used to be wooden building Welcome Hotel. My friend used to own that. And down below was a theater. Movie theater. And we used to go around looking for empty bottles . . . all the kids in a gang. Ten, twelve, thirteen years old, somewhere around there. We used to go look for empty bottles, then we'd go and sell the empty bottles, and each of us would make five cents each, you see. Two empty bottles we used to take to a secondhand store and we used to get a penny for it. And make five cents, and we'd go in that theater. And all we saw was a movie . . . cowboy pictures. To this day I love cowboy pictures. And by the way I like country music. I like Roy Acuff. Red Foley."

Ford,
The Universal Car

FORD MANUAL
MODEL T

For Owners and Operators
of
Ford Cars and Trucks

What must be done before staring the car?

Answer No. 1

Before trying to start the car, fill the radiator (by removing cap at top) with clean fresh water. If perfectly clean water cannot be obtained it is advisable to strain it through muslin or other similar material to prevent foreign matter from getting in and obstructing the small tubes of the radiator. The system will hold approximately three gallons. It is important that the car should not be run under its own power unless the water circulating system has been filled. Pour in the water until you are sure that both radiator and cylinder water jackets are full. The water will run out of the over flow pipe onto the ground when the entire water system has been properly filled. During the first few days that a new car is being driven it is a good plan to examine the radiator frequently and see that it is kept properly filled. The water supply should be replenished as often as may be found necessary. Soft rain water, when it is to be had in a clean state, is superior to hard water, which may contain alkalies and other salts which tend to deposit sediment and clog the radiator. (See chapter on Cooling System.)

What about gasoline?

Answer No. 2

The ten-gallon gasoline tank should be filled—nearly full—and the supply should never be allowed to get low. When filling the tank be sure that there are no naked flames within several feet, as the vapor is extremely volatile and travels rapidly. Always be careful about lighting matches near where gasoline has been spilled, as the air within a radius of several feet is permeated with the highly explosive vapor. The small vent hole in the gasoline tank cap should not be allowed to get plugged up, as this would prevent proper flow of the gasoline to the carburator. The gasoline tank may be drained by opening the pet cock in the sediment bulb at the bottom.

Kentaro Takatsui, Kibei-Nisei

THE FIRST CAR

"**W**hen we were in the Paris Hotel. Our first car, a Model A Ford. Father and Mother did not drive. I looked at the book. I drove it. You know, in those days, they didn't have driving school because there weren't many cars on the streets. Scarce. There were still lots of wagons being pulled by horses.

"We used to go in the car, and we'd drive out in the country, where it was a little more cleaner air. And we'd visit his friends. Out in Auburn. I hear nowadays those farmlands are gone now, but in those days, it was all empty farmland out there. White River, Auburn, Puyallup, Renton, South Park. All that area used to be nothing but farmland. And my father's Issei friends used to own small farms out there. We used to visit them on weekends with presents. Like *senbei* (rice cookies), Japanese *okashi*, from the Japanese candy store on Maynard and Jackson. And they came into Seattle for shopping and visited us. That was a big deal. The whole family would get in the car, drive out in the country. Dad would tell a story. Long drive. Long story. *Shiju shichi Ronin, The Forty-Seven Ronin,* That's *Chushingura*. And *Miyamoto Musashi, Iwami Jutaro, Awaki Mataemon*.

"Well, Dad taught me many things I remember, while we were working in the hotel, working together, making the beds, sweeping up the floors. Everybody pitched in. I remember while we were working, he used to tell me,

44

he says, 'When you grow up, don't ever lay your hands on another man's wife.' I remember that. He said this in Japanese, '*Hito no okusan ni, omaye wa zettai ni te o dasuna*.' See, he taught . . . Issei taught morals. All these morals came from your Chinese teaching: Confucianism, Taoism. There are many other Chinese poets that you don't hear about. But the Japanese know.

"When the Great Depression came on and the stock market crashed, I remember you know. One of the customers would come hollering down to the office, 'There's gas all over the place near room so-and-so!'

"And we know which room the gas came out of because it was the strongest there. And knocked on the door, and they wouldn't open the door so father had to crash in the door and get in there. This man was laying on the bed, and he had the gas turned on. And he put paper around the window, and the door to keep the gas in. And they were all nicely dressed, fingernails were all polished. And father said, 'He must have lost money in the stock market.'

"Maybe once in every two weeks, once a month, somebody would always be doing that."

That Tango Tokio

words by ALFRED BRYAN

music by JACK WELLS and ARTHUR LANGE

Oh, oh, you sly little, sly little, sly little Japanese!
You are a fly little, fly little, fly little Japanese!
Tho' you sometimes make us mad,
If you want to make us glad,
Do that teasing Tango Tokio

Kentaro Takatsui, Kibei-Nisei

PICTURE OF THE JAPANESE NAVY VISITS

"There were antique battleships used during the Russo-Japanese War. They came once a year maybe. Once in two years. All the Japanese welcomed them. You see, in every Japanese family, especially after the victory over Russia, the Russo-Japanese War of 1904–1905, remember Admiral Togo at Tsushima Strait wiped out the Russian fleet? General Nogi took over the Russian fortress in the Port Arthur area, remember? That's history. So they were the first Orientals that had beaten the white race in modern warfare. You see, up to then, all you had to do was to look at the map of the world. Every country, colored race people were occupied, conquered by a white race. The Issei taught us that.

"So, especially after the Russians were defeated, the stories of Admiral Togo, General Nogi were repeated over and over among the Japanese. Wherever they gathered. Not only to the children to pass on to the next generation, but you went to see a movie, the silent movies. We saw movies about the Russo-Japanese War. You see the Japanese soldiers conquering the famous Nirei zan Hill. That is known in English as 'Strategic Point 103 Meter Hill.' That was where General Nogi sacrificed hundreds of thousands of Japanese soldiers to conquer that Kinshu fortress of the Russians, at Ryojun (Port Arthur) on the southern tip of the Liadong Peninsula. You saw that movie. You saw the navy victory, Tsushima Straits. Admiral Togo defeating the Russians. Not only the movies, but the books that you picked up written for Japanese children: Admiral Togo, General Nogi."

The old man recites:

KINSHU-JO

Tsukuru

NOGI MARESUKE

Sansen somoku utata koryo
Juri kaze namagusahshi shinsenjo
Seiba susumazu hito katarazu
Kinshu-jo gai shayo ni tatsu

He offers a word-by-word literal translation:

KINSHU-JO

composed by

NOGI MARESUKE

Mountains and rivers, grass and trees so desolate
Ten-*ri* wind bloody smell newly fought battlefield
Military horse will not move forward men are appalled into silence.
Kinshu-fortress outside sunset at stand

Then he offers his own translation where "no poetic interpretation" is attempted. Only the feeling:

How ever more desolate is the scene before me
The mountains, rivers, green grass and trees are mostly withered and
    deathly silent.
For over ten *ri* [each *ri* = 2½ miles], the wind carries the sanguinary odor
    of a newly fought battlefield.
My war horse is stunned and will not move forward.
My staff members are appalled into silence, transfixed,
Speechless and hurt to the quick, I stand outside of
Kinshu fortress at sunset.

Dr. Clifford Uyeda, Traveler

"**Y**ou just completely believed in the propaganda that had been given to you. Especially in the Japanese community, often they look at the leaders and put them up too high on a pedestal, and everything they say is always right. It isn't right. I still remember when I was going to Japanese language school, the teacher used to talk about Nogi Taisho, Gen. Nogi.

"Gen. Nogi was possibly one of worst Japanese military ever to exist. Everything he did, he did wrong. He was a failure."

"He was a hero of the Russo-Japanese War," Paul Tsuneishi says.

"The only reason that he was a hero was because he committed suicide when the emperor of Meiji died. His command was even taken away from him in Manchuria later because he was so inefficient, so incompetent, and they replaced him with someone else. Yet this is the person that is just talked about almost like a god."

"There's the other side of the story, which is really fascinating, and that is, that other side of the story, he knew what tremendous cost in Japanese lives [it took] to win that battle, so he wanted to commit *hara-kiri*. The emperor forbade him from doing that. But after the emperor died, he did that, and his wife followed him in *hara-kiri*. That's the other side of the story."

"I wonder if that's an excuse that was manufactured after the war, because before the war, he was in command of a lot of Japanese troops and failed everywhere."

Shosuke Sasaki, Japanese American Conscience

HIGHER STANDARDS

"**M**y father and mother made it very plain to us that we were different. That we were expected to behave and live according to higher standards than the ordinary run of people. Sometimes when I would see other children doing something that I wanted to do, my mother would tell me, 'You're not supposed to do that!'

"I remember eating while walking in the street. Now, in Japan, that's considered poor manners. When I came to this country, now, all my Caucasian friends, they'd think nothing of buying a bar from the candy store and come out eating it. I came home one day munching on a bar and was immediately taken to task by my mother. 'Well, why can't I do it? The other kids do!'

"'Well, it doesn't make any difference what the other kids do. You come from a Samurai family. You're supposed to behave accordingly.'

"My father was a graduate of Japan's First Merchant Marine School. He later studied English from a British tutor in Kyoto. And as I grew up in this country, when he would hear me using a new word, he would once in awhile stop and ask me, 'What is the definition of that term you just used?' And if I was unable to give him an exact definition of that term, I used to get a severe scolding for using words I didn't know the meaning of. I was told only fools did things like that.

"The only time they spanked us was if we came home late. We were expected to be back home at six o'clock, and if we didn't show up till seven or so, well, naturally, they'd get worried. And the minute we entered the door, well, whoosh! my sister and I, we'd both be spanked! So we wouldn't forget the next time.

"The most lasting impression that my father left on me was that he was a man who insisted on absolute and total honesty and integrity. And that he was not the kind of man who would easily accept insults from Caucasians.

"When I came to this country at the age of seven, I was naturally small, in relation to my Caucasian friends. And getting into fights was fairly frequent, because I, too, was not the kind who would take insults from Caucasians easily.

"They used to call me a 'Jap.' I remember, I used to get furious and start fighting back. And I would occasionally come home with a bloody nose. After this had happened a few times, I thought, 'Well, I'm going to fix that kid!' One morning I was going to school. I picked up a toy wooden mallet. My father saw it, and he said, 'What are you doing with that mallet?'

"I said, 'Well, I'm going to fix that kid I've been getting into fights with.' And upon that, the color of his face changed. He became very serious. He said, 'If you go out and get in a fight and use that mallet, don't you dare come home without having killed your man!'

"I was about eight. That was a shock to me when he said that in absolute seriousness. And I don't remember the exact words he used, but he impressed upon me the importance of fighting fairly, if it was merely a matter of a dispute.

"My father was a graduate of Japan's First Merchant Marine School, and apparently he had been taught or had learned judo there. I never realized it at the time. He never boasted of it. He said, 'You're coming home with a bloody nose like this has got to stop! I'll teach you!' And he showed me one judo throw. I didn't realize it was a judo throw at the time. He never said it was. Just a way of throwing an opponent. He made me practice every day after I came home from school for about a month. And he said, 'All right, you've got it.'

"Then I went back to school and provoked the other kid. And I had no difficulty just flipping him flat on the ground. And after that my fights came to an end. Kids left me alone.

"My father and mother were Buddhists. But the whole town had no Buddhist church. And so my father felt that rather than grow up without any religious instruction, we should go to a Christian church. And one of his friends happened to be Methodist who gladly took us in tow. And after that introduction we went to church, without fail, every Sunday. That is my sister and I. I enjoyed those days. The pastor and his wife were most kind. The other people in the church were also kind.

"My father died in a sudden hemorrhage.

"I was in school. Both my sister and I were in school. And someone came to the classroom door and told me I was needed at home. So I left the room, and this man who came to notify me went to the next classroom and got my sister and told us both we had better hurry home. We didn't know what had happened and thought that perhaps my mother had become seriously ill, because my mother had been in what we thought was more fragile health than my father. When we came home and discovered that my father was dead, it came as a complete shock. I never dreamed that he would pass on.

"Then we sold the business and moved up to Seattle, because we wanted to be near other Japanese. My mother had never bothered to learn to speak English. My father was bilingual in the real sense of the word. He could read, write, and speak both languages before he came over."

Nobu Kawai,
The Volunteer

Nobu Kawai was a city boy, grew up in a white neighborhood, and went to a white high school and junior college, all in Pasadena, California. Like the JACL's leader, Mike Masaoka, Kawai did not enjoy reading, but did enjoy writing and speaking. He has a bachelor's degree in journalism. During the war, while he and wife Miye were interned at Gila, he founded the only chapter of the JACL to be formed in camp. Gila was one of the two camps, out of nine, that had no draft resisters. When he moved to Heart Mountain Relocation Center, he became an editor of the camp newspaper, the *Heart Mountain Sentinel*, founded and edited by Bill Hosokawa of the Seattle JACL.

Nobu Kawai is in his eighties. He's a well-built, very fit-looking man. His flesh is not an embarrassment to life. He moves without any visible complaints. His voice is full and fills the room. He's proud of his English. The Nisei city boys are proud of their accents, their vocabulary, their persuasive way with words. He tells a story of how his good English and non-Japanese ways make him likable. What he says is one thing; what makes him likable is another. Like what he says or not, he is a very likable man. And his wife, fit and crocheting in a chair facing the TV that is turned off, is a very likable woman, making them a very likable couple. Ozzie and Harriet, with a little edge of Maggie and Jiggs.

Most of the time she listens, hums, and grunts and mumbles agreement and emphasis. When she jumps in to finish his thought and flash him a caution, they sound like a well-rehearsed comedy team. A little Burns and Allen. A little

Judy Holliday and Broderick Crawford. A little "Lum 'n Abner" of the radio of their time.

"My father's name was Toichiro Kawai, and my mother's name was Hama Kawa. My mother was from Kanagawa-ken. She was from Yokohama. My father was from Shizuoka-ken, which is the next *ken* over. He was from a town called Ainshu.

"My father first came to America in 1898. He came over alone as a seaman on an American naval vessel. It was a sailing vessel, a training vessel. And this American naval training vessel was in Yokohama. They were ready to sail back to America. But evidently, in those days, the crews of naval ships would get awfully drunk. And so the crewmen didn't all show up when it was ready to sail. They were short a ship's carpenter. They had to have a ship's carpenter, you see. Because they had to climb the mast and repair it and things like that.

"Father was a ship's carpenter. He used to work on sailing vessels between Yokohama and the south Pacific there—Hong Kong, Singapore—and places like that, on merchant vessels. When this American warship in Yokohama asked for volunteers, dad wanted to come to America, so he volunteered as a ship's carpenter. His chief mate was the original Jack Sharkey."

"The boxer?" Miye asks, lifting her head.

"Well, yeah. It was his forerunner. The Jack Sharkey that most of us know, came after this Jack Sharkey."

"Oh," Miye says dryly.

"This ship set course for San Francisco. My dad got the idea that if it would dock, he'd be shipped back to Japan. So he jumped overboard. He came in as a wetback. He swam ashore."

"He was a wetback," Miye echoes her husband and laughs. This is radio vaudeville. George Burns and Gracie Allen again.

"So he took a job in San Francisco. He worked until he had enough money to return to Japan to pick up my mother and an older sister who was born in Japan. They came over in 1902. I guess, it was somewhere there, I don't know the exact date.

"The older sister was four years old when she came over. She was a noncitizen. But the rest of us six boys and two girls were all born here. I was born here in Pasadena. March 21, 1907, across the street. I don't think they were born in hospitals at that time. Most of the births were by, what do you call these?"

"Midwives," Miye prompts.

"Midwives. Yeah. They had big families all around at that time.

"Dad was a carpenter, but he did a lot of carving and art work. He worked for this importer of art goods, Victor Marsh Corporation. They had a place in San Francisco and a place in Pasadena. They would import these Oriental art goods from Japan. They would get pieces of carving that were knocked off and unsalable. My dad would carve a piece to fit in there and restore them and lacquer it to match the rest of the thing. Then they would be able to sell it. He did a lot of repair work on things that were imported from Japan. He worked for them a long time.

"We had birthday parties. Well, not elaborate things as they have now."

"Maybe they'll give you a dollar or something to keep you quiet with something," Miye says laughing.

"I think mother baked a chicken or something like that. Or roasted a chicken. We never made a fuss about birthday parties. We didn't have money to celebrate like that anyway."

"They would have to work when they were young. And then they would have to turn the money into mother. Mother would put it away," Miye says.

"I started working when I was eleven years old."

"Get up five o'clock in the morning. Deliver the milk," Miye says.

"Well, it was about four o'clock in the morning. And we would make the morning deliveries before school. I was a milk shagger. I don't know if you know what a milk shagger is or not. But in the olden days, we used to make house-to-house deliveries. The milkman would drive the truck and the shaggers would run the milk into the homes.

"So, we were milk shaggers. My brother and I worked off of one truck. We drive up the streets here, and one of us would jump off with two carriers of milk, and we'd deliver at the homes here, while the other would deliver at the houses at the other end of the street. And then we'd come back and pass the carriers with the empty bottles and shelf them, and take another street.

"Then we would go to school. The milkman would park the wagon over there, and as soon as school was out, we'd run out and jump on the wagon and deliver the afternoon milk."

"There was no child labor law," Miye quips.

"Well, that was our job. It was either be a milk shagger or a newspaper boy. And some of my brothers were newspaper boys. And I was a milk shagger.

"My mother would get up and feed us before we left the house. She had to get up early, too. We had American food. Toast and coffee—cocoa or something like that. I don't remember what we ate. But we didn't have a traditional Japanese breakfast—*miso-shiru*—something like that—"

"Rice and maybe a little fish or something like that," Miye says. "Oh! Tell them about your underwear!"

"My mother used to sew underwears out of flour sacks and stuff like that. She used to make our shirts out of materials she would get from Japan. And I was very conscious of my Japanese heritage. We lived in a strictly Caucasian community. It wasn't like Li'l Tokyo, where you have a lot of Japanese friends around. We were referred to as Japanese all the time.

"It was a question of identity with us. We knew we were Americans, but we were referred to as Japanese all the time. And even in our family, we talked about Americans as being whites. And you talk about other Nisei. They are Americans. But we talk about them as Japanese. It was hard to look at ourselves as Americans. Mother used to make our shirts out of materials she would get from Japan, and they were recognized as Japanese materials. And I would just hate to wear them to school. But I had nothing else to wear. We had snide remarks of being 'Japs' or 'skibbies' directed at us."

"I heard that," Miye says. "I heard that when I was growing up. Skibbies. I would be walking up a street and a couple of young boys would say 'skibbies!'"

"I don't know what it means," Nobu says.

"I don't either," Miye tells her husband.

"I went to Japanese language school on Saturday. My brother-in-law happened to be the teacher in Pasadena.

"There is another thing! We tried to avoid everything that reminded us of our Japanese heritage. It was embarrassing to me to bring Caucasian friends home and have my father reading a Japanese language newspaper in the front room. Or have them see us eating with chopsticks. Or my mother wear *zorii*— everything that pertained to Japanese culture was kind of embarrassing to me.

"It's quite a change now. You see Americans, the Caucasian Americans adopting so many of the Asiatic cultures. The hot tubs, which are Japanese *furo*. Most Americans use chopsticks now. Fall, the kids are wearing zoriis. Hibachi are household appliances. You don't think of those things now. But when we were kids, we were very conscious of those things. Yes, I tried to avoid all those things.

"I spent fifty-two years in the dairy industry. I started out with a small company out on a dairy farm. I lived on a dairy farm. They sold out to a company called Crown City Dairy. They merged with Creamery of America. Then it became Valley Maid Creamery. Then it merged with Beatrice Food Corporation, and then it became Meadow Gold. I couldn't stick with Meadow Gold.

"I had continuous employment with the company. Seniority for fifty-two years' employment. I did just about everything. I worked on the dairy farm feeding cattle, washing milk bottles, bottling milk, and so forth. And then when they sold out to Crown City Creamery, I worked at the milk plant here as a pasteurizer or bottler.

"Yes, I started in the dairy business in 1918, when I was eleven years old. That's the only work I've ever done.

"I think I became involved in journalism at Pasadena Junior College. Pasadena Junior College was just a new school in 19. . . . And I was in the second class. I think, altogether there were still less than a thousand students. So it was a very small school. It gave us an opportunity to participate in a lot of student activities. That was the reason I was involved in news writing on the newspaper and student annuals.

"And I was hoping to go into chemistry as the major. But I lacked the background in mathematics. I got through qualitative analysis fine. But when I got into quantitative analysis, which required higher math, I was completely lost. And I decided after that, chemistry was not my field.

"Like I said, I was very active in student affairs. I was involved in school publications, sports, and so forth. For the first time in my life, I felt that I was part of the crowd. It was the first time that I felt I was a part of the student government. I had never run for office, because it was sort of accepted, in my mind, that a Nisei would never be elected.

"Although there was discrimination still, I had the support of my classmates. I was induced to run for student body office. And, lo and behold! They elected me secretary of publicity! From there on, one thing led to another, and I started an honor society over there. It is one of the few organizations that still exists at Pasadena City College.

"I enjoyed journalism so much that I went into journalism. As a matter of fact, one course I flunked was English. And the reason for that was, I despised English. I'm a very poor reader. In fact, I don't know whether I have ever read a book cover to cover. Unless it's a small book—but I don't like reading. I like reference books. I do use reference books quite a bit. But as far as novels, fictions, or stuff like that, or even historical materials, I'm not too keen on it. I'm not that much of a scholar."

"Well," Miye says, "his Bible is his dictionary. And also he has his thesaurus."

"At that time, I think I was five-eleven. I think I shrank. I don't think I'm more than five-ten now. We were big guys in those days."

"In those days," Miye says.

"Big guys!" Nobu says.

"Yeah, at that time," Miye says in rhythm. "It was a novelty to see a Japanese play football. Like, when he went to Hawaii. Everybody came out to see this big guy play football."

"I think it was 1928, wasn't it? Oh, you don't know. I think it was 1928."

Miye says, "If it wasn't '27 it was '28."

"I played fullback. Number 34 for the Pasadena Pirates. I weighed 152 pounds. It was quite a novelty for a Japanese to come from the mainland and play in Hawaii, see."

"You ought to see how many pictures he put away," Miye says.

"They gave me a lot of publicity when I was over there."

"You see, the previous year, Pasadena Junior College had won the state championship. So, we were invited to play St. Louis College in Honolulu. One of our team members was a Japanese American from Honolulu, Torao Inouye. And he made arrangements to get invited to Honolulu. It was the first time that a junior college team had played in Hawaii. So we grabbed the opportunity and we made this trip to Hawaii.

"We didn't have transoceanic flight at that time. We went over by boat. Well, it was the L.A. Steamship Company. We went over on—No! It was the *President Taft*! That's right. We went over on the *President Taft* and came back on the L.A. Steamship Company's *Kuali Wei*. It was really a barge. It took us seven days going over and eight or nine days to come back. We all got seasick.

"One of our assignments was to write several themes for English, while we were on this trip to Hawaii. It you know football players, when they are on a trip like that, they don't spend any time studying. You could imagine the dean who came along with us, and he was supposed to get us to study. But none of us football players were studying."

JOURNALISM

"We had a very interesting instructor in journalism. He taught English in such a different way than your English teachers teach that I really enjoyed it.

"I never never knew what a dangling participle was. I still can't tell. He had a way of explaining things. He said, for instance, 'Turning the corner, the building came into view.' What you're saying is the building turned the corner. He said that is a dangling participle.

"For the first time, I understood what a dangling participle was.

"He had other ways of teaching writing. Instead of calling them 'themes' he would call them 'feature stories,' or 'news stories.' So, he sent us out on a news story, and he assigned me to a meeting. I went to the meeting, and the meeting was cancelled. And so, I came back. He asked me, 'Where's the story?' I said, 'There is no story. The meeting was cancelled.' He said, 'There's always a story, and you write a story on how it was cancelled.'

"So, I had to write a story on how it was cancelled.

"He was a German. He had a moustache. He was full of theatrics. Von Grinigen was his last name. I can't remember what his first name was. He would send me to cover a lecture. So I go there. And I knew I would have to write something, so I would have to stay awake and listen to what that speaker was saying and make notes as to the points he was making. And so when I came back, I knew what he was talking about. And I wrote the story.

"In journalism, they teach you the meaning of a lead and you answer the questions: 'Who?' 'What?' 'When?' and 'Where?' And so he says, 'Answer all your questions in your opening paragraph, which is your lead.'

"He would get up there in front of that class and say, 'Now words that so often are misspelled, often enough are words that end in ceed. Proceed, succeed, and so forth.

"'All you have to remember is pro—suck—and—S-C double E-D! All the others are c-e-e-d except hayseed. Remember pro-suck-and —S-C double E-D.' He gave all sorts of things like that. That made journalism, or the English, interesting. We didn't have to diagram sentences or anything like that. But we did have style manuals.

"I don't know how familiar you are with journalism, but every news organization has a style manual because the English language is so pliable that two newspapers can't agree on a perfect style. Especially, right now, when you have sexism and so forth. Some newspapers would talk about a 'chair person.' And they used the title 'Ms.' instead of 'Mrs.' and 'Miss' and so forth.

"It is the option of the newspaper what style they would use. And so you would have to know the style of the particular newspaper in order to write and conform to their particular policy. And we studied these style manuals. And in there it gave different rules for capitalization and terms of address and so forth. It made writing very interesting. That made writing easy. So, I began to enjoy writing. So, I decided, I would go into writing. I spent part time as a stringer at the Pasadena newspaper, and got to know the editors and people there.

"Then this schoolmate of mine and I were both journalists. And we decided we would go on to college and get a journalism degree. The managing editor of the *Pasadena Star-News* was from Columbia University and the city editor was from Missouri. They were kind of influencing me to go to either Columbia or Missouri. Lee Merriman was the city editor. And he said, 'Nobe, if you're going to college, you may as well go to the Number One school.' He said, 'When you finish, you'll get a journalism degree, instead of bachelor's degree in journalism.'

"So he was telling me about Missouri. I decided to go to Missouri. This friend of mind didn't have any money. So he took a city news job in Los Angeles. And he went from there to become a very outstanding journalist in southern California. He was public relations man for the All Year Club of Southern California. And he's done a lot of feature stories for them. But he never did go on to get his degree. I went on and I got my degree. Yeah, I was a novelty back there, too. You see. . . ."

"They'd never seen a Japanese back there," Miye says.

"I didn't make the varsity team at Missouri. I made the traveling squad, and I got a lot of travel out of it. We played in Yankee Stadium and all the other Big Eight schools. Nebraska, Kansas, Kansas State, Oklahoma. . . .

"I was virtually promised a job on a newspaper in Pasadena when I came back. But I finished in 1930, which was the beginning of the Depression.

"In Los Angeles, the *Tribune* went out of business. Several newspapers consolidated. In Pasadena, we had the *Star-News* and the *Pasadena Post*. And the *Pasadena Post* went broke. So they consolidated. And, gee, here I just got out of school and was trying to get a job when a lot of seasoned newspapermen were looking for work. It wasn't possible to get a job. And so I reluctantly went back to working at the dairy. As the economic conditions began to get better, the war clouds got darker. It made it impossible for me to change professional fields. I was offered a job with the *L.A. Times*, as a copy runner. But it was at such a small salary, I couldn't afford to take it. So I stayed at the dairy."

Momotaro, The Peach Boy

Here we are in a beautiful mountain region of Japan near the sea. An old samurai and his wife have packed up the sword and picked up the plow. They are old and childless. They grow rice.

One day he's out cutting firewood and she goes down to the river to beat dirty clothes on wet rocks till the clothes are clean.

The old woman looks up from washing clothes to see a huge peach, larger than a beach ball, bobbing down the river.

"Oooh," the old woman says, "this is going to be good to eat tonight after the same old rice."

And after dinner the old man picks up his knife and slice! "Whoops, what's this little naked baby boy doing standing up in the middle there? This peach has no seed, only a little boy! He's perfect. He's the child we have always wanted."

Life is good where Momotaro, the Peach boy, lives by the sea. The weather is always perfect and the crops always full. And there are no pirates and marauders. This is because this part of Japan is protected by the *oni*. In return for their protection, all the oni ask is children.

Every now and then the oni come from an island across the sea to collect payment for their protection, in children. The oni are demons, monsters who eat children.

Momotaro does not think giving up children to the oni is such a good idea. His parents tell him, he's a little boy. He's young and doesn't understand politics.

But Momotaro insists he's going off to fight the oni. His parents relent and make him kibidango rice cakes to eat along his way to war. They give him armor, a long and short sword, an iron fan. They give him a flag with the peach crest on it and the slogan "Nippon Ichi"—"Japan First!"

On his way to the sea, he gathers three allies. The dog, who asks for something to eat, the monkey, who asks for something to eat, and the pheasant, who asks for something to eat. Momotaro shares a kibidango with each.

The dog can bite through trees and fell them. The monkey can climb like the dickens. The pheasant can fly high and scout what's ahead and dive and peck. Momotaro, the dog, the monkey, and the pheasant build a boat, cross the sea. They massacre the oni. They capture the oni chief and he surrenders by breaking off his horns and giving them to Momotaro. Momotaro and his friends free the children, return the treasure.

Momotaro goes home because the old man and old woman kept their word. They did not sell Momotaro to monsters for the good life. And everyone who'd had it so easy for so long has to work for a living again, and they have to raise their children instead of selling them to monsters for good weather, good crops, good money, and the good life.

James Omura,
Nisei Newsman

"ALL MOTHERS COOK"

"All mothers cook. What I remember is she prepared the rice mash out of which dad made his homemade whiskey—remember this was the Prohibition Era—in such a way that it was a treat we children looked forward to. It was yum, yum!"

James "Jimmie" Omura was born on Bainbridge Island, in Washington's Puget Sound, in the Year of the Water Rat, 1912. In a little town named Winslow, on the eastern side of the island. The ferry from Seattle docked there.

"Dad also cooked. When he had the time, he'd really prepare sumptuous eats, bake bread—there was a lot of that and it was good good—and other pastries, cakes, pies, etc. He was a damn good cook and had to take over after mom went to Japan.

"When we got older, my brother Casey did most of the cooking. I occasionally helped, and I probably learned how to cook that way. Of course I cook. I'd starve otherwise. I picked it up working as a schoolboy in people's homes, and later batching. Nothing complicated, just simple home cooking. Oh, yes! I used to ingratiate myself with the cooks at the Alaskan canneries to obtain special favors. I just got this thing about eating.

"I don't know too much about my dad, except for the fact, during the First World War, he was foreman of the carpenters at the Marine Shipbuilding Company. Then, after that he had a little problem when my mother got sick.

"My dad decided to take her and three of the kids to Japan and then decided to come back. So, there were three of us left. The older ones.

"We were given the option of remaining or going to Japan with our folks and never coming back. We didn't like this never coming back business, so we elected to stay with a guardian.

"Well, from six years old until my father came back, we didn't get along with the guardian, so were running away from home all the time and causing him all kinds of grief. My oldest brother ran away the first day. And they had a hell of a time getting him back. They called the police and everything. We stayed in Seattle. They finally decided that if we were going to run away, anyway, we should go back to our home on Bainbridge Island.

"We had a big house, two-story house on ten acres. That's where we had lived all our lives. We were born there. So we went back. This was a different story. We're not going to run away from our real home, you know. But we didn't get along with our guardian. We were always having trouble with our guardian.

"I suppose you could say my dad was a carpenter, but in his time, he was considered a builder. He built residential homes and industrial and business buildings throughout the Puget Sound area. Port Angeles, Seattle, places like that. I don't know how he learned carpentry. He came to America as a cabin boy. In fact, he stowed away. I just don't know how he learned. But he could read blueprints and start from scratch. He'd install the plumbing and string the electric wires where necessary. Soup to nuts! He had the general tools of the time. He had handsaws, bucksaws, etc. All manually operated. He sharpened his tools himself.

"We had pedal-powered grinders. He was not a cabinetmaker or an artisan making artcraft. He did not spend much time around the house, although, the last two years before I left, we lived in a house he built. It was the Johnson house near Rolling Bay. We lived there in lieu of payment.

"One of our problems was that my father wasn't a strawberry farmer like the rest of them on the island. After awhile things got a little tough for him. He couldn't make a living there. That's the reason he had to go to Port Angeles and Seattle to build homes.

"I was never at any site where he was working. I have never developed any interest in carpentry. I couldn't cut a straight cut with the saw. My older brother, Casey, had some of my dad's carpentry traits. I was just a useless boy around the house. Played a lot; read a lot; and ate a lot. No sheds. No truck. No phone.

"We had a dog. One dog. He was a big dog.

"Dad had a Ford touring sedan. He was on the road all the time for long periods of time. I remember one summer, my father took me to Bellingham. He had a summer-long carpentry job at the fishmeal manufacturing plant. In retrospect, I think the reason he did this was the previous year, I had a long struggle recovering from a gunshot wound. That trip to Bellingham was the first and only time he took any of us with him. So, in his own way, he favored me. At that time, I lacked the perspicacity to understand.

"I did fret about spending a whole summer picking berries in the hot sun and never being able to see the result of my efforts. Growers paid my wages to my father, which was a Japanese custom. What I would get would be five or ten dollars and a large bag of peanuts. And probably some candy bars.

"I knew he was sending money back to Japan to support my mother, my two younger sisters, and a younger brother. I didn't object to that. But I sure would have liked to have seen what I had earned. I never knew how much. That irked me.

"I wasn't interested in comics, because I didn't feel they did me any good. I started reading other books. I read *War and Peace* and all those things. I read the Greek and Roman histories and stuff like that. I read the philosophies of Aristotle, Kant, Nietzsche, and Spinoza when I must have been ten or twelve—all on my own. I had nothing else to do, so I would go up to the library and pick out a book. Not just one book. I used to take out six to eight books at a shot. I didn't want to be going back each week. It was a little ways to the library. And I had to walk each time I went. That was the reason I took out six to eight books.

"If you have conviction, you will make a stand, even if it hurts. They tell me I have some of that quality. I supposed I acquired it somehow from such immortals of the past as Sir Galahad of King Arthur's Round Table. Roland! And Oliver in Charlemagne. I forget now, but who was it that stood at the bridge in the pass? Horatio? Sparta or someone in the old Greek history who had the courage to stand and defend the pass against insurmountable odds. People who stood and fought when the odds were all against them.

"I thought my father was just as good in his community as any hakujin. He was well-liked by the hakujins. My dad knew good English. At home, all we spoke was English. Perhaps that encouraged my reading. Well, we didn't have anything else to do. Either we read or we wrote. I did a lot of reading.

"He was the contact for the Japanese on Bainbridge Island, with the hakujin. If any problems arose, the Japanese would come to him and he would negotiate with the hakujin for them. I never saw my father ever kowtow to any hakujin. He and I didn't get along, but I respect him for maintaining his own self-respect.

"When I was a small boy, we always began our day's studies with the Pledge of Allegiance. My father was one of those who believed in America and he believed in our being Americans. I was brought up believing in the principles of democracy. I think eventually that got ingrained in me. Maybe more than in some, because as a young kid I did read those heavy philosophers. Lot of them I understood. The one that gave me trouble was Nietzsche. The others I understood.

"I followed things from way back. I know something about the discrimination against the Chinese. I know what happened in Seattle and how they drove them out. I know what they did in the early mining days. They got treated worse than we got treated. Did you know that? We got it easy compared to the Chinese people in the United States.

"I knew the history of the world. I knew the history of warfare and the history of the United States from its inception. I knew it well enough to be regarded as a top student. I think that might have sort of gotten under my skin, I guess. I was as good an American as the next one.

"Not better! But just as good."

In his trial, he name is listed as "James Royal Baking Powder Matsumoto." Where did the FBI find that name?

He says, "In junior high school I played Chief Somerset in *The Song of Hiawatha*. I was a good enough baseball player. They tried to distract me when I came up to bat. Brownie Elingsen used to call me 'James Royal Baking Powder Matsumoto.' He was the only one who called me that. But all that was done in fun. A joke!

"We were called 'skibbee' from when we were little kids. Other kids. Hakujin kids called us that. At that time I didn't know what it meant. But I knew it wasn't a good word. They didn't use the word 'Jap' on the island that I can remember—not in my hearing. I was quite popular with the hakujin people because of my athletic abilities. I never heard them use that term 'Jap' towards me. My dad was well known to the hakujins because he was a foreman. I don't think I got to that point of personally feeling racial discrimination until I came out to Seattle, to look for a job.

"I first faced it, a little, in my old country school days. We would start each morning by rising and saluting the Stars and Stripes. We would place our hand over our heart and Pledge Allegiance to the Flag. While we were learning the lessons of democracy, we weren't practicing it. Socially, the Nisei were ostracized. I was fairly proficient in athletics, so for me personally, there were more inroads socially. Still, I knew—

"My teammates said maybe I could get a job at the strawberry cannery on the island. I applied for a job down there with my teammates. Just my teammates were hired. I was told they wouldn't hire Japanese.

"Some families invited me to partake lunch with their kids, but such occasions were rare, far and few in between. Only a couple of families did that.

"The only place I could get a job was in the strawberry fields. That didn't look good to me. So I figured that there was no opportunity on Bainbridge Island, and I might as well get the hell out of there. After all I was thirteen and a half now and couldn't get along with my father anyway. So, in 1925, I got my first job in Alaska. I went up to Alaska about seven seasons, altogether."

Seed of the Sun

By

WALLACE IRWIN

Author of "The Blooming Angel,"

"Trimmed with Red,"

"Letters of a Japanese Schoolboy," etc.

G. H. Doran Company

New York

"Our mutual friend, Baron Tazumi, has broken out again," he announced, squinting into the perpendicular lines of the front page.

"Has he?"

He glanced sharply at her over the top of the paper and prefaced his reading with the explanation: "The Japanese have a proverb which says, 'You cannot tear paper the wrong way,' much as you say, 'You cannot float upstream.' You know how hard it is to whistle and sing at the same time? Well, our distinguished racial half brother seems to have perfected himself in the art. A sweet song of love for American interviewers. A sharp whistle of hate for Japanese readers: I wonder what has happened to the Baron? Never before has he been so openly bitter against the blond race of which I am a poor half portion?"

"I can't imagine," answered Anna, though she had made her guess. "But what does he say?"

"He has gone to Seattle, it seems, and was given an ovation by the Japanese there. It was one of those spontaneous affairs carefully arranged by the Beneficent Society. The account of his speech is headed 'Jewel Words from Great Lips.' Here is a handful of those gems:

"'Be of stout heart, my people for ye are sprung from the land of the gods. Even though you go forth into the outlands to toil among mocking tribes, yet heaven is with you because the divine Emperor is with you.

"'They cannot check our peaceful progress in this land, or in any other where our divine Emperor has sent us to toil in his name. If they built laws to wall themselves about and exclude us we will tear down those laws or dig under them. In America we are already inside, and we shall remain for the glory of the Emperor.

"'Small as we are in numbers here, let us see to it that our race shall increase. Seed of the Yamato germinate anew! Beget, beget, beget! While the Emperor permitted it, it was well that you brought wives from the homeland—young wives and fertile. And now it is more important still that we marry into this American stock. Prove your race equality in the blood of your children. Choose white women if you can. Where this is not practicable, marry negroes, Indians, Hawaiians.

"'Do not fear that our race shall be lost in such a mingling of blood. The blood of Japan is immortal, because it is descended from the sun goddess, Amaterasu. Plant it where you will, Yamato's seed shall never die. Even unto the tenth generation Japanese with blond skins and blue eyes will still be Japanese, quick with the one God-given virtue—loyalty to the empire and the Emperor.'"

Henry Johnson ceased to read and permitted the paper to fall across his shabby shoes.

"What else did he say?" asked Anna in choking voice.

"Not much," smiled Henry. "After these few remarks ice cream was served and a good time was enjoyed by all present."

She struggled a while with a difficult question, then said, "Henry, do many of the Japanese want to—marry white women?"

"Well," he informed her, "you have just heard the Baron's speech translated."

"I can't believe that he could suggest anything so cold-blooded."

"The temperature of the blood," drawled Henry Johnson, "is merely a relative matter. What seems cold in California may seem warm in Japan. Suicide, for instance. Here it is a crime, there a virtue. Nippon applauds the hero who operates upon himself with a short sword."

"Henry you exaggerate," her employer cautioned him. "Harakiri has gone out of style in Japan."

"Yes? Not so many years ago General Nogi murdered himself in order to join his old Emperor in the land of souls. He had no sooner struck the blow than all Nippon cried, 'There dies the last gentleman in Japan!' To-day Nogi is enshrined as a god with an altar of his own and plenty of priests to comfort his spirit with incense. It makes a pretty picture. Religion and politics again, you observe."

"Why do the Japanese want to marry into other races?" Anna broke in.

"Just look at me!" snarled Henry Johnson. "Am I not a noble example of intermarriage?"

"But why do they want it?" she persisted.

"They want to borrow your stature," he said. "They have already borrowed your telegraph instruments, your educational systems, your military equipment, your advertising methods. They have borrowed your brain, but they cannot change their bodies without one thing—intermarriage. Don't you see? Four feet six wants to become six feet four. Then Japan will have everything."

"A Bright Morning after the Rain"
by
Shisei Tsuneishi
(English translation by the poet)
August 1921

I open all our little windows wide,
And let the breeze and sunbeams' flooding tide
    Dispel the damp and gloom
    Out of our dusty room;
And the dreary memory of the rainy night
Away, like dreams, does vanish out of sight.

We let our laughing children totter out
Into the sunshine warm to run about;
    And the tears my grief betray
    As I watch them at play.
Ah, we are of despised and hated race,
To call our own, we have no single place!

Yet, somewhere, with our minds as calm and sane.
As the stainless atmosphere after rain,
    Yet once, oh, let us sing,
    With voices cheerily ring:
"This is our farmland, this our home,
Forever ours: no more we roam."

Paul Tsuneishi

"DAD WAS WRITING HAIKU ALL HIS LIFE"

"He was writing haiku all his life and was submitting it to this national Japanese magazine. And it's the traditional haiku, it's not any of the spin-offs. And, as I said, he became one of these editors at large, whatever you call them honorable editors—contributing editor—and he had a minimum of one and sometimes two haiku in this regularly published haiku magazine. His lifetime goal was to have three in one issue. He never made it. But he also started —I don't know when—but certainly in camp—haiku clubs, and when he came out of the camps he started one in L.A. and one in San Diego, and he went down by bus to San Diego Haiku Club once a month and he had students all across the country. And that's why he needed a typewriter. So he did all of this and published, and compiled a lot of his haiku later, and published them privately.

"He also tried English poetry—sonnets—other things. He translated a lot. Rubiyat of Omar Khayyam into Japanese. He loved Tennyson. When I used to go with him to the produce market in L.A. in the middle of the night he'd be quoting all the poems he knew. Tennyson's 'Crossing the Bar' was one of his favorites."

Jimmie Omura would have loved that! Tennyson's "Crossing the Bar"—"Out of the dark that covers me black as the night from pit pole to pole. I thank whatever God there might be for my. . . ." Yes. This idea of an unconquerable spirit.

Frank Seishi Emi, Leader

Gold, wood, fire, water, and earth are the five elements in Asian cosmology.

The dragon is the most powerful and volatile animal in the twelve-animal lunar zodiac. The dragon is the fighter, the idealist, the leader.

In the family of Yanusuke and Tsune Emi, there are two dragons. Their first-born, Hisako, sometimes called Alice, was born in the Year of the Wood Dragon, 1904. The second child, Frank Seishi, was born twelve years later in the Year of the Fire Dragon, 1916. Kaoru, the baby of the family, acts as hostess, fussing and serving little salty things.

In their seventies and eighties, they laugh about fighting. Frank would always win, Hisako says, and it used to make her so mad. He was fire, and she was wood. Fire consumes wood. She'd be so mad she'd mutter and fume all day. But then Frank always won. The Fire Dragon is a born hero. He looks like a hero. Handsome, square-jawed, muscular. He looks like Superman with his curl combed back into his hair. He sits and listens to his sister Alice talk of life before he was born.

"My father came, I think, to Texas first. He didn't come to Los Angeles. He came to Texas with this group made up by wealthy people in Japan. You know, like peers—professors of Kyoto University—like a congressman in Japan, you know." She wears a plain, straight haircut, and no makeup. She sits on a well-cushioned couch, hands piled neatly on her lap, her back straight, her head still.

"They all formed a group, and they came to Texas to start a Yamato Colony. But they didn't succeed because they have no experience working. Texas. They work with their barefoot. They wanted to start a rice plantation. But they didn't succeed so everybody drifted apart. Mr. Saibara was the only one who stayed in Texas. That's what I heard."

"Where did he go?" Kaoru asks her sister.

"Papa went to Alabama. And he imported Japanese orange trees, *mikan*, you know. Then he planted all the plants on the company land. And he became a foreman at the company. He rode horses and watched the workers, you know. Then he quit and went to Georgia. All the southern states. Then he ended up in Los Angeles, because my mother wanted him to come back to Japan.

"We lived in my grandfather's place in a small town. My mother is an Okayama, but she has nobody there. So she's an only child. So she came over to just one more mountain and the other side of the hill working." The grammar is Japanese. It's a pun: *yama*, mountain. It must have been difficult to have such a quick sense of humor in America, where no one catches her jokes 'til days later.

"Tell them when mama went to Korea," Kaoru coaxes gently.

"Oh, yes. After my father came to America, he could send money because those days, ladies were very low, you know. So my mother had to make a living. One of her friends—he was an artist. He was drawing pictures for the school textbook, you know. He sent her a letter, 'You could make better money than in Japan, so why don't you come to Korea?'

"He used to be a Kaicho. He got her a job as a seamstress at the Kaijo—Japanese Government Hospital. Big hospital there. She worked at the president's home as a seamstress. She had a nice life there because no hardships. My mother was good at sewing.

"But when she came back, I saw a strange lady coming toward our house. I was kind of bashful. I remember that time because I didn't want to see her because she seemed so strange. I don't know her, you know. I hid somewhere, but I finally came out. It was my mother. I think I was about eight.

"So papa came to Los Angeles and he was farming in El Monte. Then, finally, my father told us to come to America. So we came."

"We came on a boat called *Mexico Maru*. It was around Thanksgiving time. We landed in Seattle. I passed my medical examination. Nothing wrong with me. But my mother got caught with—what is that?" Alice asks Kaoru.

"You mean *mushi*? Worms?"

"When Japanese came to America, they had to pass the examination, you know. My mother had a hard time getting in. We landed from Kobe. Then, finally, she passed at Kobe. Then she came to Seattle. And got caught again. So she had to stay at the Immigration Office for a long time."

"Two months? Three months?" Kaoru asks.

"We arrived there, I think, 1915. Thanksgiving time. My father took me out of Immigration Office to the Fujii Hotel. But I couldn't get used to him, so I went back to the Immigration Office.

"After Christmas, she finally got okay. So we came out of the Immigration Office. Then came to Los Angeles, by first-class boat, 1916. January first.

"We landed at San Pedro. And it was raining so hard. It was so dreary and dark. I thought to myself, I thought America was more beautiful country than this.

"We stayed in the Japanese town for awhile. Japanese town wasn't too bad. I didn't feel at home. Japan was better. Then my father got a job at San Fernando and we moved to San Fernando. Those days we go on wagons. Horse and buggy. Those days San Fernando was one-sided street you know. There was a mercantile store, like you see in those cowboy pictures. And the other side of the street had posts you tie horses to.

"Oh, my father, he moved around so much," Alice says. She attended nine schools, in almost as many years, following her father. "First, I went to San Fernando. Then my father moved to Venice, and went to school there. Then, after that, Hope Street School, in Los Angeles. He started a store there, you know. Sixth and Flower, between Flower and Hope. We used to live upstairs. And Frank was born there, 1916. September."

"What kind of baby was he?" Kaoru, the baby of the family, asks.

"He was all right," Alice answers.

"Spoiled," Frank says.

"Yeah, I took care of Frank after school out in a buggy. Oh, I used to change his diaper. That's what I did to everybody."

"Three of us!" Frank adds.

"Mom worked out in the field?" Kaoru asks.

"Yes," Alice says. "My father started a farm, so my mother never worked so hard in Japan, you know. But I felt sorry for her. She got up at 5 o'clock in the morning and prepared breakfast. Then she'd go out in the field and work. That's what all Japanese women did in those days. Either they had a business or farmed. They couldn't find a job, you know. They had to do something. So most Japanese had a farm."

"We call Alice 'Cha-Chan,' because Frank couldn't say 'Ne-chan,' which is 'Older sister' in Japanese. He said 'Cha-chan.' So we all call her Cha-Chan. Even mama and papa called her Cha-Chan," Kaoru says.

"Oh, Art was born Sixteenth and Vermont. That's where my father had a farm, on Vermont," Alice continues.

"He had farms everywhere," Kaoru says.

"So Art was born over there. After that, I went to Manchester Avenue School; I went to Burbank School. Anyway I spent four years. My father started a hotel in San Pedro between Ninth and Tenth. I had to move to Ninth, you know, Stanford Avenue School. Ninth and Stanford. That school. Those days there were several Japanese children."

Cherry Blossom

Lyrics by GUS KAHN
Music by HARRY RAYMOND

In the time of Cherry Blossoms
Far away in old Japan
Sailor boy lov'd geisha girlie
Making eyes behind her fan
Soon she learn'd to say "I love you."
Soon she learn'd to sigh
For the hours pass'd like moments
'Till he said "Goodbye"
But just before he sail'd away
She heard him tenderly say
Just wait for me Little Cherry Blossom
Across the sea I'll come to woo
And when the spring brings cherry blossoms rare
I'll bring a ring to you I love you I do
You'll always be
Just a little flower
That blooms for me
I will cherish ev'ry hour
My Cherry Blossom I love you
When the spring brought Cherry Blossoms
Down beside the dreamy sea
Lonesome little geisha girlie
Sat and waited patiently
For the boy who said "I love you."
Thought she would forget
Just a summer's day flirtation
But she's dreaming yet
And in the mating of the sea
She still hears this melody.

CHORUS

Gordon Hirabayashi, On Civil Disobedience

WHITE MAN'S COUNTRY

"**Y**ou know ever since that Columbus story: wading ashore with his men, and landing on his knees and kissing the earth while strange, lightly clad, dark skinned nonhuman, nonpeople come bringing food, this was a white man's country, because whites discovered America," Gordon Hirabayashi says.

"I really think that is instilled in the genes and permeates American society. Fundamentally this is a white man's country. They tolerate us. They give lip service to equality and so on. I think that this is a white man's country comes in whenever a crisis crops up. It's a powerful thing."

Gordon Hirabayashi was born in 1918, the Year of the Earth Horse, in a Japanese Christian commune in Seattle, Washington. His brother James was born in 1921, the Year of the Golden Rooster.

"There is a movement in Japan called 'Mukyokai,' which is a Christian non-church movement," Gordon says.

"The spearhead of the Mukyokai movement was a man named Uchimura. Kanzo Uchimura. And there is a legend about him. He was one of these nonconformists. He used to say, 'Well, the Emperor is a nice man, but he is a man. There is no need to do these special imperial bows.' And since he said this sort of thing all the time, people suspected that when the royal family went by, he didn't really bow.

"It's like he didn't, but nobody could testify when he wasn't bowing because, if he could testify, he wasn't bowing either!

"This group, my dad's group, would tell that story with a lot of laughs.

"This Uchimura went to a theological seminary in Massachusetts somewhere to get theological training. He became a Christian at university in Hokkaido. And he decided that Christianity has some value and would be useful in Japan, but we didn't need all this church and clergy claptrap and organization this and that. He said, 'Heck with that.' And so he would join any church movement or the missionaries over there. The Mukyokai was a very strong group in Japan but it didn't spread widely. But those who were converted to it were very strong.

"It so happened that the guy who was teaching English to the people who wanted to go to the U.S. as immigrants was a disciple of Uchimura's Mukyokai brand of Christianity. He was the only English teacher around. So, everyone in Hokata, intending to go to settle in the U.S., took English from him, and some he converted. My mother, who came over seven years after dad, studied English with the same man, and both became Christians.

"Dad came over with eight young guys between eighteen and twenty. Dad was nineteen. All from that village. It was 1907.

"One of dad's motives for leaving Japan was economic. Another strong motive was Japan had begun to militarize more intensely after the Russo-Japanese War, and he didn't want to go into the army. A few of the other guys had that same motive: get out of the army."

"Uhhh, no. . . . " Jim the younger mumbles.

"Part of the reason dad left was because he was opposed to being conscripted into the army. Japan was militarizing after the Russo-Japanese War. He and his group didn't want to be in the army," Gordon insists.

"No, I think that's one of the myths," the younger brother says.

"That was one of the reasons. Maybe the more powerful reason was economic, trying to find something for the family."

"Well, I'll play you some tapes," Jim the anthropologist says.

"Okay."

"I collected from my . . . You see, I collected tapes from my father," Jim says.

"He did some interviews before I got there," Gordon says.

"All this time, I had a notion that he was a protestor. But what he says is, he was swept up in this post–Russo-Japanese War period and he went off and tried to join the army. He was too young.

"So Dad and that group came out and they were headed for California. Dad said that was the original plan. The ship stopped in Seattle. And I guess they were on a ship until they could be cleared by Immigration.

"Dad had a name of a man given as a contact in Seattle. So he came off the boat to visit. And he said, 'Why don't you stay here? There is a lot of opportunity here. This is not a bad place.'

"And they said, 'Well, there's eight of us. If there's something you can get for the eight of us, we might consider it.'

"He got them a railroad job, two handcar teams of four men each. Dad was on a section gang. That was his first job. And so they came out and stayed her in Seattle, instead of going to California.

"Dad worked on the railroads for a little over a year. I think the whole group worked outside of Seattle up in the Cascades.

"He was telling me the first time he rode on a passenger train, it was following an accident. One guy on his group—when they would be going around a bend, there are trees growing—so they send someone out to see if it's clear.

"The guy that did this got excited when the whistle of an oncoming train blew and was coming so he jumped off in front, and he fell over. And before he could recover, he was halfway over the tracks. And they just cut him in two. It was a shocking experience for Dad. Nobody wanted to go back to the railroad again. So they got a job in the city.

"And he was working in the city for three or four years. When the guys were thinking of getting married, they figured, Gee, they should have something. You know, a home and some business. They decided they would go into agriculture. So the four of them rented a farm. And they had a sort of co-op farm. One of them was Dad's cousin. And the others were distant cousins. Three of them were Hirabayashi surnamed. They were first cousins. The other one grew up in the same village. He was not a close relative. He wasn't a first or second cousin. More distant. But somewheres along the line, they were all tied up.

"Dad was a single man when he came over. All of them were. And he was single for seven years. The picture brides marriage system wasn't really all that different from what would have happened had he married in Japan.

"Instead of pictures you've got the go-betweens and the families are involved in selecting your wife. Except, at some point, in Japan, you are going to meet the girl before you marry. You'll get to see each other. You'll get to peek at each other physically. So, that part was skipped and only pictures sent, and letters.

"He was about five foot three-and-a-half inches tall. Roughly we said five four, but I think he was five three and a half.

"He was a pretty hefty guy when he died. When he got older he'd gotten down to about 130 pounds. But in his working days, he was 145 or 150. Well-built guy.

"Even when he was in his eighties, the doctor said, 'From the waist up, you're like a young man, twenty or thirty years younger.' But from the waist down . . . he had stomach cancer and liver cancer, which finally did him in. So, below the waist was not in good shape. But up here above the waist he was in good health. He looked young. He looked like he was in his sixties when he was in his eighties.

"Mom came from a village about ten miles from Hokata in the same prefecture. This is in the shadows of Matsumoto. Mitsu Tzuzawa was her maiden name. She came to the U.S. when she was nineteen. Seven years after Dad came.

"Dad was born in 1880. She was born in 1895.

"I was born on the co-op site, near the university. This was Sand Point, 'Kumiare' they called the co-op. Kumiare."

"There was one other family from the same area. When I was about a year and half, they moved to the White River Valley, between Seattle and Tacoma, in the valley there.

"A fellow named Katsuno had a piggery near where dad was farming. He made a lot of money there, during the war, selling meat to the army and getting garbage from the army. He said on a weekend or holidays there would be whole meals thrown into the garbage.

"They cooked the same anyway. Even when people are on leave on holidays, they cook anyway, only to dump it, and Katsuno got it. And so he made quite a bit of money. And it was his money that afforded the purchase of forty acres in the valley.

"When the Alien Land Law came in, it had to be registered in some name. It was registered under Katsuno's daughter's name. She was the oldest of the Nisei. She was ten at the time. She was born in 1910 and this was 1920, when they purchased the land. And they formed another co-op. One of the Hirabayashis, my dad, and Katsuno, and one other family. They had Katsuno's house built first. His is a nice house. It's even up yet. It was two-story with a cement basement. He had two sections of forty acres. So, he had sixteen acres. His was a very good house. Dad had the next eight acres. And there were two more lots with eight acres each.

"Our house did not have cement foundation. It was open, just up on struts. And we were crawling under there. We had lumber stored there and so on. It was just unfinished. It wasn't even dug out. We used to keep cats because they used to keep it rat-free. It was one of the better ones in those early days. The others were shacks, right on the ground, practically. We had a fairly spacious kitchen, which had what we called a family room attached. We ate there. I think, throughout most of my growing up into the thirties, it was a wood stove.

"Then, there was a living room which the folks used for meetings. The living room was like sixteen by sixteen. The kitchen was maybe ten by twelve with a table in there for the family. And the front end: no door, but a doorway. Our whole family lived there. Two double beds. One bedroom upstairs. We had an upstairs that we finished as we went. We had about four kids. Two of us were in one bed with Mom and two with Dad. That's when I was in grade school. Mom and Dad didn't sleep together when we had that system. They must have gotten together when we were asleep because kids kept coming.

"We had running water, electricity. No flush toilet. Outhouse. Periodically we would dig another hole. So, we were there.

"I remember they would make homemade paste out of rice, and put it on the wallpaper and then put it up. Some homes had newspapers on. We had wallpaper instead of newspaper plastered on.

"Oh, dad was a good carpenter. He did the shelves and so on. And so we had relatively good furnishings. He always built the bath. I miss that. If I had room in my house, I would put in a hot tub right now."

"Later on, we had one of those kind. . . . " Jim begins, and Gordon knows what he's talking about.

"The co-op had one," Gordon says.

". . . cultivator with a motor on it," Jim says.

"Largely in charge of Katsuno's. But dad drove it, too. We were poor. Maybe not unusually poor. We were just making out. But so were a lot of others," Gordon says.

"Every spring Dad would have to get a charge account to be carried on seeds, fertilizers, and things like that. Then, towards the latter part of summer, he would pay it off.

"So, these guys always had to carry us. Then it seems in the fall, we pay off the thing and borrow again. That seemed to be a cycle."

"This ten-acre truck gardening was sort of a norm, I guess. Peas, carrots," Jim, the younger says.

"It was a truck farm, celery, cauliflower, peas, tomatoes."

"No allowance for his kids," Jim says.

"Not in a regular monthly amount," Gordon Hirabayashi says.

"Maybe we would ask for four bits to do something or other."

"And we'd get praised if we brought change back. And that was reward we always tried to gain. We always tried to—"

"No!" Jim protests.

"I did!" Gordon says. "I always tried to bring something back to gain a verbal reward."

"This happened with us, in grade school, going to the country fairground," Jim says. "Yeah, and the thing was to bring money back. We'd ride some things and buy some things."

"Lunch would be hamburgers," Gordon says.

"We'd always bring back some money. I remember hanging on to my younger brother Dick," Jim says.

"I never went to a barber in my life until I left Seattle. Haircuts: the old man. He had the barber equipments in a box. And all of us got it. I learned to do some haircut because he wanted a haircut. He was willing to have me cut his hair. And I learned to taper it around. Jim got to be good at it. Jim had some experience even when I went to school, I'd come home and give haircuts or get a haircut when I was home.

"Yeah. You see, I'm getting thin up here. Dad had a thin spot here, but he had his hair. And he wasn't greyed all that much either. I'm quite a bit like him.

"And that's where my older brother died shortly after. Technically, I'm the second son. My older brother died when he was five. I was only two, so I don't remember him. My younger one lived about a week and died. We had seven born and five are still around.

"And that's where I grew up all the way through high school."

"What kind of fairy tales stories did Dad tell when he was going to sleep?" Jim asks.

"You know the stories of raccoons and fox, all the Japanese folk tales," Gordon says. "There are books of Japanese folk tales for children. We'd say, 'Oh, read this over again! Tell us this story and tell us another one you haven't told.'

"'I don't know anymore.'

"'Oh, read me another story! Oh, read me another one.' And he would tell us, embellish it and so on. If he embellishes it too spicy, Mom would be reprimanding him. 'Hey! You're getting too rough there.'

"You know all those stories have morals in them. And we picked up on those things. *Chushingura*? So the loyalty and so on that is demonstrated in that story. We probably got it in other forms. I don't remember that in particular. They kind of avoided this samurai, the violent-type models for us. By the time Dick came along, Dad was too busy, and Dick never had that. He didn't have all that interaction. So, he's trying to learn about it.

"And we didn't have *odori*, artistic sort of things," Gordon continues, "Mom was literary. We all figured that under other circumstances, like in this era, she may have been a magazine editor or teacher or something.

"She was a frustrated farmer's wife. Both Mom and Dad finished middle school, *chu-gakko*. Between high school and junior high.

"And after that, there was senior high. The system is just slightly different from ours, but essentially chu-gakko was high school. The Japanese group that came over in that valley there were much above the average of other rural populations who came from Europe, in terms of education.

"You know they had Nihonjin-kai, A Japanese Association. And that Japanese Association for the Japanese population is a male-chauvinist group. In that era, in the twenties, she became the vice president of the Japanese Association! That's as high as you could go!

"Yeah, the Japanese Association! That indicates the kind of outwardness she had. Dad had high respect and was a good worker, but he wasn't as articulate as Mom was in meetings. And Mom used English a lot. We were unusual in having Caucasian friends drop over. You know, socially, not just for business.

"Yeah. We had a language school and association. There was a Buddhist Church as well. The Buddhist Church had their own building. I remember sitting in at the Japanese school meetings, when I was in my early grade school, because I just tagged along. All the kids would be playing outside, but now and then, we'd sit in.

"We had been meeting in the Buddhist Church when they finally decided to get that building when it became available for the association. In Japanese-style, they'd say it cost so much. 'If we would put up a hundred dollars each, we could meet most of it. We want to get commitments now.'

"There's a guy writing it down. I remember one guy saying, 'I'm a bachelor. I'm operating on a small basis. I'd like to be allowed to participate, chipping in even for the language school, even though I don't have any kids at half, fifty dollars,' and so on. Then they got him strung up there on the wall.

"Every time there is an occasion, they put that down. The group pressure to contribute. And Japanese always contribute. I find this true even when I got to equivalent of Snake River Valley sugar beet farmers up in Canada, south of Lethridge—south end. I went over there for the Centennial to get them to get organized. And in the city we have been working a whole year on various types of fund raising and we got up to about four thousand. There, on one shot, they got six thousand. Smaller population but those guys give two hundred, five hundred. We're giving twenty-five bucks, fifty—just like Japanese-style to being '*kifu*.'

"I went to the Nippon *kan*," Gordon says, beginning something, and Jim perks up.

"Uh, huh! That's right," Jim says.

"For movie time."

"Yeah."

"That was before the war in the thirties. I went there to see movies as well as to line up movies for the valley," Gordon, the older brother says. "They showed Japanese movies, silent movies with the guy on the side doing all the voice and dramatics. And of course at the movies we used to kid the Issei, especially the women. They used to have one handkerchief, two handkerchief, three handkerchief movies. 'God! You people cry all the time and it's all sad stuff!'

"'Ah!' they say, 'Unless, it's that way, it's not a good movie.' And boy, they really liked it.

"I don't remember Dad being the Japanese Association president or anything, but he was on the board. I've already mentioned that Mom was a vice president, the only woman to hold any position. But in this Mukyokai, the religious co-op group, he was right in there assuming, you know, they had a core of three or four people holding responsibility. He was one of the three holding it."

"He was not the kind of out-front leader type," Jim says. "There is some kind of connection and continuity between parents and boys. That there is a continuity in taking an idealistic stand on things. I don't ever recall them coming and apologizing."

"You accept that," Gordon says. "You don't expect them to come out and say so. In terms of their subsequent behavior you could interpret some of that."

"Yeah. Acknowledgment of a mistake?" Jim thinks a moment. "I don't recall any. . . . "

The Pride of Palomar

by

PETER B. KYNE

Cosmopolitan Book Corp.

New York

1921

She smiled ruefully. "I am just about to let them out for recess," she replied. "Your friends may remain in their car and draw their own conclusions."

"Thank you," Don Mike returned to the car. "They're coming out for recess," he confided. "Future American citizens and citizenesses. Count 'em."

Thirty-two little Japanese boys and girls, three Mexican or Indian children, and four undoubted white parentage trooped out into the yard and gathered around the car, gazing curiously. The school teacher bade them run away and play and, in her role as hostess, approached the car. "I am Miss Owens," she announced. "And I teach this school because I have to earn a living. It is scarcely a task over which one can enthuse, although I must admit that Japanese children are not unintelligent and their parents dress them nicely and keep them clean."

"I suppose, Miss Owens," Farrel prompted her, having introduced himself and the Parkers, "that you have to contend with the native Japanese schools."

She pointed to a brown house half a mile away. Over it flew the flag of Japan. "They learn ancestor worship and how to kowtow to the Emperor's picture down there, after they have attended school here," she volunteered. "Poor little tots! Their heads must ache with the amount of instruction they receive. After they have learned here that Columbus discovered America on October 12th, 1492, they proceed to that Japanese school and are taught that the Mikado is a divinity and a direct descendant of the Sun God. And I suppose also, they are taught that it is a fine clean manly thing to pack little, green, or decayed strawberries at the bottom of a crate with nice big ones on top—in defiance of state law. Our weights and measures law and a few others are very onerous to our people in La Questa."

"Do you mean to tell me, Miss Owens," Parker asked, "that you despair of educating these little Japanese children to be useful American citizens?"

"I do. The Buddhist school over yonder is teaching them to be Japanese citizens; under Japanese law all Japanese remain Japanese citizens at heart, even if they do occasionally vote here. The discipline of my school is very lax," she continued. "It would be, of course, in view of the total lack of parental support. In that other school, however, the discipline is excellent."

She continued to discourse with them, giving them an intimate picture of life in this little Japan and interesting revelations upon the point of view, family life, and business ethics of the parents of her pupils, until it was time to "take up" school again, when she reluctantly returned to her poorly paid and unappreciated efforts.

Uhachi Tamesa

EARLY SEATTLE

Today he's an old man. A rich old man. He has friends who speak Japanese, so he speaks Japanese, "I have four older sisters, two older brothers, and one younger brother. The younger brother was hospitalized after sudden hemorrhage. Father said, 'I wish I could send him to the best doctor in Tokyo.' We couldn't afford it. It occurred to me to go as an itinerant worker to the States and send money home. My father and brothers opposed me, but I was supported by Chuzaburo Ito, principal of the grade school. I left for Kobe, the fourth of October, 1899."

His mood changes, and he continues in English, as if English is more comfortable in his mouth, "Then, it's right after war, with China, 1899, you know. Everybody want come but no work. Everybody wait in hotel." He came to Seattle in 1899, according to his papers, he was born in June 28, 1884, making him fifteen on the day he sailed.

"Parents don't come boat. We lived on small island. I come from farm family of Yamaguchi Prefecture. I think mother tears when leave home. Then little boat about eighteen foot long, take fifteen miles to big ship Kobe. The *Ryojun Maru*. We get on late night, and was early morning when we get Kobe.

"They have immigration hotel. They have regular hotel. You stop there and have examination. You must pass physical examination.

"I go Kobe and told I want to come Seattle. Ito, old timer, was my teacher. My school teacher was in Seattle." So, he sails for Seattle.

"At that time, no Japanese captain. No chief engineer. All white. White was captain. Just six months before, I learned A-B-C."

"I could understand Good Morning and Evening! and you know, ten cent. That's all."

On American soil, in 1899, Tamesa was one of approximately 250 Japanese, compared with approximately three thousand Chinese, in the Seattle area. He set about learning English, doing housework, and helping in the kitchen for bed and board while going to school. "I went schoolboy, you know. When I first went Cascade School. Then I went to Sumner. I stayed there about nine months." He was a live-in houseboy, in Sumner, a town twenty miles west of Tacoma, and thirty miles south of Seattle. "It was an American school. That is more than eighty-eight years ago."

By 1900 the Japanese outnumbered the Chinese in Washington: 5,432 Japanese men and 185 Japanese women to 3,550 Chinese men and 79 Chinese women.

In Seattle, two brick train stations rise from the level of tracks at the bottom of the railroad, cut to the bridge over the railroad. The stone entrances were at the level of the bridge crossing Jackson Street. In the cut, there were no build-ings, other than the stations. The railroad tracks came from the south and Mount Rainier, and ran north into a tunnel, under the city.

Union Station, built in 1904, serves the Chicago, Milwaukee, and St. Paul, and the Union Pacific. King Street Station, built two years later, serves the Great Northern and the Northern Pacific. King Street is the taller of the two stations, with its conical clock tower showing one face to the Japanese hotels, shoe fac-tories, working men's restaurants, and the docks and the water of the water-front on one side of the railroad mainline, and its opposite face to the whorehouses and gambling in Chinatown and more Japanese hotels: The Fujii Hotel, Eastern Hotel, Umemoya Hotel. Since 1901 Japanese hotels burgeoned in Seattle—and Tacoma, and Portland, Oregon—since immigration to Hawaii was no longer possible, thanks to a ban, the Chinese and Japanese populations flourished. The Japanese more than the Chinese. And Seattle, the Gateway to Alaska, attracted Japanese gold hunters bound for Alaska.

Tamesa's wife entered the country in 1906, four years before the entry of women was banned.

"I went to Japan 1906 to marry my wife," having introduced the marriage, he backs up to tell the story. "When twenty-one years old, I go back Japan. Never go marry or anything like that. I go see parents. Mother said, 'Marry and then go!' She don't want me anymore. Then I changed my mind. Was 1906. Same year I come back United States.

"That time don't talk minister at all. I think China same thing. Everything Japan come from China. Chinese think Japanese," Uhachi Tamesa says. Marriage was a contract, an alliance between families, not a contract with the state, not dedication to organized religion.

"At that time, mother home. During that time Japan, devotion between wife and husband. I think China same thing long time ago, wasn't it? If you going marry, the wife's side get together and everything have satisfy them. In this country, you do what you want. They don't care about mother. Only both get together. Two people decide.

"My side people and wife's people both get together. Mostly man and wife. And then they all go away and everything satisfied, they marry," the old man says in English, then in Japanese, "When the event is agreed upon, the person who brought them together performs the ceremony. Go-between. Go-between is mostly women. It could be a man or it could be a woman. In any case, minister. He just do talking. I had already handled everything. Had explained that living would come \$30–\$40 a month. So, I had quite a bit of money before I married Natsu Okamoto. I told her not to worry about that."

"You told her how much money you had?" Kay, his daughter, an attractive woman in her seventies, asks. She hasn't heard this about her late mother.

"Sure! Before we married, I had to tell everything!"

"Big wedding ceremony?"

"No very big ceremony. But all relative get together. Husband's home. If husband's home too small, hold at relative's. Just borrow. Now, today, some Christians after atomic bomb quit being Christians. Where I come from island, we had church and quite few people—Christians—since they dropped bomb Hiroshima and Nagasaki, don't want to be Christians. Want be Buddhists. Buddhists don't do things like that; only Christians." He laughs. She smiles.

"We stayed about month and half before we come over. Before marriage, we well acquainted. Wife knew something about United States and everything. I don't want anything that she would be disappointed."

As many times as Kay has heard her father interviewed by reporters from the local newspapers, TV news, and university students researching a paper, she has questions of her own. "What ship did you return on the second time?" she asks in Japanese.

"*Tosa Maru.* Big boat. Eleven thousand ton. It biggest boat that time. This time: Japanese captain and Japanese chief engineer.

"Only one day stormy. Not very bad. It was a little rough. When *Ryojin Maru* come over first time twenty-four hour buck waves. When waves come like this," the old man says, one hand playing the waves, his other playing the *Ryojin Maru*, "You can't run like this. We had to wait.

"*Tosa Maru* would go just like this." His hand as the *Tosa Maru* knives through the crunch of the waves. "But smaller boats have to wait until smooth, like this," he smiles.

"When mother saw this country for the first time, how did she feel?"

"Everything she satisfied. She stayed home. She don't work. Now, women have all sorts of jobs. At that time, women, before marriage work all over. But after marriage, they stay home and take care of children."

Japanese hotels were meeting places for the Japanese and Chinese picture brides and their correspondents in Seattle, until the entry of Chinese women was banned by the Gentlemen's Agreement. After 1908 only Japanese women freely traveled between Japan and the United States.

"Only trouble, picture marriage, some people sent picture before go railroad. They get all black," Uhachi Tamesa, remembering the days he had horses and a wagon, says.

"Young picture. They marry young picture. Ten years younger. Then come over this country have lots trouble when meet. At that time, I operating express business. Only expressman could go aboard after all immigrant get off boat. Other people had to get permit to board. Only expressman could board inside ship.

"I see many women with husband waiting on dock. She crying no husband in sight. Different picture. Some husband would not board ship but go away. Quite a few disappointed.

"Some women come off anyway. If they don't marry or not satisfied with marriage, they don't have to marry. From United States, if you go back you have to pay fare anyway. Seventy-five to 80 percent married; everything goes smooth." The rejected picture brides, who didn't go back across the Pacific, found a way to stay in Seattle. They say there were three hundred-fifty whorehouses spread out through Chinatown.

In 1907, there are 5,000 Japanese, and fifty-three Japanese hotels in Seattle. By 1910, there are forty-five Japanese hotel owners in Seattle, and they form the Seattle Japanese Hotel Operator's Association.

"When papa came here, there was an area of prostitutes," Kay says in English, "Drinking and gambling was conducted," then asks her father in Japanese, "You didn't go there did you?"

The old man answers in Japanese, "I never went."

Tamesa talks as if he was more interested in making money than chasing women.

"And then I can read quite a bit. When I come Seattle, I went housework one year. When come over Sunnydale, 1908, people here very, very nice. Come over riding bicycle. They don't want hurt—throw rocks like that, you know. But here they really nice.

"Yeah. Mrs. Olive Roberts. She's the one surgery for twenty years at Orthopedic Hospital. When I come over, I wanted a little money, so go housework." I guess that's what sticks in the memory, the money you made, not the women you had.

"She was the original founder of the Children's Hospital," Kay adds. "Today there's an Olive Roberts Guild."

"Mr. John W. Roberts's the husband. I go work for him. One kid worked for him had small incubator to raise chicken. Yeah! surprised. Never heard before. Thought chickens raised chicken. Hen, you know. One hundred-twenty small one.

"At that time, work railroad. One day, day for ten hours. Dozen eggs cost twenty cents. Five dozen make day's work. So I thought raise chickens myself.

"At eighteen years old, I am South Park. Friend farming. We have chicken house. Asked him if I could work. Sure. He paid for four them pullets! you know. They grow in three months.

"I got scarlet fever and lost my money. I stay hospital only two weeks and have stay friends three weeks before could come back. When come back, somebody eat—not pullets—but older chicken.

"Same time his friend thought good future. Want to buy some geese! I glad sell because I got no money. So, I sold them. Then, I buy team. Two horse and wagon. And I returned Seattle do express business.

"Then, three years later Okuda, Yamamoto, and three of us get together form Oriental Express. Buy a little wagon and haul stuff for Furuya Company, Hirade Company." Furuya and Hirade were trading companies, rice, dried foodstuffs from Japan, sake, locally made tofu and soy sauce. The men sewed. And the women sewed. They extended their trade beyond Seattle with route men, men with horse-drawn wagons, visiting the milltowns north of Seattle. The express companies had larger wagons and worked for hire. Tamesa hauled for Chinese and Japanese and white.

"At that time, three-ton wagon. On three-ton wagon could load four ton, maybe five ton.

"We had about ten horses. When load it, need helpers. Three people. Mostly two people for extra work. Yeah, all Japanese. Yeah, before got together, three of us incorporated. I used to haul—Oh, I think it's gone now—Quong Tuck Co.—Chinese, you know. I don't know if around anymore now."

Quong Tuck Co. was a Chinese import-export house and herb shop, established in 1868. The sign on the street advertised Quong Tuck as importers of opium and stayed up for years after Quong Tuck Co. closed.

"I used to haul lot of things and working company had forty acres in Georgetown. Then, fire broke out in Winner Street. Winner Street—it isn't there now. Every day. Every day, I hauled firecrackers because city told too dangerous to keep in store, out of town. Georgetown.

"Yeah. Six days, I haul every day only watching firecrackers. At that time, there was only Chinese firecrackers. American had no firecrackers."

Kay had believed her mother had harbored a wish to return to Japan to live, but in talking with her father, she becomes momentarily confused. Her mother lived and died here happily? She did not suffer in silence?

"When I moved her to Sunnydale, in 1908, I decided not to go back to Japan," Pop says.

"When mother married and came over here, didn't she intend someday to return?" Kay asks, and looks at him askance.

"Yeah, just visit," answers the old man.

In Japanese now, Kay asks him again, "Oh, she planned to stay here briefly and return?"

"No, no!" the old man answers. "Visit there."

"She understood she was staying here, but she might visit Japan?"

"The Tamesas were the slaves of their American-born children. They liked the room, the space, and the money in America," he says. We hold our breath. It was a joke.

The year 1910 brought new, tougher immigration laws, and a new immigration center, in sight of Chinatown. There were 860 Chinese men and 72 Chinese women in Chinatown, and 7,497 Japanese, including Japanese women, whose numbers equaled the total number of Chinese men. The Japanese in town called the town "Nihonmachi." *Nihon* means "Japanese." And *machi* means "town." The Chinese called the same town "Tangyun Fau," or "Tangyun Guy." *Tangyun* for "Man of Tang." And *fau* for "town," or *guy* for "street." White newspapers called it "Chinatown."

Young laborers gathered at the hotels, awaiting clearance from Immigration before moving on. Out of town, Japanese hotels mixed in with old Chinese and Japanese businesses, old Chinese and Japanese curio shops, groceries, and Chinese and Japanese restaurants. But the Japanese ran the larger businesses, the hotels, banks, newspapers. Read the signs. The Chinese have blocky, complex characters. The Japanese have a combination of Chinese style and a more streamlined and spare writing style. And curves. Chinese were interwoven with Japanese, shop next to shop, but the Japanese had larger shops on every block of "Chinatown."

There are 9,000 Japanese in Seattle in 1920; 5,000 in Tacoma. The Japanese government's ban on picture brides goes into effect on February 25. Picture brides are no longer issued passports. California passes its Alien Land Law, and the next year Nebraska, Texas, and Washington pass theirs. Anti-Chinese and anti-Japanese sentiment is rife throughout the country, from states with two "Oriental" residents, like Nebraska, to those with thousands. Smith Towers is finished and serves as a magnet for white businesses moving in and Chinese and Japanese moving out. They had moved from the waterfront to Third Avenue, and now they moved from Third to Sixth Avenue, around 1925. Chinese and Japanese cannot buy land or lease. Tamesa's English is deceptively simple. People forget his Japanese is alert and canny, and deep with understanding.

"Yeah. I stayed Columbia little while. Had more chickens. Then come over Sixteenth Avenue, first. Across street worked eight acres where apartment. Bought in my boy's name. I couldn't buy land myself. Had boy at time. Minoru. I can't buy my name, come Japan. You can buy anyone born this country. I buy Minoru's name and he guardian for me. That way could see that okay. When grow up, twenty-one, no longer need guardian. And I sold place in 1964. Sold fifty times over what I paid." He laughs in triumph.

As a Japanese he has no rights. All of his rights are in the hands of his children. And he openly defends his children's rights as American citizens—from the simple things to the complex.

"My first daughter, Kimio, was thirteen years old. She was chosen out of forty-three members of Girl Reserves, sponsored by YWCA, to attend the Washington State Conference. But, saying that she was not good at singing, they repeated the election several times until a white girl was elected. I felt it was strange.

"During that period, Ichitaro Takada was a journalist for the *Hokubei Jiji*. He wrote an English editorial in the Japanese paper accusing the YWCA as a religious group for sponsoring discrimination against Japanese citizens, and mailed copies of the paper to churches and religious groups.

"Then Reverend Murphy reported this to Mrs. Case, the general manager of YWCA. She was very surprised, saying it was the first time she had heard such a thing, and immediately she published an apology.

"Later two representatives of the Ministers' Alliance Association came and requested, 'Since it is a time when anti-Japanese feeling is so high, please don't stir up the situation any more.' I answered them, 'If it were my personal affair, I would keep my mouth shut. But it is a matter of my daughter who is an American citizen, so I will push on. We really need the help of religious people in such a situation.'"

Number One Hotel

The N.P. Hotel, named for Northern Pacific Railway, opened in 1914, as the "first number one hotel among Japanese hotels on the Pacific Coast." The symbol for the mighty N.P., the circular yin and yang, was displayed without explanation. An attraction to railroadmen perhaps. The lobby took up the entire first floor and displayed a portrait of Admiral Togo on the bridge of the *Mikasa* during the Japan Sea Battle, framed in gold, that dwarfed the guests standing in front of it. Behind the desk was a huge switchboard, connecting every one of the 130 rooms to their own phone. And an elevator zipped up and down six floors of the hotel, enabling the hotel porters to carry up luggage without climbing stairs. A sink in every room, and a bathroom and toilet on every floor.

When the famous Takarazuka troupe of girl dancers visited Seattle in 1928, half the girls stayed at the N.P. Hotel and half stayed at the Mayflower, downtown. Eventually they ended up all staying at the N.P. They might have been influenced by local journalists, who also kept rooms at the N.P. Seiran Takeuchi of the *Taihoku Nippo*; Ichitaro Takata of the *Hokubei Jiji*; Toshiro Nakamura, nicknamed "the Red Dragonfly of Literature"; and Emile Masatomi helped make the N.P. the center of Japanese society. They wrote about the dancers. Their papers were landmarks in this part of town. Chinatown had four established Japanese newspapers, while the first Chinese newspaper, which began printing in 1921, went belly up in 1927. In terms of numbers, seventeen thousand Japanese to two thousand Chinese, in terms of the cultural institutions they ran—the Nippon Kan with the only Hanamichi on the west coast—the banks, the newspapers, the tofu factory, the wholesale fish stores they ran, the Japanese had made it in America. The Chinese were a few quaint shopkeepers, running one tong.

Is it any wonder James Sakamoto, to make a splashy opening for the first all English-language Japanese newspaper, the *Japanese American Courier*, chose to place its offices on the first floor of the N.P. Hotel, in 1929?

Moving to Town

Pomeroy is a town of about a thousand people, near the southwestern corner of the state of Washington, about twenty-five miles from Lewiston, Idaho, on U.S. 12. Shosuke Sasaki moved with his mother and sister to Seattle from this town after the death of his father. They bought an apartment house, and subscribed to the all-English-language *Japanese American Courier*.

Mukilteo is a milltown, north of Seattle, on the water. Kentaro Takatsui was born in Mukilteo's Japtown, and after a time in Japan, where his father recuperated from an illness, he and his family settled into the hotel business in Seattle and subscribed to the *Courier*.

Frank Emi's older sister, Hisako Alice Emi, remembers their father meeting her ship in Seattle and staying at the Fujii Hotel. Monica Sone, author of *Nisei Daughter*, grew up in the Occidental Hotel, run by her family. John Okada, author of *No-No Boy*, a post–WWII novel, grew up in a Japanese hotel. The Japanese who ran hotels in Seattle were an association unto themselves, if not a class. They formed the Seattle Japanese Hotel Operators Association.

James Omura was born on Bainbridge Island, a bit of jungle green unto itself, isolated, and steamy enough for a family of bigfoot, a ferryboat ride away from Seattle. He knew Seattle as it was defined by the *Japanese American Courier*.

These people all came to the Skid Row–Chinatown of Seattle for the city, the J-Town, the Japanese hotels, the Japanese restaurants, and the *Japanese American Courier*. In a few years they would all come smack up against WWII, make decisions, make enemies, make friends, and make history for one side or the other. One of the names in the middle of that history—like him or not—was

Gordon Hirabayashi. But now, in the 1930s, he was just another Japanese kid looking for a good time with his family in the city.

"Going to Seattle for dinner would be a treat for the family," he says. "I was growing up in grade school days, so this would be in the twenties and early part of the Depression, the thirties. Maybe twice a year we'd go in as a family in the truck. When we went in as a family, Mom and Dad and a couple of the younger ones would be in the cab. The rest of us, there would be two or three of us sitting in the back with the vegetables. We had half a day like toward the latter part of August, we aim to go to the [Puget] Sound and to the big Sears Roebuck store. We'd get outfitted for school. Then, we had about ten families we are going to visit, where we run into families with kids our age. Oh, we'd have a great time.

"We had fresh vegetables arranged. They had it all planned who they're going to see; who they're going to give. That was all that we could give. And that was appreciated because the vegetables they had to buy were not as fresh. So, that is what we did. And when we came home, it was close to midnight by the time we reached home. It was a big trip, about twenty miles.

"When we ate on family trips, we would be eating several times in various homes. When we ate out, we'd go to Main Street.

"At that time, Main Street was Japan-town. We usually went to Chinese restaurants run by Japanese. You know Kinkado, Nikko Low [Chinese and Japanese food], and so on. They are all Chinese foods but operators were Japanese. I think the cooks were Chinese.

"I'll tell you. We have the wrong habits in Chinese restaurants. We learned to fill up on rice with relatively little relish. These were expensive. When I went to Chinese restaurant, with our basketball team, we would have a contest. Who could eat the most rice. I used to enter that vigorously. You know the big Chinese bowl? I'd eat two or three of those. Well, we were farmers' kids.

"I got wise and let the others win. And I'd eat as fast as I can, the more expensive stuff. Even today though I'm eating the expensive stuff. I like to have my rice. I like the rice more than I should.

"Egg foo-young is still one of my favorites. If you go to a nice dinner, I mean it's still on the spread. You get chicken something or other, steamed fish.

"I have a Chinese friend, my son-in-law's father. He died now. He used to run a restaurant and then went into investments and so on. He is an excellent cook. He taught me how some of the dishes are made, too. You know like won-ton and steamed fish. How you steam it and pour hot oil over it."

Uhachi Tamesa, the old man who saw Seattle Japanese America grow and defended the civil rights of his American-born daughter, with his bankbook. Come 1941 and WWII, the world changed. And come 1942, it would change more. And so would he and his family. They would be evacuated to a concentration camp, Heart Mountain Relocation Center, Wyoming. Uhachi, the Issei, and Minoru, the Nisei, would become prominent in an organization dedicated to proving, in a court of law, that concentration camps wrongly imprisoned American citizens. Minoru was an organizer of the Heart Mountain Fair Play Committee, and Uhachi was a supporter of the Fair Play Committee's legal fees.

Meantime the Nisei have time to dream their American dreams. The new writers of Japanese America, the first generation born to use English, in their newspapers, stories, and poetry, will write their way into America.

The Japanese Sandman Song

told by RAYMOND B. EGAN

set to music by RICHARD A. WHITING

Won't you stretch im-ag-i-na-tion for the mo-ment and come with me
Let us hast-en to a na-tion ly-ing o-ver the west-ern sea
Hide be-hind cher-ry blos-soms a sight that will please your eyes.
There's a ba-by with a la-dy of Ja-pan sing-ing lu-la-bies.
Night winds breath her sighs

CHORUS
Here's the Japanese Sand-man. Sneaking on with the dew
Just an old second hand man
He'll buy your old day from you.
He will take every sorrow
Of the day that is through—
And he'll give you to-mor-row
Just to start life a-new—
Then you'll be a bit old-er
In the dawn when you wake
And you'll be a bit bold-er
With the new day you make
Here's the Japanese Sand-man.
Trade him silver for gold
Just an old second hand man
Trading new days for old.

PART II

The Nisei Dream

The Nisei and the News

The Nisei are graduating from college and high school in large numbers. They speak English as if born to it. The Issei help the English-speaking Nisei by turning their newspapers into dual language entities with a separate English-language staff and a Japanese-language staff. Is this the dawn of Nisei journalism, or something to keep the Japanese printers busy while their job printing expands into English? English wedding invitations. English menus.

Nisei who know that being born American means they were born to become publishers. They want to grab their generation, which was born to speak English. And some of the newly minted publishers think of themselves as political organizers and political thinkers and their newspapers as political organs. Dare they dream? The first Nisei to reach elective office is coming!

All over the country Japanese American newspapers are popping up like mushrooms: Seattle, Portland, San Francisco, San Jose, Fresno, Los Angeles, Denver, Salt Lake City. It is a new age.

L.A. JAPANESE DAILY NEWS
Sunday, February 21, 1926

L.A. Japanese Daily News
(The *Rafu Shimpo*)
104 N. LOS ANGELES STREET, LOS ANGELES, CAL
TELEPHONE TRinity 0667

SUNDAY ISSUE

This section aims to publish important news from the Orient, thoughts and comments of prominent Japanese writers together with the news and activities among the younger generations in Southern California. News from any gatherings either social or educational among our second generation are especially welcome.

Please send in the news so that it will reach us Wednesday evening to be published on following Sunday.

Announcement

This is the resume of the news among those who live in Southern California. Our long-hoped-for wishes are materialized, and so here we have a medium to publish news of the second generation, for the second generation, and by the second generation. Therefore, you people of Southern California, get busy and send in some news, news of general interest to everybody.

All dispatches must reach us not later than Wednesday in order to appear in the subsequent Saturday issue.

The Editor

James Omura, Nisei Newsman

IRON CHINK

"I was probably the only Iron Chink operator signed up with the American Federation of Labor, the A. F. of L. labor union," James Omura says.

"I don't mean it that way," he says, as if he caught a look in my eye. "The Iron Chink is a big machine. It slits the belly of the salmon, and it takes out all that gunk, intestines and stuff. That's the machine they call the Iron Chink. I suppose I was fifteen when I was put on that machine."

The Iron Chink is a famous machine designed by a man aptly named Smith to do the work that used to be done by Chinese. Japanese who worked the canneries knew it. Filipinos, everybody who worked the canneries in Alaska in the summer knew the Iron Chink. It was famous for taking and chewing off arms at the first wrong move. Young Jimmie Omura lived the entire Japanese American adventure, from the fields to the canneries, to the hitch hiker, to boxcar traveler, to Nisei journalism.

"I got blackballed because my name was on the A. F. of L. list. The C.I.O. won," he says.

"I went over to the C.I.O. and talked with the vice president. I got nowheres. I practically pleaded, you know—that I needed the job to complete my schooling.

"He didn't care. No.

"Someone told me of a different contractor who was in Portland, Oregon. For some reason when they unionized, they only unionized the Seattle companies. So other companies, operating elsewhere, were nonunion. They hired me. I went north several times after that.

"I had some good fellows teaching me how to operate the Iron Chink. You have to know how to put the tails into the machine just right. If the tails don't go in right, why the tails would knock the pins off. You could have all sorts of problems. Mess up the fin grippers, you know, and they'll have to replace it. The engine would get stuck. They'll have to replace it. Sometimes, it ties them up two hours or more. The mechanics don't like it. You know. It makes him work too hard.

"I picked it up pretty fast on putting the tails into the machine. But I didn't like it toward the end there. During the Depression, why they dropped the wages like mad.

"Most of them working were getting thirty-five dollars a month. And they paid only fifty-five dollars a month for Iron Chink operators. And fifty-five dollars for pitch fish too. So, since they paid the same, I'd rather go pitch fish.

"The salmon comes in, you pitch it from the boat to a conveyer. So, it's work like hell, when you're working, but a lot of the time you don't do nothing. When boats aren't coming in, it'll be slow. You can loaf and don't do nothing. So I signed on as a pitch fish, and went to the Bering Sea.

"The foreman knew I was an Iron Chink operator. The foremen were Japanese. Superintendents were white. But foremen were Japanese. And he kept on asking me if I would switch my job. I refused because the pay was the same, while, if you're an Iron Chink operator, you have to go and work in the warehouse and do other things. And if you're a pitch fish, you didn't have to do other things. You could go bear hunting or something.

"They had started their season with their Iron Chink operator, and he was so terrible, the superintendent was raising hell. So, the foreman came to me and he just wanted me to switch to the Iron Chink and he begged me. I don't know how many times he begged me during a period of two weeks. He was having all sorts of problems because the superintendent was jumping down his neck. Eventually I gave in and took it over. No more problems.

"That particular season was up in Nusugak in the Bering Sea, way up there beyond Kodiak Islands. The season generally ran somewheres from April to September. Room and board was provided by the cannery. I slept in a large bunkhouse with everybody in it. Mostly young dumbbells like me. During the height of the season, because I had to run the machine, I would get about three hours sleep.

"If it wasn't too busy, I'd get about six hours. And that's not bad, if you get six. So, I'm used to sleeping six hours now.

"I must have made about three hundred and fifty dollars that season. Then from Alaska, I had a job at the Anacortes cannery, when I came back. Then I went to Pocatello, Idaho, and lived there a year and a half, almost two years."

NIKKEI SHIMIN

October 15, 1929

Nikkei Shimin

Semi-Monthly by the New American Citizens
League of San Francisco

Subscription Rate: $1.00 Per Year

Business Offices, 1623 Webster Street, San Francisco, Calif.

Publisher editor..............................Iwao Kawakami

OUR PURPOSE

By IWAO KAWAKAMI

One of the purposes of this publication is to give the new Japanese-American citizens an appropriate medium through which they can express themselves. Before proceeding further, however, I would like to give my own opinion of the phrase "creative expression."

"Creative expression" is perhaps the finest record of man, or it determines the cultural progress of a nation or a race.

Contemplating the present quality of "creative expression" in art and daily life, if one compares it, let us say, with those of the "Golden Ages" in Greece, Rome, England and France, the comparison reacts most unfavorably on the "creative expression" of our day. The reason is not hard to find—peoples everywhere are becoming more standardized and less individual in their ways of living and thinking. Also, they are content to follow the "Old Masters" or to imitate them whenever possible.

That it is at this point that the solution appears. We, the Japanese-Americans, are in a position where we represent the blending of two races or, in another sense, we are an entirely new group of young people in America. It would not be amiss, therefore, to believe that new forms of creative expression will rise from our group. Let us first, however, consider the basic soil in which our creative expression will take root.

There are, to my conception, three promising aspects of Japanese-American life. In the first place the agricultural aspect; secondly, the industrial aspect; and lastly, the social or intellectual aspect.

The agricultural aspect is, despite the various legislative restrictions placed on it, a steadily progressing one. The first generation of Japanese farmers have learned bitter lessons from Mother Nature, and are now in the position to reap the honest efforts of their toil; and without doubt they shall reap moral rewards as well as material ones. Their sons and daughters have been given a splendid heritage of patient pioneering.

The industrial aspect is, perhaps, the most practical and lucrative one. As the Japanese population in America increases, there will constantly grow a demand for well-trained, efficient business men and women. This will inevitably lead to the social aspect which is based, in majority of the cases, on industrial success.

The social and intellectual aspects are, by far, the least developed by the Japanese-Americans. There are, to be sure, individual examples of social and artistic leadership; yet they cannot begin to compare in quantity or quality with those other races in America. The Japanese American, in most cases, confronts the pitfall of imitation or unoriginality; and those are precisely the things that one must learn to avoid.

It is in order to help the New American citizens avoid these pitfalls and in order to encourage the development of healthy sincerity in the matter of expression that we wish to introduce this publication to the Japanese and American people. If it is not taking too much for granted, I would like to conclude with the following two stanzas which I wrote recently:

> From America's oft-quoted "melting pot"
> Have bubbled out thousands of newspapers
> With their editorial fire or rot
> Catering to—or cutting up capers.
> Some may be fit to read, others not—
> Though all, at times, indulge in hot vapors.
> We rejoice at the power of the press
> For good, but not its abuse in a mess.

> At first, all our papers were in English
> (Though even that speech has undergone change.)
> But when the aliens came, (by our wish
> To clear away the wilderness and range),
> They settled and then started to publish
> Needed news in their own tongues—some quite strange.
> If we promise no transient example,
> Before you cast your ancient eggs sample!

CONGRATULATIONS

By SABURO KIDO

President of New American

Citizens League of San Francisco

It is with great joy and pride that I write this message to the members of the staff for making our dreams of having a publication come true. Ever since the organization of the league, the Board of Governors have recognized the necessity of a newspaper or magazine which would serve as a mouthpiece. Though the English section of the Japanese-American News gave us wonderful support by giving all our undertakings full publicity, still we felt something lacking.

Oftentimes, we have read in the Japanese section of local papers articles pertaining to us, second generation members; and we have had the desire to express our ideas and thoughts as a reply because we thought our elders misunderstood us. Inability to write in Japanese, however, has been the chief handicap. Also, the Board of Governors have done their utmost to stimulate interest in the league and build up a strong, unified body; but they have fallen short of the goal they have set up. A publication such as we now have will be of great aid.

The publication can be the connecting link between the first and second generation Japanese by trying to dissolve any misunderstanding which may be existing at the present time. It can portray to the American public what we, American citizens of Japanese ancestry, are thinking in regards to our duties as a citizen as well as our diverse problems. It can give expression to what is considered true American ideals and guide the growing generation to become American citizens we can all be proud of.

Considering the potential power of the publication to do good, I cannot help but impress on the members of the staff the grave responsibility that lies on their shoulders. In their hands lies the power to help mold the second generation members for good or bad.

The public is expecting great things. I am confident that the members of the staff will do their utmost so as not to disappoint these supporters. Of course, we cannot expect perfect models of journalism from the beginning; but we hope that improvements will be made gradually as time goes on. We all appreciate the great sacrifice that is being made by the members of the staff.

In closing, I wish to congratulate the members of the staff for the splendid work they have done. This venture is a great and noble one. Everyone is expecting that this work, once launched, will be continued. I hope and feel sure that the sincerity of the members of the staff will make this publication the voice of the American citizens of Japanese ancestry of the Pacific Coast in the near future.

Blinky Winky

By JACK CADDIGAN

and CHICK STORY

Writers of: "The Rose of No Man's Land"

"Salvation Lassie of Mine," "Mammy's Honey Boy"

In a maze of oriental haze
Way down in dreamy Chinatown
Nightly 'neath the Jack O Lantern rays,
A lonely lover can be found
He sighs for his almond eyes,
While he is waiting there.

CHORUS
In the little Hinky Dinky land of Blinky Winky
There's a weary sad, and dreary, lonely little Chinky,
Waiting for one that he left at home, 'cross the foam,
All alone she was only a China rose
When the weepy sleep creepy shades of night are falling,
To his God of Oriental love you'll hear him calling,
Bring me the breath of the Rose I had,
Make me glad, I'm so sad,

Tell her that I'm waiting down in Blinky Winky Town.

JAPANESE AMERICAN COURIER
JAMES Y. SAKAMOTO

Jimmie Sakamoto's judo instructor, Tokogoro Ito, a *go dan*, fourth-degree black belt, told young Sakamoto he would do better boxing. And it was no put-down. Ito entered him against an "older and more experienced" fighter, and though Sakamoto doesn't say, he must have done all right, because he quit Princeton after two years and took up boxing. Sometime in this period, Sakamoto met and married Frances Imai, a half-white woman, a Eurasian. He doesn't talk about her. He doesn't write about her. The only one who knows and writes about her seems to be Bill Hosokawa, the designated Boswell to the JACL's Mike Masaoka. The Sakamotos had a baby. A girl they called Blossom.

He worked at Japanese American newspapers and boxed, as a bantamweight, a featherweight, and junior lightweight. He fought for three years in three different weight classes covering a weight difference of forty pounds. In camp in 1942, the War Relocation Authority (WRA) at Minidoka touts Jimmie Sakamoto as "probably the first person of Japanese ancestry to fight in Madison Square Garden." A probable accomplishment.

In 1955, Sakamoto recalled that in the 1920s he taught the European manly art of boxing one night a week at the Japanese Christian Institute, in New York, the same place Sessue Hayakawa taught what Sakamoto called "fencing," which is probably misleading.

Hayakawa was an actor, a vaudevillian, a bon vivant and a Zen man. He turned his 1926 novel *The Bandit Prince* into a forty-five-minute piece for vaudeville and performed it 1926 and 1927, at the Palace, in New York, and on tour of the United States and Canada. In 1928, he performed another vaudeville piece, *The Man Who Laughed*, by Edgar Allan Wolf, opposite Lucille Lortel (who later owned and operated the Theatre de Lys in Greenwich Village, filling it with *The Threepenny Opera* in 1955, the year of Hayakawa's fame for *Bridge on the River Kwai*). In 1927, during his vaudeville period, Hayakawa started a Zen study group. Japanese "fencing," or *kendo*, was a part of it. In 1933, he made his first sound picture, *Daughter of the Dragon*, with Anna May Wong and Warner Oland (as an Asian). Hayakawa played an American-born Chinese police detective. "I enjoyed it very much," he said of the experience.

Jimmie Sakamoto mentions Hayakawa, to link their names, ever so briefly with his boxing experience. It's obvious, at the time that they might have met, Jimmie wasn't interested in the world that Hayakawa knew. It's a pity. If he had become acquainted with Hayakawa's multicultural world, the *Japanese American Courier*, and Japanese America, might have developed differently. As fate would have it, Jimmie's world was getting smaller and smaller.

His wife died. He gave the baby up to her parents.

Sakamoto had the retina of his left eye knocked loose in a fight in Utica, New York, in 1926. Then a blow detached the retina of his right eye, in 1927. In those days there was no way of reattaching the retinas. Blindness was inevitable. As the world went dim, Sakamoto walked up and down stairs, turned corners, and went in and out of rooms blindfolded. Brave, stoic, and alone. That was his preparation for blindness.

Blind, twenty-four years old, and back in Seattle, he married Misao Marietta Sadie Nishitani (called Sadie), and started the first all English-language Japanese American daily on January 1, 1928, the Seattle *Japanese American Courier*.

"So we started, or rather, revived, a defunct organization called the Seattle Progressive Citizens' League back in 1928."

HOT OFF THE PRESS!

JAPANESE AMERICAN COURIER

Vol. 1   SEATTLE, WASH., JANUARY 1, 1928   No. 1

THE COURIER

Without a gesture of ceremony that attends almost every launching of a new enterprise, "The Courier" makes her introductory bow to the public in modest form, but without the subservient indication of an apology. Beset by a lean treasury, the sails cannot be filled to show swiftness with which she can apply her speed, but "The Courier" will endeavor to make up for all her inceptional defections in other ways best able to serve the public and purposes.

With the ever increasing number of American born Japanese in Seattle and the outlying districts, the fact is patent that there must be established some organ to be used as a medium in expression of their opinions and to guide them in the most commendable fashion, in their political actions as well as their social activities....

James Sakamoto

JACL 1929–1930

The Progressive Citizens League was founded with an Issei board. The Issei were interested in civil rights. They were interested in overturning the anti-alien land laws of 1919 and 1921. James Sakamoto writes, "The League was formed more or less to combat any anti-Japanese legislation or reactions, but as you know, and as the records will show, it proved of little avail or usefulness. When we reorganized the League, we eliminated the three first-generation advisers, as well as its negative stand to a positive one of Americanism." So an interest in civil rights and the first-generation Issei, "ineligible for citizenship," were removed from the Progressive Citizens League as being too negative. Membership was conveniently confined to "citizens only." The Progressive Citizens League was a positive, all-American, all-citizen, all-English performance for whites and that became the JACL.

"Now, a movement was started up and down the coast that resulted in the organization of a national body here in Seattle in 1930. During the latter part of August and September of that year, we organized the Japanese American Citizens League as national body with 9 chartering groups, Seattle, Portland, Newcastle— that is in Placer County—Stockton, San Francisco, San Jose, Fresno, Los Angeles, and Brawly were represented, with total membership of less than 1,000."

In 1936, James Yoshinori Sakamoto was elected fifth president of the Japanese American Citizens League.

"Today, we have 60 chapters with an approximate membership of 20,000, which I believe will be increased to larger number very, very soon.

"Now, this organization has been working on a program to make the American-born Japanese realize their duties as American citizens, based on the principles of Americanism."

Blind Jimmie Sakamoto hung out with reporters from the *Post-Intelligentser* and the *Times*, in his bow tie and round, dark glasses. In Seattle, his voice remembered as being rough, gruff, and tough by the Japanese and gentle by the whites, he was a news mascot or a news equal, a part of the Seattle news scene.

Then Pearl Harbor. Seattle's Japanese American streets were emptied into Puyallup Fairgrounds, renamed Camp Harmony by the new JACL camp staff, headed by James Sakamoto. He divided Japanese America by publicizing JACL loyalty and the JACL Intelligence Unit that worked with the FBI. "May I also state, right here that we have, under this emergency defense council, a civilian protection corps, a Red Cross corps, a general welfare corps, a national defense stamp campaign corps, and an intelligence unit. This intelligence unit is cooperating directly with the Federal Bureau of Investigation. The only man that I know who is in that unit is the chairman [Clarence Arai], and that is only because I appointed him chairman."

HOT OFF THE PRESS!

JAPANESE AMERICAN COURIER
"FOR TRUTH, JUSTICE & TOLERANCE!"

Vol. I   SEATTLE, WASH., JANUARY 7, 1928   No.2

AWAKE! CITIZEN'S LEAGUE

There is in this community today an organization which by virtue of its importance and political prestige, should be the outstanding association. Probably no mention need be made as to its entity, but it might just as well be said that the Citizen's League is deep in slumber and needs a thorough awakening....

James Omura,
Nisei Newsman

OMURA AND SAKAMOTO

J immie Omura was eight years old when he met Jimmy Sakamoto, the boxer blinded in the ring who became the publisher-editor of the first and only all-English Japanese American newspaper, the Seattle *Japanese American Courier*. The blind publisher summoned Omura to his office and lectured him on getting along with his father. Little Jimmie Omura thought it presumptuous of this stranger to talk about his relationship with his father, and did not take to the man.

"No, I stayed away for a very good reason. At the University of Washington, I asked a professor of journalism speaking in the circular amphitheater on campus, what my prospect was as a journalist.

"I was told none whatsoever except for Sakamoto's *Courier*.

"It was well known in Japanese circles that the *Courier* was dying on its feet. Everyone knew it was barely making out. Most people wondered how it managed to exist.

"Hosokawa come on in '33, I think, and helped them. He was going to the University of Washington at that time. He was the associate editor, but his name was not generally known in Nisei journalistic circles.

"I went in there with some poems I wrote in August of 1934 and inquired whether the *Courier* would be interested in printing them. Hosokawa glanced at them and turned away, but, as an afterthought, took them in to Jimmie Sakamoto. He was in Sakamoto's office a very brief time, when he came out he again turned them down. I told Hosokawa, it didn't matter. 'I'll get them printed elsewhere.'

"One of the poems was read over an Oakland radio station. I don't know who read it. I received a postcard stating, 'Your poem entitled Solitude will be read on so and so evening over this station on the Song of Eventide program.'"

HOT OFF THE PRESS!

LOS ANGELES RAFU SHIMPO
July 30, 1932

XTH OLYMPIC GAMES OPENS TODAY WITH CEREMONIALS

The greatest athletic gathering this nation has ever known opened its 16 days of competition for world laurels this afternoon at the Olympic Stadium with impressive ceremonies.

ELEVEN JAPAN ATHLETES SEE ACTION SUNDAY

Anno, Sasaki Race Against Ralph
Metcalefe and Jonah
of Germany

Eleven Japanese athletes who bear the colors of the Land of the Rising Sun will see action tomorrow, and six more on Monday.

Announcement

All Japanese taking part in the pageant, "California We Are the World," are requested to be at the Bowl by 9:45 A.M. the practice will commence immediately at 10:00 o'clock. It is imperative that all singers and dancers attend this practice as it will be the only one with the orchestra.

I.A.A.A. NAMES FIVE JAPANESE TO OFFICIATE

For the first time in the history of the Olympic games Japanese have been appointed to help officiate at the various events.

James Omura,
Nisei Newsman

TAJIRI WAS A SHREWD POKER PLAYER

"Well, after I graduated from Broadway High, I first went north. To Alaska. There wasn't any opportunity in Seattle. I should know. I had lived there several years. Several years. Tough times. So after Alaska, I headed down to California. Everybody thought California was the golden land. People in the Northwest thought money grew on trees in California.

"So, I decided the place to go was California. I stayed right downtown at the old Iowan Hotel, on [Third Fourth or Fifth] Street. Then the old Ohio Hotel on East First, near San Pedro, in Li'l Tokyo and took over the English-language section of the *New Japanese American News* for fifty cents per day plus room and board. People were lucky to have any type of work at the time. Soup lines stretched for blocks, and men were selling pencils, neckties, and apples on city streets.

"I worked at the *New Japanese American News* just four months. That's how I got to know Larry Tajiri and Brownie Furutani of the *Kashu Mainichi*; Louise Suski and George Nakamoto, coeditors of the *Rafu Shimpo*; Ken Tashiro and all those Nisei journalists of the Deadline Club. Newspaper people always have a club. And if we had a few spare dollars, we'd play poker. Larry Tajiri was a shrewd poker player.

"Oh, yeah. We liked to scoop each other. But there was no problem. Nisei newspaper people were all in the same boat. They were hard up for cash, and always on the lookout for anything interesting. And after hours we enjoyed getting together. We would play poker at someone's room sometimes, at a professional office and in homes. I don't remember names because we never had a set group. I remember the *Pacific Weekly* group playing cards. I played poker at the home of Mr. Izumi, managing editor of the *Shin Nichibei*, and I won, but it went on the tab. I never got paid, and when my newspaper salary became irregular, I quit.

"Lawrence [Steven Taniyoshi] Tajiri was without exception the finest journalist the Nisei ever produced. He was the most liberal of the Nisei editors, although he pursued no causes. He would not damage his own personal image but recognized those who did. I do not recall any divergence of vision on the Nisei dream. We have differences on the approach. Tajiri was more of an idealist. I feel I was more impatient and eager to prod the Nisei and the community towards that end.

"Few Nisei editors had the breadth of knowledge at their mental command as did Larry Tajiri. He was especially well versed on Hollywood, including of course, Toshia Mori, the Wampus Baby Star of 1932, and other Japanese actors and actresses. What's a Wampus Baby Star? Wampus's first name was George. He was a casting critic of considerable note. In 1931, he began his list of the thirteen most promising young actresses. The press called the selections Wampus Baby Stars.

"It was the early thirties. Sessue Hayakawa, the Japanese screen idol, had returned from France after a long hiatus to recapture his stardom in Hollywood. He teamed with Anna May Wong in the Oriental vehicle *Daughter of the Dragon*. The film historian W. E. Crane says it flopped at the box office. For some reason, I always thought Toshia Mori won acclaim in this movie.

"Toshia Mori caught Hollywood's attention for her role in *Fury of the Jungle*. In 1932, the second year of Wampus's Baby Stars, Toshia Mori was named as one of the thirteen Baby Stars of 1932. She was cast in the role of Mah-Li, a Chinese attendant to Barbara Stanwyck in Frank Capra's Oriental vehicle, *The Bitter Tea of General Yen*, starring Miss Stanwyck and Nils Asther. Miss Stanwyck was Caucasian in this movie. Nils Asther played the Chinese General Yen. Toshia Mori played a Chinese servant. Frank Capra directed. Larry Tajiri wrote: 'Frank Capra considers *Bitter Tea* in many respects as the best film he ever made.'

"I have no knowledge whether Larry Tajiri met Toshia Mori [Ichioka] or not. She was not that easy to reach. I met her through a mutual friend, Bill Kono, a commercial radio operator.

"Later when Bill lost his life in a boating accident at Lake Arrowhead, I tried to reach Toshia. But she was off somewheres. Toshia Mori married a San Francisco Chinese American—Alan Jung, who piloted her career after her break with Columbia Studios. She played in number of—but never reached her previous high.

"I do not know if Larry Tajiri aspired to be an actor, but he was interested in drama and once participated in a play, in San Francisco. Larry organized the Li'l Tokyo Players in which he also acted. Tajiri's handicap was diction. He spoke fast, staccato, like Walter Winchell, and not always too clearly.

"Nisei newspaper journalism was a prosaic occupation. It had one specific benefit. It was a source of contacts with the white establishment that may some day blossom into opportunity. I don't believe any of us felt progress could be found in the Japanese racial community. It was a dead end!

"Nisei newspapers at that time just wrote up club news and took things off the AP and wire news from the INS. We used to take whatever referred to Japanese and feature it and obtain stories pertinent to the Nisei from the Japanese-language section. The Japanese section had the Domei News Service and occasionally we would run across something interesting.

"When I first started in Nisei journalism, I soon found that the English-language section was dominated by the Japanese staff, insofar as editorial policy was concerned. I didn't like that. I was fortunate that on the first two newspapers on which I worked, the editor-in-chief of the Japanese Divisions were congenial and tolerant persons. They gave me a free hand and allowed me to dictate my own policy and, in fact, cooperated with my efforts.

"I wrote an editorial in the *New Japanese American News* that perked the complaint of the Little Tokyo bigwigs and Central California Japanese Association powers. I was told that Katsuma Mukaeda and Gongoro Namura had visited the newspaper to file a complaint. The Japanese editor was Sakaguchi. He reported the matter to me. Then he said, 'Don't worry about it!' He had a big smile. I didn't worry about it.

"I flayed the Nisei for indifference and inertia. Urged them to get out to legitimate theater and opera, expand and become a part of the mainstream of America. I argued that the political process was the route to overcome the barriers of discrimination and prejudice. No Nisei editor had the effrontery to criticize their own racial people. That was courting economic and social sanctions. I told them to shape up and spruce up their establishments, their cluttered homes. I encouraged the literati as another method of pushing our way into the mainstream. I spotlighted talented Nisei as symbolic achievements. I sought upward mobility and uplift of my racial people instead of engaging in useless idealism. I reviewed books.

"Right here, in Los Angeles, one week in 1933, I read two racist books. Peter B. Kyne's *The Pride of Palomar*. The theme of it was that Japan was going to invade California and overrun the state and take it over. They were going to rape all the white women. That's a real cute one, because that would create hysteria. And they showed pictures of a Japanese bucktoothed with long scraggly hair and leering features. Oh, boy! Just looking at it!

"The other racist book I read was something by Gene Stratton-Porter, *Her Father's Daughter*. It is in one of my columns. I reviewed it. To the Nisei literati, it was probably better known than Wallace Irwin's *Seed of the Sun*. The sad fact is few Nisei were acquainted with either book. Nor was much reference made about them by English section editors of newspapers."

AMERICAN BOOKSHELF

PRESENTS

Her Father's Daughter

by

GENE STRATTON-PORTER

Frontispiece by

Dudly Cloyne Summers

Doubleday, Page & Company

Garden City, N.Y., and Toronto

1921

CHAPTER XII

The Lay of the Land

"Messy idea," said Linda promptly. "Thing to do, when you build a house, is to build it the way you want it for the remainder of your life, so you don't have to tear up the scenery every few years, dragging in lumber for expansion. And I'll tell you another thing. If the home makers of this country don't get the idea into their heads pretty soon that they are not going to be able to hold their own with the rest of the world, with no children or one child in the family, there's a sad day of reckoning coming. With the records at the patent office open to the world, you can't claim that the brain of the white man is not constructive. You can look at our records and compare them with those of countries ages and ages older than we are, which never discovered the beauties of a Dover eggbeater or a washing machine or a churn or a railroad or steamboat or a bridge. We are head and shoulders above other nations in invention, and just as fast as possible, we are falling behind in the birth rate. The red man and the yellow man and the brown man and the black man can look at our eggbeaters and washing machines and bridges and big guns, and go home and copy them; and use them while rearing ever bigger families than they have now. If every home in Lilac Valley had at least six sturdy boys and girls growing up in it with the proper love of country and the proper realization of the white man's right to supremacy, and if the world now occupied by white men could make an equal record, where would be the talk of the yellow peril? There wouldn't be any yellow peril. You see what I mean?"

Linda lifted her frank eyes to Peter Morrison.

"Yes, young woman," said Peter gravely, "I see what you mean, but this is the first time I ever heard a high school kid propound such ideas. Where did you get them?"

"Got them in Multiflores Canyon from my father to start with," said Linda, "but recently I have been thinking, because there is a boy in High School who is making a great fight for a better scholarship record than a Jap in his class. I brood over it every spare minute, day or night, and when I say my prayers I implore high Heaven to send him an idea or to send me one that I can pass on to him, that will help him to beat that Jap."

"I see," said Peter Morrison. "We'll have to take time to talk this over."

"You let that kid fight his own battles," said Henry Anderson roughly. "He's not proper bugcatcher. I feel it in my bones."

For the first time, Linda's joy laugh ran over Peter Morrison's possession.

"I don't know about that," she said gaily. "He's a wide-awake specimen; he has led his class for four years when the Jap didn't get ahead of him. But, all foolishness aside, take my word for it, Peter, you'll be sorry if you don't think this house is big enough for your dream lady and for all the little dreams that may spring from her heart."

"Nightmares, you mean," said Henry Anderson. "I can't imagine a bunch of kids muddying up this spring and breaking the bushes and using sling shots on the birds."

"Yes," said Linda with scathing sarcasm, "and would our government be tickled to death to have a clear spring and a perfect bush and a singing bird, if it needed six men to go over the top to handle a regiment of Japanese!"

"I am in the deepest kind of earnest," said Peter Morrison. "What Miss Linda says is true. As a nation, our people are pampering themselves and living for their own pleasures. They won't take the trouble or endure the pain required to bear and rear children; and the day is rolling toward us, with every turn of the planet one day closer, when we are going to be outnumbered by a combination of peoples who can take our own tricks and beat us with them. We must pass along the good word that the one thing America needs above every other thing on earth is homes and hearts big enough for children, as were the homes of our grandfathers, when no joy in life equaled the joy of a new child in the family, if you didn't have a dozen you weren't doing your manifest duty."

NEW WORLD DAILY

DRIFTS

By JIMMIE OMURA

A Novel

Gene Stratton Porter is generally regarded as a character and nature writer. He is known for authoring "The Keeper of the Bees." But what is not so well known is that Porter penned one of the most unjust novels ever to come off an American press. The novel in question is "My Father's Daughter."

Porter draws the picture of a Japanese student in a Los Angeles high school, Oka Saye, with the implication that he is subsidized by the Japanese government. Although Porter sets forth no concrete proof, it is asserted that middle-aged Japanese who have graduated with high honors from a Japanese college are being sent to public schools on the coast to learn the American system of government and to study its weaknesses.

Ths fellow, Oka Sayye, is painted as a venomous type. Porter makes us believe menace fairly springs from his character. He is allegedly about thirty years of age, but passes off for nineteen. We would like to meet Mr. Porter and ask him if he really believes what he wrote.

James Omura, Nisei Newsman

THE GREAT NISEI NOVEL

"**L**arry Tajiri and I discussed it in L.A. 'It' was The Great Nisei Novel!" James Omura says. "We started to talk about it when we were in Los Angeles and discussed it some more when in San Francisco. I came up in the fall of '34. He came up and took the Nichibei job about a year later, I think.

"We had a newspaper club in San Francisco too, naturally. But that wasn't our only connection. We did a lot of slumming around together in San Francisco. After hours," Omura says.

"You know it's odd. Stirring up all that hellishness, I had plenty of friends and the respect of my Japanese editorial counterparts. I always was sought after by Larry Tajiri to write for him. Rural readers came up with support in surprising fashion. I'd be invited to holiday dinners. To weddings. To a dying girl's goodbye party. To farewell celebrations of departing friends; to slumming at night. I never felt any hostility . . . except from the JACL. And fanatics.

"In those days the JACL was an anathema to the many. And those who adhered to the organization were low-key about it. Take the editor of the *Nikkei Shimmin*, Iwao Kawakami. He was out with us frequently. We never had a serious discussion about the JACL. On rare occasions when the JACL came up, Larry would say, 'It wouldn't hurt to jump on the bandwagon.' He was a real bandwagoneer.

"The Nisei editors were tremendously conservative and on the whole were content to put out bulletin board-style publications, spruced up with reprints from the wire services and the metropolitan dailies. None would attempt to disturb the status quo. No Nisei editor had the effrontery to criticize their own racial people. That was courting economic sanctions, from the advertisers whose money almost supports their newspapers. I flayed the Nisei for their indifference.

"Rival editors scrutinized what I said in my *New Japanese American News* editorials and were quick to note any boo hoo."

NEW WORLD DAILY

DRIFT TIDES

By JIMMIE OMURA

The Brothels....

The girls who work at the Ginza, the Poppy and other such establishments are human under their veneer of make-believe. They must make their bread and honey in some way, and this is the path they have chosen. We should not forget that emotions and feeling still live in the heart of these entertainers.

Their profession may be an ignominious one, yet that should be no reason for us to treat them like animals. Are they not our sisters? Sometimes we seem to forget that we aren't such fine beings ourselves. Those who habit these haunts are themselves not much better than the average brothel girl.

James Omura,
Nisei Newsman

"I'M LIKE POPEYE"

"**L**arry Tajiri wrote a satirical piece on my describing San Francisco drinking parlors, called *rioyas*, as prostitution joints. The *Hokubei Asahi* blasted me for Seattle's *Great Northern News* reprinting something I wrote with a Louisville dateline instead of a San Francisco dateline.

"After four months on the *New Japanese American News*, I left, and wandered over to Hollywood for awhile. A group trying to republish the old *Pacific Weekly* called me back to Li'l Tokyo. Franklyn Suiyama, Ruth Kurata, Dick Takeuchi, and George Nakamoto, who used to be editor of the *Rafu Shimpo*, six or seven in all, had an office right across from what they used to call the old Tomio building. Most people never heard of the *Pacific Weekly*. It was weekly that did with the Orient All-English. They used to comment on situations between the United States and Japan and anything along the Pacific seaboard.

"The six were positive they could get the paper going again. They wanted me to stand by. So, I came down from Hollywood to the Ohio Hotel, a few blocks from the produce market, where I ended up working. At Ninth Street Market.

"I worked for a commercial merchant and had to sleep in the daytime. I just couldn't sleep. It was too hot in L.A. Too much noise. I had to be up and at work at four o'clock in the afternoon and work 'til three in the morning, trucking to the farms in Orange County to pick up their vegetables and fruits, then come back and sell them in the city. I also worked on these fruit stands, too, like the rest of the college graduates. They worked right beside me.

"I'm like Popeye. I'm what I am! And that's what I am! In Los Angeles and San Francisco, why, I used to hobnob with Larry Tajiri. We would sit in Foster's after a movie and discuss the cinema world. We were literary comrades more or less strangers in a then somewhat strange city. We had developed some kindred friendship in the Los Angeles journalistic world. None of us were Clark Gables and none of us were obsessed with the Casanova virus. That didn't mean that we didn't engage in affairs with Nisei girls. It happened some times. And Brownie Furutani and after Brownie left for the Islands, with Larry, Curtis Otani, Iwao Kawakami and a fellow name of Harry Hoshide. Sometimes Hauro Imura joined us. On other occasions, Dixie Koga and his group, a Kibei named Tada, a linotypist named Harry Yasuda, a boxer Joho Shiroma from Honolulu, the Yoshino brothers. Of course, there were girls. We pal-ed around and walked the streets. Telegraph Hill. Nob Hill. Coit Tower and those sort of places. Landmark areas. Do you know that's how Larry Tajiri found his wife! They met in our group. That's how he met her.

"I think just he and I had ambitions to write The Great Nisei Novel. The others discussed it, but they all agreed that somebody else should write it. They didn't have any ambition to author The Great Nisei Novel. Tajiri and I had the ambition to write it some day. Of course, there were a number of writers who were more or less a part of our group. Haruo Imura was one of them. Then Iwao Kawakami, Curtis Otani, Brownie Furutani, John Fujii. All male. We all discussed it, but I think only Larry Tajiri and myself seriously projected The Great Nisei Novel in our future."

He brightens and recalls his friendship with Larry Tajiri, "What we discussed was literature. What we sought out were historic spots—Telegraph Hill, Nob Hill, Alcatraz by night, the lights festooning the far shores of the Bay. We would observe the empty, littered streets late at night and relate the scene to Ben Hecht's vignettes.

"I suppose in his Great Nisei Novel, he would emphasize Nisei who had achieved a niche in their field, advanced in their profession and obtained some worth of status symbol to make their lives worthwhile. We all felt the Nisei weren't getting their proper recognition," Jimmie says.

The Great American Novel

by

CLYDE BRION DAVIS

Farrar & Rinehart Incorporated

New York and Toronto

1938

At the Louisiana Street police station they finally let me go because I wasn't 15 years old yet and because it wasn't my gun and because I hadn't fired the shot. Pete, who was 17, was held on a charge of malicious mischief, but got off finally with a suspended sentence.

But the reason for me writing about this experience is this:

There was an amazing lot of excitement over this explosion because everyone in town had heard it and wondered what had happened. And when the police turned me loose a reporter for the *Morning Journal* cornered me. His name was Hartley.

"Bud," he said, "the *Journal* wants you to write your own story of this explosion. You just tell me about it. Just tell me everything—how it looked and what you thought and all that and I'll write it in your own words. It'll be printed under your name and I'll give you two dollars."

So I told him everything and the next morning, along with the main account of the explosion, there was my story with "By Homer Zigler" In black type at the top. And Hartley gave me two silver dollars, which made me a clean profit of $1.95 after I paid Pete Buchtel the nickel I bet and lost although there was no way to know for sure Pete hit the top box instead of any box in the pile and besides Pete admitted he used a .22 long cartridge instead of the .22 short I thought he was using.

So a prank which might easily have ruined my life and which might easily have killed a lot of people gave me my first ambition.

That story with "By Homer Zigler" over it fascinated me. As a matter of fact, the reporter Hartley fascinated me too. He was a handsome devil-may-care sort of fellow with a loud, checkered cap and a very high linen collar.

And I got to thinking that a newspaper reporter led the most interesting life imaginable. Where anything was happening, there was the reporter as fast as he could go, digging into all the interesting places so he could relay the story to the public at large. He was much better than being a policeman, because the reporter was excused from such disagreeable jobs as dragging drunken men down to jail. Besides, I had no hope of growing large enough to be a policeman. And a reporter was at the front during all celebrations and political meetings. He got to meet all the prominent people that come to town and he was privileged to write how they acted and what they said.

James Omura,
Nisei Newsman

"EXPLOITATION—BETRAYAL—I ATTACKED IT"

"I was interested in upward mobility of the Nisei racial group. A few individuals gaining the brass ring wasn't going to improve the Nisei status in the totality of American society. They were merely figures symbolic of status. Not actual status. The door to opportunity had to be opened for all. In the mainstream, the Nisei came face to face with prejudice. Within their own racial community, they were exploited by Issei entrepreneurs and by their own fellow Nisei business operators. It was a hell of an economic wall to scale. Exploitation—betrayal—I attacked it. In different ways, we both, Tajiri and myself attacked the weighting of the scales against us—exploitation of labor, inadequate housing, poor diet, and the other ills of the laboring class."

JAPANESE AMERICAN COURIER

"FOR TRUTH, JUSTICE & TOLERANCE!"

Vol. VIII., No. 373   Seattle, Wash., Saturday, March 9, 1935   Five Cents a Copy

LOCAL JACL ANNOUNCES NEW PLAN FOR CITY DISTRICTS; TO AID CENSUS

New System Will Aid Organizations; Increase Cooperation;

Hashiguchi Heads Finance Group; Arai to

Preside at Meet

Repertory Group Leaders Asked to See 'Chushingura'

Mr. and Mrs. Burton James and Mr. Albert Ottennelmer, of the Seattle Repertory the-atre, have been invited to attend the all-second generation girls drama presentations which will be given. The Playhouse is planning on giving an elaborate presentation of the famous play next season.

Work on the details of the play is progressing rapidly. It will be one of the most elaborate and carefully planned presentations that the Playhouse has ever given.

CAL. JOINT IMMIGRATION LEADERS FLAY WILD CONGRESS STATEMENTS

"500,000 armed Japanese" Charge Is Branded as Utterly Ridiculous; Group Praises Second Generation as Whole

LEAGUE OFFICERS CALL ON VOTERS

Hot Fight Centers on Council Seats; Two Charter Changes Up

With city elections scheduled for next Tuesday, officers of the Seattle chapter of the Japanese American Citizens' League are urging all registered members of the second generation to go to the polls and vote.

ALL-SECOND GENERATION GIRL CAST GIVING FAMOUS PLAYS TOMORROW

Excerpts from "Chushingura" Will Be Given, "Adachiga hara,"
"Shirokiya" on Bill: Nakamuras Acting as Directors.

NIPPON KAN IS SCENE OF STAGE PRESENTATION

Dramatic scenes from this "Chushingura" will add to a cultural program when local second generation girls take the stage at Nippon Kan tomorrow at 5pm.

Besides "Chushingura" two other famous Japanese dramas "Adachi-ga Hara" and "Shirro-Kiya" are to be presented by this second generation girls cast. Rehearsals for these dramas have been going on for the past several weeks under the direction of Mr. and Mrs. Kameo Nakamura, better known on the stage as "Nakamura Namidayo" and "Omaya Tandai" respectively.

From "Kotobuki Bambaro" to the final curtains scenes from the three famous Japanese dramas are to be enacted by second generation girls.

Tura Nakamura Feature

Another feature of the program will be Tura Nakamura popular Courier radio announcer, who will star from the sidelines with his brother Nisaidayu in lyrical readings to be accompanied by Tamiji and her samisen.

Tomorrow's performance has attracted much attention, as witnessed by the unprecedented advance sale of seats. But a greater interest is reported in many circles of the possible development of feminine stars in the Japanese dramatic world here.

Japanese Kabuki dramas have not been performed here in many years and due to that reason the show is attracting wide attention.

U.S. FOLK SONGS TO BE RECORDED BY PRIMA DONNA

Hizi Koike Records Planned for Japanese Sale; Voice Well Suited

OPENED OPERA HOUSE

The plaintive melodies of American folk songs will soon be heard in Japan as sung by the sweet soprano of Miss Hizi Koike who will sing in Seattle this month with the San Carlos Grand Opera Company.

Music lovers in Seattle and the vicinity are eagerly awaiting Miss Koike's appearance here. She will sing in "Madame Butterfly" on Sunday, March 24.

Gordon Hirabayashi,
On Civil Disobedience

"I KNEW ABOUT JAMES SAKAMOTO OF SEATTLE"

"**I** knew about James Sakamoto of the Seattle JACL because one of my good friends, Stas Hoshi, student friend, lived through part of his grade school and high school days, at his home as a kind of a not officially adopted son, but living there and doing duties and taking care of things with the *Courier* and this and that. Then, he was like me, working in a home going to school. And he told me about being in Sakamoto's home."

Of course he does. The Gordon Hirabayashi, first resister, and Sakamoto, the 200 percenter. We know Sakamoto and James Omura were at the Nippon Kan for the all-girl performance of scenes from the classic samurai revenge drama *Chushingura*. How many of the JACL wartime leadership and how many of the wartime resisters and anti-JACL plotters were in the audience that night in Seattle? Why didn't Jimmie Omura mention that it was an all-girl *Chushingura*, at the Nippon Kan, in his review?

"Sakamoto was the editor of the *Courier*," Jim the younger brother says.

"Yeah," Gordon the elder says.

"His wife is Sadie. . . ." Jim says.

"He's a relative of ours now," Gordon says. "Dad's second wife is a sister of Sakamoto."

"That gives you some twist!" Jim says and lets out a laugh.

"Oh, this guy Sakamoto was a 200 percenter," Gordon says, deadpan. Does he get the joke?

HOT OFF THE PRESS!

NEW WORLD DAILY

DRIFT TIDES

By JIMMIE OMURA

Back again in Seattle, we worked a pass into the Nippon Kan, Seattle's community hall, to see a portion of the highly-publicized second generation production of "Chushingura," the tale of the forty-seven faithful ronins. The small hall was filled to overflowing with scores of people finding standing room in the rear. Interspersed in the crowd were a number of Americans, who, no doubt, were as much at sea as this writer.

The famous story of the loyal samurais have been lauded in literature, the motion pictures and the stage. The Seattle Civic Repertory Playhouse is now undertaking the production of "Chushingura" in English. The project was launched under the direction of Burton S. James last winter and is expected to be completed for presentation in autumn of this year.

Joe Hirakawa, a University of Washington grad and now employed as an actor in Hollywood authors the translation of "Chushingura," which he has halfway completed. In the meanwhile Burton S. James has been scouring every available source for detailed information concerning the dramatization of the historic tale. Inquiries have been made to the cultural department of the Japanese government.

Dr. Clifford Uyeda,
Traveler

"I left Tacoma in 1936 right after high school. I fled the West Coast. I didn't just leave. I couldn't stand the West Coast. There was so much anti-alien feeling on the West Coast, and I knew that I would get into trouble if I stayed around, because I thought I was an American citizen.

"They called you mostly 'Japs' but it was mostly the attitude that really got to you after a while. I used to talk to a lot of the Issei, because I was able to speak Japanese well. And they used to tell me how they were treated when they came to the United States. They were spit upon and they had rocks thrown at them, and all that type of thing that they would constantly hear of. And even for us, many times, we got into fights with the Caucasian fellows because they would call us names. In these days, you're not supposed to fight anyone. You're supposed to be nice and quiet.

"At least in Wisconsin they treated me more like an individual, than like belonging to a group. Wisconsin was an area were a lot of Norwegians came. They were a lot more open. Progressive.

"When I went there, there was only one other Asian person that I remember at the University of Wisconsin. He was half Norwegian. I remember going to his home. A little town called Stoughton. And you never heard any English spoken anywhere. Everybody spoke Norwegian.

"And because all the other students were from many places, they just accepted you as another student."

Honorable Spy Exposing Japanese Military Intrigue in the United States

by

JOHN SPIVAK

Author of *SECRET ARMIES*

Modern Age Books, Inc.

New York

1938

THE BOOK AND THE AUTHOR

The famous reporter-detective John L. Spivak, author of *Secret Armies* and *America Faces the Barricades,* has scored another sensational exposure in *Honorable Spy.*

As in Secret Armies, which focused on local and official attention on Nazi spy activities, Spivak gives names dates and places. Evidence of his accuracy is already plain in the frantic shiftings of registration of Japanese "fishing boats," operating off the West Coast, the shifts and registration occurring just after the author published some of these findings in a periodical.

If Japan is colonizing in strategic military areas just south of the United States border, Americans should know about it. If fuel oil for submarines is being cached within easy striking distance of American naval bases, we cannot overlook the intent of such moves. The information gathered in Spivak's lastest book points toward an enormous net which is being spun around areas vital to American defense.

Unlike the Nazis, who specialize mainly in internal disruption, the Japanese apparently lean toward direct military plans of attack, but Spivak found both Nazi and Japanese agents working together in the common aim to defeat the interest of this government. However, the author cautions against loose talk about "yellow peril." The real peril it seems to him, "lies either in ignorance of what the secret agents are doing, or indifference, because we feel ourselves too strong to be perturbed by their activities."

That is why this book was written.

[Excerpt from the book]

There was a cultured language student; a photographer with no visible means of support but plenty of money in his pocket; a Japanese lady answering to the Irish name of Betsy O'Hara and with a story of being fired off the *Tatsuta Maru* in San Francisco for an indiscreet love affair on board ship. She had checked into the Miyako Hotel and quietly announced that she would live there while taking a course in "beauty culture."

Ohtani, like other "language students" at present in the United States, is a lieutenant commander in the Imperial Japanese Navy; his real purpose in this country was to act as chief of the Japanese intelligence for southern California, which includes the Japanese "farmers" south of the American–Mexican border and some of the Japanese fishing fleet active in American and Mexican waters.

Shortly before the mysterious German chemical capable of sinking the American fleet without firing a shot was being secretly cached in Lower California, Ohtani left hurriedly for Washington D.C., where he conferred twice with the Naval Attaché at the Japanese Embassy—the same attaché who directed espionage work in the United States and under whom John Farnsworth, a drunken former lieutenant in the American Navy, worked for the Japanese intelligence.

Early in May, 1938, Ohtani vanished from his usual haunts in the Japanese settlement. It was not until six o'clock on the evening of May 27, 1938, that he drove up to the Olympic Hotel in a 1937 Chevrolet carrying District of Columbia license plates DC 57-512. To Chieko he confided that he expected to return to Japan and that he had driven the car across the country for his "relief" who was expected soon. Apparently he himself didn't know the "relief's" name, for when she asked who he was and what he looked like, the language student just shrugged his shoulders.

Three days later (May 30, 1938) a serious looking individual quietly checked into the Olympic Hotel. He registered as Ko Nagasawa, also a language student. Commander Ohtani, who had been informed the day before that he was coming, made reservations for his room....

One of the fascinating quirks about Nagasawa is his reading habits. Every Japanese, especially every naval officer on intelligence duty in a foreign country (and Nagasawa, too, was a lieutenant commander in the Imperial Japanese Navy), is naturally interested in the war in China. The newcomer was no exception; he was always asking persons around the Hotel to tell him what the late editions had about the war and to interpret the news broadcasts over the radio.

His chief source of news was the *Rafu Shimpo*, a Japanese language newspaper published in Los Angeles. Every morning, with the regularity of a man punching a time clock on his job, Nagasawa would get the *Rafu Shimpo* and settle himself comfortably for an hour's reading. The war news was on the front page; but despite his interest in it, the language student glanced only casually at the headlines. He never read the news reports until he had first studied the market page containing vegetable quotations. He glued his eyes to that column as if hypnotised. Sometimes he stared at it for as long as half an hour as if trying to memorize it—or find a hidden meaning in the list of vegetables and their market prices. At no time did he ever use a pencil or make notes. He just sat and stared at the column and when, apparently, he had concluded his study, he then turned back to page one and read the war news.

Whether or not the vegetable quotations contained code messages for him, I have not been able to establish definitely; but there are several interesting aspects in his fascination for vegetable prices. With none of the persons with whom he associated did he ever disclose the slightest interest in vegetables except at meal times. But early on the morning of June 16, 1938, the market on vegetables apparently upset his plans and sent him hurriedly on a two-week trip.

[The complete vegetable quotations from the *Rafu Shimpo*. If there is coded message here, it is still here.]

RAFU SHIMPO
June 16, 1938

FRUIT PRICES

Valencia	50	100
Market Pack	125	150
Same Pack	130	150

Lemon		
Same Loose	150	225
Same Pack	425	450

Grapefruit		
Local Loose	50	75
Arizona Loose	75	100
Regular Loose	75	100
Good quality	100	125
From Other Areas Pack	150	250

Apples		
Roman Beauty	2	2½
Jonathon	3	
? Pippin	1½	2½
Winesap?	3	

Others		
Banana	4	4½
Avocado	15	18
Cherry	3	10
Apricot	2½	5
Peach	3½	5

VEGETABLES & FRUITS (June 14) Quantity

Watermelon	150
Asparagus	2065
Beans	3412
Lima Beans	62
Corn	5576
Cabbage	2464
Cauliflower	615
Celery	7568
Chickory	253
Lettuce Pack	4246
Same Loose	586
Romaine	792
Peas	898
Pepper ?	1522
Parsnips?	257
??	591
Summer squash	1089
Same Italian	676
Cucumber Lug	2284
Cantaloupe	7778
Egg Plant Lug	1799
Tomato Lug	2292
Same	12922
Potato	
100#bag	4049
Same lug	8878
? Lug	1898
Same 50#	909
?	495
Strawberry	
tray	10351
Tree	
Strawberry	421
Same Lug	550
Same Young	9479

EASTERN MARKETS

Beets	887
Carrots	3520

EASTERN MARKETS (continued)

Mustard	282
Green Onion	360
Parsley	377
Radish	898
Spinish	1811
Turnips	944

VARIOUS FRUITS: LUG

Apple	2044
Grapefruit	813
Lemon	1813
Orange	8048
Avocado	
average	707
Cherries	6480
Peaches	2809
Apricot	2149

L.A. FLOWER MARKET

Cut Flower Prices

	Low	High
Rose	25	150
Same Outside	15	75
Carnation		
Inside	100	250
Same Outside	75	200
Sweat Peas	25	100
Star ?	25	50
Green ?	75	75
Lark Spur	25	75
Gardenia	75	200
Gladiola	25	75
Aster	25	75
Centuria	25	50
Phlox	25	50
Daisies	25	75
?	25	
Corn Flower	25	50
?	50	

Marigold	50	
Same African	35	75
Scapiosa ?	25	50
Gladiolus	35	50
?	75	300
Stocks?	50	75
?	35	75
Straw Flower	35	75
Delphinium	25	75
Rhinoculus	25	150
?	25	50
Snap Dragon	25	100

VEGETABLE PRICES (June 16)

Cucumber	150	175
?	150	160
Flat	50	70
Honey Dew	100	175
Casaba	100	125
Watermelon ?	25	?

Asparagus		
Special Good		
Quality	11	12
Big	9	10
Same Average	7	8
Same Small	3	6

Strawberry Tray		
Torrance Good	90	110
Local Good		
Quality	80	90
Watsonville	70	100
Central &		
Northern		
California	40	55
Tree Strawberry	50	80

Raspberry	60	100
?	120	135

VEGETABLE PRICES (June 16) (continued)

Young Berry	45	60
Boysenberry	60	75
Logan	65	100

Sacked Items: Pea

Bowl	6	$8\frac{1}{2}$
Bush Peas	3	6
China Peas	12	15
Kentucky Local	2	$2\frac{1}{2}$
Same Bowl	$3\frac{1}{2}$	$5\frac{1}{2}$
Was	$3\frac{1}{2}$	5
Lima	9	10

Crate Items

Lettuce Loose	50	100
Central Coastal area	325	350
Same 5 doz	250	300
Romaine	15	40
Cabbage	40	100
Same Red Cabbage	40	100
Same Red Cabbage	75	115
Cauliflower	760	90
Chickory	40	75

Celery

White	35	50
Same High Quality	60	50
Same Heart Utah Area	50	70
Same Good Quality	75	80
Utah Heart	50	80

Lug Box Items

Cucumber Lug	75	115
Parsnips	30	50
Rhubarb Local	20	35
Same Grass Strawberry	30	45
Egg Plant	50	60

Summer squash		
Lug	75	100
Artichoke	75	115
Okra 1#	8	11
Tomato		
Local lug Large	200	275
Same Small	100	150
Regular Crate		
9 top	135	1854
12 top	125	160
16 Top	75	90
Regular 5x5		
& 5x6	125	160
Same?	75	115
Same?	70	75
Loose lug	40	50
Pepper Products		
Bell (within the state)	3	4
Green Chili Same	6	9
Yellow Chili Same	5	$5\frac{1}{2}$
Bunch Items		
Beets 3 doz.		
Crates	35	45
Carrots (this		
area)	30	40
Same Good Quality	45	60
Mustard 4 doz.	25	40
Spinich Same 4 doz.	25	65
Parsely Large		
Bunch 6 doz.	40	50
Radishes Same 6 doz.	30	60
Green Onion 2 doz.	100	130
Same Good Quality	150	200
White Radish	40	50

VEGETABLE PRICES (JUNE 16) (continued)

Leek ?	50	75
Celery root		
1 doz.	20	25
Watercress 1 doz.	25	30

Potato & Round Onions		
? Potato lug	30	45
Same 100 lbs	150	
Russet Potato 100 lbs	200	
Sweet Potato lug	100	150
New Onions Lug	20	45
Spanish Same	20	40
Garlic Pound	4	5

Eggs	
Large	27
Medium	25
Small	20

LOS ANGELES WHOLESALE AGRICULTURAL PRODUCE MARKET
THURSDAY'S MARKET:

Strawberry, bean products
Lettuce and Bundled Products very weak.
Cucumber, Bellpepper dropped in price.
Tomato, flowers, corn strong.

Due to cool weather, order light, market slow especially strawberries, cucumbers, bellpeppers, cabbage, summer and yellow squash, melons, cherries, majority of fruits.

—Cauliflower, corn, asparagus and tomato strong.
—Celery, melon, eggplant, onion, potatoes, beets, and spinich,-WEAK TO FAIR.

Beans
—Too many; price down
1 lb. = 2 to 3½
Lima = 9 to 10

Pepper Products
Green chili:
    small quantity   6, 7, 8 cents
    good quality   9 cents

Tomato
(Illegible)
Peas
weak (Illegible)
Strawberries
Lowered prices, some leftover
(illegible)

Lettuce
    4,800 large quantity   15 to 25 cents
    300 left
    Loose   900   Some left

Cucumber
    Local species increased
    Central California's down in price
    Lug   25 to 80 to 90 cents.

San Pedro as well as Blue Hill
    Good Quality   1.00 to 1.50
    Many left

Corn
    Small quantity
    Lug average   80 to 90
    local   75
    good quality   100 to 125

Others

Flower: small quantity, sold well

Cabbage: 50 - 60-100
Celery: weak market

LOS ANGELES WHOLESALE AGRICULTURAL PRODUCE MARKET
THURSDAY'S MARKET (continued)

Eastern Market: June 15th

Weather = New York 65 degrees, cloudy
Chicago 69 degrees, cloudy

Lettuce
Chicago-weak market
California Salinas good quality

Cauliflower
Chicago-?

City of Tacoma
Washington
J. J. Kaufman
Mayor

Aug. 7, 1939

Japanese-American Citizen's League
1532 Market Street
Tacoma, Washington

Greetings:

It is a privilege to extend a welcome on behalf of the City of Tacoma to the members of the Japanese-American Citizens' League for their Northwest convention September 3rd and 4th.

It is gratifying to note that better citizenship will be the theme of your convention sessions. In these days of world-wide turmoil, with subversive forces attempting to discredit American institutions and ideals, it is fitting all groups should re-dedicate themselves to America's principles and should rejoice for the blessings of liberty which our American form of government guarantees.

May your convention be so successful and so enjoyable you will anticipate with pleasure your return to Tacoma in the future.

Sincerely,
J. J. Kaufman
Mayor

Dr. Clifford Uyeda, Traveler

"THERE WAS A JACL CONVENTION"

"**I** had gone back, from Wisconsin, one summer, to Tacoma, before going up to Alaska. And there was a JACL convention going on. That surprised me. I didn't know that it was being held in Tacoma, so thought 'Well. I'll go in and see what it's like.' I walked in, and I almost walked out, because the first thing I noticed was that the first row was taken up by American Legionnaires with their Legionnaire caps on."

"You're talking about Nisei American Legionnaires?" Paul Tsuneishi asks, slightly confused.

"No, no, no, no. These were hakujin, white folks," Dr. Uyeda says.

"Oh, really."

"Because there were no Nisei legionnaires in Tacoma at that time. I thought, what are they doing here? Because, the most anti-Japanese organization on the West Coast, before the war, was the Legionnaires.

"Then I found out that what the JACL was doing was they were honoring them. They gave them a place of honor because they wanted to be on the good side of the American Legion. That surprised me. I stayed to listen to the oratorical contest that was going on. And then I walked out. When I got back to Wisconsin, I wrote a letter to the *Japanese American Courier*, in Seattle, saying that if those speeches that I heard in Tacoma, at the JACL—if the words 'United States' were changed to 'Japan,' it would be just like the speeches being made in Japan.

"Mr. Sakamoto, the owner, sent a letter back to me saying that you can't print anything like this in a Japanese American journal."

Nobu Kawai,
The Volunteer

COURTING, DATING, AND RADIO

"**I** married quite late in life. You see, I was thirty-three when we were married. I was trying to hold down two jobs at the time and so my time was very limited. I was at the dairy and I was working for Investors Syndicate on the side. Or what was it?" Nobu Kawai asks.

"Investors Syndicate," Miye says.

"So, I was selling Investors Syndicate as an investment. And I had interviews like that and everything, so I didn't have any time for courting or anything like that. Besides at the time, I first met Miye, she was pretty much involved with a boyfriend. She had a boyfriend. And she wasn't about ready to give him up. But I persisted. She finally relented and consented to have a date with me.

"I really didn't know Miye too well. I knew the rest of the family. She comes from an old family in Los Angeles. Her father was very active in the Japanese Association and so forth. And, of course, my family was more or less a pioneer family in Pasadena."

Miye says, "My father was from Aomori-ken. That's way up north. And my mother was from Shizuoka. Fujioka is my parents' names—"

"Shiro Fujioka."

"And my mother's name was Chiyo," Miye continues.

"They came over, early 1900 wasn't it?"

151

"He was an editor."

"He was the editor-in-chief of the *Rafu Shimpo* way before the war. You know, he was the editor. So during the signing of the Russo-Japanese peace treaty, which was held at Portsmouth, Massachusetts, he went there to represent the *Japan Times*."

"They're originally from Seattle."

"Yeah, originally. Some of my sisters and brothers were born in Seattle. Then, they came to Los Angeles. I was born in Hollywood in 1917. We have ten in the family. Twelve to be exact. Ten are alive."

"She's from Hollywood High."

"Well, I went to high school for just a little while. That's all the education I've had. I did graduate. Class of '35," Miye says.

"We have five children."

"Five boys," Miye says. "He happened to know me through my brothers and sisters."

"In the early days, the Nisei had a lot of clubs and athletic organizations. And we would go to Los Angeles to play football and enter track meets and so forth. Pasadena had quite a reputation. And we would go over and play Bukkyokai and some of the other Japanese teams in Los Angeles.

"I used to do quite a bit of bowling, and I bowled with Miye's brother quite a bit over there. And I got to know her family quite well. And so one thing led to another."

"I think what happened was, you had two tickets to go to see something in Hollywood. Horace Heidt's . . . Horace Heidt's. . . ."

"Ohh. Talent show. Yeah."

"It must have been a radio show. TV didn't come until later."

"Yeah, we didn't have TV then. We were in the studio audience at a radio show."

"Yeah! That's it! That's it! All I remember seeing is an orchestra and a man up there talking through the mike."

"We came out and he said, 'You want to eat?'" Miye says. "And so we went to eat. That was about it. We were very civilized then. There wasn't a hangout at that time."

"I don't remember any."

"He did not have to take me to a place like that."

"There may have been in Los Angeles. See, I lived in Pasadena, and commuting to Los Angeles made it kind of bad. The freeway wasn't even there then."

"No," Miye says, correcting her husband, "just finished."

"Just building, yeah. . . ."

"Pouring it. That's when we were there," Miye says with finality.

"Oh, yeah, before the war, we had a radio. We would listen off and on. The only program I can remember very definitely was Orson Welles's *War of the Worlds*. I can remember that. I turned the radio on and I listened to it. It was unbelievable, you know. They were invading New York. Now, I said, 'Wait a minute! If this is really happening, it must be on all the other channels.' There was no word about it, see."

"I didn't know it was even on," says Miye.

"That's one thing that made me doubt the authenticity of the *War of the Worlds*. Because it wasn't on the other stations. It was very realistic, you know. And I thought, 'Oh boy! Something this important: Every radio station in the country would be on it.' So then, I thought, 'Ah! This is a hoax!'"

Gordon Hirabayashi,
On Civil Disobedience

GOLDEN

"Everybody in the community called me Gordon. My Japanese name is Kiyoshi. That's my regular name. Some people have it. But we never used it. Always 'Go'den.' The Japanese—they skip the 'R.' 'Goden.' And so when they Anglicize it, those who know a little English, they say, 'Golden.'

"AND AFTER MY BROTHER PAUL DIED, THEY SPOILED ME"

"We had a pet for awhile. We always had cats. We had a dog for awhile. In addition, we had chickens but Mom got rid of that. Gave it to relatives because a rooster chased my brother. And he ran and fell against something. And medical services weren't that sharp then. They didn't discover he had a kind of injured intestine until several months later.

"And he was too weak. I mean they operated. The operation was okay. But he was too weak to survive it. So he died. He died at age five. So Mom didn't want chickens around anymore. And after my brother Paul died, they spoiled me.

"They spoiled me at first. They groomed me, unknown to me, as the other brothers came along; and especially after we were grown, they forced me to be the *chonan*. I resisted. I didn't want to play that role. I wanted to be one of the sons, democratically, you know. Like when I came home from Edmonton for the first couple of hours I'm listening to one grief after another. I said, 'Why don't you talk to my brother there or my sister?'

"They said, 'No, no! It's just for you. Can't you talk to them about it?' You know, that sort of thing. And Dad played that thing out whether I'm willing or not. And he forced me in my relationship and my mother. She died early so she didn't reinforce it as much as he did.

"He just quietly treated me as a first son, Japanese-style. And my brother Jim and so on, now and then would say, 'God, you're getting dictatorial!' "

DRIVER, NOT A FARMER

"I was in the Model A and wanted to start to drive when I was seven or eight out on the farm. My friend Peter Katsuno was driving already. He was four years older. And so Peter would coach me. I was in there driving before I could reach the foot pedals. I took over the driving early. It relieved Dad to do other things. When I was twelve, I was taking loads to the packinghouse because it was back roads off the highway, not patrolled gravel roads. It was illegal, but I was managing to do it. Mainly to get out of doing the field work.

"I didn't like farming. The dirt part. So I used to do a lot of the driving. I used to take it to the market. That made me deal with adults, like sales agents and so on.

"Let's say you have a load of lettuce you've driven in. You know the price range. If your product is pretty good, you try to sell it at the upper end. That one cost a little more but it's better. Dad was one of these guys that for beauty's sake, he would put the nice ones on top. But he hated to do that. He was so straight. So he wouldn't stick any lousy stuff down, although they're a little smaller. And Mom would argue with him 'This is business. This is normal.'

"And cauliflowers, you put in about eleven or twelve all Number Ones. Most people stick in couple of them that are borderline. And Dad would stick it in only under pressure from every one of us. So buyers would take his stuff without any question. But he wasn't a very good bargainer. And that was good for me. Because I was fairly shy in those things.

"I'd take our produce to the Farmer's Market! It was a Ford truck. I guess it always was a Ford when we had a truck. It was one-and-a-half ton flatbed truck. Staked. With sides put up for certain occasions. I'd start about three-thirty and get there by six.

"Down below on Western Avenue. There were these various houses, including some Japanese. Then, there was a place south of Seattle. Well, it was on

First Avenue or Fourth Avenue, there was a place where trucks could back up early in the morning.

"And the grocery companies would come and buy from us. It was just like a wholesale public market. And we used to be reprimanded by other farmers saying, 'Don't undercut us now! Don't sell it cheap.' You're getting scared. They force me to take some of the stuff home sometimes."

THE RADIO

"Dad being a Christian objected to my playing baseball. I played a lot of basketball because that was in the winter and not on Sundays. Baseball was played on Sundays.

"He used to object to it. Finally by the time my younger brother grew up a little, we broke that restriction down. The only time we did anything on Sunday was when it was crop time, when we had to get out there. So we break the Sunday Law. We get out there and work."

"We were not allowed to play cards in the home," Jim says.

"It was sinful." The Deadpan Brothers laugh their deadpan laugh.

"No drinking or smoking or that stuff," Jim, the younger, says. "No cards. Sundays was sports."

"How about the radio?" Gordon asks.

"It was Ota," Jim says, "the storekeeper, who came around the farm and left a radio for us to listen for awhile. And I had it in my room. Then, mom was going to return it to Ota. I was so upset about it that I made a long statement in Japanese when I returned the radio. It was like here's my life!" The brothers laugh in perfect sync.

"And they were so surprised!" Jim says, "I just blasted out my feelings in Ota's presence. Dad was like this—frowning, arms crossed around his chest, listening.

"And Mom told me in mixed English and Japanese how Dad felt that it was stupid and she did, too. She said, 'I didn't know you felt that way about the radio, and didn't know you could articulate yourself so well in Japanese. We were impressed with that. We were upset you would say those things in front of an outside person.' And she said, 'You embarrassed him.'

"Dad was speechless there and felt very uncomfortable. But because of that incident, Ota-machi said, 'I'm not going to pick that radio up. I'll leave it here.'"

"Then they agreed to pay for it or something," Gordon says. "It was one of those little ones."

"Table one," Jim says. "Small table one."

"Yeah, table one." Gordon says.

SOMEBODY SOLD MY PARENTS THIS
ONE VOLUME OF AN ENCYCLOPEDIA

"Somebody sold my parents this one volume of an encyclopedia. Some Japanese probably. I don't know what it cost. It's a big fat thing. I used to look at that a lot.

"That was one of the few things I could look at. There are the presidents and then samurai on one page. President Buchanan's term and the main force thing that happened in his term just before Lincoln's. And then, there were the cities and the ranks of population. I just loved that one volume of an encyclopedia. That's how I skipped one grade.

"We were in a rural school. Two grades in one room. While the others were doing something, we're supposed to be studying. But I can listen.

"I did well on things like geography. I was better than those guys in the upper grade. So the teacher said, 'Why don't you take this state test? Try it out.'

"I took Arithmetic, Geography, Spelling, and whatever else they had. I passed those. So, he said, 'Try the others.' And I graduated suddenly a year ahead of my group—which was a bad mistake because I was small.

"If I stayed one more year in grade school, I would have been on the first team in basketball, baseball. I was first-line sub. In fact, my colleagues all became regulars. So I missed out on that thing. Otherwise, I held my own through high school."

Jim says, "Dad bought life insurance on himself. Because he's the one who's earning and we are going to suffer, only if he goes. So what's the use taking it on me. That would be like endowment. We weren't in that stage at all. The only reason he bought insurance is because some friends would come and, you know how the Japanese visit and talk. After the tenth visit, you get down to brass tacks, then out of obligation as well as being talked into some deal. 'Why, you could pay it this way and so on.' We had Sun Life Insurance. This guy—in fact, he's the one to whom Ann Fisher dedicated her book."

"Terazawa," Gordon says. "He was an insurance salesman. He used to come out and visit the family and all the farmers around there, and stay with one of us. He was a promoter. Operator, you see. And so, if he thought this was a good deal, he probably played that part. And he knew some English."

THE FIRST NISEI

The first Nisei is the first to confront the American custom of dating. "You see, I was one of the first—and I was among the older Nisei in the area—so the American custom of dating and other kinds of things that aren't generally accepted in Japanese expectations," he lets the thought trail off, then says with new energy, "We had to do the ice-breaking. We started in our junior high school days breaking the ice in dancing.

"My parents kept friends with this missionary. This was a hakujin, Caucasian minister who learned Japanese. And so he used to come and lecture in Japanese. What do you call it? Sermon!—on the second Sunday of each month. Fundamentalist, you know.

"He came because these people weren't Methodist or Baptist or anything. And he was one of these—American Bible Society and not of the other regular denomination.

"We could be in group relations, group dances, and so on. And so they would hear something. This minister would say to us as well as to the parents the only reason they dance is so they can get close and make body contact and sex! He said it's just a subterfuge for sex. They got the dirty mind, you know.

"And so they used to oppose dancing. They tolerated it later. But I broke from that group about my senior year in high school."

AUBURN HIGH

"Half the students were Japanese in my grade school. The high school became about twenty percent. Auburn, it was in between Kent and Auburn, Thomas Grade School. And every year at least one Japanese would be valedictorian or salutatorian. And several of the years, both of them would be.

"When we got to high school, it became dominantly white for many of the activities.

"Because of talent, you know, Japanese wouldn't be trying out for the school play. Some of those who could sing, they would be up there. I was really chicken with girls. I wasn't chicken with boys. I wasn't chicken in mixed groups.

"And I participated a lot. I did a lot of those things. I knew during that time that you're Japanese and you're limited in opportunity. I knew because I hear about it. The outstanding engineer graduate, Tak Tsuchiya, number two in his class, can't get a job except in a Japanese firm, and things like that. And we knew 'bout the court case on the Alien Land Law. We lost it, you know. They said this is a subterfuge. They put it in their daughter's name, but the real owner is the father who is an alien. And they took the land away—I remember that in grade school. Even before grade school because the thing went on for five years all the way up to the Supreme Court, which refused to hear it. In other words, let the State Supreme Court decision stand, you see. That was 1928. So it started in 1922.

"I couldn't sing, but I got in the Glee Club. I could sing but I couldn't go any higher. I would be in the middle there. I like activities. So, I was in the Glee Club and through that I was in the operetta. And I turned out for the junior play *Tiger House* and I got the part, partly because they need an East Indian. I played the part of a swami.

"Later on another fellow and I—he is an engineer for General Mills in Minneapolis, now—we went through trade school, high school, and university together. We were both in the High 'Y,' that's a high school YMCA.

"In our school, that was the elite club. They had Knights of Columbus and some other clubs, too. But this was the elite. I don't know if it was a token or not, but they always had one or two Japanese in there—before and after me. I was in there for two years. They always had dates. That was a crisis. I had to get dates.

"I didn't have the nerve to ask girls out although we were in groups sometimes, meeting out in the streets, two, three, four of us. It's like a group. They're going to coffee shop and then out somewheres. They could be mixed groups. Caucasian girls, my classmates, and so on. They'd say, 'Come out to dance,' dragging me out."

"Caucasian girls?"

"Yeah. I did have that kind of exposure more than the others. Most of the activities were pretty ethnic.

"We have to ask to go to a junior prom. You see, going to a junior prom, you have to know how to dance. We knew dating was an issue. And so we avoided it frequently. And the girls did, too. The Seinenkai dance, picnic dance, we'd go like in group-dating.

"And the girls, we'd say, 'Shall we pick you up?' They'd say, 'No, no, no! Don't come to the house. We are telling our folks we're going out with a bunch of guys!' Even when we are dating, it was that way. We're going to a dance with a bunch of guys. That was the early part.

"And we arranged to meet some of the girls there, and in some cases, they weren't very one-to-one, although a few had their picks in there. And others had their wishes come true, but they were too chicken. I was one of those!

"Then Tak Tsuchiya joined the High-Y, following year. He got elected in. I didn't know these girls. I began to date them later. But they were attractive and cute. They were the twins. The twins were Maxie and Dixie. Their Japanese names were Yoshiko and Hidako. I couldn't tell them apart. Tak and I got another person to negotiate a date to a house party. Just a house party. I never talked to them at all before the date. And Tak hadn't either. He knew them. He talked to them.

"We say to Mom, 'We have to take a girl out. Everybody is doing it. And Tak and I are doing it. The families know each other. And we're taking these girls.'

"I guess they heard of the twins but didn't know the family. Mom and Dad didn't object to it then.

"We didn't have a jacket, but we had one of these triangle emblems that said 'High Y' with a 'Y' symbol. And it was a thick emblem. I sewed it on a sweater. And I had a pin with that same emblem with a chain and an 'A' over it. 'A' for Auburn. And that's how we pinned my girlfriend, one of the twins. Maxie and Dixie. They were identical. None of us, until we got acquainted, could tell them apart. She wore it for a year."

MOM RESOLVES A STINKO

"I was about eighteen. We formed a basketball team on our own, independent of the Auburn Senior Association. And through my high school contacts, I managed to get the gymnasium for the winter season.

"I kept telling the superintendent that the Association had been using it for several years, but this is a new team. And I'm representing them and it's not the Association's. Well he didn't get the significance, I'm sure, even though he heard me. And he gave it to me.

"Then the Association wanted the gymnasium, but it was ours already. And so, over this dispute, they called a meeting of senior Association. The Issei called a meeting to bring us together. So, I said I would have to go to this place where they are having this stinko.

"And my mother sized it up right away and she said, 'I'm going with you.'

"I said, 'No, you don't have to go. I can defend myself.'

"She said, 'Oh, no. You're going to get creamed!' And so she came with me. And she was the only woman there.

"I was the manager, and this guy was the captain. His father came with him too. I guess he had some concerns that Connie might get stepped on.

"After the social greetings and so on, the meeting starts off. She dominated the meeting. She starts off and says in a very friendly, innocent way describing how these kids are doing all the things to form the basketball team. 'They're holding these skating nights and film nights scaring up the money to get basketball suits, and looking at samples and ordering them," she went through all of that describing it because we were doing it.

"We were sitting around like this in the living room of the president's house. And then she said kind of innocent-like, 'I didn't realize these fellows should have gotten permission for the Auburn Senior Association to have this sort of thing.'

"And they said, 'Oh, no. We don't require that.' And one after the other, they said, 'No. No. No.'"

"And after, 'No, don't do this. It's not necessary' then 'What the hell is this meeting for?'

"Well, she just sets it up at that point, just resolving it in a friendly-like way. So at the end there was nothing they could argue about. The only thing was, can we resolve this? We were willing to let them use half of the floor. See, if they had it, they wouldn't let us in.

"So, we had the upper hand. We eventually gave it to them. But we had our rights there. We had it so they couldn't say, 'We can't give you room today.' So everything worked out.

"That's the sort of thing she did. She trapped them, you see. She was more of the model for me than my father.

"She was a frustrated farmer's wife. And she used to write articles and send them to a journal in *Japan Shifunotomo*—and then didn't sign her name. She signed it, 'A Farmer's Wife' and sent it in.

"A neighbor woman—that's how I found out—was talking. She said, '*Rhoda-san, Kore antano desho*? Is this yours? This sounds just like you.' Mom's English name is Rhoda. She identified it. She had publications. I said she could have been a magazine editor or something.

"When I got old enough, like in high school, I used to argue with Dad. 'This is a helluva business. You object to gambling. This is the worst gamble of all!' You work all year; the whole family works all year. There are so many variables. The price could go down. Just before you're harvesting lettuce, it could rain and it would get slimy. I said, 'Look at the gamble.' We were struggling.

"Now, Jim don't take it so bad, playing around with plants and everything. I have a hard time mowing the lawn."

DESTINY

"I was talking to my classmates, girls, later, and they talk about boys, you know, and they said they had spotted me as one of them that's not going to be a farmer, but one who'd go on in engineering or some profession. Even though those professions weren't really open to us before the war. Going to college was one of these unrealistic, vague aspirations. Mom was always talking about it. She says, 'When you get through high school, you don't want to go to a school like Washington. Maybe Yale or Harvard.'

"Well, she reads a lot. Mainly in Japanese translations and so on. So, she knew 'bout those schools. And she said you should go to those. Now, there was no way I could afford to go to Yale or Harvard, because I couldn't afford to go to the University of Washington.

"But the idea was implanted. When you finished grade school, you know you're going to high school. I knew when I finished high school, I was going to university.

"I started school, working in a doctor's home as a houseboy. Since I was going to school and it wasn't full time, they used the word 'Schoolboy.' And I'd get a room in the basement. I'd help with the kitchen. There were other kids doing this, going to school.

"His name was something like Wilson. He was a doctor. I worked for him two years, I think. It was two years because I went two half-years, fall and winter, and I worked spring and summer out on the farm. And I repeated that the next year. And then, after that I went the whole cycle, but part time, working side jobs, getting jobs around the campus. Then, I could participate in all the activities. There was a period just before the war when activities were my main event. I'd go to class when I could.

"I'd get up and help set the table and so on. Breakfast wasn't too much. Then, I take off. Pack a little lunch and take off.

"Then, I'd come home in the afternoon, four o'clock or so, and help set the table. I'd do some cleaning, minimal during the week. But really missed extracurricular activities I was interested in, because I had to come home in the afternoon. Then, I helped in the kitchen, preparing vegetables and this and that. I helped the woman to cook rice. She was cooking dry rice, old rice you buy in the store, in a whole bunch of water.

"And so I said, 'We cook it a different way.'

"She said, 'You try it.' So I did. I taught her to get some Japanese rice. And she said, 'It's the first time my husband asked for seconds on the rice.' She thought he never liked rice.

"After I left, and started living at the dorm and doing odd jobs around the campus, a Quaker girl that I knew told me she worked at the hospital. And she said, when the war broke out, Dr. Miller became anti-Japanese. He had some Japanese stuff. You know, my mother in Japanese style gives lamp or ashtray or something. And he was bragging how he took some of these things and cracked it.

"He was just a bigot at the time.

"None of our brothers are farmers. We have an appreciation for the environment in which we grew. We think we are lucky to have grown up on a farm instead of in a city."

Frank Emi, Leader

BROTHERS AND SISTERS

"I remember once, though . . ." Art says, and begins again. "See, my dad used to get up at 2 o'clock in the morning to go to the wholesale produce market in L.A. to buy produce for the market in San Fernando. He used to come home and take a nap in the afternoon. We were on the front porch making a hell of a racket. We wore overalls, and the window opened, and when the window opened, Frank was on the other side of the block already. He just got me by the overalls and pulled me into the window."

"My reactions were faster," Frank says.

"I think Frank is most like my father," Kaoru says. "I guess it makes a difference, you know, because he was the oldest and my dad had to rely on him for interpreting. He had to do most of that for my father when it came to the nitty gritty." Frank says, "My dad used to love dogs. He used to go to the wholesale market, you know. When we're farming, he'd sell produce; when he went into the market business, he'd buy produce. Every time he'd find a stray dog there, he'd bring it home. On the farm, we had about three dogs all the time. In those days, I can't remember ever having a dog get shots or licenses. They never got sick. We had one that looked like a little snowball, which was with us for about fifteen years before he was run over. Oh, I guess it was as far back as I can remember. So I must have been three or four years old. He was about fourteen or fifteen years old when he got run over. He wasn't a pup because my dad never brought home a pup. He used to bring home grown dogs. When

163

they got sick, they would mope around and get low for a few days; don't eat and get well. Then, when the dogs died, we used to bury them out in the farm. In the city, I think we used to take them to the 'wash.' We lived in San Fernando at the time. We take them to the 'wash' and bury them. I guess it was my mother's responsibility to take care of the dogs, feed them and wash them. My mother's, or my sister's."

"Well, see my mother came from a very . . ." Art considers a moment then says, "I guess what you call an upper barrier, and my father married into my mother's family. She was the only child, and when my mother's grandfather lost it all, he didn't work and just let it go. So when my father married my mother, he made a vow that he was going to bring the family back to the position that they used to be in." He's saying their father was *yoshi*, he was adopted into his wife's family and took her family name.

"My dad was very strict with us," Frank says. "He used to beat me up. After work, I still remember he used to take me at night—we lived near the wash, the San Fernando Wash, near the river—take me out to the wash and leave me there."

"He was more intense in everything he did," Art says.

"I guess I was a little bit more rebellious," Frank says.

"I was more easygoing. I'm not him, see," Art says, meaning he's not Frank. "And he and I decided to go fishing. We said, we better make the boat. So at Compton, I pushed on the pedal and went over 55, and the timing gear broke! Remember that?"

They got beaten for that. "We used to get beat, maybe it wasn't hard," Frank says. Big boys, big enough to drive, and they amazingly submit themselves to their father's discipline. Times have changed. "I don't remember how badly we were beaten," Frank says. "It was more than just a spanking."

Art nods and hums once. "Sometimes they would give you *yaito*?" Frank asks.

"I don't ever remember getting hit. I remember yaito," Art says.

"They'd lay you flat on your stomach, take your shirt off, and put a couple of those *mokusa* on your back," Frank says.

"They really hurt for a long time. Felt like you got a hole burning in you. . . ."

Frank says, "Actually, the Issei use that as a cure for pains. When we were bad, generally, we were running so dad wouldn't catch us. He was an ex-army man. Japanese army. He fought the Russians. You didn't talk back to him. So I used to get punished, but I never lied. No. In fact, he always used to say, 'Frank is very honest. He may be slow, but he's honest.' That was one thing he said."

The father's temper raises the subject of the mother's health. Hisako Alice says, "As long as I can remember, she was very frail. She was always in bed or just barely up and around. Well, she wasn't that sick, you know. But she was always laying down. She always had stomach problems and she was very—she was always kind of tired. I think she was suffering from ulcers.

"My father used to take her to the doctor. But she is the cook, yeah.

"As kids we used to make our own breakfast or have cocoa and a piece of toast or something. And in the evening, I did the rice, and she'd cook something very simple.

"We really had some great times though, when we ate supper. We all sat around the table. We just talked all the time. I don't think we stopped talking for a couple of hours. Don't you remember that, Frank? We used to sit and talk a lot. All of us—my mother, my father—I don't remember who talked, though. I'm trying to remember who's talking!" She laughs. "Yeah, we all talked. I just can't remember what we talked about or who did the talking, but it seems like we just all sat around the table."

"We talked about everything!" Frank says.

"We really had a good time. I remember that part was a good time," Kaoru adds.

"You talked, too," Frank says.

"Yeah. Really, was Mom the one who keeps us going at the table?" Kaoru asks. "And, you know—she never went out. She was always home. But I never saw—you know, I think my mother was so intelligent, now that I look back. She constantly read—magazines, books, newspapers—strictly Japanese. And whatever she said comes back to me, I think, God, Mom was sure right."

"Yeah, she was," Frank says. "She was always full of quotes. You know, sayings—what do you call that?"

"Yeah, proverbs!" Kaoru says. "A lot of proverbs." All the Emi family laugh.

Frank continues, "Slogans, like these wise sayings. She had one for every occasion. Issei are good at that."

"No, she wasn't much of a talker," Kaoru, the baby of the family says. "I always thought of her as rather quiet," she thinks a moment and says, "But I guess she got us going on subjects."

"Yeah, she would bring up subjects that she was interested in, like reading papers and something that would worry her," Frank says. "She used to keep up with current events—world events. We would hash it over—talk about it."

"She was a very gentle woman," Art says. "She wouldn't raise her voice when she sort of scolded us. Her name was Tsune, but we never called her by that, always 'Momma.'"

"I can never picture her crying," Frank says. "The only time she would get upset was when the kids would fight among themselves. Like me and my brother would fight. Like my sister and my younger brother would fight. My baby sister and I never fought about anything because we were so far apart. But my older sister and I would sometimes, and my younger brother and I would sometimes. She would get very upset when we were very bad that way. The way she would punish us was, 'Well, if you boys are going to behave that badly, I don't want to be with you.' And she would say, 'I'm going to leave.'

"And she would put on her hat and pick up her umbrella. We would hang onto her legs and say, 'Don't go, don't go. We'll behave. We'll behave!' And we would be crying! We were little kids you know. Grammar school, pre-grammar school. I remember that. Put on her hat and get the umbrella, and then she makes as if to take off. That would stop the fighting," Frank says. Everyone mutters laughter.

"On the farm we had horses. Goats. No cows. We used the horses for plowing. Later, we had a tractor, but we had both, horses and a tractor. We had an old iron plow. Yeah. Goats for milk. We didn't slaughter any animals. I think the only animal we slaughtered were chickens, like on Thanksgiving or something. We had chickens. And we had rabbits, too. I think we all took care of them. Us kids.

"I sprained my wrist when I was cranking a Model T when I was about ten or eleven years old. I started driving the car. I learned just by watching, I guess. It wasn't too hard. I drove the Model T around the farm. When I was about thirteen, I said I was—I was kind of big for my age—so I got my driver's license. It was a little after that that I got arrested for driving a little too fast. Dad had his business in town then, and everybody respected him, so the judge—Judge Swinger was his name—straightened it out. I remember the judge said, 'Frank, I'm going to give you back your license, but don't ever break that speed limit again.' I said, 'Yes, sir!'"

Ford Manual
Model T

For Owners and Operators
of
Ford Cars and Trucks

Where should these levers be when starting the engine?

Answer No. 5

On cars not equipped with a starter, the spark lever should usually be put in about the third or fourth notch on the quadrant (the notched half-circle on which the levers operate). The throttle should usually be placed about the fifth or sixth notch. A little experience will soon teach you where these levers should be placed for proper starting. Care should be taken not to advance the spark lever too far, as the engine may "back kick."

On cars equipped with a starter, the spark lever should be fully retarded (all the way up).

What else is necessary before starting the engine?

Answer No. 6

First: See that the hand lever, which extends through the floor of the car at the left of the driver, is pulled back as far as it will go. The lever in this position holds the clutch in neutral and engages the hub brake, thus preventing the car moving forward when the engine is started. Second: On cars without starters, insert the switch key into the switch and turn the key as far to the left (counter-clockwise) as it will go. On cars equipped with starters, the switch key may be turned either to the right or left. The engine cannot be started until the switch is turned on—the turning of the switch key to a vertical position stops the engine.

Frank Emi, Leader

"FRANK SHOWED HER HOW
TO MAKE PUMPKIN PIE"

Art says, "Dad used to take us to judo, when he had the time. And then we moved. Long Beach Junior High was separate from the Senior High. In San Fernando, from seventh to the twelfth grade was one school. At that time, it was called San Fernando High School. It probably still is."

"At Long Beach, when I was playing football there, the one remark the coach made that burned the heck out of me—this one kid named Joe Takahashi was playing. He was scrimmaging, and his helmet was knocked off, so he was playing without it. One of the kids said to the coach, 'Hey, Coach, Joe is playing without his helmet.'

"And the coach said, 'Ahhh! Let it lay. If he gets hurt, it will be another dead Jap.' That got me so mad!"

Art says, "He's the coach that used to make the guys dive off of the high—how high was that?"

"You know the high diving board, twenty-five foot?" Frank says. "To make the football team, you had to dive from it backwards. Back dive. If you didn't do that, you were chicken or you were cut."

Did the Emi brothers dive backwards off the high board?

"I played end," Frank says.

"I played quarter," Art says. "When we played high school sports, the folks never came out to the games. In fact, my mother was fearful about me playing

168

football. But no way in the world was she going to stop me. I used to have nightmares about graduation, because I can't play football anymore."

"Well, you know, we had a market. And my mother cooked anything that my father would bring home, like vegetables that got a little bit old. Oh, my favorite was—she used to make homemade tomato soup," Kaoru says.

"Uh huh," Frank says and nods.

"She made it with fresh tomatoes, so that when the tomatoes go soft—they weren't rotten—they were so good," Kaoru says. "I never had tomato soup like she made. She used to make spaghetti. I think Frank showed her how to make spaghetti. Frank showed her how to make pumpkin pie."

"I was able to read and follow directions," Frank says with a smile.

"He'd tell my mother, and she'd write it in Japanese," Kaoru says. "She couldn't do any of those things, but if she got the recipe or Frank showed her how to do it—he did most the things like that. He made a pie once and showed her how!" She laughs a long time. "Then she would make a pie after that every so often."

"You know, my sister used to try to make pies, and every time she made it, the crust would come out like cement, you know," Frank says.

"Not me," Kaoru says, "Frank's other sister."

"She'd always roll the flour in water only, it would just come out like hard tack or something. One day, I finally said, 'Hey, you are supposed to mix a little shortening with it.'"

In Little Tokyo, Los Angeles, there was the sports-based Oliver group, founded in 1917 by Nellie Grace Oliver, a kindergarten teacher, at Hewitt School. She organized the boys of Little Tokyo into teams to play sports, and taught them American food, American manners, and Robert's Rules of parliamentary procedure. Not all the Olivers were well intentioned; some developed a reputation as marauding thugs, or Yogore, who chose Japanese from out of town as their victims. Paul Tsuneishi knew the Olivers as a "good sports organization." Frank Emi had seen the predatory Olivers in action.

"In fact, they picked on two guys from Long Beach, when I was going to Long Beach Polytechnic High School," Frank says. "One was a star football player on the varsity, and the other was an amateur boxer.

"The boxer and the football player beat the hell out of the Oliver bunch. The boxer was good. I'd seen him box one time, and he had a good left hook. You might have heard of him. Hide Watanabe. And then the football player, the star football player for the varsity at Long Beach Poly, was Johnny Takahashi. This guy jumped on him. Boy, the two of them just cleaned up on him. They beat up the big guy.

"I've been with judo all my life. I only used it when I was attacked. I remember one time this was about 1936 or 1937—I was twenty-one or twenty-two—when

I had a little produce stand. On one side there was a truck driver's union, on the other side was a bar. One of these truck drivers came by and picked up an apple without paying for it, so I went after him and said 'Hey, you didn't pay for that apple.'

"'Oh, don't bother me. You damn Jap!'

"Ooooh! When I heard that I grabbed the SOB and threw him with a *koshi nagi*. *Koshi nagi* is a hip throw. And just as I threw him, a car came by and his legs hit a tire and knocked his shoes off. He didn't get hurt. Came back a few minutes later and said 'You know, I'm sorry, I acted like an ass. What did you do to me?'"

Did Arthur also get involved in these demonstrations of Judo expertise?

"No. He's kind of mild-mannered. Another time, when Art and I had a store at another place, two guys went by and took a bunch of flowers from us. My brother asked them to pay. And they got real snotty. One of them took a swing at me. When he did that, I threw him. Then I grabbed him, and pulled him back to the store. He was about six feet, you know. Much bigger than me.

"We called the cops. The cops looked at me and said 'How did you control this guy?'"

On the eve of Pearl Harbor, in 1941, the Oliver Gang was still terrorizing Little Tokyo in Los Angeles.

"One time, before the war, they had a bazaar at Union Church where East West theater is now. In those days the Oliver Gang was a tough bunch in Japanese town. It was a bunch of young Japanese guys. They used to pick on guys that were from out of town, so I guess they thought that myself and my friend were from out of town, and one of these guys went around pushing everybody around; when he pushed me, he had his glasses on, so I grabbed his glasses, took them off with one hand, and I slapped him in the face with my other hand.

"My friend went over to the car, and I saw this bunch of guys following us. The leader of the gang, the guy I slapped, came over to me and said something. So I said 'If you want to start something, come ahead.' And they didn't do anything. They kept mumbling, so I said 'Can't stay here all night,' and turned around to get in the car. Then the guy hit me from the back. That really pissed me off, I grabbed one, and threw him. Then his friend was next to him, so I grabbed him and threw him. Then the other people took off.

"There's one story that stuck in my mind," Frank Emi says. "When I was real small. Mother was telling us. This was about being bad, a story where a thief was caught and he was put in a big bathtub of boiling water. He had a little son. Because his son was his son and carried bad blood, he was also put in there with him. And as the water kept getting hotter and hotter, the father kept holding his son up, until finally he was boiled in the water and he died. And the little baby boy died with him. That made an impression on me. I felt so sorry for the little boy. Just because his father was a thief. And I think that had a lot to do with some values, as far as taking somebody else's things."

"The thing that I remember best is when the Issei parents—I don't know if they ever, what they call *amaeru*, love their kids to the point where they would show it—I remember, I don't know what it was, but some friends of ours, they were over, and my mother said that I'm a real nice boy," Art Emi says.

"I've never forgotten that. It was so unusual, I think at that time, to have the parents say things like that to other people."

"Oh, yeah," Frank says. "All I can remember is my parents telling me off. 'Frank, you're stupid!' 'He's a bad boy. He never minds.' I guess I was a little more active, more rambunctious than Arthur. I was fairly *atarashii*—kid."

JAPANESE AMERICAN CITIZENS LEAGUE
ARTICLES OF INCORPORATION

June 21, 1937

KNOW ALL MEN BY THESE PRESENTS:

That we, the undersigned, a majority of whom are residents of the State of California, do voluntarily associate ourselves for the purpose of forming a corporation under Title 12, Article 1 of the Civil Code of the State of California, for purposes other than for pecuniary gain or profit to the members thereof, and WE DO HEREBY CERTIFY:

I   That the name of said corporation shall be "JAPANESE AMERICAN CITIZENS LEAGUE."

II   That it is a corporation which does not contemplate pecuniary gain or profit to the members thereof.

III   That the objects and purposes for which said corporation is formed are:

1. To promote the welfare of the Americans of Japanese ancestry in a program of education to forward and high purposes of American citizenship and ideals.

2. To promote, encourage, and foster a feeling of good fellowship, friendship and good will among the members of this corporation and all peoples.

3. To have, hold, buy and sell any real or personal property that may be necessary to carry out the objects of this corporation.

4. To make, perform and carry out contracts of every kind and description pertaining to the purpose of this corporation and for any lawful purposes necessary and expedient thereto with any person, firm, association or corporation.

IV   That the principal office from the transaction of the business of the corporation will be located in the City of Sacramento, county of Sacramento, State of California.

V   That said corporation shall exist for an indefinite term beginning upon the filing of these articles of incorporation in accordance with law.

VI   That the number of directors of this corporation is seven (7) and the names and places of residence of the Directors, who are appointed to serve until the election and qualification of their successors, are as follows:

NAMES	RESIDENCES
JAMES Y. SAKAMOTO	SEATTLE, WASHINGTON
WALTER T. TSUKAMOTO	SACRAMENTO, CALIFORNIA

The first two names on the list (shown above), the blind Seattle publisher and the Sacramento publisher attorney, will grow in importance with the JACL.

Dr. Clifford Uyeda, Traveler

"I REALLY DIDN'T HAVE ANY AMBITION"

"You know, I really didn't have any ambition, except that I enjoyed literature. I changed after my freshman year because I realized that literature in the United States meant an extension of European literature. You ever have hardly anything else except mostly European literature. So I said, 'This is nonsense.' You don't get much Asian literature—just a cursory review. If it was going to be this way, I might as well change, and I changed to English. So that's how I finished college.

"I had already planned that after I got my B.A. at Wisconsin, I was going to go to England to do my graduate work. Then when I was doing the investigation to see which university I should go to, Hitler invaded Poland.

"That was in 1939. When England declared war, I thought, 'That's the end of all my plans,' because I couldn't go to England anymore.

"So I thought maybe I should do something else, especially with a war going on, that maybe I should have something more concrete than just the appreciation of literature. So I got an appointment, thinking that medicine might be interesting, with the dean of the medical school at Wisconsin. He looked at my transcript and shook his head. He said, 'In four years of college, you've only taken five credits in science.' He said, 'You don't have any scientific background so I'm not going to recommend you're going into medicine.'

"I left his office and went to the registrar's office, and I started Chemistry 1, Physics 1, and all the basic courses. I finished all my science requirements in my last semester and graduated English."

173

Tom Oki,
Fair Play Committee

COSMOPOLITAN

"**I**n those days, when you went into town like that, were there any signs in any of the stores saying 'White Trade Only?'" Paul Tsuneishi asks.

"When we were kids?" Tom Oki asks.

"Yes."

"No. No. Because we lived in a cosmopolitan-like area. We had Russians, Jews, Armenians, Mexicans, and what else? Germans—Poles. That's why on the football team, there was myself, there was a Mexican, Jew Armenian, Russian—you know, German. We all are different nationality.

"Just one of the guys. Our school was cosmopolitan, international, you know—even the guys around Boyle Heights—Roosevelt High School, there was no such thing as 'I'm better than your people,' you know. Same thing in high school. I never had any experiences about race problems. Every kid was a friend.

"After I went to junior high school, I associated with hakujins more times than with my own childhood friends.

"That's why, until the war started, I figured there wasn't an enemy in the world.

"In the ninth grade, I was on the C team. And then, from sophomore year, I was on the B team. But never grew big enough to be on the varsity. When I was doing judo, I weighed about 135 pounds. But now a little different. I was shorter than my dad, five foot six and a half. My brothers were taller, though.

174

"Well, at that time we were more busy with athletics, and we didn't bother with girls. No kidding. Basketball, football, and stuff like that. And then, this friend of mine that's in Oakdale—on weekends or summer vacations, if I'm not busy—we used to go to Irwindale, hunting.

"Those days, we used to go out rabbit hunting out there. There were no homes out there. All orchards. If it wasn't orchards, it was rock quarries.

"I used to shoot shotgun—a twelve-gauge shotgun when I was fourteen years old. Go rabbit hunting right around our farm. There used to be hayfields.

"My first brother—he graduated, I think at Garfield, and my second brother, the youngest brother, graduated from Heart Mountain. I graduated in '38."

"Valedictorian of the class?"

"No. No—not that good—I was—in junior high school. I didn't do that much, but in high school I got into the CSF—California Scholarship Federation—not on the top, but on the bottom side. So you can't brag about it. I liked math. That's why I wanted to go to that aeronautical school, see?

"My shop teacher's brother was a personnel enrollment person at Glendale Airport on San Fernando Road. That's where all the Hollywood celebrities used to fly out from, you know. Anyway, there was an aeronautical school there. One year from high school we went there on an excursion. The shop teacher's brother—I was introduced to him. He told me that if I wanted to come to that school, that he'd help me get in. So I was all hepped up, because I wanted to go to aeronautical school, somehow. Not to fly, but to be a mechanic or engineer.

"So I went home and then I kinda hinted to my dad. After I got out of high school, I asked him again, and he said, "No. If you do, I'll have to hire somebody else to—"

"Your father didn't want you to go to college?"

"The thing was, Nisei at that time didn't have a chance to get into any kind of profession in the United States. But I told him, 'If I finish this school, I'll go to Manchuria.' At that time, Japan was big in Manchuria." [The Japanese army invades Manchuria in 1931 and defeats the Chinese in 1932. The Japanese government is not consulted by the army before, during, or after the action. The Japanese now have a source of coal. Manchuria is renamed Manchuko.] "Japanese was overseeing, and Manchuria was the thing.

"But he told me, 'If you stay, I'll let you run the farm. I'll give you the checkbook.' So, he gave me a small sum of money for a checkbook to run the farm. So, right after high school, I started—not everything, you know, but I started going to the market. Buy this and buy that."

"So how big a farm might this be?"

"Oh, about fifteen acres." Tom Oki says. "It was '39 already. I was drafted before the war started. And I went. And then I got deferred. I'm a farmer. I was running the farm, you see, so I get deferred."

ENTER: "THE MAGAZINE FOR THE AMERICAN BORN JAPANESE"

RAFU SHIMPO

PUBLISHED DAILY EXCEPT HOLIDAYS

No. 11,516   LOS ANGELES, CALIF., SATURDAY, FEB. 18, 1939

As Fair Opens in San Francisco

San Francisco Japanese today were getting their first taste of the whirl and excitement of the greatest World Exposition ever held in the west as thousands thronged to Treasure Island following the opening yesterday. Above is picture part of the Japanese parade which featured festivities prior to the opening. Below is the million-dollar Japanese pavilion in the fair grounds on Treasure Island—New World-Sun photos.

Legionnaires to Attend Defense Week Event

The Commodore Perry Post of the American Legion will be among the hosts to those attending the gala Nation Defense Week program sponsored by the County Legion posts—and all nisei are cordially invited. Among the speakers on the program will be Edward Arnold, motion picture star whose talk is entitled "The Meaning of American Democracy."

CURRENT LIFE

The Magazine
for the American Born Japanese
October, 1940

THE CURRENT LIFE
Published Monthly in San Francisco

Bus address...............1737 Sutter St.
Phone...........................Walnut 0315
Editor.......................James M. Omura
Bus. Mgr.................Miss Fumi Okuma
Composing Editor.........Harry Yasuda

WHO'S WHO IN THE NISEI LITERARY WORLD

By KENNY MURASE

Scanning the nisei literary horizon, we see a galaxy of literary lights—many of them we know. A short stay in the South, while attending school, and a hitch-hike trip up North have etched impressions sharply into our mind. With some of these writers it was just a "Hello" and a "Glad to have met you." But with most of them we've come to know as real friends—the kind of friends what would augment your dreams and your hopes of a brighter tomorrow—the kind of friends that gives you a bit of confidence, a dash of optimism, and something of a reassurance that perhaps humanity is good, and that life might not be so bad after all.

CARL KONDO—pioneer nisei journalist; edited Sangyo Nippo; columned in Rafu Shimpo; wrote for pulps; now has a typewriter shop in Li'l Tokyo; writes a swift, sure prose and a sort of cold hard brilliancy; his probing pen explores mental recesses of mind with keen analytical, calculating thoroughness.

LUCILLE MORIMOTO—considered one of leading nisei poetess; extremely introspective, profoundly contemplatative; very delicately poised emotionally; and intriguing esoteric personality; appears the classic Grecian type—stately, elegant, patrician.

BOB OKAZAKAI—veteran nisei scribe and soldier of fortune—"I worked every damnsheet on the Coast"; managed publicity for Nisei Festival; voluble, suave, debonair; has barbed, pointed sense of humor.

MOLLY OYAMA—(Mrs. Frederick Mittwer) frequent contributor to vernaculars; earnestly interested in promoting better race understanding; active in civic bodies; an affectionate young matron—poised, neat with a tranquil informal charm all her own.

JOE OYAMA—travelogues, descriptive sketches, personal briefs; writes with a sustained style—lean, lithe, powerful; has tremendous perspective and a far-sighted clairvoyance; substance of writings indicative of a profound wisdom, an understanding of and a sympathy for the Common Herd of simple people; bids fair to rise forth with that Great Nisei Novel before being scooted off into those ultimate realms of some astral limbo—and shuffled from this mortal coil; has his hands full: one hand jammed down into Gabriel's Horn; with the other he goes about interjecting social consciousness into Ivory Towers of mentally bankrupt nisei; peripapetic, iconoclastic, intelligent with a good sense of self-proportion.

ART TASHIRO—of the well known Tashiro clan; lives with brother Aiji (an instructor in creative writing) while going to Appalachian State Teachers College (Tennessee); spends summer vagabonding around—has covered most all of Atlantic Coast states, deep South and was in California last summer; very interesting conversationalist; has an active; expressive face that becomes a swift-changing scene of fluid and kaleidoscopic activity.

BEAN TAKEDA—editor-publisher of all-nisei Japanese-American Mirror; writes column "Typetown Talk"—personal heart-to-heart, E. V. Durling-ish; has penetrating sense of humor and pertinent observations; Man-About-Town—claims he has all desirable girls of Li'l Tokyo catalogued in his mind but can't decide who is most desirable; dapper, energetic, genial, and a hard-working hustler.

WARREN TSUNEISHI—writes crisp caustic, incisive satire; brilliant UCLA student in political-science; political tendencies; an ultra-reactionary and rugged individualist (weak emphasis on "rugged") adores girls with "exquisite lips," Westbrook Pegler, the L.A. Times and James Thurber, but mostly girls with "exquisite lips"; admires Hitler, looks like Hitler (without the mustache), and employs Hitlerlistic tactics in subduing unwitting, unsuspecting victims; a short-stocky peasant-like fellow—entirely innocuous, though fearsome spectacle.

HISAO HATA—writes intense short stories—powerful, sweeping, panoramic; scholarly student at UCLA, and an embryonic writer who promises to blossom out into an author of note—shows occasional spurts of dazzling, inspired writing which rockets to magnificent heights; writes Thomas Wolf-ish, acts Thomas Wolf-ish, looks Thomas Wolf-ish—huge physique (shade under six feet) strong, able, but repudiates, rejects America's past and present gospel of work—general locomotion akin to that of Model T Ford, 1912 vintage (but with little more finances and a little less noise).

TOGO TANAKA—English editor of the Rafu Shimpo—handsome, hard hitting, dynamic; acknowledged outstanding spokesman for nisei; vitally concerned with leading nisei out of the darkness and chaos of confusion and pessimism; a UCLA Phi Beta Kappa grad at 20—extremely cordial, gracious.

HELEN AOKI—columns "Printer's Ink" for Rafu —brief personal essays, political commentaries, lyric prose; has polished, mature, craftsman-like style; observes human foibles and frailties with startling clarity; endowed with sensitive poetic soul, and temperment that runs entire vicissitude of emotions—subject to varying moods and whims; intensely social and political conscious—pensive, free thinking, raciocinative; has faith only in interrelationship of science, philosophy and religion; quiet, restrained and courteous.

BOB HIRANO— sport editor of the Rafu has colorful, graphic style—fluent precise, compact; modest, retiring sort, and despite being dubbed "Mrs. Hirano's tragedy," Bob is a regular fellow. (But he is a sports writer.)

ROY TAKENO—English editor of the Kashu Mainichi; has a clear insight and an understanding of nisei problems; a soft-spoken, affable, and conscientious gentlemen—clean cut, manly, and with an inevitable grin.

TOMOMASA YAMASAKI—once hell bent, obstreperous, irresponsible—now considerably pragmatic and docile through marriage, job (assistant editor on Kashu) and arrival of baby girl to Mrs. few weeks ago; one of so-called "lost generation"—led by vanguard force of Oyama, Furiya, Iki—whose emergence from adolescence was met

178

by the impact of economic chaos; to escape from the frustration of his depression era, frequently indulged in unrepressed, uncontrolled rampages; went to college on poker earnings; worked in Alaska, the Northwest, and the Coast in general, now lives comfortably in cozy little home where friends wander in and out at all hours of the night to drink beer and talk.

RUTH KURATA—(Mrs. Yamasaki formerly assistant editor the Kashu before hubby took over; leader in organizing Young Democrats; active in JACL; was wise-cracking, tom-boyish hoyden—now sweet, doting Mama; bouyant convivial, Emily-Post-be-damned-and-make-yourself-at-home-ish

CHICO SAKAGUCHI—writes "Fuges" (Kashu)—sprightly, pungent, and not without verve; UCLA English honorary society grad this year—belligerant, independent intensely individualistic; scorns idealist puritan conscience and priggish indecisions of great nisei mediocrity; defies conventions, despises cant and dogma and people who kow-tow to them; has insatiable intellectual curiosity about people, ideas and things; trying to discover distinguishing points between a philosophical and political liberal; has rich earthy humor, and a common-sense approach; insists, "Hell, I'm no lady." (But we insist otherwise.)

LILY YANAI—"Telephooie" (Kashu) chatty, light, spontaneous; a veteran columnist—"I write on and off—mostly off." bonnie belle of Orange County—youthful, abounding vitality; tsk, tsk, tskable—loves motorcycle riding, sweet innocent little boys, and candied yam—and the city of Bakersfield (ask her why—and run); dainty, pretty . . . nice.

HISAYE YAMAMOTO —"Napolean's Last Stand" (Kashu)—naive, cute niceties; an intellectual giant weighing 89 pounds—graduated with top honors from Compton JC this year; deceiving, enigmatic, fascinating personality—tries to look at the world through pair of rosecolored pinze-nez; toddles about in size 12 rompers, hop-skotches on the Primrose Path, studies "Superman Comics" for intellectual stimulation; ambitions: go to Wichita, Kansas next year, entering convent at 24, jump off the Olive Blvd Bridge in to the L.A. River at 26. (Pardon while we chuckle.)

MARY KITANO—"Pulse of the Southland Beats" (Sangyro Nippo)—frothy frivolous pleasantries a-la Walter Winchell; desk-edited Compton JC sheet last term, now slated to take over editor's un-easy chair; pert, petite and piquant, with a trim jaunty figure; disconcertingly charming manners—abrupt, aggressive, spontaneous; twirls a mean baton—would make a high-stepping, fancy struttin' drum majorette, but tragedy: no bands.

AYAKO NOGUCHI—"Merry-Go-Round" (Rafu)—lively, spirited, efferevescent; veteran columnist of 3 years; special corresponent of Rafu and Nichi-Bei; refreshing, vivacious, winsome little country lassie; a whirlwind of activity; helps Mother with cooking and house-cleaning; packs melons and vegetables; acts as Amicable Relations Department for family; cabinet member of CYBL; vice-president of Cen. Calif. div.; reads couple books a week; writes feature stores; keeps all her notorious

179

cats feeling find and dandy; designs and sews all her sartorial needs; does credit to "Emily Post" as charming hostess to huge number of company; and the rest of the time, squanders on eating and sleeping.

YORI WADA— Cal graduate this year; worked his way up to post of Associate Editor on Daily California; was active in campus "y", member Race Relations Board; now has article under consideration by Louis Adamic for publication Common Grounds; extremely alert and conscious—has electric quickness of ideas; critical, restless, energetic—handsome, husky, likable.

BOB IKI—once edited Sangyo Nippo (l.A.) with George Furiya; now Public Relations Director for government agency in Oakland; has option to write article on nisei in asparagus camps for Scribner's Magazine; went to Cal with Yamazaki; roomed with Eddie Shimano and William Saroyan at time of Saroyan's writing of "The Daring Young Man on the Flying Trapeze"; bar-tendered in Havana; rode the rods with Oyama and Furiya; happily married to sweet charming Fumi Katsu; intellectually bent, intransigent, unconventional; active member Oakland Young Democrats; if-you-don't-like-me-may-it-please-yourself-to-go-to-hell-and-give-my-regards-to-every-one-down-there-ish.

YAS ABIKO—English editor Nichi-Bei; capably filling in after Larry Tajiri's departure for New York; considerate personable, and industrious.

VINCE TAJIRI—"Rigamarole" (Nichi-Bei)—pleasant, whimsical absurdities; talented short-story writer—suggestive of stream-of-conscious medium; handles subjective states of feeling with deft skillful adroitness; has clean, forceful, vigorous prose; is yet to clamber out of diapers, now teething on Sir Walter Raleigh; stayed over at Murase Mansion with Joe Oyama one night—for breakfast, had buttered toast (grated), coffee (two teaspoonful in a cup of sugar) and asked for a hatchet to break the yolk of his egg (slight exaggerations but you get the general idea); sly, waggish, droll-a swell fellow. (But he's a sports writer.)

Well, that's about it. And thirty.

Nation Awaits Call to Military Training

October 16 will be a memorable date in the history of the American commonwealth, for on that day the SELECTIVE TRAINING AND SERVICE ACT of 1940 will go into operation, requiring the registration of 16,000,000 men 21 to 35 years old, inclusive. The immediate objective of the act is to raise an initial protective force of 1,200,000 men for the Western Hemisphere.

Included among the sixteen million American manhood, who are subject to compulsory military training, are an approximate number of 210,000 U.S.-born Japanese, 14,000 of whom reside in California.... A large percentage of the Nisei will probably be deferred due to the rigid physical requirements of the Army, which exempt persons of less than 5 feet 4 inches in height from military service.

An Editorial

OUR POLICY

The Current Life magazine is built upon an altruistic foundation. It believes in the Nisei, and it dedicates itself to the stupendous task of presenting a true picture of the life and thoughts of the U.S.-born Japanese.

The lives of the Nisei have been a constant struggle. They have been faced with prejudice and intolerance. Their economic opportunities have been limited. In many instances attempts have been made to deny them their inalienable rights, and often enough the foes of the Japanese people have failed to take cognizance of the fact that there is a gulf of difference between U.S.-born Japanese and the immigrant Japanese or to distinguish between Japanese who are citizens and Japanese in Japan.

It is one of the fundamental purposes of this publication to seek a better understanding of the U.S. Japanese. In order to facilitate the program we believe that encouragement of Nisei talents should be made and that accomplished U.S. Japanese should be given greater recognition. Current Life will endeavor to be a true mirror of Nisei life. It will reflect the opinions and sentiments of these people. It will be a defender of the American-born Japanese against the unscrupulous politicians and rabble-rousers.

Current Life is the first magazine of this type and scope to be launched by an American-born Japanese publisher. It is predicted upon its confidence in the Nisei, and the Nisei, we hope, will have confidence in us.

CURRENT LIFE

The Magazine

for the American Born Japanese

November, 1940

The Day Came Not So Soon

It is dawn, but stars still swing
    Between the earth and sky,
And darkness keeps the wind,
    And not a sound blows by.

Slowly the night will lift, and morn
    will flower into noon,
Yet may the heart recall
    The day came not so soon.

               —Toyo Suyemoto

181

The Nisei's Problem Is Difficult but Natural

By LOUIS ADAMIC

Mr. Omura, the editor of this magazine, asks me to write for him a brief article or editorial. I can do no better than quote the hero of my story "A Young American With a Japanese Face" in my last book.

From Many Lands

"I spent my Easter vacation in 1938 trying to write an essay on the Oriental Americans. I held that the first thing for us to do was to realize that our situation, while difficult, was perfectly natural; in fact inevitable.

I saw it this way: we are the most recent immigration, and so still in the acute stage of adjustment to the country, as the country is, in turn, in that stage in relation to us. We have our problem, to be sure; but what can we expect?

We are marginal people, but more important than that fact is the need or us to see that we are that naturally.

To cease being marginal, we must proceed from this realization, the only point from which we can proceed. We must look both within and outside ourselves, especially for the good and weak things within us. We must start working against our disadvantages ... which, to repeat, are perfectly normal: but their being normal does not mean we need to put up with them.

In America it means the exact opposite. It means we must try to overcome them. If we try, we will do something.

We must prove ourselves. All the people, groups and individuals, who came here had to prove themselves. We must stand up and face the situation, and not withdraw from it and lie down, or sneak around with it with various dodges...."

CURRENT LIFE
The Magazine
for the American Born Japanese

Nisei Loyalty Challenged

Sensational charges of "Fifth-Column" menace levelled at Nisei as the nation calls citizens of very racial descent to the colors.

The All-American Girl
By TOSHIO MORI

The story of a passive attraction subtly told by the rising literary comet of San Leandro, California.

Who is the Nisei of the Year 1940?

The Nisei of the Year contest was launched in early 1940 by a committee of the Chicago Japanese Young People's Society. Its primary purpose is to uncover an individual among the Americans of Japanese descent, who by his achievement and conduct has best exemplified the sterling qualities of his race, and by thus awarding him recognition to inspire others to emulate his success.

Your nominations will help to uncover the individual most worthy of the honor. If there is a person in your community of outstanding merit, don't let him languish in provincial obscurity. He is probably deserving of national recognition, and you can be the instrument for his selection as the Nisei of 1940.

The following candidates have already been nominated:

1. George "Pop" Suzuki, enterprising Stockton, California, Buddhist and prominent organizer of valley athletic activities.

2. Kazuko Tajitsu, internationally known Seattle violinist, acclaimed for her excellent Pacific Coast concerts.

3. George Furiya, author of the novel "Act of God" and numerous short stories.

4. Togo Tanaka, dynamic English editor of the Los Angeles Rafu Shimpo and organizer of Nisei projects.

5. Masao Yoshida, violin virtuoso of Alameda, California.

6. Sono Osato, ballerina of de Basil's Ballet Russe, now being acclaimed as a promising and talented terpischorean after years of arduous devotion to her art.

7. Hitoshi Yonemura, Los Angeles youth attending U.C.L.A., believed only non-Caucasian to be accorded the Blue Key, a national upper division honorary.

8. Mike M. Masaoka of Salt Lake City, Utah. An outstanding Nisei leader in the Rocky Mountain region and university instructor in drama.

9. Tomiko Kanazawa, Los Angeles soprano and winner of Treasure Island talent contest.

10. Chiyoko Matsuda, Petaluma, California, coloratura soprano.

11. Kenny Murase, prolific Central California writer.

12. Lillian Lida of Berkeley, social worker stationed at the Japanese Children's Home in Los Angeles.

Entry deadline is February 15th. The selection will be announced in March.

In making your nomination, tell why you think your candidate should be accorded the Sansho Yamagata Award, giving specific data on achievements accomplished or acts done in 1940. Substantiating data in the form of letters, biographical material, photos, etc., while not necessary, is requested.

Send your entry to Franklin Chino, chairman of the Yamagata Award committee, 160 N. LaSalle Street, Chicago.

NISEI LOYALTY CHALLENGED

SLEEPY, OBLIQUE-EYED Nisei in the "Li'l Tokyos" dotting the coast awoke from their peaceful slumber one day recently, and read their morning papers and blinked—and blinked. Headlines shrieked at them that Senator Guy Gillette, Democrat of Iowa and member of the Senate foreign relations committee, had charged the Japanese government of "conscripting" American citizens of Japanese ancestry on the West Coast and Hawaii for espionage and military purposes....

YELLOW

The other children pointed fingers at me
And cried, "Yellow, yellow inside and out!"
Because my skin was a shade different from theirs.
They ringed me in a circle of distrust
And mocked me with repeated taunts
I held my hands fisted against my ears
And shouted, "No ... no ... no!"
And still the words crashed heavily
And thundered in the brain:
Yellow ... yellow ... inside and out.
See, my skin has not changed color,
But it may be that I am stained inside.

      —Toyo Suyemoto

JAPANESE IN SPORTS

By JIMMIE OMURA

Invades East

FROM THE shores of the Pacific, the paths of Japanese pugilists have led invariably to eastern fight centers since the days of mysterious Young Togo who, it is believed, was the first of the fighting sons of Nippon to lace on a glove in U.S. rings.

Young Togo, of whom little is known except for the fact that he met the great Bat Nelson in a 12-round engagement in 1912, fought in the era of Jack Johnson, then the Black dynamite of the heavyweight ranks.

The latest of the Japanese fighters to campaign in the east is the tough, little Honolulu featherweight, Hitoshi Tanaka. On April 17, 1940, Tanaka dropped a decisive eight round main event decision to Harry Jeffra, present featherweight champion, at Hagerstown, Md. It was a disheartening setback for the Honolulu battler who was making his first mainland start.

Tanaka, like his predecessors, is finding the road to fistic fame a rough one. From a main event billing he has been dropped to a preliminary spot. In a recent fight, the Honolulu boy took another lopsided beating, this time at the hands of Vince Tumminella in a four round affair at the Century Club in Baltimore.

One of the better Japanese fighters to step into a ring before a fight crowd in New York's famous Madison Square Garden was Jimmy Sakamoto, who is now a publisher in Seattle, Washington. He fought nearly a decade after Young Togo quietly disappeared off the fistic scene in the golden era of postwar America, popularized as the Roaring Twenties.

NISEI FASHIONS

THE MUSIC was enchanting . . . the setting elegant. Girls in soft flowing evening gowns; boys in tuxedos and dark suits swayed gracefully to the rhythmic tunes and between numbers exchanged social amenities or conversed in trifle excited tones. The occasion was the JACL Inaugural Ball; the setting, the spacious "Empire Room" of the hotel Sir Francis Drake in San Francisco.

There were many well dressed Nisei who had come from far and near to attend this outstanding social function of the year. Dresses vied with each other for attention. Mrs. Saburo Kido, wife of the national JACL president, appeared in a charming chiffon gown of white studded with tiny rhinestones. . . .

CURRENT LIFE
The Magazine
for the American Born Japanese

Berkeley Hills Covenant
Latest move to discriminate against racial minorities.
North Berkeley property owners propose restrictive measures
DEATH ON A HOLIDAY

by Hisao Hata

A story in two installments

Nisei of the Year—Mike Masaru Masaoka

April, 1941

In Canada

THE CANADIAN government's policy in discouraging applicants of Canadian Japanese ancestry for service in the dominion's armed forces is not meant to discriminate against them but rather to protect them. asserted Prime Minister MacKenzie King in the Canadian Parliament at Ottawa.

Improvement Meeting

HISTORY MAKING was the meeting held in Los Angeles of representatives of 15 Southern District JACL chapters with southland peace officers and chiefs of the Army and Navy Intelligence Service. Questions discussed were: "What is the out-look on a possible conflict in the Pacific among resident Japanese, Issei and Nisei?" "How predominant is the viewpoint of wholehearted American loyalty among the 145,000 Japanese in the United States?" "What is the chief concern among American born Japanese and their parents?" "What steps should be taken now to assure the greatest degree of normalcy in event of an emergency?" Leaders at this conference were Col. Kimberly, Fort MacArthur commandant; Lt. Commander Ringle, Chief of Naval Intelligence; and Sheriff Eugene Biscailluz of Los Angeles County. The Nisei were represented by Ken Matsumoto, national JACL vice-president; Dr Y. Nakaji, Southern District chairman; and Togo Tanaka, Equality Committee head.

Selective Service

THE SPLENDID response of Nisei draftees to military training is a fine reflection on resident Japanese, and an opening wedge toward acceptance by Caucasian Americans. In a San Francisco address Frederick Vincent Williams, veteran writer, newspaperman, and author of the novel "Behind the News in China," declared: "The record that the Nisei have made in the draft has been the first step toward breaking down prejudice." Mayor Claude Crawford of Santa Monica believes that "through the Nisei entering military service will come a better understanding."

Fish Harbor

THE GREAT fishing industry located at Terminal Island, Calif., is to be evicted in the near future by federal mandate and the area converted into a naval base. Residents, including a great number of Japanese, have been harassed by press reports of "Fish Harbor" demolition, and in order to check the customary furor, caution against "undue alarm to the industries" located at Terminal Island has come from high sources.

Mike Masaoka Named Outstanding U.S. Born Japanese

THE 1940 Yamagata Award for distinctive service went to 25-year-old Mike Masaru Masaoka of Salt Lake City, Utah. His selection was based particularly on his sterling public service in pioneering racial comity and understanding throughout the Rocky Mountain regions and for his outstanding and manifold participations in civic and in educational channels.

Recommendations for his selection came from many quarters—from people high in the state affairs of Utah. He was endorsed by such prominent public figures as U.S. Senators William H. King and Elbert D. Thomas, Gov. Henry H. Blood, Mayor Ab Jenkins of Salt Lake, and Chief Justice William H. Folland of the Utah Supreme Court. The *Salt Lake Tribune and Telegram* and the *Desert News* also endorsed his candidacy.

"It is rare indeed that any young American, regardless of parentage, renders the service to his community that Mike Masaoka has done in Salt Lake City," wrote Mayor Ab Jenkins in his letter of recommendation to the Nisei of the Year committee. "As the president of the Utah Japanese-American Citizens League, he helped organize the Japanese-American Council for the Intermountain States. In anticipation of the trying times we are now going through, these American activities bear a deeper significance than perhaps any of us realize. The thanks of his community were expressed to him last year when he was awarded the Salt Lake City Junior Chamber of Commerce Americanization Award. There is no higher honor that can be paid a person of foreign ancestry in this state.

Mrs. Burton W. Musser, woman diplomat and lecturer and delegate to the Pan-American Conference at Buenos Aires and to the Lima Conference, says: "Mike Masaoka represents the outstanding example of a youth born in America of alien parentage who has assimilated himself into the American cultural pattern."

The judge's committee, composed of Franklin Chino, chairman; Dixie Ishida, Lillian Sano, Kanjii Nunome, and Cecile Kuroki, announced from their Chicago headquarters that "Masaoka was selected because he particularly distinguished himself in concretely working to spread the actual, the seldom recognized, fact that the Nisei are in every way upright, loyal and progressive American citizens. Few Nisei have ever attained the high regard of their fellow Americans as has Masaoka." The award is to be presented by Gov. Herb B. Maw in the near future.

JACL Convention
in Monterey

Summer: 1941. They sense war with Japan is coming. President of the JACL Saburo Kido calls a special meeting of the ruling body of the JACL, to hire a full-time spokesman to speak for the JACL and to organize new chapters in new areas with Japanese American populations off the West Coast. The members of the National Council wanted someone who was fluent in English and Japanese, who had the "poise to meet with government officials on their own terms," someone who had an understanding of Issei and Nisei psychology and knew the history of Japanese Americans.

Kido had his own ideas. An articulate spokesman was more important to him than someone who could speak Japanese and knew the Japanese American community. Mike Masaoka came from a state that had few Japanese. His friends were "Caucasian" white American Mormons in Utah. His friends were his teachers. And his teachers were politicians who shared their interest in "intellectual matters" and "socioeconomic status" with Mike, in their homes, rather than ethnicity. Masaoka, in Kido's eyes, was the perfect Japanese American. He was an American who one day woke up in a Japanese skin. He was not uncomfortable with non-Japanese. Kido did not want a Nisei who "could not or would not articulate his thoughts in a mixed group and preferred being among his own kind." Kido did not want a typical Nisei—men who were "polite, conservative, reliable but quite unaggressive. They seemed to lack spontaneity. They . . . were careful not to . . . cause anyone to lose face."

The council members favored Togo Tanaka, who seemed to satisfy everyone's criteria for an aggressive spokesman, including Kido's. But, no. Tanaka was UCLA and Phi Beta Kappa and the English language editor of the *Rafu Shimpo*, the largest paper in Los Angeles; that made him too knowledgeable and possibly too beholden to the Japanese American community. Even Saburo Kido himself might be too Nisei for the task. He too had edited a newspaper. His speaking had a Hawaiian pidgin lilt. Masaoka was fresh from Utah! Kido offered the job to Masaoka.

On the advice of his friend Senator Elbert Thomas, who sat on the Senate Committee on Military Affairs, and Foreign Relations, and Labor, Mike Masaru Masaoka set aside his part-time job and political ambitions to speak for and lead the JACL, for $135 a month.

CURRENT LIFE
The Magazine
for the American Born Japanese

May, 1941

William Saroyan Salutes Current Life

Nisei publication receives singular attention from current America's outstanding literary figure. William Saroyan foresees magazine's vital role in national affairs, and declares: "…future issues of the magazine will be increasingly interesting and important, both to Nisei and to outsiders.…" Emergence of an outstanding Nisei writer is predicted.

THANKS AGAIN for the nice sukiyaki supper and a very delightful evening. I have been wanting to meet Japanese-Americans of California for some time.

I look forward with eagerness to the emergence of an outstanding Japanese-American writer. I believe this event cannot be avoided; that sooner or later one of you must write that story—if for no other reason than this: that I, for one, want to read that story. Now, if I want to read it, you may be sure that almost everybody else wants to read it.

I will predict for this writer these things: that his source of material will be his race, the memory of the old country in his parents, his own personal experience, and the experience of his own kind about him—but—at the same time—I will predict also that everything he writes will be as valid for me as for himself; that, while his work will spring from his own inner life, it will be universal.

The emergence of this writer is not going to take place tomorrow, or three months from now; it may be five years, or ten or twenty but my hunch is that now is the time for this writer to begin his work.

I wish you and Current Life and its readers all the best.

Yours truly,

William Saroyan

THE SWEET POTATO

It was the last day at Treasure Island. The lights were going out at midnight. Two Nisei youth muse over memories and in the crowded tearoom of the beautiful Japanese Pavilion they hear the story of the sweet potato.

By TOSHIO MORI

IT WAS the last day at Treasure Island and Hiro took me around for a fast look. Time after time he shook his head as he fondly gazed at the buildings. The lights were going out at midnight.

"Gee, it gets me," he said, his eyes becoming red. "I don't like it."

All summer we had gone to the Fair together. There were days when I would rather have stayed at home, but Hiro would come and pull me out of the house.

"I'm sick. I want companionship. Please come with me and make me happy," he would beg.

Each time it ended the same way. We would walk for miles, and he would talk. We saw very little of the exhibits. When we became tired we would go up on the Temple Compound and rest. Each time we would look below and watched the crowd coming and going. And each time Hiro would comment, "Gee, look at those people going back and forth. Wandering forever . . . that's what we're doing. Searching for something, searching for the real thing . . . everyone of us. Look at them going in circles. That's us when we go below and join them."

I knew what was coming next. All summer we had argued about ourselves . . . the problem of the second generation of Japanese ancestry. "I tell you. We're not getting anywhere. We haven't a chance," he would tell me. "We'll fall into our parents' routine life and end there. We'll have our own clique and never get out of it."

"You're wrong, Hiro," I would say. "We'll climb and make ourselves heard. We have something in us to express and we will be heard."

Hiro would shake his head. "You write stories and sing in the clouds. You dream too much."

Over and over we would talk and disagree. Whenever the situation became unpleasant we would become silent and walk. After a time the holiday spirit of the Island would take hold of us and we would become lively again.

"It's this friendly spirit around here I like," I would tell him. "I hope it never fades."

"Same here," he would agree. "But the Fair will be over and there'll be no more. Let's go and see the Cavalcade once more."

On the last day at the Fair we walked much and said little. Our legs were aching but we did not rest. Hiro was almost crying. "Here's this wonderful thing called the Fair ending tonight, definitely at midnight. The place where people came to forget awhile and laugh and sing. Tomorrow the Island will be empty and dark." I said nothing.

190

"What do you think?" he asked me suddenly. "Do you think our people will ever be noticed favorably? What can we Japanese do? Must we accomplish big things here in America?"

"Little things can accomplish big things too, I think," I said.

"That's right," he agreed. "But it's so slow. It takes time."

At three in the afternoon we became hungry. All the eating places were filled and we had to hunt around for a place to eat. "Let's go in the Japanese Tearoom today," Hiro suggested. "We might find a table there." I agreed.

The place was filled and we had to wait for a table but we finally got one. All about us were the white people munching teacakes, sipping Japan tea, and tasting green tea ice cream. Hiro's face reddened a bit. Long secluded in the Japanese community, he looked shy and awkward. But it did not last long.

An old white lady and a young man came over to the table and asked if we would share the table with them. We readily consented. Suddenly the old lady began to speak in Japanese.

"How are you?" she said. "Isn't it a wonderful afternoon?"

"You speak Japanese," I said, amazed.

"A little," she explained in Japanese. "I was in Japan for several years. I was in Yokohama during the big earthquake."

The young man spoke in English. "My mother and I love Japan. Have you ever been there?"

Hiro and I shook our heads. "No. We'd like to some day."

"You should visit Japan. It's a beautiful country," the young man said.

The old lady continued in Japanese. "I taught in the grade school for five years. When the earthquake came we lost everything. Fortunately my family came out alive."

"I was small then," the son said. "One day the houses were all standing in Yokohama and the next day there was nothing. It happened very quickly."

"It must've been terrible," Hiro said. "I guess there was food shortage."

"Yes, there was food shortage." The old lady nodded her head. "There wasn't enough food to go around. Do you know? There was one experience I'll always remember."

"She likes to tell it to everybody," the son said, smiling. "I remember."

"We were without food on the first day," she continued. "Nobody had food. A Japanese family whom we did not know, found a single sweet potato. There were four in their family, but the father cut the potato in eight parts and gave each of us a cube. The four in our family were never more filled. I cannot forget it. And afterwards a boy came along with a cupful of sterilized water and we shared that too."

"That potato was really sweet," the son said.

We nodded and said nothing. Hiro's eyes twinkled, looking first at the old lady and her son and then me. "Where do you live now?" he asked the young man.

"In Sacramento," replied the young man. "We come to San Francisco often. And whenever we do we feast on Japanese food."

"I like daikon, miso, tofu, tempura, and things cooked with shoyu," the old lady said.

"And mochi," added the young man. The old lady laughed. "My boy likes rice cake best."

"Do you like raw fish?" I asked them.

"Very much, with mustard and shoyu," was the young man's reply.

"There's the octopus," the old lady said. "It's like rubber and there's no taste."

"Say, what's going to happen to the Japanese Pavilion?" The young man suddenly changed the subject. I said it probably would be torn down.

"That's a shame." He shook his head sadly. "A beautiful building like this."

"This is a beautiful day," said the old lady. "Warm and serene. A beautiful setting for the last day."

Hiro beamed and looked gaily about, forgetting time and place. The four of us sat there a long time as if we had known one another a good many years. The people looked curiously at us, wondering what we had in common.

When the war comes and the Japanese Americans are evacuated to camps throughout the isolated parts of the country, James Omura will continue to fight for Japanese American civil rights, in the pages of the Denver *Rocky Shimpo*. He never set foot inside a concentration camp, yet he will be arrested as a leader of a group of draft resisters at Heart Mountain. He will write letters to each of the writers whose work he championed in *Current Life*, appealing for their help. In return he will receive not one answer. Not one dime. Not one letter.

PART III

December 7, 1941—
The Closing Papers

Pearl Harbor Time

Three hundred and sixty Japanese torpedo planes and dive bombers took off from six carriers. At 7:55 A.M. they struck the U.S. naval base at Pearl Harbor, Hawaii, through a rift in the clouds. They flew right over the fleet's entire supply of fuel. Ten minutes short of two hours later, the American fuel is untouched, but eight American battleships and three cruisers are sunk or disabled along with several smaller vessels. The Japanese lost 29 planes and 5 submarines. Out of 360 planes, the Japanese lost only 29? America is stunned. Americans remember where they were when they first heard the Japanese had bombed Pearl Harbor. They remember what they were doing. Japanese and Japanese American pressmen remember they were at the newspaper setting type. Japanese Americans published more "vernacular" newspapers in San Francisco (twenty-one) than they did in Oakland (three), Seattle (nine), and Los Angeles (eight) combined.

The news of Pearl Harbor arrives in San Francisco. The Army Harbor Defenses of San Francisco ready themselves for war. Brigadier General Edward A. Stockton issued a statement to the newspapers and radio stations:

> "All Coast Artillery officers and soldiers of the Harbor Defences of San Francisco are ordered to report to their stations immediately. All leaves and furloughs are canceled."

Nisei heard the words of their commanding officer on the radio and went to report to their unit.

Artillery at the Golden Gate

The Harbor Defenses of
San Francisco in World War II

by

BRIAN B. CHIN

Pictorial Histories Publishing Company Inc.
Missoula, Montana 59801

Men poured out of the Cronkhite barracks and into the 16-inch gun emplacement on the hill.... Some feared an enemy landing, especially since Battery E could not man the 16-inch guns and guard the nearby beach at the same time. "They could have landed on the beach down there," one of the artillerymen observed, "we were wide open."

... Battery I hurried from their barracks at Fort Barry to the 6-inch rapid-fire guns, bringing their lion cub mascot with them. [M]ost of the six-inch projectiles still wore protective coats of yellow paint from World War I. The men set to work scraping off the old paint so the shells could be fired. The men of Battery F, 18th Coast Artillery were firing their 1903 Springfield rifles at the Funston range when they heard about Pearl Harbor. They went back to Fort Miley and the 12-inch guns of Battery Chester. The forty year old seacoast guns and equally ancient 12-inchers of Battery Mendell at Fort Barry, together with modern 12 and 16-inch rifles of Wallace, Townsley and Davis, composed the "harbor defense commander's reserve." If the Japanese navy attacked San Francisco, as many believed possible that day, these big guns were counted upon to slug it out at long range with the enemy battleships.

• • •

Some gun batteries had no guns to man on December 7th. The 155mm armament of the 18th Coast Artillery's Battery D awaited construction of concrete Panama mounts at the southern end Fort Funston; so the men grabbed their rifles and went on guard duty.... Battery F of the 216th CA antiaircraft regiment, though not a part of the

Harbor Defenses, was supposed to defend the Golden Gate Bridge from aerial attack with 37mm automatic weapons. But these had not yet arrived.

• • •

On the afternoon of December 7th, Western Defense Command had received an erroneous report indicating a Japanese fleet thirty miles from the Presidio. The next day, more messages poured in, signaling assorted threats; aircraft carriers off the coast, submarines spotted off San Francisco....

On December 7, 1941, in the dark of night, in Los Angeles on radio station KMTR, at 11 P.M., the JACL warned the Japanese that "Any act or word prejudicial to the United States committed by any Japanese must be warned and reported to the F.B.I., Naval Intelligence, Sheriff's Office, and local police." They were also out on streets guiding agents of FBI and local law enforcement "to the lairs" of innocent Japanese in Los Angeles and Seattle. Japanese Americans hear the JACL warn the Japanese that they now are "counterespionage." Meantime in San Francisco, Brian B. Chine reports.

At 6:00 P.M. on December 8th, air raid sirens wailed over the city. Fire engines and police cars raced through the crowded downtown streets during the Monday evening rush hour.... Meanwhile, the hydroacoustic listening post near Sutro Baths picked up sounds of a submerged submarine approaching the Golden Gate. They notified Captain Jack Lehmkuhl on duty at H-Station. "Whose submarine was it?" Captain Lehmkuhl wanted to know, as he phoned various command posts.... Then someone at the Presidio mistakenly pulled the master power switch in response to the general blackout.... This shut off electricity throughout the Harbor Defenses and cut telephone contact between H-Station and the 16-inch batteries. The hydroacoustic station tracking the unidentified submarine also went out of action. When the Presidio master switch was turned back on, the underwater intruder had disappeared.... Captain Lehmkuhl at the H-Station imagined the submarine "laying in the mud alongside the net gate and then following some ships in." He thought of alerting some HDSF guns to train their sights along the net, but he realized the only ones able to point into the bay were deactivated 3-inchers at Fort Baker. The submarine, whether a faulty contact or a real intruder, did not materialize.

• • •

In the city, civilians reacted in confusion to their first wartime blackout. Many ignored sirens. Neon lights glowed from the business district and Christmas shoppers went into lighted stores. Residents on Twin Peaks saw downtown San Francisco sparkling "like New Orleans at Mardi Gras time".... Out on the bay, the Federal Penitentiary of Alcatraz observed no blackout. Its lighthouse flashed and floodlights played off the stark exterior walls of the cell house. General John L. DeWitt of Western Defense

Command angrily ordered the lights shut, but the Alcatraz warden refused, citing the primacy of prison security.

• • •

At dawn the next morning, Lehmkuhl went up to the observation deck of the command post. He had not slept in forty-eight hours, being occupied with the tactical business of the station and carrying out his duties as assistant harbor defense adjutant. Captain Lehmkuhl looked out the vision slit of the "bridge" and saw two of the promised machine gun nests. But to his amazement, Japanese soldiers manned each gun. Lehmkuhl reported this to General Stockton on the direct line. Stockton assured his aide the situation was normal. Japanese-Americans made up a part of the California National Guard infantry unit assigned to the perimeter defense of HDSF.

• • •

Battery E . . . the ammunition magazine doors were open and the 16-inch guns were ready for action. . . . Then the rains came. "It was windy, cold, and damp," so Battery commander John Schonher invited the soldiers to bring in their gear and stay in the cavernous area behind the 16-inch guns. The captain's offer "was heaven" to the infantry who gratefully moved into the tunnel. Later that evening, the sergeant in charge of the powder magazine got a good look at some of the invited troops. He went immediately to Schonher. "Captain," the sergeant reported, "you know there are several Japanese in this company." "Well, it's all right," Schonher answered, "but I better report it to the harbor defense commander." At H-Station, a duty officer handled Schonher's inquiry by replying, "I'll get back to you." A few minutes late, General Stockton came on the line, saying to Schonher: "These are soldiers of the U.S. Army. They're treated like everybody else."

Tom Oki,
Fair Play Committee

DECEMBER 7, 1941

December 7, 1941. "Well that day, I was right off of First Street. This was in Monterey Park. It wasn't Pomona Freeway yet. It was Third Street. I was right across from the Montebello Golf Course. When the war started I was during that—I was cultivating—ready to irrigate that morning. Cabbage. Somebody yelled at me. I don't know if it was one of my brothers or—anyway. That's how I found out. And that was a Sunday. So, in the afternoon, we all gathered around the radio. We had a console like about everybody had the big console like. I remember we had a Zenith, with a phonograph inside. I bought that. The radio was about a year old.

"And when the war started—that night, I went to market, too. Because, see, farmers usually harvested Saturday, and Sunday you picked for Monday morning.

"The market is open as soon as it's dark because the farmers start coming in. After evening, you can't work out on the farm, so they usually work until the evening. And after dark, you usually eat supper than you take off about eight, nine o'clock.

"So, Sunday night I was out there. And the FBI guy was already there walking around and we got to know him. Hakujin guy. Then from the next day on, we started to hear rumors, about, 'Hey!—' he says, 'So and so got pulled in tonight.'

"Sometimes you hear these produce guys—the owners of the produce—they get picked up so you hear it right away. There was a big honcho Japanese town. Those produce guys, they had money, they had power to do a lot of things. Whenever there was a big going on, between Japan, you know, like the Navy come over. Those guys were the ones who put the money to throw a party for the officers and the sailors, too. So even though they're not officers, they were helping monetarily. They got involved so they got picked up.

"And the next day, you go in, and those things keep mounting, you know. And then, they start talking about '*Inu.*' And I found out that the JACL was the 'inu'! So I said, 'God!' I said, 'I don't think I like JACL.'

"Before, until the war, I thought JACL was a pretty good thing, you know, knowing that Japanese didn't have any big brothers. But after the war started, and it's these guys were looking after their own neck and not the rest of the people, because they were kissing their ass for them to be on the good side of them.

"The reason I say that is that Kay Sugahara was in JACL, and he was married to the daughter of my dad's best friend, see. So I got to see them. We were young whenever we go visit them on a weekend. They reserved visiting to parents, see.

"So I got to know them, but being that there were a bunch of inu in the JACL, I said, 'I gotta watch my step.'

"So the FBI guy would tell us, 'So and So got picked up today.'

"But the thing is these FBI guys were deputized, they weren't." Tom Oki does not say they weren't real Special Agents.

"Everything was normal, you know, 'til they put the restrictions on you. Because the hakujins around there wasn't that hostile. Remember the curfew? I was still going to market, you know.

"So when I took over I didn't have much time, and when the war started, I called up the tractor company to see if they got certain things: plowshares and all that, you know. So he says, 'Yeah, we got plenty of them.'

"I told my dad, 'I don't think I'll have to move. Maybe you might have to move. So I'm goin' to buy some stuff and store it. Something that I can't buy later.'

"Dad said, 'Yeah, that's a good idea.' So I bought a lot of stuff, see. Like fertilizer, and equipment that you might not be able to buy after the war starts—I mean, it started already. So I bought a lot of things and stored them. I had the barn, you know, and the garage, so I stored all that stuff there.

"Well, see—I bought all this stuff! And then Roosevelt came down with Evacuation. What am I going to do with all that stuff? I can't get rid of it. Nobody wants to buy it: the fertilizer, the hay, the tractor. So finally I sold the tractor, I sold the car. But little things, I couldn't get rid of it. I just left it there.

"There was one guy. And he bought it, but you can't bargain with the guy. Because you're not going to be here. If you don't want him—whatever they want to give you."

"So you had fifteen acres. What did you sell your crops for?" Paul Tsuneishi asks.

"$500 or $700?" Tom Oki guesses. "I had five acres of cabbage. And the rest of it was open because I was ready to plant, you know, summer stuff, like cucumbers and corn and stuff and it was open, but broccoli was gone, cauliflower was gone, and cabbage was the only thing that was left. But even so, they were ready to pick, but you can't pay to pick it. Get rid of it so—Leave it for the vultures."

"JACL Statement"

By Joe Masaoka,
Chairman Coordinating Committee
for National Defense of the Southern District Council
Read by Togo Tanaka,
on Los Angeles radio KMTR, 11 PM, Dec. 7, 1941
Anti-Axis Committee Minutes
December 8, 1941

We are all American pledged to the defense of the United States. Any disloyal act or word by any Japanese or American citizen of Japanese descent harms the United States. The Military Espionage Act of 1918 provides that any word or act detrimental to the United States is duly punishable. As Americans we now function as counterespionage. Any act or word prejudicial to the United States committed by any Japanese must be warned and reported to the F.B.I., Naval Intelligence, Sheriff's Office, and local police. Any menace to the security of our country must be thoroughly and completely wiped out.

Signed,
Joe Masaoka, Chairman
Coordinating Committee for National
Defense of the Southern District Council

Frank Emi, Leader

"AROUND PEARL HARBOR TIME"

"I wanted to develop the store into a big supermarket. Up to the time that we all started this complete market ourselves, Dad was always in just the produce business. He always had the produce concessions in the market. And this one, we finally bought some fixtures and everything, and we had our own grocery department—complete meat case and everything.

"Well," Frank Emi says, "around Pearl Harbor time, Dad was more or less semiretired. He had been in an auto accident, and he wasn't working too much. Us kids were running the business at that time. But after Pearl Harbor, I think business slacked off somewhat. We didn't have any problems about supplying. We had a few more payments left on the cases and things. We planned to expand it."

Ike Matsumoto,
Fair Play Committee

"HEY, PEARL HARBOR'S GETTING BOMBED!"

"I used to deliver the *L.A. Times*," Ike Matsumoto says. "All of my buddies in this Ford from high school said, 'Hey Pearl Harbor's getting bombed!' and they drove off, and I didn't think it was anything. Just a joke. It wasn't 'til the afternoon when I was home, You can't believe nobody, what do they know, you know? For joke, they say all kinds of shit. Shoot! The radio convinced me. Sure! Shoot! Then I believed it."

TELEGRAM

SPECIAL
O
WB236 174 43 EXTRA
LOSANGELES CALIF FEB 16 1942 425P
ATTORNEY GENERAL FRANCIS BIDDLE
DEPARTMENT OF JUSTICE WASHDC

ERX WE HAVE BEEN WHOLEHARTEDLY WORKING AND STRIVING FOR THE WAR EEFORT TO DEFEAT JAPAN WE HAVE COOPERATED WITH ALL FEDERAL AGENCIES IN APPREHENDING SUBVERSIVES AND HAVE ACTUALLY BECOME INFORMANTS FOR THE F.B.I.? WE ARE DEEPLY CONSCIOUS OF OUR RESPONSIBILITIES OF CITIZENSHIP AND ARE LOYAL TO OUR INNERMOST FIBRE; WE UNDERSTAND TODAY OUR VERY RIGHT TO SERVE, OUR MOST PRECIOUS CITIZENSHIP AND THE RIGHTS AND OBLIGATIONS ARISING FROM THIS CITIZENSHIP ARE THREATENED BY POLITICAL EXPEDIENCIES OF OUR LOCAL POLITICIANS: WE UNDERSTAND THAT THEY ARE MAKING REPRESENTATIONS TO YOU ADVOCATING OUR TREATMENT AS ALIENS AND ADVOCATING OUR EVACUATION? WE PRAY THAT AS OUR GUARDIAN AS FOUNTAINHEAD OF FEDERAL AUTHORITY YOU SAFEGUARD OUR CITIZENSHIP RIGHTS THAT YOU PRESERVE FOR US OUR CHANCE TO TAKE PART IN THE WAR EFFORT HERE AS LOYAL AMERICAN CITIZENS

LOSANGELES CITY AND COUNTY CITIZENS OF JAPANESE ANCESTRY PERRY POST AMERICAN LEGION SOUTHERN CALIFORNIA CHRISTIAN CHURCH FEDERATION LOSANGELES CITIZENS LEAGUE JAPANESE YMCA FRUIT AND VEGETABLE WORKERS UNION LOCAL 1510 AFL YMBA & YWBA FLOWER MARKET ASSOCIATION JUNIOR PRODUCE CLUB JAPANESE YWCA SOUTHERN DISTRICT CITIZENS LEAGUE 104 NO. LOSANGELES STREET LOSANGELES CALIFORNIA.

FBI YMCA 15 0 AFL YMBA YWBA YWCA 104

Ben Kuroki,
Boy from Nebraska

"On December 7, we were meeting in the basement of church in North Platte—North Platte Episcopal Church—where Mike Masaoka was trying to tell us about the Japanese American Citizens League. They were young people from within a fifty-mile radius of town, Nisei, I knew them all. I think there might have been twenty.

"About halfway through the meeting, the police came and arrested Mike, and put him in jail. In North Platte. Then of course, shortly after that, he was released, because the governor of Utah phoned and told the police that they shouldn't hold Mike. That was the beginning of Pearl Harbor, of course, the news was on the radio."

JAPANESE AMERICAN COURIER

"FOR TRUTH, JUSTICE & TOLERANCE!"

Volume XIV, No. 726   Seattle, Wash., Friday, Dec. 21, 1941   Five Cents a Copy

WILL BACK AMERICA WITH THEIR LIVES

Second Generation Stand squarely Alongside Others In United Nation; 3,000 In Uniform Under Old Glory

MUST NOW JUSTIFY CITIZENSHIP

Text of Declaration of War on Japanese

WASHINGTON—Before a hurriedly-summoned joint session of the Congress on Monday, President Roosevelt informed the nation of the Japanese attack on the United States and asked for a declaration of war.

The President branded "Yester-day, December 7, a date which will live in infamy."

Remember Pearl Harbor

words by DON REID

music by DON REID and SAMMY KAYE

History in ev'ry century
records an act that lives forever more.
We'll recall as into line we fall
the thing that happened on Hawaii's shore—

Chorus
Let's REMEMBER PEARL HARBOR
As we go to meet the foe
Let's REMEMBER PEARL HARBOR
As we did the Alamo
We will always remember
how they died for Liberty
Let's REMEMBER PEARL HARBOR
And go on to victory—

FROM
WARNER BROS. STUDIOS
THE
HAL B. WALLIS PRODUCTION
OF

A

HOWARD HAWKS FILM

Air Force

STARRING
JOHN GARFIELD - JOHN RIDGELY
GIG YOUNG - ARTHUR KENNEDY
CHARLES DRAKE - HARRY CAREY
GEORGE TOBIAS - FAYE EMERSON

Produced by
HAL B. WALLIS
Directed by
HOWARD HAWKS
Screenplay by
DUDLEY NICHOLS
Director of Cinematography
JAMES WONG HOWE

93. INT. MEAT CAN [INTERIOR OF THE BOEING B-17 NAMED "MARY ANN"]
McMartin is crouched in the nose, outlined black against the increasing glare. Calls to Hauser at desk behind him.
McMARTIN:
For Pete's sake—look at Pearl Harbor!
Hauser slides in beside him, both silhouetted now.

209

94. SHOOTING DOWN PAST THEIR HEADS
Through the Plexiglass nose we see a ghastly inferno (miniature). Great fires are gushing up into a sky over hung with rolling smoke. At one side a battle-ship lies half on her side, burning fiercely, blotted out momentarily by heavy black smoke. Oil stores send up great tongues of flame. Further inland are other fires.

95. REVERSE CLOSE INTO AWED FACES OF McMARTIN AND HAUSER
lighted by the growing glare.

96. INT. COCKPIT
White behind the pilots, their faces lighted by the fires as they look down. The flickering light is bright on the ceiling over their heads.

QUINCANNON:
Pilot to crew. Take a good look at it, fellows—something to remember.

WHITE (LOOKING DOWN GRIMLY):
Mary Ann won't forget it.

97. INT. RADIO SECTION
The faces of Peterson and the kid, lighted by the glare through window from below, tighten as they watch.

98. EXT. WAIST SECTION
Faces of Weinberg and Winocki looking down, caught in the flickering light. Now Winocki has found something real to direct his embittered feeling against and his eyes grow hard and his jaw clenches.
LAP

99. HICKHAM FIELD LONG SHOT SHOOTING UP PAST SIDE OF BURNING HANGER NIGHT
We hear roar of engines and see the big airplane coming down through smoke and glare. Then she levels out along runway.

100. PAN SHOT
As her wheels touch and she bounces and bumps along the shell-pitted field and finally stops, silhouetted against fires in the distance. Dark figures of men dash out toward her.

102. GROUND FULL SHOT MARY ANN
Bright in the glare as ground crew men come running in. The door opens and
the crew piles out. The men make way for a tired-looking colonel who comes
striding in toward ship accompanied by a sergeant.

103. NEAR SHOT GROUP AT DOOR
The crew are already on the ground, including Hauser and McMartin, as
Quincannon jumps down followed by Williams. The colonel and sergeant
stride into scene. Camera moves in.

COLONEL (offers hand):
Fine job, Captain—but you shouldn't have come.

QUINCANNON:
Had to, sir. We were getting shot at by a squad of snipers. Couldn't fight 'em
in the dark, and I was afraid they'd hit a fuel tank.

COLONEL:
Mmmm, I see. We had plenty of trouble here too with the friendly Japanese.
(Grimly). Three trucks arrived from Honolulu at seven-thirty this morning—
delivering supplies. When the first Jap plane showed up, they slammed
across the field and wrecked every airplane in sight. Cut the tails off all but
three of our fighters.

WHITE (growls under his breath):
The sons of heaven!

Ben Kuroki,
Boy from Nebraska

"I FELT GUILTY BECAUSE I WAS
OF JAPANESE ANCESTRY"

Across the country, the Nisei response to Pearl Harbor is the same. A rush to enlist. Ben Kuroki, a farmer's son in Hershey, Nebraska.

"I felt that Pearl Harbor was just terrible. And I think I felt like a lot of the Caucasian kids that wanted to avenge what happened at Pearl Harbor.

"And it was the next morning that my brother Fred and I decided that we were going to enlist in the service. I felt guilty because of what the Japanese enemy did at Pearl Harbor. I felt guilty because I was of Japanese ancestry." They are refused at the recruiting station in Grand Island.

Kuroki is determined to get into the Air Force. They go to the recruiting station in North Platte. The recruiting sergeant in North Platte says, "Well what are you guys waiting for? Get an OK from the sheriff's office that you haven't got any criminal record, then bring two letters of recommendation from some responsible citizens, we'll swear you in, tomorrow, along with the next batch."

Dave Kawamoto,
Fair Play Committee

Dave Kawamoto is an NCAA wrestling champion at San Jose State College.

"I went up to the officer that was registering, and I told him I would like register too in the Air Corps.

"And he says, 'We're not taking Japs!'

"Well, I tried to find a place to hide."

Gloria Kubota, Nisei and the Zen Man

"**D**ecember 7, 1941. That was a sad day!" Gloria Kubota says. "We were just getting through planting our garlic seeds. Dad and I was in partner with Harry and Rosie."

"Oooh," Kozie Sakai groans in a whisper. The grocer knows the Harry and Rosie whom Gloria Kubota speaks of.

"On Steven's Creek Road," Gloria Kubota says.

"Yeah," the old grocer says.

"And we had the little John Deere tractor that cultivated all the different rows, and they had the big tractor. So we made a deal, and we had a certain percentage. We just got through planting our garlic. And oh, we started crying because that was terrible, just terrible. I was born in this country. I don't know anything else. And yet you feel terrible that your mother country is having a war with your country. It was really terrible."

Guntaro and Gloria's daughter, Grace, was born in May of 1941, five months before Pearl Harbor.

"This guy back of us, Mr. Olson, he always was friendly with us. Then when the war broke out, he goes and calls the Sheriff's Department. And he says, 'You know that man that lives right behind me, the teacher, and he's very educated and you better go and take a look at him.' And so the sheriff would come.

"But we knew the real sheriff, Sheriff Egan, because my folks lived on Larson's ranch by that time. And Mr. Larson was one of the sheriffs there, a deputy sheriff. So he says, 'There's nothing wrong with him. I know him.' But of course they had to come and check us out. That's when we started hiding and burying things, throwing all George's legal books away. So he really has nothing. He threw away everything."

Grace, Guntaro's daughter, says, "My father also performed—because of his judo—performed for the Duke of Windsor, the Duke of Windsor who became the king and abdicated." The Duke of Windsor, when he was the Prince of Wales, gave Guntaro Kubota a medal. He had several medals; what happened to them? His daughter says, "The real bad thing in our life is he had all these medals, and because of the Evacuation, he put it in a coffee can and buried it."

"He buried it!" Gloria says. "We never could go back there. And he did demonstrate before the Prince of Wales."

"The Duke of Windsor," Grace says.

"The Duke of Windsor," Gloria says.

"Well, I guess he was the Prince of Wales, then," Grace says.

"He said it was hard to demonstrate because, he said, you could never put your behind toward them." Mother and daughter laugh.

CURRENT LIFE

THE ONLY NATIONAL NISEI MAGAZINE

Vol. 2., No. 4   San Francisco, February 1942   15¢

EVACUATION NUMBER

SPECIAL NOTICE: -With this issue we temporarily suspend publication. Current Life will resume again from somewhere in the interior. Good luck and God be with you—

Publisher, James M. Omura

THE PASSING SHOW

By JIMMIE OMURA

The great concern of 63,000 Nisei Americans living today on the Pacific coast is primarily the threat to their civil liberties. The loss of employments and bankruptcy of businesses as results of the current conflict are secondary in importance to the free exercise of their cherished birthright as American citizens.

The rising clamor for mass evacuation into the interior of all persons with Japanese faces is a cause for alarm. Such a movement would trespass upon fundamental precepts of our constitution and would deprive one segment of the nation's citizenry a just redress of its wrongs. In this respect the troubles of the Nisei are strikingly analogous to the difficulties confronted for centuries by people of Jewish birth.

Every Nisei should be unalterably opposed to mass evacuation. Some Nisei Americans publicly encourage voluntary evacuation as a symbol of loyalty. Voluntary evacuation by the Nisei is a false idea of loyalty and is a betrayal of their inherited rights. We should not be so eager to give ground at the first threat to our civil liberties but should struggle to hold on to those inalienable privileges to which we are entitled.

In trying periods, such as the crisis we are now experiencing, false gods will appear to advise us. They will attempt to weaken us and then destroy us by subtle preachments and soothing promises for our submission. Whatever promises are made for us beyond the Sierras should not undermine our stern resolve to fight the good fight here where destiny has placed us. We ought not to barter our birthright for gold.

EVACUATION

By CARYL F. OKUMA

Officials of the Japanese American Citizens League, the recognized spokesmen for the resident Japanese offered no protest. Continued waging their fence-sitting policy of inaction and subordination. "Gladly cooperate" was the keynote of the society's pledge to the evacuation order. Meanwhile bitterness and resentment simmered against the JACL and its stand upon the problems of mass evacuation. Civil rights group among the Nisei hammered away at discriminatory features of General DeWitt's drastic proclamation. "Our civil liberties are precious rights," said James Omura, editor-publisher of Current Life, "and we should fight to maintain them. If we are willing to give up without a struggle at the first threat we do not deserve to have them at all."

James Omura,
Nisei Newsman

"THE AGE OF THE NISEI"

"In 1940, the Nisei were coming of age," Jimmie Omura says, "and gradually taking over operation of businesses. So how is the Nisei going to grab that torch without any experience? I don't think you could get them to join Nihonjin-kai or something like that. But you could have a joint participation in another organization with the leaders of the two groups. Then, you would get somewheres.

"And there was nothing like that. And I think there was some hostility among some Issei and the JACL leaders.

"I think on the whole, the Issei didn't think the Nisei were taking hold of the subject. Well, shucks, the JACL before the war was a laughing stock. Once a year they had their dance and then they had their beer-bust. That's all they did.

"I wrote an article for the *Japanese American News* for Larry Tajiri which was about the coming Nisei Age. And this was in 1940. If the war didn't come, we'd probably have had it, but I don't think we have had the Nisei Age because of the internment camps.

"All the Issei that I talked to held great hopes for the Nisei as future leaders. Right here. Right here."

"You're saying that the Issei in their way were extending themselves to the Nisei?" Lawson Inada asks.

"Definitely! And they took pride in doing that, to push the Nisei forward."

Mike Masaru Masaoka

"MR. JACL"

...I must confess that no written statement or accounting of the work of the Office of National Secretary and Field Executive has been made since the office was created in 1941. My only excuse for this neglect is that I have been too busy, either with my duties as the National Secretary or as a volunteer in training with the Japanese American Combat team to do so. Even now this paper will not be a formal and comprehensive summary but rather an informal resume of those activities and personalities which I can recall to mind at this time. Of necessity, this cannot be an exhaustive report and I regret to add that facilities here at the training center are such that I cannot document those items which ought to be supported by additional evidence. (To: National Board of the JACL 4/22/44)

But when you think back, those who are old enough to recall those dark and tragic days and remember the situations then, I think you will agree with me that all the historians in their ivory towers were never there. Or the people who want to write scenarios for books and scripts for plays, they weren't there. We were! And this is the story I would to tell you about. (JACL Convention 8/10/82)

Why do I feel so strongly about this? Because after all, I was damned as a Moses of the Japanese people who led my people, if you will, out of the civilization of the cities and into wilderness camps where many died. This isn't a very good stamp to be held on you. I'm here today because I remember that in certain camps they built little monuments to me then defecated and urinated on them. And that isn't a pleasant feeling even after 40 years.

Yes, we cooperated in our removal because we were afraid of what would happen. (In a speech before the Commonwealth Club in San Francisco in May of 1942.) And this is not reported by the historians and others.

Col. Bendetsen pointed out, and it was told to us much more in cruel detail, that the Army had two programs for removal of the Japanese. One, if you will cooperate then the Army and the United States will do its best to make that movement as humane as possible. Two, if you don't—and this is the thing to remember—the Army has a contingency plan to move you out within 12 or 24 hours.

What are you going to say in a situation like that?

You want people murdered on the streets? You want tanks to come in and destroy the little ghettoes we have enjoyed? I think we had no alternative. (JACL Convention 8/10/82)

Mike Masaoka spoke before several Japanese American Citizen League meetings. Each time he used Bendetsen's speech to verify the army's "contingency plan" to round up the Japanese within a twenty-four- or forty-eight-hour period, using "bayonets, tanks, artillery."

BEFORE THE EVACUATION

General John DeWitt, Commander Western Defense Command, Fourth Army, the man who asked for and ordered the Evacuation, talked with Major Karl Bendetsen, GSC. Assistant Chief of Staff, the man who designed and carried out the Evacuation, by telephone on Feb. 21, 1942. Bendetsen provided Secretary of War Henry Stimson with a copy of the transcript of the telephone conversation. In his accompanying memo he emphasizes that "He [DeWitt] has no mass movement in mind." In his conversation Bendetsen mistakenly concluded that DeWitt planned to accomplish the evacuation "all at once...." and DeWitt cut him off with:

General DeWitt: Oh, no, that has got to be a gradual process. Oh, yes, I am not going to have any mass movement. Oh, no, I am going to do it step by step. In other words, I have to go to work those steps out very carefully. I have got to have a lot of information together before I can even start the first one.

Col. Bendetsen: Surely so that the steps will be first to make a military area so that you have control enough to throw out any individual you want to, but from then on, the exclusion by class will be gradual, depending on the developments and the means at hand and the situation.

General DeWitt: That's it. I've got to watch my troops, you see. I can't use a whole lot of troops, and I don't want any mass movement.

Bendetsen was in charge of the evacuation program and knew the army could not threaten the Japanese with what it did not have. On April 28, 1981, a surprised Bendetsen wrote the Commission on the Wartime Relocation and Internment of Civilians:

Your question relates to an allegation that the Western Defense Command issued a preemptory order that Japanese and Japanese Americans must cooperate and that if they did not, the Army would come without notice, "with bayonets drawn, backed by tanks and artillery to force them out of their homes or hiding places one by one."

The allegation that such order was ever issued by WDC is totally false. The truth is that to their eternal credit all such persons cooperated from the beginning.

I cannot bring myself to believe that Mike Masaoka would himself fabricate such a falsehood; most certainly not one as base and demeaning as this. If it is true that he has made such an allegation, I would be compelled to conclude that someone has deceived and misled him for mischievous purposes.

Falsehoods about this regrettable episode abound in the books of self-appointed historians, of which there are several.

Mike Masaoka toured the western states on behalf of the JACL and the army, telling the officers of the JACL of his meeting with "three generals" about the unpleasant consequences of resistance to the army. JACL leaders were impressed with his demeanor and knowledge of the army's threats against the Japanese. Masaoka says he was originally disposed to resisting the army action in the courts, than abruptly changes the subject, but not his voice, and insists they could not, as leaders of the JACL, knowingly provoke a mass reaction from the army. He wouldn't go to court to defend Japanese American civil rights? Wasn't that his job? Mike implied through his manner, the way he talked, that he knew more about what was going on than the average Japanese American.

In his speech before the Commonwealth Club of California, May 20, 1942, Major Karl Robin Bendetsen does not deal in Masaoka's "cruel details"; there is no mention of "guns, bayonets, or tanks," no mention of completing the mass movement of 113,000 within twenty-four or forty-eight hours. Bendetsen is vague and general about time, manpower, and equipment:

> The second interim step was a plan for immediate evacuation if developments required. The Army needed time to prepare a permanent program and the situation called for an emergency plan. It was impossible, of course, at this time for the Army to reveal the fact that it was prepared to effect a complete evacuation, practically overnight, in the event of an emergency. Plans were made to move the 113,000 Japanese into already established Army cantonments in a Mass Movement which could have been undertaken immediately. Prepared in this way against the possibility of fifth column activity, or for any outbreaks of anti-Japanese feeling, the Army continued with its plans for a permanent program.

Bendetsen knew what the army had, and what they didn't have, which explains his vague language. Given that the "emergency" initiated by the Japanese armed forces or the Japanese Americans, or a combination of both, would be small enough, to allow the employment of every man in the army, 1,644,000 men (a convenient emergency), and they were trained (and they were not), they could round up 113,000 or 115,000 people, spread out in the cities and the countryside of the three states on the West Coast, in twenty-four hours. If they had the vehicles (they did not), the weapons (they did not), and the tanks (they did not). They had a total of three semioperable WWI tanks used for target practice. (Trainees bombarded them with sacks of flour, because the army also lacked artillery.) Most of the 1,644,000 men in the army were draftees. They trained with nonfiring training rifles, while waiting for the new .30 caliber Garand M-1 semiautomatic to be delivered. No rifles. No military vehicles to transport the Japanese. No tanks to threaten them. (According to the Office of War Information film by Frank Capra, *Why We Fight*, released in 1943.) But Mike doesn't let facts get in his way.

"MIKE, NOT MICHAEL"

My name is Mike Masaru Masaoka. Mike, not Michael. If that's an odd collection of names, it reflects both my American citizenship and upbringing and the Japanese part of my heritage.

We, the members of the National Board of the Japanese American Citizens League of the United States of America, believe that the policies which govern this organization and our activities as their official representative are best illustrated by an explanation of the alphabetical sequence of the letters J-A-C-L.

'J' stands for justice.

'A' stands for Americanism. We believe that in order to prove ourselves worthy of the justice which we seek, we must prove ourselves to be, first of all good Americans—in thought, in words, in deeds. We believe that we must personify the Japanese American Creed.

'C' stands for citizenship.

'L' stands for leadership. We believe that the Japanese American Citizens League, as the only national organization established to serve the American citizens of Japanese ancestry, is in a position to actively lead the Japanese people residing in the United States. We believe that we have the inspired leadership and membership necessary to carry into living effect the principles of justice, Americanism, and citizenship for which our league was founded.

Before the congressional Tolan Committee, which investigated the removal of the Japanese population, in February 1942, Masaoka made a point of introducing himself as having been a student of current U.S. senator Elbert Thomas and Utah governor Herbert B. Maw, in college. "They more or less looked upon me as a prodigy, and I have often visited with them. I have discussed theories of government with them and so on."

He spoke to white men as a white man, with even a condescending tone in his voice. His speaking amazed Japanese Americans.

He stressed that "I have been classified as 1-A and this may be my last appeal on behalf of the Japanese-Americans whom I believe are grossly misunderstood." Before becoming the field executive for the JACL, he was a high school speech teacher in Utah. He tells the committee:

> Our association is incorporated under the laws of the State of California June 21, 1937. We have absolutely no members in Hawaii. We have approximately 20,000 members and have chapters in 300 communities in the United States.
> And I personally say this: we are the largest group of American citizens of Japanese ancestry.
> It officially was incorporated in 1937, as I said before. The beginnings of the organization were about 1921 in Seattle. Officially the first convention was held in 1930. It is a comparatively young organization (Feb. 21–23, 1942).

Mike Masaru Masaoka is the best known and the most hated man in Japanese America. Mike Masaoka is the best known and the most revered man in Japanese America. He saved Japanese American lives by "constructive cooperation." He ruined Japanese American lives by capitulating to white racism.

"I DO NOT THINK IT SHOULD BE VOLUNTARY EVACUATION"

"But I would like to make this request of you," he says before the Tolan Committee. "Just as I pointed out, the tension is increasing all around and immediate action would be very helpful, I think, to all concerned to protect us from mob violence, to protect against sabotage, which may come. Now, I think a decision will permit us to inform our people as to proper procedure, to help them to get ready to leave, if necessary; to contact the proper Government agencies and otherwise. But I do not think that it should be voluntary evacuation for the simple reason that I am afraid of what is happening in Tulare and other counties. If they just go voluntarily out without knowing where they go, they may not only inconvenience the communities to which they go, but they may disrupt those communities."

THE NISEI CREED

Mike Masaoka would punish innocent Japanese Americans with exclusion, for inconveniencing the local law enforcement to move against racists offended by the peaceful presence of Japanese Americans. Whose side was he on? *Current Life* publisher James Omura wondered. Omura was the most outspoken Masaoka critic, but he was fair. He dedicated a full page of his magazine to printing the following, by Mike Masaoka:

The Nisei Creed

I am proud that I am an American citizen of Japanese ancestry, for my very background makes me appreciate more fully the wonderful advantages of this nation, I believe in her institutions, ideals and traditions; I glory in her heritage; I boast of her history; I trust in her future. She has granted me liberties and opportunities such as no individual enjoys in this world today. She has given me an education befitting kings. She has entrusted me with the responsibilities of the franchise. She has permitted me to build a home, to earn a livelihood, to worship, think, speak and act as I please . . . as a free man equal to every other man.

Although some individuals may discriminate against me, I shall never become bitter or lose faith for I know that such persons are not representative of the majority of the American people. True, I shall do all in my power to discourage such practices, but I shall do it in the American way; aboveboard, in the open, through courts of law, by education, by proving myself to be worthy of equal treatment and consideration. I am firm in my belief that American sportsmanship and attitude of fair play will judge citizenship and patriotism on the basis of action and achievement, and not on the basis of physical characteristics.

Because I believe in America, and I trust she believes in me, and because I have received innumerable benefits from her, I pledge myself to do honor to her at all times and in all places; to support her constitution; to obey her laws; to respect her flag; to defend her against all enemies, foreign and domestic; to actively assume my duties and obligations as citizen, cheerfully and without any reservations whatsoever, in the hope that I may become a better American in a greater America.

The Nisei Creed written by Mike M. Masaoka of Salt Lake City, Utah, an outstandingly prominent youth leader of the Rocky Mountain districts and an instructor of debating at Utah University. The Creed is believed to have been first recorded in the Calexico, California, Chronicle. The San Diego Sun later reprinted it. It has since then received wide attention.

"I SHALL DO ALL IN MY POWER TO DISCOURAGE SUCH PRACTICES . . . ABOVEBOARD, IN THE OPEN, THROUGH THE COURTS"

In the "Nisei Creed" Masaoka said, "Although some individuals may discriminate against me . . . I shall do all in my power to discourage such practices, but I shall do it in the American way; aboveboard, in the open, through courts of law."

When Mike M. Masaoka assumed office on September 1, 1941, he turned the JACL against protection of Japanese American constitutional rights and toward generating favorable publicity for himself and bad publicity for his enemies, inside or outside the JACL.

Min Yasui, of the Portland, Oregon, JACL, disobeyed the curfew order to create a test case, like Gordon Hirabayashi did 250 miles north, in Seattle. Hirabayashi was not a member of the JACL, and Min Yasui was. Masaoka rejected and denounced his fellow JACLer in "Bulletin #142: RE: Test Cases, San Francisco, April 7, 1942."

The Min Yasui case in Portland, Oregon, is gaining considerable attention. The facts seem to indicate that one Minoru Yasui, a Nisei attorney who worked for the Japanese consulate in Chicago as late as last December 7th, registered with the State Department as a propaganda agent for a foreign government, and a reserve lieutenant in the United States Army, deliberately violated the curfew regulations and surrendered to the police with the declared intentions of legally determining the right of the authorities to impose such restrictions upon American citizens of Japanese extraction. Yasui contends that such actions are discriminatory and unconstitutional.

At the present time, he is "out" on bail and is said to be circulating a petition among the Portland Chapter members demanding that the National Organization take some definite stand on the question of constitutional rights of the Japanese Americans.

In regard to this particular case, as well as all other test cases of this nature … this office releases the following statement:

"The national JACL stands unalterably opposed to test cases to determine the constitutionality of the military regulations at this time. We have reached this decision unanimously after examining all the facts in light of our national policy of: "the greatest good for the greatest number.

"We recognize that self-styled martyrs who are willing to be jailed in order that they might fight for the rights of citizenship, as many of them allege, capture the headlines and the imaginations of many more persons than our seemingly indifferent stand. We realize that many Japanese and others who are interested in our welfare have condemned the JACL for its apparent lackadaisical attitude on the matter of defending the rights and privileges of American citizens with Japanese features."

Masaoka sides with the army against the constitution, and his race. He rules his organization. He tries to create a compound of volunteer-hostages, the friends and family of Nisei who want to fight, people who offer themselves to be held as guarantees of their Nisei sons' loyalty. He writes "TO: NATIONAL BOARD MEMBERS OF THE JACL, dated April 22, 1944":

Two ideas which we seriously considered at that time illustrate to what extremes we Japanese Americans were willing to go to safeguard our homes and associations.

One was to form a volunteer "suicide battalion" which would go anywhere to spearhead the most dangerous missions. To assure the skeptics that the members of the "suicide battalion" would remain loyal, if such guarantees were necessary to quell the objections of the professional agitators of the west, the families and friends of the volunteers would place themselves in the hands of the government as "hostages." When this idea was informally discussed with a high military official, we were informed that it was not the practice of the government to require "hostages" or to sponsor such "suicide battalions."

He's determined to convince the army to create concentration camps, which the army wanted, in order to create a suicide battalion, which the army didn't want.

"CALLED UPON TO LEAVE OUR HOMES FOR HUMANE AND DEMOCRATIC RESETTLEMENT"

On April 6, 1942, on JACL letterhead, Masaoka begins a collaboration with Milton Eisenhower, of the newly formed War Relocation Authority, against Japanese American civil rights.

> Japanese American Citizens League
> An All American Organization of American Citizens
> National Headquarters
>
> April 6, 1942
>
> Mr. Milton S. Eisenhower, Director
> War Relocation Authority
> Western Defense Command and Fourth Army Headquarters
> Whitcomb Hotel
> San Francisco, California
>
> Dear Mr. Eisenhower:

There follows many eloquent, elegant, euphonious words of praise, congratulating Eisenhower on his appointment, then this sentence:

> We are grateful that our Federal Government has appointed a man of your calibre to direct the humane and democratic resettlement of us unfortunate people who have been called upon to leave our homes and businesses in order that the military defenses of our country may be strengthened.

He uses "resettlement" as a euphemism for the evacuation to concentration camps and links getting the Japanese Americans out of sight to military strength.

> In the first place, the entire evacuation program is complicated by the fact that we are dealing with a society which is composed of both American citizens and "enemy aliens." . . . Because both groups are living under the same roof in most cases, the tendency may be to treat both generations as one. This may be dangerous for the future, for the citizens have been taught that they are entitled to certain inalienable rights which no other citizenry enjoys.

Instead of arguing the injustice of denying the Issei U.S. citizenship, Masaoka, representing the JACL and the Japanese Americans, turns the Nisei against the Issei.

> Seventhly, the Japanese have no national organization except the Japanese American Citizens League, which is confined only to the American citizens of Japanese extraction. While other nationality groups may have a number of national organizations which purport to represent them, the Japanese have only our organization, which is non-partisan and non-sectarian, to speak for them on a national basis.

$$\bullet \quad \bullet \quad \bullet$$

> We are doing our best to follow out the various regulations and orders because we feel that this is our patriotic duty and not because we are submitting to the demands of the jingoists, race-haters, and politicians who have demanded that we be placed in concentration camps. We have not contested the right of the military to order this movement, even though it meant leaving all that we hold dear and sacred, because we believe that cooperation on our part will mean a reciprocal cooperation on the part of the government.

So the JACL promises not to use the constitution against the military evacuation, and they promise not to represent Japanese American civil rights. In actuality, Masaoka seems to represent white racism. What happened to Japanese America?

> . . . We don't relish the thought of "Little Tokyos" springing up in these resettlement projects, for by so doing we are only perpetuating the very things which we hope to eliminate: those mannerisms and thoughts which mark us apart, aside from our physical characteristics. We hope for a one hundred per cent American community.

He sees the camps as a behavior modification program, applied to the subjects without their will, without their knowledge. Walk into camp, eliminate your mannerisms and thoughts that aren't white. Walk out 100 percent American. What about the Japanese language?

One thing is certain: there should be no Japanese language schools.

Japanese Americans are locked in concentration camps without being charged with anything, and the JACL opposes holding judicial hearings to charge or discharge individual internees. Masaoka's argument for locking people up against their will, and keeping them locked up, is perverse:

> Paradoxical as this may seem we are opposed to Hearing or Determining Boards or Commissions which might attempt to determine the loyalty of those in these resettlement projects. . . . Should a person be adjudged disloyal at this time because of something which he might have said or done years ago, he would be branded for life and would prove useless after the war. We believe that the American concepts of justice—that one is innocent until proved guilty—should be applicable to all citizens, including ourselves. Until definite facts of overt actions of disloyalty can be shown, we believe that all persons should be accepted at their face value, as loyal and devoted citizens of the United States.

The representative of Japanese American civil rights is against the use of the courts to defend the people's rights and close the camps. He asks that the Issei, barred from citizenship by racist laws and called "enemy aliens" by the same laws be treated worse in these concentration camps than their citizen children, the Nisei.

> As far as possible and practicable, Japanese Americans should be treated in the same manner as all other American citizens, and certainly with greater consideration than the "enemy aliens".
>
> Because of the unusual and unprecedented requests made upon American citizens of Japanese ancestry, special provisions should be made to compensate them for the temporary loss of some of their privileges and rights. This might be in the form of 'certificates" of citizenship or appreciation, or some other token which will help them retain their self-respect in their own eyes and in the eyes of their fellow citizens.

Only Masaoka uses the words "temporary loss" regarding his people's civil rights. The Japanese Americans in camp are to be compensated, with a piece of paper thanking them for suffering the loss of privileges and rights? No, the government's not blind enough to provide concrete documentation of its seizure of constitutional freedoms.

> Self-government as far as possible and practicable should be the order of the day. Because most of those involved are citizens, the citizens should be given special privileges over and above those granted to the non-citizens.

We recommend that only citizens who have attained their majority be permitted to vote and to hold offices of any sort, elective or appointive.

Masaoka used the camps to turn noncitizen Issei against citizen Nisei, parents against children. He expects a reward.

> No intimation or hint should be given that they are in concentration camps or in protective custody, or that the government does not have full faith and confidence in them as a group and as individuals....
>
> Finally, in concluding this letter to you, may we reiterate the pledge of our Japanese American Citizens League to cooperate with you to the best of our abilities and to offer to you and our Government the individual and organizational facilities at our disposal.

> Respectfully submitted,
> Mike Masaoka
> NATIONAL SECRETARY—JACL
> For Better Americans in a Greater America

Mike Masaoka, Ken Matsumoto, and George Inagaki are all officers in the JACL. They also share authorship of a memo written on War Relocation Authority letterhead, as if they were WRA employees. The title of the memo is "Definition of Kibei." It goes beyond the definition of Kibei, into penalties for just being a Kibei, and the breakup of a family of Kibei and non-Kibei, people who've spent a part of their youth in Japan. The JACL seems to be working in collusion with the WRA against civil rights for the Kibei. The memo shares the date of his letter, to Milton Eisenhower: June 6, 1942.

War Relocation Authority

For: Mr. Eisenhower

Definition of Kibei: An American citizen of Japanese ancestry who has studied in Japan for a period of five or more years, all or part of which was after the year 1930, and all or part of which was after attaining the age of 12 or more.

In the case of family, if the husband is Kibei and the wife Nisei, the family should be considered Kibei; and if the husband is Nisei and the wife Kibei, the family should be considered Nisei.

Inasmuch as the parents sent the child to Japan in most cases, the parents should be held suspect, regardless of the number of other children which they may not have sent to Japan for study. In all cases, they may appeal their status.

If the child under question is 16 years of age or more, he is entitled to elect whether he chooses to be placed in the same classification as his parents or not, provided that his parents are declared suspect. If the child is under 16, he assumes the status of his parents, but on becoming of age may have the privilege of election.

Any person declared suspect may appeal to a special board of investigation, which might be composed of representatives of the military forces, the WRA and the Department of Justice. The applicant may submit the names of five persons, none of whom may be members of the immediate family or close relatives, to vouch for him or offer information regarding him. The board may call any or all of the persons so named and question them, if they so desire, or request them to make a recommendation concerning the party in question. All such persons must present their information under oath, so that all information of a false nature makes them liable for criminal punishment for perjury. The board may also call additional persons to present testimony, if they so desire, under whatever terms they may deem necessary and proper. It should be understood that all such testimony is purely advisory and is not binding per se on the investigating board.

Incidentally, we are in unanimous agreement as the principle of segregation.

Respectfully submitted,
Mike Masaoka
Ken Matsumoto
George Inagaki

THE TOLAN COMMITTEE

NATIONAL DEFENSE MIGRATION
MONDAY, FEBRUARY 23, 1942
MORNING SESSION

House of Representatives,
Select Committee Investigating
National Defense Migration
Washington, D.C.

The committee met at 9:40 A.M., in the Post Office Building, San Francisco, Calif., pursuant to notice, Hon. John H. Tolan (chairman) presiding.

TESTIMONY OF MIKE J. MASAOKA.
NATIONAL SECRETARY AND FIELD EXECUTIVE
JAPANESE AMERICAN CITIZENS LEAGUE.
2031 BUSH STREET, SAN FRANCISCO

MR. SPARKMAN: Do I understand that it is your attitude that the Japanese-Americans citizens do not protest necessarily against an evacuation? They simply want to lodge their claims to consideration?

MR. MASAOKA: Yes.

MR. SPARKMAN: But in the event the evacuation is deemed necessary by those having charge of the defenses, as loyal Americans you are willing to prove your loyalty by cooperating?

MR. MASAOKA: Yes. I think it should be—

MR. SPARKMAN: (Interposing). Even at a sacrifice?

MR. MASAOKA: Oh, yes; definitely. I think that all of us are called upon to make sacrifices. I think that we will be called upon to make greater sacrifices than any others. But I think sincerely, if the military say "Move out," we will be glad to move, because we recognize that even behind evacuation there is not just national security but also a thought as to our own welfare and security because we may be subject to mob violence and otherwise if we are permitted to remain.

MR. SPARKMAN: And it affords you, as a matter of fact, perhaps the best test of your own loyalty?

MR. MASAOKA: Provided that the military or the people charged with the responsibility are cognizant of all the facts.

MR. SPARKMAN: Certainly. That is assumed.

MR. MASAOKA: Yes.

Mike Masaoka's testimony inflamed Rev. Frank Herron Smith. Smith had twenty-one years' experience in the Orient until he was called back to America, in 1926, to take charge of the Methodist Japanese Missions west of the Mississippi River. "Since 1926 I have given all of my time day and night to these Japanese in America." He was at the Post Office Building to testify to the loyalty of the Japanese Americans before the Tolan Committee. He found Masaoka in the corridor and, according to James Omura, also there as a witness, "grasped him by the arm, spun him around and charged in a loud irate tone heard around the corridor: 'You have betrayed your people. They should ship you back to Utah!'"

MONDAY, FEBRUARY 23, 1942

AFTERNOON SESSION

House of Representatives,
Select Committee Investigating
National Defense Migration
Washington, D.C.

The committee met at 2 P.M., in the Post Office Building, San Francisco, Calif., pursuant to notice, Hon. John H. Tolan (chairman) presiding.

TESTIMONY JAMES M. OMURA, EDITOR AND PUBLISHER, CURRENT LIFE, SAN FRANCISCO, CALIF.

MR. OMURA: I appear before this committee informally. I have just come from work and I am not dressed properly for an appearance before such a committee. [He was not badly dressed; he appeared in a jacket and tie, instead of a dark suit.]

MR. ARNOLD: What is your work?

MR. OMURA: My regular work is that of a buyer and head packer for the Amling Wholesale Florists.

Of course, on the side, I publish *Current Life*, a magazine dedicated toward better understanding. It is entirely supported by what income I gain from my regular job. It was originated in October 1940. Since then we have been doing our best to present the factual side of the Nisei problem.

• • •

I requested to be heard here due largely to the fact that I am strongly opposed to mass evacuation of American-born Japanese.

It is my honest belief that such an action would not solve the question of Nisei loyalty. If any such action is taken I believe that we would be only procrastinating on the question of loyalty, that we are afraid to deal with it, and that at this, our first opportunity, we are trying to strip the Nisei of their opportunity to prove their loyalty.

I suppose you understand that I am in some measure opposed to what some of the other representatives of the Japanese community have said here before this committee.

I specifically refer to the J.A.C.L. It is a matter of public record among the Japanese community that I have been consistently opposed to the Japanese American Citizens League. I have not been opposed to that organization primarily in regards to its principles, but I have felt that the leaders were leading the American-born Japanese along the wrong channels, and I have not minced words in saying so publicly.

I would like to ask the committee: Has the Gestapo come to America? Have we not risen in righteous anger at Hitler's mistreatments of the Jews? Then, is it not incongruous that citizen Americans of Japanese descent should be similarly mistreated and persecuted?

We cannot understand why General DeWitt can make exceptions for families of German and Italian soldiers in the armed forces of the United States while ignoring the civil rights of the Nisei Americans. Are we to be condemned merely on the basis of our racial origin? Is citizenship such a light and transient thing that that which is our inalienable right in normal times can be torn from us in times of war?

JACOB GENS

"False Messiah"

Many of you think I am a traitor. Others wonder what I am doing at a literary demonstration in the ghetto. Me, Gens, I blow up the underground shelters in which the Jews hide to escape deportation and me, Gens, I go to a lot of trouble to get papers and certificates for inhabitants of the ghetto. Me, Gens, I keep track of Jewish blood, but not of Jewish honor. When they ask me for a thousand Jews I turn them over, for otherwise the Germans would come and help themselves, and they would take not one thousand but many thousands. By giving them a hundred Jews I save a thousand, and by giving them one thousand I save ten thousand.

You who devote yourselves to things of the mind, you aren't involved in the dirty work of the ghetto. You'll leave it clean, if you're lucky enough to leave, and you'll be able to say, "Our consciences are immaculate." Me, Jacob Gens, if I leave, I'll be dirty and my hands will be covered with blood.

• • •

In the administration of the ghetto, as well as in the work commandos, it is our duty to prove that the prejudice about our unfitness for work is fundamentally false. We must prove that we are indispensable to production, and that it would be impossible to replace us under present wartime conditions. At this moment there are in the ghetto 14,000 workers. We must make our objective to raise this figure to 16,000. We must make a selection among the workers so as to increase our common output, which will increase our right to exist accordingly.

> JACOB GENS
> President and
> Chief of Police
> Vilna Ghetto
> Lithuania

WERE YOU NOT TRYING TO IMPRESS YOUR NATIONAL ORGANIZATION WITH HAVING DONE THINGS THAT YOU HAD NOT DONE?

MIKE MASAOKA, FIELD SECRETARY, JACL
HEARING BEFORE A SPECIAL COMMITTEE ON UN-AMERICAN ACTIVITIES,
investigating Un-American Propaganda Activities in the United States,
on Saturday, July 3, 1943.
The chair, John M. Costello:

MR. MATTHEWS: (Staff director of research J.B. Matthews, reads from the JACL minutes)

The minutes read in part as follows:

Informal meeting was started at 8 P.M.

National Secretary Mike Masaoka started the meeting by giving a brief report of his thoughts and ideas regarding our work in the East. Mike Masaoka is convinced that we must maintain somebody in Washington all the time. It was for the reason that the hearts of all the Japanese people lie in our hands. He has met Chief Justice Stone, Mrs. Roosevelt. Attorney General Biddle, Secretary Stimson, Secretary Knox, and Sumner Welles; also Senator Thomas and Senator Murdock.

Did you meet all these persons?

MR. MASAOKA: I may have.

MR. COSTELLO: You do not recall whether you actually met each of the persons named?

MR. MASAOKA: That is right, at that particular time.

MR. COSTELLO: Do you know how many of them you did actually meet?

MR. MASAOKA: No. I do not.

MR. MUNDT: How long ago was this letter written?

MR. MATTHEWS : August 17, last year.

MR. MUNDT: Now, will you recall for the record, Mr. Masaoka. How many of these persons can you recall?

MR. MASAOKA: Now that you put it this way. Many of these people we may have met indirectly: in other words, we had our people contact them concerning their views.

MR. MUNDT: And heard them?

MR. MASAOKA: Many of these people we may have met indirect; other people may have contacted them for their views regarding somebody.

MR. MATTHEWS: You got the views of thousands of people without meeting them.

MR. MUNDT: Did you contact any of them personally?

MR. MASAOKA: Oh, yes. May I see that list again?

MR. MATTHEWS: Yes. Take Chief Justice Stone, for example.

MR. MASAOKA: Yes; I contacted him.

MR. MASAOKA: I met her.

MR. MATTHEWS: Attorney General Biddle?

MR. MASAOKA: I met him indirectly.

MR. MATTHEWS: What do you mean "Indirectly"?

MR. MASAOKA: I think other people approached him on the subject.

MR. MUNDT: You did not meet him personally?

MR. MASAOKA: No, sir. I got his views indirectly.

[Masaoka wrote Stimson a letter on Jan. 15, 1943.]

MR. MATTHEWS: Secretary Knox?

MR. MASAOKA: The same thing is true of Knox and Welles.

MR. MATTHEWS: You could have extended this list to include thousands of people, could you not?

MR. MASAOKA: Yes; in other words, being overenthusiastic.

MR. MASAOKA: Yes.

MR. MATTHEWS: Now in the next sentence you say, "They have all been very interested and helpful but wish to avoid any publicity."

Is that not a rather serious statement to make when you had not met them in the first place, to quote them directly, as wanting to avoid publicity, when there was no occasion for publicity.

MR. MASAOKA: The general problem was touchy at the time and it still is.

MR. MATTHEWS: As a matter of fact, were you not trying to impress your national organization?

MR. MASAOKA: All right.

MR. MATTHEWS: With having done things that you had not done?

MR. MASAOKA: All right; let us put it that way. I am willing to accept that.

MR. MATTHEWS: Well now, did some of these persons indicate to you that they wanted to avoid publicity, and if so, what publicity?

MR. MASAOKA: In this particular problem, when the Japanese Americans and other groups were put on the spot, it was felt that they could more effectively work if they were not too closely associated with persons of Japanese ancestry. I believe that was the thought behind unfavorable publicity.

MR. MATTHEWS: You mean some of them told you that?

MR. MASAOKA: Yes.

MR. MUNDT: At that time was Mrs. Roosevelt trying to avoid publicity? You do not have to answer that.

CIVIL RIGHTS AND THE NISEI

According to the Declaration of Independence "all men are created equal" and are "endowed by their creator with certain unalienable Rights, that among these are Life, liberty and the pursuit of happiness." According to Mike Masaoka, all rights are alienable— they can be taken away and must be reearned on demand. Waiting to be shipped overseas with the 442nd, on April 22, 1944, he writes, "To: National Board of the JACL":

> Moreover, no group of Americans ever had their liberties handed to them on a silver platter. They had to work, to sacrifice, to suffer for them. And, because of that work, that sacrifice, that suffering, citizenship means more to them today than ever before.

Is he talking about America?

They know that citizenship and liberty are not matters for the bargain counter; they are far too precious and difficult to attain.

For American-born citizens of the country where government rules "from the consent of the governed" and every individual's freedom of speech, religion, assembly, and right to trial by jury have been protected by the constitution from the beginning, Masaoka's definition of citizenship is uninformed and un-American:

Neither is citizenship and its incidental blessings a matter of right. It is a privilege. And it is a privilege which must be earned.

He's telling the JACL they need to convince the internees to use the draft to earn the privilege of citizenship. The War Department suspended the drafting of Nisei on March 30, 1942, and the Selective Service in June 17, 1942.

W. E. B. DU BOIS AND THE NAACP
and
MIKE MASARU MASAOKA AND THE JACL

"When The National Association for the Advancement of Colored People was organized it seemed to us that the subject of 'social equality' between the races was not one that we need touch officially whatever our private opinions might be. We announced clearly our object as being the political and civil rights of Negroes and this seemed to us a sufficiently clear explanation of our work."

W. E. B. Du Bois, writing in the 1920s of his work co-founding the NAACP in 1910, reminds one of Mike Masaoka in 1940. The objective distance between the speaker and what was being spoken of—that was cool. That was arrogant. That was sometimes lyrical and biblical.

"The N.A.A.C.P. years ago laid down a clear and distinct program. It's object was to make 12 million Americans:

"*Physically free from peonage.*

"*Mentally free from ignorance.*

"*Politically free from disenfranchisement.*

"*Socially free from insult.*

"Limited as this platform may seem to perfectionists, it is so far in advance of anything ever attempted before in America, that it has gained an extraordinary following. On this platform we have succeeded in uniting white and black, employers and laborers, capitalists and communists, socialists and reformers, rich and poor."

Du Bois's stately cadence brings Masaoka to mind, but the message is Masaoka's own:

> Some historians, writing from the isolation of their ivory towers, have contended the draft resisters were the real heroes of the Japanese-American story because they had the courage to stand up for a principle. These historians are wrong! The significance is in the relatively small number of dissidents in the face of gross injustice. The heroes are the men and their families who demonstrated their faith in America. (*They Call Me Moses Masaoka*, 1987)

The Japanese American Citizens League recognizes the right of the army to strip the Nisei of all civil rights. They are proxies for the army. They pretend to be the organized representative of Japanese Americans. If W. E. B. Du Bois knew of Masaoka, his organization, and the beat of his blather, what would he have said? Hadn't Masaoka read "Returning Soldiers" in a 1919 issue of the NAACP magazine, *The Crisis*? Negro soldiers went off to fight for the civil rights of whites, against white Germans in WWI, and, when they got home, did the whites thank them?

RETURNING SOLDIERS

We are returning from war! THE CRISES and tens of thousands of black men were drafted into a great struggle. For bleeding France and what she means and has meant and will mean to us and humanity and against the threat of German race arrogance, we fought gladly and to the last drop of blood: for America and her highest ideals, we fought in far off hope: for the dominant southern oligarchy entrenched in Washington, we fought in bitter resignation....

But today we return! We return from the slavery of uniform which the world's madness demanded us to don to the freedom of civil garb. We stand to look America squarely in the face and call a spade a spade. We sing: This country of ours, despite all its better souls have done and dreamed, is yet a shameful land.

It *lynches*.

It *disenfranchises* its own citizens.

It encourages *ignorance*.

It *steals* from us.

It *insults* us.

This is the country to which we Soldiers of Democracy return.... But by the God of Heaven, we are cowards and jackasses if now that the war is over, we do not marshal every ounce of our brain and brawn to fight a sterner, longer, more unbending battle against the forces of hell in our own land.

We *return*.

We *return from fighting*.

We *return fighting.*

Make way for Democracy! We saved it in France, and by the Great Jehovah, we will save it in the United States of America, or know the reason why.

FROM READER'S DIGEST

Mike went up and down the coast urging the evacuees to cooperate with the army in the evacuation even though their constitutional rights were being violated. His listeners had misgivings. And when they found themselves in wretched camps behind barbed wire, with little to keep them occupied, they blamed him personally for their plight. Some camps hung him in effigy, and one camp erected a Masaoka tombstone.

• • •

To his supporters he is known as "Messiah" Masaoka. No matter how much he protests that he cannot promise success, they scoff at him. And no wonder! (5/49)

FROM MESSIAH TO MERELY MOSES

"Perhaps we Japanese Americans have not yet earned our right to unqualified citizenship," Masaoka wrote the National Board, on April 22, 1944.

"Therefore, in order to be in a position to legitimately demand that our full citizenship rights and privileges be restored and maintained for all time to come, JACL has worked unceasingly for the reinstitution of the Selective Service ever since the War Department changed its policy and announced that Japanese Americans were not wanted for military service. That arbitrary classification of 4-C granted us was embarrassing and humiliating."

FROM *THEY CALL ME MOSES MASAOKA*

"More than half of the 33,000 Nisei who served in the war were from the mainland. 20,000 had been in detention camps. Compare that number to the 267 who refused induction, demanding restoration of their rights before they would serve their country."

And he closes with words he wishes others to say of him: "Some of my friends and some who are not my friends, also call me Moses. Moses Masaoka. They say that like the Biblical prophet, I have led my people on a long journey through the wilderness of discrimination and travail. They say that I have led them within sight of the promised land, justice for all, and social and economic equality in our native America, but that we will not reach it within my lifetime."

Nobu Kawai, The Volunteer

"I ALWAYS ADMIRED MIKE MASAOKA"

"Oh, yeah. And every once in awhile somebody would make a remark against us that we would have to ignore. But we expected that," Nobu Kawai says, recalling that life in Pasadena was not that bad. "Probably you heard that if you went into a barbershop, you didn't know whether that guy was going to cut your hair or not. Sometimes they let you just sit there and never called you.

"They would let you have a chair but they wouldn't even call you.

"You go to a restaurant and you didn't know if the waitress was going to serve you or not. Some were very direct. They hung signs out there: 'No Japs Wanted.' So you knew that you wouldn't be served." But life after Pearl Harbor wasn't that bad for the Japanese.

"It was a pretty good-sized population around here. We had a fair population. It wasn't large. But we had a good-sized population of Japanese in Pasadena."

In Pasadena, Nobu Kawai was in the JACL before the war. He takes on, as do all JACL Nisei under Masaoka's shadow, the pompous manner and language of false modesty of Lionel Barrymore, of W. C. Fields, of FDR, and of Mike Masaoka himself when talking about the JACL leader.

"Well, I always admired Mike Masaoka. He was a young fellow. But he was a very brainy person, and he had a very mature mind. Very mature outlook on everything. And I always admired Mike. And I think that he conducted himself real well. He has poise before big people. He doesn't let titles intimidate him."

Miye nods, smiles knowingly, and crochets.

"Oh, yes. I was very friendly with him. In fact he was to our home several times. And just before the outbreak of war when things were getting very critical, they often stopped by here. I was very close to Mike and George Inagaki, Fred Tayama. I associated quite closely with Larry Tajiri and Hito Okada. Mas Satow, of course, I grew up with Mas Satow.

"I always admired Mike," Nobu Kawai says again. "I know that he has been the butt of a lot of criticisms and so forth and everything like that. But I don't think he has been fully appreciated for all of his contributions to the Nisei.

"I didn't know Sab too well at that time. Saburo Kido was a lawyer and he was working behind the scenes most of the time. But I didn't know him too well. I knew George Inagaki. And let's see, some of the others who were there.

"Oh, Ken Matsumoto wasn't too active.—"

"He's a really tall guy," Miye says.

"Yeah. Bushy-haired guy. Yeah, Ken wasn't too outstanding in my mind. I don't know what contributions that he made. I know that Mike Masaoka was very strong. George Inagaki? He wasn't too outspoken, but he was a very dedicated worker. And he just did an awful lot of travelling at his own expense and everything throughout the country.

"Jimmy Sakamoto from Seattle? Well, I didn't know him too well. He was a blind fellow."

"Yeah, that's it." Miye says.

"Yeah. No, I didn't know Jim too well. I knew him through correspondences and through the *Pacific Citizen*. I was never in the, which you may call, the cabinet of the association. I was just a president of the local chapter. But I did participate in conventions. And I got to know these people through my association as a chapter member. Then, of course, at the conventions that I associated closely with all the leaders of the JACL. So I got to know them quite well.

"Larry Tajiri, of course, was an editor here before he took over the *Pacific Citizen*. And I think he did a marvelous job with the *Pacific Citizen* at the time of the war.

"In fact just before Evacuation, I was on a group that went to San Francisco to meet with Colonel Bendetsen to discuss evacuation and so forth. We asked him several questions. And I asked him, you know, 'In the event of Evacuation what we could take and so forth,' And he cut me off! He said, 'You're asking for too much.'"

Mike Masaoka writes of this meeting as a secret one with Colonel Karl Bendetsen, "three generals," and the JACL's Masaoka and Kido. The generals told Masaoka and Kido that the Army had two plans for evacuation, one with Japanese American cooperation and a second "Contingency plan," with tanks, troops with fixed bayonets, gas, and live ammunition to swoop and scoop up all the Nikkei people of Japanese ancentry on the West Coast without warning and put them behind barbed wire in twenty-four or forty-eight hours.

Years of searching by those who believe no such plan ever existed, and those determined to corroborate every word Masaoka ever uttered, have turned up no such contingency plan or orders at any level. I don't want to force Nobu Kawai to take a stand on the ultimatum Bendetsen threw at Mike Masaoka, to cooperate without protest or resistance or face murder in the streets. If Nobu Kawai heard Bendetsen or a general make such an ultimatum and describe such a threatening plan at that meeting, he might spontaneously remember.

"What was your impression of Karl Bendetsen?" I ask.

"I don't recall what it was. I had a lot of questions to ask. Of course, it's my nature to be outspoken. Sometimes I say things probably that are not too diplomatic and so forth. Whether it is a JACL convention or whatever it is, I usually try to speak my mind. Sometimes it invites—"

"He's too forward," Miye says laughing.

James Omura,
Nisei Newsman

"I PINNED 'SOLD DOWN THE RIVER'
ON THE JACL"

"When this Evacuation came along, my father had been dead long before," Jimmie Omura says. "I think that if he were alive, he would definitely not approve of the Evacuation. Because he was looking forward to a better America for us than the one he lived through. That's just what I think, you know. Knowing him, that's what I think. There are only a few Nihonjin left who knew him. I think they would say the same."

Once they are convinced that the Japanese Americans were put into concentration camps, and not wilderness resorts, the first question everyone looking for the story asks is, "Why didn't the Japanese Americans resist, get arrested, go to court, test the constitutionality of the camps in court?"

The JACL's Bill Hosokawa, a fellow journalist and senior editor of the *Denver Post,* answers the question by blaming the Issei and passive Japanese culture, a pathological victim culture embodied in the word *shigatagenai* or "it can't be helped." And the question of Japanese American resistance ends there. How can one question the JACL about Japanese America's response to the constitutional issues raised by the camps? The JACL defended Japanese American civil rights, didn't it?

The JACL spokesmen and Jimmie Omura, for all the differences they sensed between themselves, sounded very much alike before the war and the Evacuation. But they were different. The JACL said they had to prove Nisei loyalty, through Nisei obedience, Nisei sacrifice, and Nisei cooperation. Going to court was obviously antagonistic. The JACL simply avoided all constitutional issues in their efforts to make the Nisei internee and the JACL dream of a Nisei soldier acceptable to the army.

Omura said the leaders had to protect the constitutional rights of the Nisei. Of course, the JACL could have done both, cooperated with the army in the Evacuation and defended Nisei civil rights from the excesses of the army. But it chose to woo the army with the sacrifice of those rights.

Jimmie Omura recalls February 17, 1942, when Mike Masaoka testified before the Tolan Committee in the morning. Omura denounced the JACL before the committee in the afternoon. Earlier, Omura had been face-to-face with Masaoka, at a meeting of the Bay Region for Unity, in Berkeley. Nisei church group leaders, political leaders, and representatives of Nisei newspapers and magazines came to discuss a united Nisei response to talk of removing the Nikkei population off the West Coast and deal with "wartime hysteria."

Omura was interested in the Bay Area Council for Unity, as a voice for the Nisei that was not the JACL.

"The first thing that happened when I got to the meeting was Larry Tajiri asked that I be barred from participation. The JACL wanted to have me read out of the group. Isamu Noguchi was the first to support me. He said that if *Current Life* is written out, he has to be written out, too. The *Doho* representative present stated that he was in the same boat as *Current Life* because he represented a newspaper. He was followed by Lincoln Kanai. So, a vote was taken. And I was accepted as a member.

"The problem was that we have to pick a chairman. I proposed the man who originated it, Isamu Noguchi. He was a real active person. He tried to form a group in L.A. first. That went to pot. He founded the idea of an organization to start with. There were five or six people representing the Young Democrats, the so-called Red group, from Oakland. I didn't take note of them at the time. Our interest mainly was that the JACL not head it. I didn't think we were getting the proper backing from Noguchi. He wanted to become subservient to the JACL. I wasn't about to accept that.

"What they did was engineer it so that Larry Tajiri would get the vote. He was popular, so he got the vote, he's supported by the Young Democrats. One thing we never considered at the time was that there were about six representatives of the Young Democrats, and only one of us; they all voted for Larry Tajiri."

Omura and Mike Masaoka clashed over the Evacuation at this, the one and only meeting of the Bay Area Council for Unity.

"Masaoka had just returned from a trip to the Southland. Plans were being discussed for evacuation of the Isseis in military areas," Jimmie Omura says.

"Masaoka urged evacuation of all persons of Japanese ancestry, without consideration of violation of constitutional guarantees. It was the action subsequently followed by General DeWitt. Mass evacuation was not under consideration at the time, although the newspapers were whipping up support of it!

"Because Mike Masaoka didn't know the Nisei, he made a lot of boo-boos. We would hear about it.

"Then Masaoka goes down the coast and talks before some group down there in San Luis Obispo. We were told that he was making a bad impression with statements that weren't true. It wasn't helping the situation. It was hurting it. So before he came to our Unity Council meeting, I brought this matter up that Masaoka was making a lot of statements that were hurting the Nisei. Larry Tajiri represented the JACL at this meeting. And he agreed with me. He advised us that they were trying to get Masaoka back to headquarters so they could brief him. In fact, Tajiri stated that they intended to write Masaoka's speeches. But I don't know whether they ever did or not.

"Masaoka was caught up in the hysteria. You could tell by his fears. He was caught up in the hysteria.

"Masaoka: We must keep the families together.

"Omura: It is better to break up families than to violate constitutional rights of the Nisei.

"Masaoka: They shot into a farmhouse in Parlier and killed an Issei couple. There will be mass killings.

"Omura: There will probably be some killings, but I don't believe there will be mass killings. The authorities would not tolerate it.

"Masaoka: We should all get out.

"Omura: What about our constitutional rights?

"Masaoka: Who would want to stay under this condition?

"Omura: I would.

"He just looked at me. He was scared. He was practically shaking."

"He was?" Lawson Inada the poet asks, his voice rising in questioning disbelief. Was it fear or anger at being contradicted in public that had Masaoka shaking?

"But because he is scared, why should he make the rest of us scared?" Omura says. "He was personally really scared when he came to the meeting.

"Masaoka gave us several catchy slogans such as 'Greatest good for the greatest number,' 'The End justifies the means' and '100 percent cooperation for future considerations.' At some point cooperation translated into collaboration. The Niseis were betrayed.

"There was a YMCA leader named Lincoln Kanai, in fact he was so disgusted with them that he walked out of the meeting. Later when I asked him about it, in Denver, he said he didn't think the group would accomplish anything the way it was constituted. He was right.

"That's what killed the organization. Tajiri represented the JACL and the *Pacific Citizen*. The vote was overwhelming. I, like Lincoln Kanai, recognized the ball game was over. So, it is possible that Noguchi may also have thought that the die had been cast and that he might as well go along with the majority. But the moment they elected Larry Tajiri, why—dead, you know. There was never another meeting.

"It was after this meeting that I pinned the phrase 'Sold down the river' on the JACL leadership."

SEATTLE POST-INTELLIGENTSER
February 29, 1942

JAPANESE PREPARING TO QUIT WEST COAST

LOS ANGELES, FEB. 28- (AP)

Mike M. Masaoka of San Francisco, national secretary and field executive of the Japanese American Citizens' League, disclosed late today that his organization is preparing all Japanese—American and foreign-born alike—for an ultimate mass evacuation of the Pacific Coast.

Circulars have been sent to key places telling all Japanese to get ready for a movement to some inland location under government supervision and to abandon property in California, Oregon and Washington.

"We are preparing our people," said the youthful official, "to move out. We want them to go without bitterness, without rancor and with the feeling that this can be their contribution to the defense of the United States. . . .

"We want to convince them that it will be patriotic to make this sacrifice, and a sacrifice it will be."

Masaoka said the campaign was undertaken voluntarily by the Japanese American League, and was not guided by war developments "or the work of pressure groups seeking the ouster of our people."

"Why jeopardize this country or our people by trying to insist on staying, or even by pursuing our legal rights as citizens of this country to contest evacuation," Masaoka asked referring in the latter phrase to American-born Japanese.

"Naturally our people would leave instantly on orders from the army, but we hope to leave you might say, before the army sees fit to kick us out."

Masaoka said the league of 30,000 members represents more than 100,000 Japanese on the Pacific with property he estimated at one hundred million dollars.

The first group of sixty-three draft resisters from Heart Mountain face trial in Cheyenne, Wyoming.

Heart Mountain Relocation Center, Wyoming, 1943.

The Heart Mountain sentinel, Nobu Kawai, stands fifth from the left, next to Vaughan Mechau, the reports officer (or censor).

McNeil Island Federal Penitentiary, Washington.

The Emi family poses for pictures in the camp firebrake on the eve of their expected arrest. Art is at the extreme left, and Frank is at the right.

Frank Emi poses with his wife and children, well dressed before his arrest.

Nobu Kawai, The Volunteer

"I WAS PRESIDENT OF THE JACL CHAPTER"

"**W**hat were you doing around Pearl Harbor?" Lawson Inada asks.

"What was I doing?" Nobu Kawai answers.

"Yeah," Lawson nods.

"You know, it's a very funny thing. I have a very poor memory for one thing, and I can't remember where I was when I first heard Pearl–"

"Dayton," Miye his wife says, as she works yarn around knitting needles, and knits.

"What?"

"In Dayton. You, you were at work, that's right. And I was in this housing project. The word came around to the housing project that Pearl Harbor–it happened. It was a Sunday morning."

"What are you talking about? You are talking about Pearl Harbor when we were here," Kawai asks his wife.

"Oh, that's right!" she says.

"December 7, 1941," Nobu Kawai says.

"Oh, that's right! What am I thinking about?"

"It must have been when the war was over," Lawson Inada says.

"When the war was over," Miye says, springing back to the here and right now.

"Yeah. Yeah." Lawson Inada soothes.

"That's it! Yeah, Pearl Harbor we were here," Miye says. "That's right."

"Yeah," Nobu Kawai says. "I know I was working at the dairy but I don't recall now. I was evidently at home, because I was working the swing shift. I didn't go until the afternoon. Still it must have happened about noon, wasn't it? Yeah, when the news got here because of the time lapse.

"So it must have been around noon. I know it was a big shock to me. My first reaction was, well, what is going to happen to us? It was a shock to everybody. The first thing that appeared in the *Star News* was a letter asking for fair treatment of Japanese Americans by William C. Carr.

"Well I was president of the Civic Association and the JACL chapter. And so as president of the JACL, I immediately went down to call on him and to talk to him in his office. And he told me his viewpoints and everything. And that's how I got to know Bill Carr.

"Yes they bucked public sentiment to support us. My own boss, Aron Markus, at that time he had a lot of pressure brought to bear upon him to fire me. He was president of the creamery in Pasadena. But he kept me on. And when I came back from the Evacuation, he put me on.

"And so, I have a tremendous amount of respect for these people who weren't fair weather friends.

"And so when I went on to camp, I was able to ask Dr. Harvison to send us books for the library and school there. He arranged to send a lot of surplus books to Gila, Arizona, for us."

"THE JACL HAD TO TAKE LEADERSHIP"

"Well, I don't know how much you know about camp days and relocation centers. But before the war, the Japanese American Citizens League was probably the most representative organization for the Nisei. It could not represent the Issei because they were noncitizens. But when the war broke and the Issei were interned in internment, then the responsibility fell on the shoulders of the older Nisei. And I happened to be among the older Nisei.

"And the JACL had to take leadership. And now I don't think the JACL leaders have been credited with all the honors that are due them. I have a high regard for our JACL leaders at that time. I refer to people like Mike Masaoka and Saburo Kido, George Inagaki, Larry Tajiri, Hito Okada. And I worked very closely with those people because they were the leaders among the Nisei.

"And when they had this responsibility thrown on their shoulders, they had to take the place of the Issei. They had to think in terms of the future of the Nisei.

"And I have a lot of admiration for the maturity they showed in the decisions that they made and the criticisms that they have faced, and the threats to their lives and so forth. And there are a lot of people who didn't agree with the JACL in their stand on Evacuation.

"And they wanted the JACL to fight Evacuation. Well, we fought as hard as we could. But there was so much public opinion against us that it was almost a losing battle. There was no way we could prevent Evacuation. Because there was no way we would counteract all the propaganda that was thrown about by the newspaper and the columnists. If you read some of the columnists at that time and some of the hate they expressed and some of the lies they told about rumors and so forth, and the public gobbled that up. And it became actually unsafe for us to be here."

Unsafe? He feared walking the streets of Pasadena? He feared bodily harm?

"No, I don't think it was to that extent. We were uneasy. We had a lot of discrimination. We had a lot of snide remarks directed at us.

"I don't recall any outright violence. It was uneasiness and so forth. We heard violence in other areas in southern California. But so far as Pasadena proper is concerned, I don't recall anybody complaining of vandalism or outright attacks. Pasadena is a pretty well-established community.

"So, even right around here. Oh yes. There was curfew. And we felt discrimination every place we went. We had a lot of very strong people behind us that supported us. But they were at a minority and they were labeled 'Jap lovers.' They were ostracized and so forth for even speaking out in our behalf.

"Well, I was fortunate in that I had personal friends that were very influential. I had the president of the junior college, Dr. John Harvison, and the editor of the *Star-News*, Lee Merriman. And so when the war broke out, I went to see Lee Merriman. I said, 'Lee, we are sort of behind the eight ball. I would appreciate everything that you can do to give us fair treatment in your news column.'

"And he said, 'Nobe, I believe in you. I want you to write an editorial explaining your side. I'll put it on the front page of the newspaper.'

"And so I wrote this editorial and pleaded to the people to consider us as American citizens. And to treat us fairly. They published that on the front page of the newspaper. And I corresponded continuously with Lee Merriman and the other people in Pasadena who were supporting us. I don't know if you knew Jerry Voorhees or not. He was a congressman from this area.

"But his father was Charles B. Voorhees, president of the Bank of Pasadena. And I went down and had an interview with him. And I appreciate Jerry Voorhees, because his stand in our support led to his defeat in congress.

"Jerry Voorhees and his father, Charles B. Voorhees, are very strong people in this area. Dr. Milliken, president of Cal Tech. His wife, Mrs. Milliken, was a very strong supporter of our cause, too. I have any number of people.

"I have a file that big of letters I have from these people. And I hope to document that some day. Not for publication, but no, rather as a historical document so that the people in Pasadena will not forget those in our area who stuck their neck out in our behalf. You take people like William Carr, who was a real estate agent. Oh, that man was a wonderful person! Herbert Vic Nicholson. And there were some people who went so far out of their way to help us. And I'm very grateful to them because they suffered a great deal more than a lot of us suffered.

"You know, this one person, Bill Carr, he was a real estate agent in the west side of Pasadena. He had a marvelous business. And he supported us. His partner left him and he went around to all of his customers and said, 'Carr is a Jap lover. He is selling his property to Japs over here and they are going to bring down your property value.' And he went in competition to Bill Carr. It almost ruined him. Yet he stuck it out. I have all these fine letters from him. He told me about the Fair Play Committee in Pasadena. This is a different Fair Play Committee than the one in Heart Mountain. This Fair Play Committee in Pasadena really did go out. It had people like Mrs. Milliken, the officials at Pasadena City College, and a lot of very fine people in Pasadena that supported the Fair Play Committee."

THE JACL ANTI-AXIS COMMITTEE

Anti-Axis Committee Minutes,

December 8, 1941.

PURPOSE

We pledge the facilities of our entire organization and our individual services to our government in this great crisis.

We pledge our unequivocal repudiation of Japan and bend our energies to the common objective of an American victory and the defeat of the Axis powers.

OBJECTIVE

1. To cooperate with all national, state and local government agencies in their program in this emergency.

2. To coordinate the activities of all citizens and alien residents in the successful prosecution of this war.

3. To secure national unity by fair treatment of loyal Americans.

PROGRAM

1. To take charge of all press release.

2. To send mimeographed programs to all government agencies and nisei and alien resident organizations.

3. To inform and instruct nisei and resident aliens as to their course of conduct as groups and as individuals and how they may serve for the best interests of our government.

"English Translation of Japanese Translation of PROGRAM OF THE JACL ANTI-AXIS COMMITTEE, approved by Chairman Fred Tayama"

PROGRAM

To supervise all language press and news.

To distribute to government organizations and to issei and nisei organizations our mimeographed program.

By giving direction to both nisei and issei, as individuals and as groups, we endeavor to make them conform to the policies of the American government.

"Duties and Powers of Dr. T. G. Ishimaru, Anti-Axis Committee chair of the Control of the Vernacular Press Committee."

Anti-Axis Committee Minutes,
December 7, 1941.

To keep in close check on the vernacular newspapers to see that all the contents of the newspapers are entirely in accord with the spirit of national defense. The committee derives its powers from U.S. Attorney William Fleet Palmer and Postmaster Mary Briggs.

The U.S. Attorney and the Postmaster had no authority over the free press—be it American or Japanese American. And they had no authority to appoint the JACL, Junior G-Men policing the Japanese press's adherence to the "spirit of national defense."

Anti-Axis Committee Minutes,
December 8, 1941.
STATEMENT BY CHAIRMAN FRED TAYAMA

The United States is at war with the Axis. We shall do all in our power to help wipe-out vicious totalitarian enemies. Every man is either friend or foe.

We shall investigate and turn over to authorities all who by word or act consort with the enemies.

We must and will mobilize our maximum energies to facilitate America's War Program.

We must not play into enemy hands.

American must be permitted to render his services. The enemy will try to sabotage our usefulness by inciting race hysteria. Let us be vigilant.

The die is cast. We face the issue with grim determination.

America we are ready!

PASADENA STAR-NEWS
DECEMBER 10, 1941
American-Born Japanese Pledge Lives
To the Defense of the United States

(Editor's Note-Hundreds of Pasadenans know Nobu T. Kawai, a Pasadena native son. They know him because they went to school with him here. They shouted for him and his teammates when, in 1927, he played fullback on the state championship Pasadena Junior College football team. They remember him as a member of the first junior college team to play in Hawaii, and as an organizer and first president of the Order of Mast and Dagger, leading honorary club on the junior college campus. Nobu continued his studies, being graduated from the University of Missouri School of Journalism in 1930, where he also played football. He returned to Pasadena, married, has one son and holds a responsible Pasadena position. So does a brother, Harry, an old and valued employee in a Pasadena home. A second brother, Aki, enlisted in March and now is on duty with the U.S. Army tank corps. A third brother, Hiro, also a Pasadena native son, offered himself for enlistment and was rejected for faulty hearing. America has a right to be proud of this son, who today, by invitation of the Star-News, speaks to you as president of the Pasadena Chapter of the Japanese-American Citizens League. Nobu Kawai, the floor is yours.)

By NOBU KAWAI

In the calm that follows the anxiety and near hysteria which gripped the nation for several hours after the first announcement of the bombing of Hawaii, we wish to appeal to the rational thinking of the American people to correctly establish the status of the Japanese population within our borders.

Let us not lose sight of the fact that more than two-thirds of the entire Japanese population of the United States are American citizens who happen to be born of Japanese parents instead of English, French or some other nationality. Some 20,000 of these Americans of Japanese ancestry, known as Nisei, are residents of Los Angeles county.

Their parents, who have been permanent residents of the United States since the period prior to the Alien Exclusion Act of 1924, are here today because they have chosen the American way of living instead of taking advantage of the many opportunities they had of returning to their old country. They are alien Japanese who would be good American citizens had the privilege of naturalization not been denied them.

Many of these alien Japanese have been peaceful residents of the United States for more than 40 years.

Because we are at war with Japan, we need not look upon these Japanese residents as enemy aliens who would turn against the country they have adopted and learned to love. At the very moment hostile action broke the peaceful ties between Japan and the United States, the long arm of the Federal Bureau of Investigation was already picking up those aliens who have for months been listed in their files as suspicious. For the individual to attempt to do the work of the FBI is to risk doing an injustice to an innocent resident.

The Nisei are definitely in a tough spot. The have professed their loyalty to the United States and have won the confidence of federal, state and local authorities. Their problem now is to demonstrate their loyalty during this major emergency to the "man on the street," their fellow Americans.

Because they believe in the principles of democracy and fair play, they are confident that right thinking Americans will give them a fair chance. America, to them, is the only country they know. To them, it is not only a place to live, but a country they want to defend.

With hearts filled with emotion and minds stunned by the reality of war between their own country, the United States, and that of their parents, they lost no time in pledging their lives to the defense of America and the crushing of Japan and her Axis partners. Through their national organization, the Japanese American Citizens League, they have formed an Anti-Axis Committee which will co-operate with local and state defense councils and aid federal agencies in apprehending members of their community who are disloyal to America.

The Nisei's choice of America as their country has been deliberate and without reservation. They have made known their pledge and ask now that they be given opportunities to show their patriotism.

THE JAPANESE QUESTION IN THE UNITED STATES

A COMPILATION OF MEMORANDA

By LT. COM. K. D. RINGLE

6-0058

FOREWORD

The accompanying statement of views of the Japanese question in the United States was prepared by Lt. Com. K. D. Ringle on the basis of his acquaintance with the problem over a period of years. Commander Ringle's background and experience with the Japanese include the following: (a) three years' study of the Japanese language and the Japanese people as a Naval Language Student attached to the United States Embassy in Tokio from 1928 to 1931; (b) one year's duty as Assistant District Intelligence Officer, 14th Naval District (Hawaii) from July 1936 to July 1937; (c) Assistant District Intelligence Officer, 11th Naval District, in charge of Naval Intelligence matters in Los Angeles and vicinity from July 1940 to the present time. . . .

"The Japanese Question in the United States"

The Nisei

I have stated above that seventy-five percent or more of the nisei are loyal United States citizens. This opinion was formed largely through personal contact with the nisei themselves and their chief organization, the Japanese American Citizens League. It was also formed through interviews with many people in government circles, law-enforcement officers, business men, etc., who have dealt with them over a period of many years. There are several conclusive proofs of this statement which can be advanced. These are:

(a) The action taken by the Japanese American Citizens League in convention in Santa Ana, California, on January 11, 1942. This convention voted to require the following oath to be taken, signed, and notarized by every member of that organization as a prerequisite for membership for the year 1942, and for all members taken into the organization in the future:

"I _____, do solemnly swear that I will support and defend the Constitution of the United States against all enemies, foreign and domestic; that I will bear true faith and allegiance to the same; that I hereby renounce any other allegiances which I may have knowingly or unknowingly held in the past; and that I take this obligation freely without any mental reservation or purpose or evasion. So help me God."

SEATTLE TIMES
February 22, 1942

The intensive campaign which Japanese-American citizens are making to establish their loyalty to America has been carried even to the comic strips.

The following is an interchange of letters between Ham Fisher, cartoonist who draws Joe Palooka in the *Times*, and William Hosokawa, University of Washington graduate and secretary of the Seattle Japanese-American Citizens League.

Dear Mr. Fisher:

For a long time many Americans of Japanese descent of the Pacific Coast have followed the adventures of Joe Palooka in the Seattle Times.... We have seen the fine example Joe has set in the way of clean American living and unselfish patriotism, and now we feel Joe can help us with our particular problem. He would not jeopardize his popularity, and he would be continuing to act in the finest American traditions of tolerance and understanding....

Our problem is this: There are approximately 135,000 individuals of Japanese parentage in the United States. Some 80,000 are American-born and therefore American citizens. The remainder are foreign-born and ineligible to citizenship although they have resided here for two-thirds of their lifetimes.... The vast majority have proven themselves good Americans, and have gone on record as unreservedly loyal to the United States in this war.

More than 4,000 of the young Japanese Americans ... are now serving in Uncle Sam's armed forces.... They are serving their country willingly, but sometimes the general public is not so understanding of their families at home....

We believe it would be a great step toward national unity if Joe could meet one or two of these American-born Japanese in the Army so that the general public will realize that we of this group are doing our part in national defense.

Joe would find these Japanese Americans slighter of stature than other Americans. They would have straight black hair, and perhaps slightly slanting eyes. But the most outstanding thing about him would be his language, which would be as American as swing.

We do not presume to suggest this proposed Japanese character be any sort of hero [but] an intensely human character, an eager little fellow anxious to do his duty to the country of his loyalty.

Two of these American-born Japanese, you may be aware, distinguished themselves at Pearl Harbor and received mention in Secretary [of the Navy Alexander] Knox's report....

In closing, may I extend my regards to Joe, a swell fellow, and wish him the best of fortune wherever his duties may take him.

Very sincerely yours,

William Hosokawa

Ham Fisher's answer apologizes for putting words in Joe Palooka's mouth that "might have caused some loyal American citizen of Japanese descent some pangs." What those words were, the *Seattle Times* story does not reveal. Fisher goes on to say:

...I can deeply sympathise with the Nisei and I am sure that every American or most Americans feel the way I do about it. We realize they are in no way accountable for the acts of the Nazi Japanese for the horror the vicious attack made while peace negotiations were in progress and would undo it faithfully and loyally if possible....

I am so glad you didn't take Joe's remark in the wrong way and your own answer to it I wish every American could read.

Thanks again for your grand letter. With most cordial regards and hopes for victory for all men of good will against the mad oppressors.

Sincerely,

Ham Fisher

Accompanying the story of the exchange of letters between Hosokawa and Fisher is a drawing of Joe Palooka and a Nisei, both in khaki uniform. Togo, a Pfc. in the U.S. Army, stands at attention and salutes Pfc. Joe Palooka and says, "We both stand for one thing, Joe—Victory for democracy!" And Joe Palooka answers, "You said a mouthful, Togo," returning the salute. Fisher's caption reads:

A salute from Pvt. Joe Palooka to the soldiers of Japanese descent in the United States Army, loyal and faithful Americans, and another salute to the vast number of other loyal Americans, the Nisei, who are bitterly angry at the brutal, Nazified Japan as their fellow Americans are, and whose one wish is victory for America and her allies.

NATIONAL DEFENSE MIGRATION

FRIDAY, FEBRUARY 28, 1942

Testimony of James Y. Sakamoto, GENERAL CHAIRMAN

EMERGENCY DEFENSE COUNCIL, JAPANESE-AMERICAN

CITIZENS LEAGUE, AND EDITOR, JAPANESE-AMERICAN COURIER

MR. SAKAMOTO: We have an intelligence unit cooperating directly with the Federal Bureau of Investigation.... I know definitely that our organization, both locally and nationally, has, let us say, "turned in" people whom we thought should be checked into.

"FOR BETTER AMERICANS IN A GREATER AMERICA"

JAPANESE AMERICAN CITIZENS LEAGUE OF OGDEN

Ogden, Utah

March 23, 1942

Brigadier General Lewis

Hdq, West Defense Area

Ogden, Utah

Dear General Lewis:

The Japanese residents of Ogden City and Weber County find it imperative to submit the following objections to the influx of Japanese evacuees from the restricted coastal areas:

1-This is the Central Defense Area.

2-Problems of housing, lack of available farming areas, and all other means of livelihood are acute.

3-The influx of new Japanese inhabitants would be a hazard to those already established here.

Weber County and Ogden Japanese of First and Second generation have established a reputation through industry and good behavior in appreciation of the privileges given them to contribute to the general welfare of the community. It appears exceedingly unwise to disturb and disrupt this status, for the most important reason the strangers from other localities might be undesirable in adjustment to these settled conditions.

We, therefore, emphatically and sincerely oppose the entrance and settlement of these people, at the same time express our regrets that the war situation compels our position in this emergency.

Very truly yours
/s/ Jiro Tsukamoto
Jiro Tsukamoto,
President, Pro. Tem.

MEMBER; INTERMOUNTAIN DISTRICT COUNCIL,
JAPANESE-AMERICAN CITIZENS LEAGUE

George Townsend,
Project Director

"I WAS BORN AND RAISED IN THE TOWN WHERE JOHN DILLINGER ENDED UP"

George Townsend was born February 8, 1903, the Year of the Water Rabbit.

"I have had a very interesting career," George Townsend says. "I wouldn't trade it for anything in this world. I moved into many different jobs at the request of somebody else, because I guess I have the talent for getting things done. Therefore I never lost a day's work in my life. I always had something to do. I was born and raised in this little town of Mooresville, Indiana. That is the town where John Dillinger ended up. He and his family. His mother is dead, but he had an older sister who was acting as the mother of the household. He was sixteen when he moved from Indianapolis to this town of Mooresville. He and this older fellow got into trouble down there. I knew him only vaguely because he came here my senior year in high school, and I went away to college. But my brother who is in business there, and my sister, of course knew him very well. Actually when he was first paroled, my wife's dad, who is a dentist in this town . . . that's another story.

"Anyway, I went to Earlham College, Richmond, Indiana, for three years. I decided to get into YMCA work. After three years at Earlham, I went to

Chicago YMCA College, which was professional school for YMCA secretaries. I was in YMCA work for twelve years.

"I started in Burlington, Iowa. Then back to Chicago where I graduated from the University of Chicago. Then I became program secretary of the downtown branch in Pittsburgh. This is June 1930. In '32, the depths of the Depression, I was loaned by the Y to set up a program for homeless men there in Pittsburgh. At that time there were thousands of men, single unattached men, just roaming the country looking for work. It became a real burden on our social agencies because they had no money. There was panhandling, crime, and living in shacks that they constructed themselves. These were just ordinary fellows, carpenters, operators of heavy equipment, just anybody. We had some professional people, dentists, architects, and engineers. I was supposed to go back to the Y after nine months after I got that program started. In the meantime the federal government got the program set up on a national basis. They prevailed on me to go down to Harrisburg, the state capital. They had that program for the state. That's when I left YMCA work and got into social work, administration. We had twenty thousand of these homeless men under care in Pennsylvania at that time.

"From that I went into personnel director for the National Youth Administration.

"Then the war broke out. I was driving. It was a Sunday afternoon. I had the family out. We were in Eastern Pennsylvania when we heard it over the radio.

"I suppose I'm biased with the kind of background I have against war. I wish to see that we could be smart enough not to go out and kill one another. I mean, it is just so stupid to have another war. I suppose most people had a terrific feeling for those 'Damn Japanese.' Of course, I condemned them for what they did at Pearl Harbor. It was a dastardly thing. But dammit, I knew some of the background, too. I knew that we were refusing to sell them scrap iron. We had done a lot of things against the Japanese government. I thought, 'My God! Here we go again!'

"I knew I was too old at that time that I didn't have to fight to stay out, like a lot of other people who had the same feelings that I did. I was just completely floored by this. There were a lot of tears when we heard the thing as we drove back.

"My son Lemond graduated from high school at the age of sixteen. He had a year of college. Now he faces being drafted. He did not feel as strongly as I did about this thing. I did not try to influence him. There's no point. I was at the point that I would go to jail rather than go. He wasn't. He was drafted and went into the Marines. He served two years until he gets a discharge because of over height. He was six foot five. One day he saw a bulletin board, everybody over six foot four can get a discharge.

"I GOT A CALL FROM THE WAR RELOCATION AUTHORITY"

"Monday morning, first Monday in May 1942 I think. I got a telephone call from the War Relocation Authority in Washington, asking me if I would come to Washington. They wanted to talk with me. Come immediately, like tomorrow morning. I said, 'Okay, I guess, I'll come down.'

"I thought what they wanted to talk to me about was a matter of care because we had built ten camps for projects, each of them about 250 men. Two of them were to go to the emergency airfields up in the mountains. Another was cleaning up streams for fish, that kind of thing. They were rather remote areas for the most part. At least we got these fellows off the road. They got good food and clothing. It was a temporary sort of thing until the economic situation improved.

"Anyway these two fellows started to talk to me. After a few minutes I stopped them by saying, 'It appears the way this conversation is going that you are recruiting personnel.'

"They said, 'Yes.'

"I said, 'Well, just save your time and mind. I want you to know that I'm violently opposed to this whole thing. I think it's unconstitutional. It's undemocratic. It's against everything I hold important in my own life.'

"They smiled and said, 'Yes, we assumed that would be your attitude. And that's why you're here.'

"They pulled out a folder and began to read some of the things I had done. I had been active in the Peace Movement. I've been active in racial matters and so on. They knew all about me. They gave me the reasons why I ought to be in this program during the war. That I could probably make a greater contribution. Number one, I was too old for the draft. I knew as far as I was concerned, I wouldn't be drafted. But I had registered as a conscientious objector.

"So these men said to me after a discussion of about one hour and a half, 'We'd like for you to go out to lunch. Think this thing over, and we want you to meet Colonel Wood [who was the liaison officer between the War Department and the War Relocation Authority] at one.'

"I don't know how much you know about the Society of Friends or Quakers, but traditionally, they have been a peace organization, believing that there were alternatives to war. To demonstrate that, many times they have reconstruction programs on both sides—refusing to take sides. The Russians, the Germans, and the French after the First World War. Herbert Hoover was a Quaker and head of the big relief program. In the Spanish Civil War they served on both sides. In Vietnam the same thing. They were greatly criticized because they were doing relief work where Vietnamese were supposed to be our enemies. This corresponds to what I'm going to tell you next. It will have more meaning to you. This Colonel Wood had an office over away from the military. I frankly do not remember the building, but it certainly was not the Pentagon. It was nowhere near the military. He was the liaison.

"I knew something about Milton Eisenhower, too. You know his brother Ike? He was of a different breed, too. I think at that time he was the president of the University of Kansas. He was an educator.

"I walked into this Colonel Wood's office. He was a man about my build, but ramrod straight. He was a cavalry officer. He'd sit up behind his desk briskly and put up his hand. These were his first words to me. He says, 'I understand you are a Quaker.' With those words coming from an army officer, I wondered what was coming next. I said, 'Yes sir.'

"He said, 'I have great admiration for the Quakers. Don't agree with everything.' He said, 'I was in Tokyo in 1923 at the time of the earthquake.' He said, 'I observed very closely the work of the Society of Friends. Quakers. You've been asked here because you are a Quaker.'

"It was very interesting. He went on to say, 'The army has an interest in this thing, getting the kind of personnel that will treat these people fairly. We don't want anybody in there with racial prejudices. I don't mind telling you the army point of view. It is a selfish motive on our part. There ought to be three neutral powers that will be going around these camps and inspecting them, then making a report to the Imperial Japanese government.' I think it was Sweden, Spain, and Switzerland. 'Anyway, we would hope that the report that these representatives make to the Imperial Japanese government will have some effect on the way the Japanese treat our prisoners of war.'"

"Did that strike you funny?"

"Of course it did. Very very at first. But after all that's the army. They were going after their own interest, you see. He was being very honest with me. It was always very interesting to me that the army said we are interested in sending personnel in there because it might have some effect on our prisoners of war.

"Well, that's all right, as long as they turn it over to a civilian agency who will do the job. Whether that was to influence me in making a decision, it might have been, I don't know. I got the feeling from the very beginning that, by golly, maybe this is some way to help out humanity. I began to see that maybe this is the place for me.

"He wanted me to leave immediately, that afternoon. They could get a special airflight. He said, 'The first group are being moved to the assembly center. I want you there by next week.'

"I said, 'I've been working terrifically hard on a classification survey. I couldn't possibly think of that. I'd have to talk to my boss.'

"He said, 'This is a war situation. Of course he would have to release you. Who is your boss?'

"I said, 'Judge Sutton, who is the commissioner who stayed in Pennsylvania.'

"He gave Judge Sutton a spiel on the thing. He said, 'We have to fast move on this thing. We have George Townsend down here and we ask you to release him immediately.'

"Judge Sutton said, 'If that's what he wants to do, sure, we'll make out without him.'

"So then he turned to me, and I said, 'I haven't talked with my wife.'

"He said, 'Go in that room right there and be private.' I had a long talk with my wife, and I had two kids at the time in junior high school. She said, 'Well, if that is what you think you ought to do, of course.'

"So I went back and said, 'Okay.'

"He asked me if I could leave tomorrow. I said, 'Impossible.' I said, 'Furthermore, I don't want to fly out. I'm tired and old.'

"So he went out, got on the telephone, came back, and said, 'Okay, if you take such and such a train on Pennsylvania Railroad for Chicago on Friday night, you transfer to a train for San Francisco. It will get you there by Monday morning.' So I packed up real quick. That was on a Tuesday. So on Friday I left.

"I got to Oakland early in the morning, 7 or 8 o'clock. I had a trunk. I left it there and took the ferry over to San Francisco. I reported in at the Whitcomb Hotel, which was the regional office, downtown, eleven hundred something Market. It was a second-class hotel. The WRA had taken over suites and rooms for the regional offices.

"I introduced myself. The receptionist said, 'Sure glad to see you. Where is your baggage?'

"I said, 'I left it over in Oakland.'

"She said, 'Oh, that's fine. You are scheduled to take the Cascade Limited tonight at 5:00. And you'll be met tomorrow morning at Klamath Falls, Oregon. They'll take you down to Tule Lake, about thirty miles away. Because the first group from Portland or Seattle are landing there tomorrow morning and we want you there. Then we'll talk to you later about your assignments. But we want you to be there and help out any way you can. You report to Mr. Terrell.' Terrell was a high school principal from somewhere in the Bay Area. He was head of that camp at the time.

"So I got off into a blizzard. This was in May in Klamath Falls, Oregon, with a straw hat from Pennsylvania. I was going to sunny California and didn't expect anything like this. I arrived there about ten or fifteen minutes before that train arrived. Terrell said, 'Get in one of those cars lined up there and follow the rest of them.'

"The camp was located just off the state highway. This was down in Godforsaken country. What they did: State troopers were there, and they blocked off that road when the train came in. Here the bottom steps were this high off the ground. I was cold anyway. I was sitting there in this car and I noticed the Military Police get off with guns over their shoulders. They started helping these people . . . having to literally lift them, every one, from these high steps, to down on the ground. Then the people walked over to the road where we were and got into the cars. When I saw that happening, tears came to my eyes. I sat there and just bawled. It was cold, and they were cold like the rest of us. My immediate reaction was, God, what is this country coming to?"

Until this moment in Tule Lake, he had had little contact with Japanese or Japanese Americans. "I had a roommate in college for one semester. He was from Japan. He couldn't speak English, and I couldn't speak Japanese. But we got along beautifully.

"Then I had had a Japanese American kid about thirteen our fourteen who hung around the Y an awful lot. He was the only Japanese in Burlington, Iowa, when I was in YMCA work. When he went to Knox College I kept in correspondence with him. He wrote me and talked to me about his job and his future. He goes back to Japan to visit his grandparents. He gets over there and he's in the consular service way up in China at the time of war. He had dual citizenship, you see. Toshi Yamamoto. He was taken prisoner by the Russians. Then he repatriated to Japan after the war, and served with MacArthur there as an interpreter and other things after the war. Then he came to the United States as a member of the staff of the Japanese government at the peace treaty held in San Francisco. Then later he comes, gets a job with the United Nations, in New York. Now, I pick him up again. He and his family visit us out in St. Paul. They visited us here. We went to their home lots of times. We correspond regularly. He's now retired from the United Nations and living in Tokyo. Those were the only two Japanese that I had anything to do with.

"When I sat there at Tule Lake, and those people were getting off of that train—this is one of the most moving things that ever happened to me. I felt like I wanted to crawl on the ground. God! To think of putting American soldiers and bringing people in here to a thing like that. I traced my ancestors back to my great-great-great-grandfather in North Carolina in 1730. William Townsend. [There was no 'D' on it at that time. The 'D' was added later.] I found the original will, and also the will of his son. There was a packet the archives gave us. Here they were, nineteen male Negroes with flesh marks and so and so. Cows with them in the room together. Sure, I know we had slavery in this country, but when I saw that damn thing. Then the horrible treatment of Indians in this country . . . picked up whole tribes and made them walk hundreds of miles. Gee, you don't see that in our history books.

"Now the MPs were wonderful. They were very kind. They were well instructed. They were doing everything they could to help, which was encouraging.

"The evacuees themselves were in a remarkable frame of mind. Whether they felt differently than they acted I don't know. They were smiling, and they were taking it.

"I wouldn't have taken it. I couldn't have. We used to remark a great deal, if we had a group of Italians to deal with instead of Japanese, it would have just been hell. But the Japanese cooperated. There were about twenty cars. And I had about five or six passengers. I took them over to the reception place in the barracks. There was heat in those barracks because they still had to get their baggage. Then you go back and get another load.

"That afternoon, after I got the people in, I'm freezing to death. I got to have some clothing. So I went back to Klamath Falls that afternoon. I bought some wool underwear, wool this, wool that.

"Now they did have state trucks there. There was a crew among the evacuees that they assembled, young couples for the most part, who drove the trucks. They pitched in. They unloaded the baggage and brought it in. People selected their baggage, and we soon learned after the first day how to handle it more efficiently and everything.

"What we did was string rope across the ends of the barracks building here and at the other end. In between that vacant space we unloaded all the baggage. While we were doing that I heard a conversation between two young women. Around twenty.

"They were talking about what a horrible place this is. They were singing the blues. They were by themselves. I just stepped up to them in a kidding way. I was just trying to lift their spirits really. A little sarcastically I said, 'You don't like this place?'

"They said, 'No we don't.'

"I said, 'What's so bad about it?' I knew they could take this kiddingly.

"They said, 'Oh, there is not a tree in sight!' They went on and on, 'What a horrible place! And these Japs!' To me that was a terribly interesting remark.

"I knew 'Japs' was a derogatory term like 'nigger.' I said, 'My God, this is strange.' So I said to them, 'Oh, you're not Japanese?'

"One girl looked at the other and said, 'I suppose we are, but we've never been around Japanese before.'

"That's when I said, 'Where are you from?'

"They said, 'Redmond, Washington. Have you ever been there?'

"I said, 'No, I've never been to the State of Washington.'

"They were the only Japanese family in Redmond, Washington. I asked one girl what she did there.

"She said, 'I was the secretary to the superintendent of Weyerhauser Lumber Company.' The other girl clerked in a store there in town. They were sisters. And

I found out they had been active in the church there. They dated Caucasian boys. They were so out of place. They didn't ever think they could ever stand it there. I read an awful lot into that.

"Here these people were physiologically Japanese, socially they were not. They came out. They came out of a different culture. They became so Americanized or Caucasianized that these were a bunch of foreigners.

"I said, 'Here we have a problem on our hands right now.' I said, 'How would you like to keep up your stenographic skills and work here?'

"She said, 'Do you suppose I could?'

"I said, 'I think you can. Here's my card. You meet me at such and such a building tomorrow morning at 9:00.'

"In the meantime I talked to the personnel man. I said, 'Here's a couple of gals who should really be put to work.'

"So he did.

"I can't speak for the others because I was only at Tule Lake and at Mindoka. Tule Lake started out all right, but then . . .'"

JAPANESE AMERICAN COURIER

"FOR TRUTH, JUSTICE & TOLERANCE!"

Volume XV, No. 745   Seattle, Wash., April 24, 1942   Five Cents a Copy

JAPANESE U.S. COAST PRESS ENDS
AS THE COURIER BIDS FAREWELL

All Japanese operated newspapers on the American Pacific Coast have ceased publication this week-end. The Japanese American Courier being the last to suspend with this issue.

THE PACIFIC CITIZEN

Official Publication of the

Japanese American Citizens League

Thursday, November 12, 1942

FROM THE FRYING PAN

By BILL HOSOKAWA

The Other Side

We have been reading and hearing at some length of the unkindly and in some cases downright mean treatment given some of those who left relocation centers to help with the sugar beet harvest. Such actions have no defense. In fact it's a matter of cutting off one's nose to spite one's face because next season there aren't going to be any workers for places that mistreated their help this year.

Here is another story that deserves mention because it is at the extreme of good treatment. A group of boys went out to work on a farm with the intention of roughing it and didn't bother to take along sheets. When the farmer's wife discovered this, she took some sheets out of her own linen closet and loaned them to the boys, and then proceeded to do the laundry for them each week.

And the story goes further. The boys dined royally off the farmer's own table every day, and enjoyed bed-time snacks of cakes and cookies from the housewife's oven.

When the harvest was finished the farmer and his whole family piled into truck with the boys and drove down to the project together with them bringing gifts for the boys' families.

This, we hasten to reiterate, is an extreme example and such fine relations probably are impossible without the accidental meeting of ideal circumstances. Yet, it shows what is possible.

The moral of this story is, perhaps, that while a great deal depends on the attitude of the employer and the natives of a district, much also depends on the personality of the evacuee employee.

There is such a thing as abuse of temporary liberty. It makes a great difference whether a man runs for town and the beer tavern when he has finished a day's work or whether he retires early to rest up for tomorrow's labors. It makes a difference in reception and acceptance whether a man speaks good English or talks in Japanese to his fellows, whether he is boisterous or quiet, whether he is cooperative or sullen.

This business of acceptance and assimilation is not entirely a one-sided affair. Often in the past there has been a passive accept-me-if-you-want attitude. The Nisei must come to realize that now as never before the old adage about hewing one's own destiny is true.

We may be wards of the government temporarily, but how soon we may strike out again for ourselves as free and independent Americans depends to a great measure on our own efforts. If this lesson can be brought home to the 100,000 behind barbed wire, then the bitter experience of an unfortunate few in the beetfields will have been worth while.

Gordon Hirabayashi,
On Civil Disobedience

"I COULD TAKE A STAND"

"**W**e had some vigilante groups come looking for Filipinos," Gordon Hirabayashi says. "I was a kid then. I heard them. I was scared. We hid our two Filipino people. They heard about it and they asked Dad. They were trusting of their employers like Dad. They were like the early Issei. They were young, all in their twenties. They were great patrons of taxi dance groups in Seattle. Because they were all singles.

"They use the Latin 'Papa-san.' Everyone was 'papa' and 'mama.' They lived in the house just behind our house. Dad took them to the community barn. We had a co-op bar with crates and so on. He said he stuck them back there and put a lot of crates in front. And he bent down.

"He said, 'Before I could put the crates up, you could hear them snoring away. Gee, they're carefree.'"

"The vigilantes didn't come in there looking for the Filipinos. But we didn't have any vigilantes looking for us.

"We had the Remember Pearl Harbor League and things like that. Ben Smith, the dairy guy right in our area, was the leader. But we didn't have vigilantes coming in as far as I know." Gordon Hirabayashi pauses and asks his brother, "Did they have some in L.A.? Because I was in Seattle then."

"It was just Mr. Boddy. Remember him?" James Hirabayashi says, talking in the brotherly shorthand only Jim and Gordon understand completely.

"Talking about race prejudice, and about the 'White Gentiles Only' rule that fraternities had, I used to debate with them. So, I was used to encounters of that type without feeling personal guilt. And I'm one of the team of the independent, nonfraternity group. I'm not debating like the Japanese are debating. I'm with the independent student group, Eagleson Hall at the University Y.

"We were the center of the independents versus Greek Row. And other times I guess, Eagleson Hall was accused of being the center of Reds and things like that. It was a place minorities could come and have a platform. I learned I could be a minority but that didn't mean I had to keep my mouth shut. I could take a stand. And others were standing with me, so I didn't feel that this was a stand only a minority could take.

"If I'd been in the Japanese Students Club half a block a way, I would have less of a chance to gain this feeling. I was not the only Nihonjin in the program, but I was the only one living there. There were others. Kenji Okuda, he was valedictorian at Franklin High, a debate specialist. He was president of Oberlin College after the war."

"Student body president," Jim says, deadpan and slow.

"Yeah." Gordon says, "He got out," in the same tone of voice.

"Civic citizen," Jim says, completing the iron molecule.

"Yeah," Gordon says. "You know he was accepted at Oberlin. He's six feet. And he was articulate. Slim, tall guy, articulate. During the war, at Oberlin, which is fairly international and liberal, he became the center of expression of Gethsamanae. He became president of the student body."

"He's now teaching at Simon Fraser," Jim says.

"Yeah," Gordon says. "He's an economist. You know when I came back from the university on one of my leaves, there was this debate on conscription. And I was chopping down the president.

"And Roosevelt was making a speech. And then, we listened to Senator Borah of Idaho. He was a critic of the president, especially on conscription. I was talking to Dad about conscription, and said, 'Listen to that! Boy!'

"Dad's kind of laughing. I think he was finding it interesting. God, here this guy was doing the same thing I was doing."

Gordon Hirabayashi tells the story of becoming the first case to challenge the constitutionality of the military Exclusion Order banning the entry of citizens of Japanese ancestry from areas within the city open to whites and his violating the military curfew order that applied only to people of Japanese ancestry. He tells the story deadpan. His family is evacuated to a concentration camp, and Gordon awaits trial in the Federal Tank, in Seattle. People from the American Friends Service Committee form a committee to press his case in court. And romance, in the form of two women, seeks him out.

"Well, Eleanor Ring was a fellow student in YWCA and I was in the YMCA. And we had a lot of joint work together. And our offices were in the same building. And she was a pacifist. We belonged to the Fellowship of Reconciliation. Her parents were also. They were supporters of my [defense] committee. I used to date her for the university events for a couple of years. Yeah. I used to date her, but it wasn't like we were going steady.

"I used to wonder what she would have said if I had the nerve to ask her, if we could have been married. Her mother had visited my parents after I was in jail and came to the railroad station to see them off to Pinedale. And then came out to Tule Lake once to visit. And they would also send my parents items in camp and at Weiser, Idaho.

"People from outside . . . Seattle, Portland, Tacoma . . . they seemed to go to Minidoka. But the valley people who went to the railroad station were taken to Pinedale. That's near Fresno. Hotter than Hell! This is '42. They had quick camps built. I don't know what Pinedale is like normally. What is there? Nothing?" Gordon Hirabayashi laughs.

He continues, "They said they had asphalt base and the cots would go just right down through it! They said Mom suffered so much from the heat. My brothers tell me she'd wet newspapers and take the mattress off and put them on top of the bed and get under the bed to get a little bit of cooling.

"Then they moved to Tule Lake from there. They were there a couple of months.

"Mom wrote me that, shortly after they moved to Tule Lake, there were two women who came looking for her and saying they are from California somewhere, and they had walked all the way over to meet her and to say, 'Thank you for what your son is doing.'

"Eleanor's mother used to send packages of things like a dress or something. Eleanor would come visit me in jail periodically because I didn't ask her to come. Esther Schmoe used to come weekly. She used to come weekly and started to take over on all my needs and so on." Esther Schmoe was the daughter of Floyd Schmoe. Schmoe and the American Friends had taken up Gordon Hirabayashi's cause.

"In retrospect, that was a courtship. I had a feeling when I got married to Esther. She came on strong and sort of usurped Eleanor after I was in jail."

THE TANK

He was in the Seattle tank so long, he became its senior resident. "The maximum was forty in our tank, and periodically, we would hit the maximum. But we always had over thirty. The tank is a wing that sticks out, and there's a hallway all around it with barred windows. And this tank here is divided into halves. One half is what they call the 'day tank' or 'bullpen,' with a steel table and bench in the center.

"And then, there is a visit slot with windows. That's it. Simple stuff. Then, the other half is divided into five, and there is a wall separating. So there are five units this way and five units to this hall with bunks on each wall. So, there's four bunks in each cell. And there are five facing this way, twenty, and five facing this way is twenty. So, it's forty. And 6 P.M. to 6 A.M., we're in there. And at 6 A.M., the door opens, and we're supposed to move into the day pen. And we are in the bullpen for twelve hours. Each tank has a 'mayor.' It's purely internal, nothing to do with the outside."

THE MAYOR AND THE SERGEANT

"You know they said, 'The Mayor and the Sergeant.' Whenever a guy is sent in like when I'm sent in, a sergeant comes out and says, 'I'm sergeant here, and that's the mayor. We have this system. You're charged with breaking and entering. How much money do you have?' Whatever he has he turns it over. And they keep it. The mayor keeps it. And the sergeant gets some of it. And that's it. And the mayor runs the tank and he assigns the inmates to their cells. And if there's any internal decision, he makes it. It's a dictatorship, and it's done for his benefit. He takes everything. It's not one where you have long-term people there. They're shifting in and out. So, that works.

"We're in there. When the mayor left they said to me, 'Well, you're the most appropriate one to be mayor.'

"I said, 'No. There is a kangaroo court here anyway. I don't go for that. So, I don't want to have any part of it.'

"'Yeah, but you're the one who has been here the longest, and you're the most appropriate one.' Several of the inmates were saying this. We gathered around one part of the tank there. When I argued, they said, 'Well put in what you like. Do it the way you like.'

"I said, 'Oh, no. You wouldn't like what I'm going to do.'

"They said, 'How do you know? Whatever it is, we'll support you.'

"I said, 'Well, let me tell you what, because you're not going to like it.'

"I said, 'There are guys that come in here, you know this is during the war, so there's lots of transients who come in and haven't any friends. Lot of them don't have any money. They can't even contact people and don't know who to contact. So, if I'm mayor, I would change it into some kind of welfare service. And I would set up a fund. If guys coming in, if they could afford it, they could chip in two bucks. We'll have stamp money and a little bit of emergency money we could use for that. We'll send out for aide. We have Traveler's Aid and Goodwill. We had some contacts. I know of some. And say this guy is leaving and he doesn't have anything. He needs clothing and this and that. I do have that kind of contact. I'd send a letter out for somebody.'

"'Well,' they said. 'We'll support that. Whatever you want, we'll support it.' But that time I said the only way I was going to get this going is if everybody supports me strongly. I made them egg me on a lot after I knew they would support me, and after I decided I would do it. I made them egg me on a lot!

"Then I said, 'I'll do it.'"

MOM AND DAD IN JAIL

"I was mayor at the time dad came in. He was with me in jail about ten days. I was in county jail five months before my parents came in October.

"See, my trial came about five days after he arrived. Then, he was taken home about five days after. He was in good health at that time. While he was in Seattle, Jim left with the first contingent out of Tule Lake, sugar beet call for workers. Well, I think that, like every parent, every chance they get they'll think of the part they could be proud of. I think that, on the whole, there was real overwhelming pride in what I had done. Along the way, there were disagreements that I should do this or that. In total, I think their conclusion was very positive.

"Dad didn't understand the whole reason why he was there. He came as a government witness. I could figure out why they were going to put him on the stand. I know the only reason they would bring him was to ask him if he was a Japanese national and if he was my father. And I expected both Mom and Dad to be on the witness stand to prove I was of Japanese ancestry. But they only put Dad on. When Dad was standing there in the hallway when I was talking to the night sergeant, he made not a peep. He did not ask why. He explained quietly what's going on in camp and so on, as far as he knows. But in the course of our stay, I would be explaining what I was doing. He could see most of it, day-by-day things. So, conversation wasn't all that full, you might say.

"If it was Mom and I was talking to her, I would have to explain more things to the point of exasperation. She begins probing and arguing and so on. Dad would accept and make his own assessment and not necessarily probe. Yeah, with him, I was talking English mixed with Nihongo. Well, gee, we were there twenty-four hours. So, there are times when we are walking around. Other things happen such as writing letters, visitors coming in on certain days, and so on. There were times we had meetings. You know, like council meetings of the tank there.

"I had been in King County jail five or six months. For about the last three months, I was the mayor. I was, by the time dad came, trying to step down. I was tired of all that haggling and responsibility. We had a meeting. At one meeting I said, 'Hey, I want to step down. I want somebody else to do it.'

"'No, there's nobody else who can do it,' they say and that sort of thing. And Dad's listening in, and he says to me later, 'Gee, if they feel that way, how come you want to step down? Why don't you stand?'

"Both parents told me not to talk half-baked when my position was half-baked. 'Think it out and don't make a fool of yourself.' 'It's stupid to say that. What the hell, it's just stupid,' and so on, 'Talk when you have something sensible to say,' and so on. I got a lot of that. Dad always made friends because he wasn't the antagonistic type. There are always people in prison who are attracted to quiet ones rather than the ones who are boisterous. So he had his contacts there. He spoke English. I mean he could talk with the rest of them. He was hesitant about making speeches in English and so on. He was . . ."

"He was low-keyed or something," Jim, the younger, says. "It was just during high school when the evacuation order came. I was sophomore at the time. By the time that I was coming into high school age, I knew Gordon more as the brother ahead of me. He was a jock, kind of smoothie. I knew his reputation more than I knew him. Gordon was off to college, so we didn't really get to know each other until, I think, the strike period at San Francisco State in the sixties. He came visiting and stayed.

"Before Gordon's trial, we contracted for work in Idaho. Then afterwards, my father came back from the trial and came out and joined the group to work sugar beets. Father and I stayed out together."

"According to a letter Mom wrote to Mrs. Ring, Eleanor gave us a copy of it, Mom said while they were gone [they were gone about ten days in Seattle away from the camp] things developed. Did you have discussions with the family about you going to Idaho?" Gordon, the elder, asks.

"I don't remember anything," Jim says.

"Anyway you were gone with the group."

"Yeah, before my father came back."

"So Dad came back," Gordon says. "The next day there was a bus going, and while he wanted to rest up a bit from the trip, he was worried about Jim out there alone, so he took the next bus the next day, and he was gone. That's what she was writing. She said he left right away."

James Omura,
Nisei Newsman

"TOKIE SLOCUM WAS ROUGH AND GRUFF"

"Tokie Slocum. He was rough and gruff and talked like a miner. And he doesn't give any quarter. He tells you what he thinks of you. If he considers you a friend, you would know it right off the bat.

"Do you know he is somewhat like Jimmy Sakamoto? They are both rough and gruff in the way they talk. About the only difference, I would say, is that Sakamoto was not inclined to use the term 'Japs,' but Slocum used it constantly. He threw it down the hakujins' throat, even in his testimonies before congressional committees.

"He doesn't say he's not a 'Jap.' He says I am a 'Jap.' Throw it right at 'em so it makes them hesitant to use the terminology. He does it to them every time. He shames them into not calling him a 'Jap.' I don't like the use of that word."

Tokie Slocum, Togo Tanaka, Sam Minami, Fred Tayama, and Joseph Shinoda of the JACL appear before the Tolan Committee under another name, giving the impression that the JACL's opinions of other Japanese groups is universal among "patriotic" Japanese Americans.

"THE TOLAN COMMITTEE"

NATIONAL DEFENSE MIGRATION
SATURDAY, MARCH 7, 1942
MORNING SESSION

House of Representatives
Select Committee Investigating
National Defense Migration,
Washington, D.C.

Mr. Arnold. The United Citizens Federation.

Now, will each of you give your full name for the reporter?

TESTIMONY OF TOKIE SLOCUM, TOGO TANAKA, SAM MINAMI, FRED TAYAMA, AND JOSEPH SHINODA, MEMBERS OF THE UNITED CITIZENS FEDERATION

MR. SLOCUM: My name is Tokie Slocum.

MR. TANAKA: Mine is Togo Tanaka.

MR. TAYAMA: My name is Fred Tayama.

MR. SHINODA: Joseph Shinoda.

MR. BENDER: For the information of the audience, there must be no demonstrations of any kind and there must be a courteous and respectful hearing accorded every witness or the hearing room will be cleared.

MR. ARNOLD: I shall address these questions to Mr. Tanaka and he can have any one of the panel answer that he sees fit.

What is your occupation and the occupation of those appearing with you, Mr. Tanaka?

MR. TANAKA: I am editor of the *Los Angeles Japanese Daily News*.

MR. ARNOLD: In what representative capacity are the others appearing?

MR. TANAKA: Mr. Slocum is a member of the Veterans of Foreign Wars, and on the Board of the United Citizens Federation. He is also a member of the American Legion, having served overseas.

Mr. Tayama is chairman of the Southern District Japanese-American Citizens League and an insurance man by profession.

And Mr. Shinoda appears here as a representative of the United Citizens Federation. He is in the floriculture business as head of the San Lorenzo Nursery Co. of California.

MR. ARNOLD: Have your usual social contacts with the Caucasian citizens been disrupted because of the war? Have there been the same contacts with the white race as you had before?

MR. SLOCUM: No. In that instance, I would like to say that in some cases, anyone who is politically minded seems to have dropped us, whereas, those who are truly Christian or right-down good folks have been more sympathetic than ever before, and they have gone out of their way to try to understand our situation.

VETERAN OF LAST WAR

Now, permit me to say, sir, that I happen to be a veteran, having had three immediate relatives in the last war, one of whom got killed and is buried in England. The other one got his eye knocked out at Viny Ridge and is a disabled veteran, and I am, myself, a disabled veteran. I have four relatives in this war; three in the Canadian Army and one in Fort Snelling, Minn. Consequently, I am glad to hear Joe Shinoda's side being presented to you.

The side that I present to you is one of a veteran's viewpoint. I served as sergeant major in the Three Hundred and Twenty-Eight Infantry in the same regiment with Sergeant York, of Tennessee; I am department chairman of a naturalization and citizenship commission for the Veterans of Foreign Wars of California, which may seem very funny to you, but that's where they put me. I am a member of the department of public relations committee for the American Legion, and I am chairman for the anti-Axis committee which is the only war cabinet ever existing in Little Tokio, so to speak.

Such being the case, my view is one of "militantly winning the war policy." As this gentleman of Congress stated a little while ago, this is wartime, so any price we pay is not high enough for us to win the war. That has been the policy of the anti-Axis committee. I do not mean to be disrespectful to Mr. Hood of the F.B.I., but I want to say this: That practically every member of my committee of the anti-Axis committee of the Japanese-American Citizens League of the Southern District Council has cooperated to the best of his ability at his own expense, time, and energy, by exposing what they term to be "subversive activity" here in our part of California. We really have.

COOPERATION WITH FEDERAL AUTHORITIES

Not only that, but if you will kindly investigate you will find that the anti-Axis committee has also cooperated faithfully, sincerely, and diligently with the United States Naval Intelligence and the United States Army Intelligence. In many instances when we were called upon to do so, we cooperated with the police and sheriff, and district attorney.

You take Lieutenant Commander Ringle, you take Lieutenant Commander Stanley, we have never gotten better treatment. My God, if it weren't for their guidance and inspiration in the dark days, I don't know what we would have done. They have been our counselors; they have been our advisers. My goodness, they have done everything for us.

APPRECIATES CITIZENSHIP

Now, if I may go on a little more, sir. I happen to be born in Japan. Consequently, my citizenship was given to me by a special act of Congress. As you remember back in 1935, there was a bill called "Nye-Lee bill." I may have met some of you gentlemen. I know I called on everybody. By golly, I was a Jap. Yes, sir; we got that bill through and I benefited, Koreans, Chinese, and Japanese, a bunch of them, about 1,000 of them benefited. Consequently, having fought for the country and then having to fight again for my citizenship, I appreciate the meaning of citizenship. Everybody admits that. The most militant organization in California, the Veterans of Foreign Wars, made me their state chairman, which, by golly, I'm doing a good job, too. Check up on it.

And let me tell you, sir, if evacuation is what you want, evacuation is what you're going to get, and I'll lead them, by golly. Let me tell you, sir, no one appreciates the spiritual value of citizenship more than I do, because I can prove to you, I fought for it. Look it up in the Congressional Record. See about Tokie Slocum.

MR. BENDER: Will the gentleman comment, if he cares to, regarding this: When Mayor Bowron testified before the committee yesterday he indicated, in substance, the thought "Beware of Greeks bearing gifts." You heard that statement.

MR. SLOCUM: I wasn't here, to be frank with you.

MR. BENDER: I am reading from his testimony, for your enlightenment. I would like to have your comments regarding the statement of Mayor Bowron.

As I look back on some events after the 7th of December, I am quite convinced that there was a large number of the Japanese population here locally who knew what was coming. They were setting themselves, adjusting the scene for the out-break of war between this country and Japan. I think that they somewhat over-played their hand.

Now what do you say, briefly, regarding that particular observation where the mayor said in his statement, "I think that they somewhat overplayed their hand"?

EXPOSED SUBVERSIVE GROUP

MR. SLOCUM: Well, I would like to answer that this way: I believe Mayor Bowron is right to this extent: I believe that there existed in our midst before December 7, nefarious and vicious elements known as the Central Japanese Association. I believe so.

I also think that the Japanese Association itself is a very undesirable element. However, please bear this in mind: That is the element that I fought. And it gave me great satisfaction on the night when the war was declared and I was summoned by the Naval Intelligence and the F.B.I., to go over the top with them, lead them to their lair, to arrest their leaders. It is so. It is so, sir, that there did exist such influence in our midst against which I really did fight tooth and toenail, and by golly they don't like me. I don't care. They are in a concentration zone now. It is on.

MR. BENDER: All along the Pacific coast, there has been testimony offered that there has not been a disposition on the part of the Japanese aliens, or the American citizens of Japanese origin, to inform the authorities of disloyalty and that there have been more than one or two rotten apples in the barrel, but the information regarding rotten apples in the barrel has not been readily made available to the authorities.

MR. SLOCUM: If I may reply to that, sir.

As chairman of the Anti-Axis Committee, I can speak with some authority on that.

This is what I have said: "Get these rotten apples out of here; if you don't, the whole basket is going to suffer."

Now, that kind we certainly wouldn't tolerate, and we report that right back to the gentlemen of the F.B.I like Mr. McCormick, in whom we have much trust. I hope Mr. Hood doesn't mind my using these names, Mr. Brown, and Mr. Finley, and other gentlemen. We try to be fair. We realize that this is the most that we can do. That is the most immediate service that we can render America in time of crisis now.

Therefore, that is the reason we have been doing it. Really, lots of the people haven't been credited for what they have done and Mr. Hood really does not know the true picture of it because he is so big, he is so way up. He doesn't see the things that are happening in the Japanese section maybe. Honest, we have been working; yes, sir.

RAFU SHIMPO

March 22, 1942

WHAT'S THE USE?

"What's the use!"

You've heard that expression, time and time again. Perhaps you've even said it yourself.

It's a common expression today, now that things are beginning to look dark for the nisei.

We are fortunate to be born in the United States. Our parents came to this country, seeking a new place where they could start a community as they pleased, just like the Pilgrims who left homes in Europe for strange lands, seeking freedom of religion, freedom of speech and freedom of livelihood.

We were born in this land of the free. Some of us have grown to manhood and womanhood enjoying the privileges of American citizens as we rightly have as native born sons and daughters.

Now that right is about to be taken away from us. The "nisei are not loyal" some of them cry as they try to take away our American citizenship. "Born a Japanese, always a Japanese" others cry as they point suspicious fingers at us, throwing us into the same class as enemy aliens.

For the first time we are confronted with the question: If we are rightly American citizens, why can't we be treated as such? Why should all of us suffer for the crime of the few, if any?

What are we going to tell our children? How can we explain to them why we cannot stand up for our rights as American citizens? How can we convince them that this is a democratic country, the melting pot of the world, a country comprised of all peoples of the world?

As nisei, are we going to be trampled down without a fight? George Washington and his tired men met many hardships in the cold winter nights but won in the end. Why shouldn't nisei fight for our rights, even if it is a losing battle? At least we nisei can say that we lost but only after a hard battle.

—Louise Suski

James Omura, Nisei Newsman

"VOLUNTARY EVACUATION"

"Right after E.O. 9066 had been announced, and before the people of Japanese ancestry were moved out of California, I was trying to obtain a legal counsel to sue the government for reparations, and we were communicating with Colladay, Colladay and Wallace in Washington, D.C., a big law firm. My understanding was that Colladay, Colladay and Wallace were one of the leading constitutional law firms. They indicated to me that they were willing to take up the Nisei cause if we were able to foot the bill.

"They asked for $2,500 retainer and $1,000 backup and expense money. I tried to get the evacuees interested in supporting it but failed. Tokie Slocum was in there. Our difficulty was that the evacuees were scared or something. They didn't want to do anything. When you start talking money, everyone falls away. And without money, we wouldn't do anything. So finally we had to drop it.

"And here, 1982, there is no suit yet.

"I was also investigating other things such as student relocation and releases of those persons frozen following the ending of voluntary evacuation. I asked for the release of those who had prospects and job offers."

FROM PUBLISHER TO EMPLOYMENT AGENT

"Well, the Evacuee Placement Bureau was wished upon us. We had hoped to resume publication of *Current Life* in Denver. That is why we set up the office in advance. When I arrived I had an office already set up. The first week, I was visited by four different FBI men, on four successive days. They showed me their badges. I remembered only the last one. Carpenter.

"Then there was a Japanese jeweler whom everybody said was Inu coming in all the time. He must never take care of business. I had an office just between him and uptown, so he obviously goes up to police or FBI, and on his way back he'd come in and chat.

"He was Issei, married to a hakujin. He was a resident. But then this jeweler—his wife's brother was on the police force, so we knew he was all over town, you knew what he was doing. And then we had this police trainer, Matsuyama, San Francisco Police, judo, stuff like that. He used to drop in on me every day. See, I was being watched every minute.

"Then because it was an office, a lot of the evacuees began coming to it. They didn't have any jobs. They'd go up to the employment office and get turned down. The employment office did very little for the Japanese in the early years. In fact, there was a Nisei who worked in there. I was drawing compensation at the time. We got to talking, and he told me that he hadn't seen a single Japanese sent out on a job prospect. That's how it was! And this is run by the federal government and not by the state during the war years.

"So the Nihonjins would check the advertising in the newspapers and go out on even a dishwashing job, busboy job. At that time, a lot of places were against hiring Japanese. The *Denver Post* was really stirring things up, and it made it through on the Japanese. So, they kept coming around to the office I had established. We developed a liaison with the governor's office. We met a hakujin who had some connections. They sent referrals to us, and we proceeded to place the evacuees.

"Eventually we went to advertising. In addition, some friendly patrolmen brought in job offers. We got jobs for the guys. So, we actually fell into placement.

"There are a lot of things the JACL accused me of. This stuff Kido said about *Current Life* money from subscriptions and advertising, that's where it went. Besides my own money. That's where it all went. The JACL stated that I who oppose the JACL was living on the misfortune of the Nisei. That's because I was operating the Evacuee Placement Bureau in Denver. That is quite an accusation, for we charged no fee. It cost us. The maximum amount that was donated from those we helped obtain jobs I think was less than thirty-six dollars. We didn't keep track of but only two groups—one an Issei person and the other three girls I brought out of Amache—gave anything. I put up everything.

"In order to operate the Placement Bureau, we had to engage in landscape service or gardening work. And believe it or not, many places wouldn't take Japanese. It was hard working jobs even at the cheap rates offered. It was schoolboy wages. There were no Japanese gardeners. If you got a contract, it was tough to lose one.

"Nobody ever came up to me to say, 'You're a dirty so and so,' or anything of that sort. Or criticized me. And that's the bad part of it all. I don't know which way they are because they would come up and talk with me and act like human beings. But the point is, what's going on behind you?

"I hired a Nihonjin from the Brighton area, and he came to work for me. About two o'clock, I left him at the final job and told him to complete the job himself, while I go downtown on business.

"When I came back at four o'clock, he wasn't there and I noticed that no work had been done. The lady of the house called me in. She used to make dinner for me whenever I was working late in the area. So, I went inside. Her lawn hadn't been cut, and I was supposed to cut her lawn.

"I asked her, 'What happened to my helper?' Well, she told me he had told her he wouldn't work for me. He told her that he wasn't going to work for 'a guy like Omura.' He is telling this to my customer. I wasn't aware that he had that kind of feeling when he hired on. He wouldn't tell it to me, but he would go and tell my customer. And then he disappears.

"He worked about five or six hours. But he didn't wait for his pay. He never came back again. That left a sour taste, telling that to my customer. It was toward the end of the season. The following year, we lost that account.

"A WRA official came from Washington, D.C., to see me and to suggest that I get out of the employment business. You know, the WRA asked me to get the hell out of the employment business?" Jimmie Omura says slowly, angry and amazed.

"And the funny thing about that is that I was doing a very good job of placement. I was bringing people out of the relocation center without a single incident. I don't know who was behind it, because at that time I said little about the WRA and I was cooperating with them. I was hollering about the JACL. Very few people would come out against the JACL. Anybody would be a damned fool to come out against an organization, because you would be dead, right there. You would have to be slightly tetched. I had to be. I had to be slightly tetched, one of these don't-give-a-damn sort of guys. If you care for yourself, you're not going to say these things. Because they are going to hit you hard.

"I was doing it for the principle. My wife said, 'Why fight for the principle? Why fight for Nisei rights? Because they don't care.'

"Well she was right! Bingo! Here comes the WRA! Get out! And turn all my files over to them, they said."

JAPANESE AMERICAN COURIER

February 27, 1942

CAN PROTECT THEIR RIGHTS

A report from New York this week stated that the president of a certain organization had protested as "unprecedented and unfounded on no specific evidence of good" President Roosevelt's executive order establishing military areas from which citizens or aliens may be removed.

It was further said that this official had instructed the offices of his organization in San Francisco and Los Angeles "to assist in protecting the civil rights of Japanese American citizens."

There are two conclusions to be reached from a reading of the news dispatch.

One is that the President of the United States had issued an unjust order. Japanese people of all classes repudiate any such suggestion as reflecting on the honor of the President. They concede that the Chief Executive is better informed than they are.

Another inference to be drawn from the news dispatch is that the Americans of Japanese ancestry need the assistance of the organization in question to protect their civil rights. This also is rejected. Americans of Japanese ancestry on the West Coast are fully informed as to their rights under the law, and capable of presenting them to those in authority. Further, these young Americans still have full confidence in the courts. They have always had justice, and believe this will be extended to them, despite the troubled conditions that now prevail.

The young Americans and their parents are thankful for any sympathy and courtesy extended to them in this hour of trial. When such is offered it will be gratefully received.

However, when it comes to a matter of protecting their civil rights before constituted authorities, they will be the judges of those from whom such assistance will be accepted.

These people wish to keep themselves clear from any entangling alliances, to chart their own course, and make their own record, which they hope to build in such a matter that when the dark days are over people can only wonder that their Americanism would have been doubted.

CIVIL LIBERTIES GROUP TO CONTEST REMOVAL OF JAPS

NEW YORK, March 4.—(AP) —The American Civil Liberties Union today asked its California branches to try to obtain modification of an order to evacuate all Japanese, United States citizens or aliens, from the Western Coast.

The area was designated yesterday as a military zone.

The union said in a statement that the order was "far too sweeping to meet any proved need" and should be modified to give hearings for citizens before evacuation.

If military necessity made modification impossible, the union added, then martial law applying to all citizens should be declared.

Shosuke Sasaki, Japanese American Conscience

FROM HIS DIARY

EVACUATION

The evacuation of the Seattle area was carried out over a period of several days. And I was among those who comprised the first large group to be removed from Seattle. We were ordered to appear at Eighth Avenue and Lane Street, on the morning of April 30th, to board buses which were scheduled to leave at 8:30 A.M. for Puyallup. For five years prior to that date, I operated an apartment house on Jackson Street between Twenty-fourth and Twenty-fifth Avenues. In leaving for the Puyallup prison camp, we were allowed to bring only what we could carry.

THURSDAY, APRIL 30, 1942

Today it rained ceaselessly from morning to night. I woke at 5:30 A.M., dressed, started the building furnace for the last time, and had hardly finished breakfast when Mr. Yamada, an Issei family friend, came at 7:30. Nobe Takaike, a Nisei family friend (who is now a professor at Stanford) arrived soon after. And the three of us loaded the baggage of my mother and me on Mr. Yamada's car. We left the apartment at 8 A.M. And as I closed the door to the apartment office, I quietly spoke a word of thanks to the apartment building, which for five years had been my home. It had seen me finish college, had witnessed the preparations for the marriage of my sister, and had enabled me to save up a little money in the bank for such a rainy day as this.

When we got to Eighth and Lane, which was Seattle's red-light district of that day, both sides of the street were lined with baggage and around them stood the Japanese waiting for the order to get into the buses.

My sister was standing beside her family's baggage with her two children. One was a baby of four months, and the other a child not quite three. It was raining, but since my sister assumed that the buses for Puyallup would depart on time, she had brought no umbrella and was vainly struggling to shield her children from the drizzle. Suddenly the door of the house adjacent to where my sister was standing, opened. And to my sister's great and unexpected surprise, she and her children were invited by the madam into the madam's parlor for protection from the rain. To this day, my sister and her family revere the memory of that poor woman who demonstrated by that act of compassion a level of kindness, unequaled by any other woman of Seattle.

It was not until almost 11 A.M. that the caravan of buses and trucks finally started out. We stopped at Beacon Avenue and Columbian Way to pick up people from Beacon Hill. Quite a number of people, since they had been waiting in the rain for about three hours, needed access to a rest room. An Associated (Flying A) gasoline station on the corner was the nearest comfort station, but to the dismay of the Japanese, the gas station attendants had locked the doors to the toilets and refused to allow the Japanese to use them. Fortunately, there was a Maxwell service station, across the street, which was good enough to not lock its toilet doors and allowed us free access. I swore to myself that in the future, I would see to it that none of my close friends or relatives ever used a drop of Associated gas if they could possibly avoid it.

In the bus, I sat beside my sister's father-in-law. He does not talk much, from habit. And since I do not feel like talking, we both watched in silence, the landscape pass by. The grass was lush and green on the roadside and field. Here and there: apple trees with pink buds and blossoms dot the countryside. Only a year ago, a friend and I had passed over this same road in search of scenes of pastoral beauty to photograph. Today I pass many lettuce fields lying fallow for want of Japanese farmers to cultivate them. Soon they will be covered with weeds.

On reflecting on this waste of land and manpower, for some reason conveniently ascribed to "military necessity," I could not help but laugh bitterly at the stupidity of man and his callous disregard of justice, productivity, and even self-interest, for the mere sake of catering to an unreasoning mass hatred directed at an innocent people.

In the seat behind me, there sat a Nisei Communist sympathizer. For reasons best known to himself, he has changed from a sharp critic of the American government into a person almost indistinguishable from some of the Nisei super patriots.

As we came within view of the concentration camp and saw the fenceposts around it, I said, "Barbed wire, I'll bet."

"I don't think so," said he. He was wrong.

We got off the busses and were herded into the gate. And the first thing to impress everyone was the quantity of mud on the main "street" of the camp. This section, known as Area "A" was formerly a parking lot for the fair. I am glad I wore boots. Those who did not got their shoes full of mud in short order.

This apartment or room in which I write this is about seventeen feet by twenty feet, with more than adequate ventilation through the cracks and knotholes, and is separated from adjacent apartments by wood partitions, which are only seven feet high and do not reach the ceiling. The wood-burning sheet iron stove in the center of our apartment has no damper on the stovepipe. Most the heat goes up the stovepipe, keeping the fire going is a real job. In the next apartment is a young couple with two children, who keep crying almost incessantly, either singly or in duet. I was told that one of the children is mentally retarded. She has a peculiar cry, like some woman sobbing in rage. The sound is becoming increasingly difficult to endure.

The toilet facilities here dirty. For lunch and dinner, we had canned tuna, beans, and potatoes. The cots, for sleeping, have real mattresses. The one surprise I did not expect to see here.

FRIDAY, MAY 1, 1942

It is still raining. The main street is almost impassable without boots. Several hundred new arrivals today.

SATURDAY, MAY 2, 1942

Today the rain has stopped. And in the blue sky float big white clouds. Last night, the next door children cried almost continuously. It is unfortunate that the partitions between apartments do not go all the way to the ceiling. I feel sorry for the father of those children. He took them outdoors in the middle of the night to look for a doctor to quiet them. I am getting tired of the food. Nothing but wieners, canned salmon, beans, potatoes, and bread. No fresh vegetables, butter, or milk, except for children.

Built a table from scrap lumber with my brother-in-law.

I had prepared with a little more care than some of the other people for one thing. I didn't think the sleeping accommodations would be good, so I had brought brand new sleeping bags. One for my mother. One for me. I figured that I would not have access to hot water for shaving in the morning, so I bought myself an electric razor, which came in very handy.

And we had been told to bring our own plates, so in order to keep the weight down, I had bought two sets of plastic plates, which we really didn't have to bring. We really didn't have to use them, because when we got into camp we found they had brought in army plates and so forth to use in the dining halls.

I guess the thing we missed most there were fresh vegetables. I remember, I thought that might be the case, so I had packed two or three packages of radish seeds in my baggage. And as soon as we got there. . . . Well, first they told us what the apartments we were in, we might be shifted later. So we waited till the shifting was finished. And as soon as that was completed, my mother, who had a green thumb all her life, immediately got busy and planted those radish seeds outside our so-called apartment. In the course of about a month or so, they came up. And I had also brought along a half a pint bottle of soy sauce, which we couldn't get at all in camp. I remember when these radishes finally got large enough to eat, we went to the dining hall. And by that time I think we were getting some rice. So, instead of going down to eat there, we brought these plastic plates along and had them put the food on the plastic plates. And we brought them back to the room and my mother cleaned the radishes, washed them, and we got the soy sauce out and put it on the radishes, you know. And I don't think any vegetable has ever tasted better in my life.

Shosuke Sasaki, Japanese American Conscience

PLOT AGAINST SAKAMOTO'S LIFE

"Within a month after we got into Camp Harmony, people started to be shifted from Camp Harmony to other camps. These notices of being sent to other camps would often be brought—these people would often be told at nine o'clock in the morning to pack up your things, you're going to be shipped to camp so-and-so, in California, or wherever. They were given no reason. Nothing. This occurred to two or three of the Seattle community lawyers, including Kenji Ito and Tom Masuda. And it happened to a few other people too.

"The only reason that I could imagine for those people being sent to other camps was that these people were regarded as having some influence in the community, occupying positions of leadership. They were apparently being shifted to other camps where they would not have a following.

"I couldn't understand the reason for shifting them out in the first place. None of these people, to me, looked like troublemakers or rabble-rousers, in any sense of the word, but they did have certain prominence in the Japanese community. The Nisei were being stripped of leadership. The Issei had already been taken. Right after Pearl Harbor, the FBI rounded most of these people up, and sent them to Department of Justice camps."

There were twenty-six small camps for the Japanese, in Alaska, Arizona, California, Colorado, Hawaii, Idaho, Louisiana, Maryland, Massachusetts, Montana,

New Mexico, New York, North Carolina, North Dakota, Oklahoma, Tennessee, Texas, Utah, and Wisconsin.

An Issei group hatched a plot to take the life of the JACL's James Sakamoto. One thing was lacking in their plot.

They needed an Issei man who spoke fluent English. English to stand up to the ear of any white authority, to explain their act, as revenge, similar to the revenge against the self-importance of Kira, an instructor in court ceremonials, who demanded bribes from his noble students.

One nobleman, Lord Asano, failed to pay his bribe and received no instruction, and was humiliated. He draws his sword on Kira and so angers the Shogun that he orders Asano to commit immediate ritual suicide, *seppuku*. The Shogun breaks up Asano's estate and retainers. Forty-six of Asano's samurai stay loyal, plot against Kira, and eventually take their revenge. The Shogun orders them to commit suicide, as their act was also an act against the rule of the Shogun.

The Issei plotters chose Shosuke Sasaki because he was Issei, spoke English, and had an impeccable reputation that echoed his father's impeccable reputation.

They assured Shosuke Sasaki that he would not get any blood on his hands. He would not know how, when, or where, till after the deed was done. When the deed was done, they would come to him, and he would explain their act to the authorities.

"I knew Sakamoto from before the war. I thought he was a pretty decent sort of fellow. I rather liked him personally. And I think he sort of personally thought well of me. My name used to appear in his paper when I was going to school because I was usually making the honor rolls," but, "the desire to get rid of Sakamoto's influence, to me, was perfectly understandable. Had the situation been totally hopeless, and the length we'd be in those camps seemingly endless, I might have given him a more affirmative answer.

"But I knew we were being moved in a few months, so I suggested we delay until we get to the next camp, and we try to approach the administrators there. And if after those attempts, Sakamoto still continues to wield his influence, then I would agree with their plan."

The people from Seattle and Portland were moved into Minidoka, a camp in southern Idaho, miles from any town, that held ten thousand people. The first week at Minidoka, Sasaki and the Issei noticed that every morning, Sakamoto walked to the administration building. Shosuke Sasaki and a number of Issei met with the administration and complained about Sakamoto. The next day they watched. Sakamoto walked to the administration building and immediately was seen walking away. The next day there was no walk to the building. And the next day, and the next. The walks were over. The plot against James Sakamoto fizzled away.

MANZANAR FREE PRESS
EDITORIAL
INDEPENDENCE DAY 1942

Fourth of July this year will have poignant meaning and value for an America gripped in a death struggle for the very principles affirmed in the Declaration of Independence.

For American citizens of Japanese ancestry herded into camps and guarded by the bayoneted sentries of their own country, it will be a doubly strange and bewildering day. For they remember, too well, the carefree Fourth of last year, when they stood along Broadway to cheer the nisei soldiers who marched shoulder to shoulder with American soldiers of all races.

• • •

It is too late to argue on the injustice of this gigantic upheaval that finds us today in Manzanar. Our leaders had repeatedly reiterated our willingness to evacuate our homes should it ever be considered a military necessity. Now we are here.

• • •

We, nisei, have temporarily put our individual freedoms on ice so that national morale might remain sound, and the fight for world democracy might continue unfettered. Of all diverse American groups, we are in the best position to appreciate the blessings of liberty.

THE PACIFIC CITIZEN
Official Publication of the
Japanese American Citizens League
Thursday, July 23, 1942

FROM THE FRYING PAN

By BILL HOSOKAWA

Our fight is the Fight of America

Our fight is the fight of America, and America's fight can never end. We have given up certain rights temporarily. That does not mean we will sit by while others try to deny them to us forever, merely because of the accident of race.

At the same time we must remember that those rights were inherited as the birthright of all Americans. So far we have done very little to demonstrate that we deserve them.

True the circumstances make it difficult to demonstrate in any spectacular manner the loyalty and love of country that motivates us. I will have to be in little, unobtrusive ways, the difficult way. And as in all other things the harder the task the more satisfying the solution.

Admittedly these sound like platitudes. They are without meaning unless accompanied by a spiritual factor. Most of us Nisei have lived shallow lives. We have not undergone deep spiritual experiences, not necessarily religious. Most of us are in the process of learning for the first time that there are other things in the world beyond the confines of the wall that we have erected in our cliquish communities.

Part of that experience is in learning the meaning of freedom and actually going through the experience of paying its price. Most of us, fortunately, are likely to come out of this wiser, with greater depth of character and better prepared to go through a difficult post-war life.

NISEI USA

By LARRY TAJIRI

Japtown was always on the wrong side of the tracks.

In Los Angeles it was called Little Tokyo, a collection of cafes, drug stores, noodle joints, department stores, barber shops and a store with live eels swimming in a tank in the window. It once had three daily newspapers, each with its page or two of English type for the nisei. Before Roosevelt and 3.2, it had its bootleggers and its speakeasies. Before Mayor Bowron and reform drove the underworld further underground, it had its gambling hall and its bookies. The *Daily Racing Form* was available at the magazine stand alongside the Boston culture of the *Atlantic Monthly*. And in those days when jobs were scarce the boys from Hawaii would stand on the street corners with their guitars and sing soft island songs. Little Tokyo had its share of love and laughter, births and deaths. It was Middletown with an Oriental accent.

We remember Little Tokyo best the day of the earthquake in '33 when panic hit Los Angeles and the 28-story city hall did a hula. The window of the store with the eels was shattered and the eels went slithering down the walk into the gutter. Most of the people of Little Tokyo gathered in the big parking lot back of the Tomio building and waited for doomsday. We rushed back to the news plant and put out an extra. Looking back now, we wonder why. The earthquake was hardly news to the people of Los Angeles and of Little Tokyo but it seemed the thing to do. Later, past midnight we climbed into a jalopy and went down to Terminal Island where the fishermen lived. That was the other time Terminal Island was evacuated. The fishing village was deserted, except for a few sturdy nisei guards warming themselves over a fire. There had been rumors of a tidal wave and the pole had evacuated to the heights of the Dominguez Hills. We came back in the dawn past soldiers on guard in the debris-cluttered streets of Long Beach and through the fallen store-fronts of Compton. A lot of people had been killed that day and the story had an angle for the vernacular press because several Japanese had been among the dead.

Everything revolved around First and San Pedro streets in those days. Little Tokyo had its share of excitement. The publisher was shot one night by a pair of would-be assassins and for a while we worked behind steel-plates on the windows. They used to change the lock on the door every week, and we were always getting confused about the keys. On New Year's eve, the night of the big flood, somebody tore down the back door of the plant and set fire to the press. The reasons for all this were immersed in Japtown politics. The nisei never cared enough to figure it all out. The world of the issei was an alien world, clouded by the intricacies of the Japanese language.

Little Tokyo was home, Little Tokyo meant America to a lot of nisei but it was just a curiosity to the tourists. . . . Little Tokyo was a place to work and a place to sleep to most nisei. Sometimes it was a place to have fun and a place to eat chow mein or "nabeyaki-udon," which are noodles cooked in an earthenware dish with mushrooms, chicken and green onions.

In a few months the people of Little Tokyo will be scattered via wartime urgency to the deserts of Arizona, the bottomlands of the Mississippi or the ranchlands of the Arkansas valley. Little Tokyo today is a ghost town with only the signs of the three Chinese cafes to give it light at night. The Miyako hotel is now the Civic and the "America We Are Ready" sign of the JACL's anti-axis committee hangs wanly now over an empty storefront. The mice and the rats in the aging buildings must be having slim pickings.

All the Japtowns are ghost towns now—on the wrong side of the tracks.

Ike Matsumoto,
Fair Play Committee

"**T**hem days you're not supposed to have no lights at night. We didn't really live in no house. We had the cleaners in front. And we lived in the back of the cleaners in some rooms back there. Chinese owned that building. We lived under a chop suey place. We been there since 1923. I was nineteen years old.

"My friends went to Manzanar. Well, I said, shoot, I'll stay one more day, and be the last one out. Have Little Tokyo to myself. Then the next day they say we're going to Pomona!

"My parents went to Pomona on the bus.

"I bought a 1926 Chrysler. We had a caravan. A bunch of us fellas met in our cars, and we all drove to Pomona. Soon as we were into camp they impounded it. They give us a little piece of paper and we never saw our cars again. I think there were about a hundred of them. Six months later, I get $25, for the car, from the government.

"I went to Heart Mountain on the first train. Seventy-five of us. Old train. It started to smoke. They thought it was on fire. They stopped the thing and looked all around it. It was just old.

"They justa taken the southern route, 'cuz we went by the Salton Sea, the Great Salt Lake, we stopped in Denver, and a lot of us never been to Denver! You know. Stuff like that. I'm a nineteen-year-old kid, and all I know is the cement of San Pedro Street. Gee, that's Denver.

"Outside of Las Vegas the train stopped one day. A flash flood washed out the tracks. There we were stopped in the middle of the desert. We didn't see no guards the whole trip. They had to be on the train, but I didn't see any."

He caught his first sight of his new concentration camp home from the train. "Barracks. MPs. The train stopped right there. Nobody there. Nothing moving. Three P.M.

"We were lucky. We got mattresses. The guys that came later had to fill bags with straw. They had a pile of straw. They give 'em this bag and tell 'em go fill it, for their mattress. They handed out pea coats.

"I worked in the mess hall. Get it ready, you know. Wipe off the tables. They had oil-fired stoves. The stoves were already there. The cooks went with us. Actually I was just a mess boy. Each block had two mess halls.

"I quit the mess hall and went to work for the fire department. I liked the fire department because they work one day and get two days off or something like that. And the mess hall was $8 a month, and the fire department pays $10 a month.

"Man, those Washington guys! They played pinochle. Everybody plays stud poker. I learned how to play cards in the fire department. Never played cards before. They say, 'How 'bout playing some cards? You can't be a fireman unless you know how to play some cards.'

"'What're you playing?'

"'Stud poker!' they say. And they did. But those guys from Washington, all they want to play is pinochle."

BASEBALL IN CAMP

Ike Matsumoto, Los Angeles city boy, met the San Jose boys playing baseball in Heart Mountain. "The San Jose guys had their own team. The San Jose Zebras. And the San Gabriel guys had their own team from before, the Valley Sportsmen, they called themselves. And they were pretty good.

"Heart Mountain had a pretty good high school football team. Undefeated. They played other high school teams from outside. Every weekend a different team. Never defeated once."

Yosh Kuromiya,
Fair Play Committee

"When we got to Heart Mountain, none of us knew we were going to be prisoners of war, heroes or resisters or whatever. All we knew was we were all called 'persons of Japanese ancestry' and we all from the West Coast. And all of us were profoundly affected by our new surroundings—and the sight of the mountain.

"I did sketches of the mountain itself. It was my way of relating to my environment and accepting it as my home. I thought it was a thing of beauty. Maybe it was the only sanity that I was experiencing at the time. There was something permanent about it, and something that was all-knowing, and like it had been there a long time and we were just passing through, and in time it would all blow over."

HEART MOUNTAIN SENTINEL
October 24, 1942

Heart Mountain Relocation Project is in Park County, about midway between Cody and Powell, not distant from world famed Yellowstone Park. The project takes in roughly 46,000 acres, of which 27,000 are considered irrigable. The elevation of this part of the country is around 4,600 feet above sea level. The temperature ranges from approximately 100 degrees maximum to 35 degrees below zero. Rainfall is from 6 to 8 inches per year. Principal crops to be raised are alfalfa, small grains, sugar beets, beans, potatoes, and sweetpeas.

Truck crops have not been raised in this vicinity on a commercial scale, but experience indicates that they are well-adapted to this area.

Heart Mountain Center is directed by C. E. Rackford, for many years with the U.S. Forest Service. A great measure of self-government will be practiced and the Caucasian staff will serve primarily in an advisory capacity.

MINIDOKA IRRIGATOR
Internee newspaper of Minidoka Relocation Center, Hunt, Idaho
November 25, 1942

Editorial-
"NISEI, YOUR MOVE NEXT"
Min Yasui faces the prospect of a year's confinement in a "road camp," of paying a 5,000 fine for having failed to win his test case, as he termed it, in Federal District Court last week.

The sentence by Judge James A. Fee has terminated the first phase of Yasui's case which began last spring when he deliberately violated curfew laws, taking it upon himself to test the validity of what Senator Robert Taft termed, "The sloppiest criminal law I have ever seen or read anywhere." Senator Taft doubted its constitutionality.

Yasui also doubted its constitutionality and his doubt was subsequently proven justified with Judge Fee's ruling that without declaration of martial law, the military has no power to regulate the life and conduct of the ordinary American citizen.

We feel with Min when he writes that he is not in a position to "carry the fight further because of my personal citizenship status."

It is perhaps too much to expect Min to carry on when his right to American citizenship is challenged.

Is it too much for us to carry on where Min cannot? Is it too much for the JACL, the national JACL, upon which Min has pinned his hopes to clarify his case's wide implications, to actively see it through? His appeal should not remain unheeded.

Nor should the Citizens' League be burdened with sole responsibility. What of the mass of us who have never closed that gap between ourselves and the JACL, who have stood at arm's length and criticized the organization?

Min's appeal to the JACL is an appeal to all nisei.

MANZANAR FREE PRESS
November 26, 1942

"THANKS GIVING 1942."

We have long dreaded this editorial as well as the one we wrote for the Fourth of July, and the one we must write on December 7. It is easy enough to sit back smugly and scribble a few pretty platitudes.

But whatever we say, be it an expression of solace in the many things for which we can still be thankful, or cynical bitterness in the mockery of the word "thanksgiving" will not assuage the poignant desolation that assails the heart as all file into the mess hall for the slab of Thanksgiving turkey.

Lest the public think us "ungrateful," let us remind them that it is not the overloaded table we miss, but the warm coziness of home. Man is so quick to adapt himself that he soon accustoms himself to a new mode of life. But when the holiday season draws near, the nostalgia for the old remembered things again tugs at the heart strings.

Shhh! It's a Military Secret
(ALAN COURTNEY-EARL ALLVINE-WALTER BISHOP)
GLENN MILLER and His Orchestra;
MARION HUTTON, TEX BENEKE, and THE MODERNAIRS

Shhhhhhh!
Shhhhhhh!
Take a tip. Button up your li-i-ip/
Don't get yourself unstru-u-ung/
War ma-a-ay come
Just from a slip of the to-ongue

Don't talk about the weather
Shhhhh!
It's a military secret!
Just keep your wits together
Shhhhhhh!
That's the safest way to keep it!

These are critical times
Be careful of espionage!
In such critical times
You've gotta watch out
for
Sabotage....

THE WRA ALL-JACL MEETING

The WRA was hoping for a conference of two elected internee delegates from each camp. They would discuss problems that occurred in the first year of the camps and plan for the future. The conference was actually the November national convention of the JACL in Salt Lake City. Every event was hosted and moderated by Mike Masaoka.

CALLING
ALL CHAPTERS!
By TEIKO ISHIDA

BUSY AS A BEE-HIVE

in our office these days, in preparation for the emergency national JACL conference, Nov. 17–24, inclusive ... general arrangements are being handled from Washington by Mike Masaoka, as well as George Inagaki and Hito Okada, the latter also attending to financial matters ... press and public relations, editor Tajiri; and secretarial-recording, yours truly. ... we were really in a dither today in our efforts to mimeograph and mail the 10-page conference call and agenda to some 50 delegates and guests, with Hito in his shirtsleeves operating the mimeograph, assisted by Tats Koga prexy of the Ogden Chapter, who happened to be visiting, and Scotty Tsuchiya, the material was ready in record time. ... pleading press of heavy preparation details, we tried to defer this column till next week, but apparently we couldn't plead hard enough, for here we are on Tuesday evening trying to make the deadline.

THE AGENDA

calls for intensive sessions for a full week, with most meetings to be held at the Civic center. ... guest speakers scheduled to speak during the conference include Dean Bob O'Brien of the University of Washington, new director of the National Japanese American Student Relocation Council; Dr. Galen Fisher of Berkeley, California, Executive Secretary of Northern California Committee for Fair Play, Institute of Pacific Relations and Writer; George E. Rundquist of New York City, National Director Committee American Japanese Resettlement of the Federal Council of Churches and the Home Missions Council; Al Wirin of Los Angeles, West Coast Representative ACLU; Miss Dora Maxwell of Madison, Wisconsin, Organization Director of Credit Unions National Associations, Inc. ... the guest speaker commanding the most attention will probably be Dillon S. Myer, National Director of the War Relocation Authority, who will confer with the national conference on Saturday, November 21, and speak at the public meeting on Monday afternoon, November 22. ... invitations are being sent to all interested nisei and Caucasian groups in the Intermountain area....further details of the conference appear in a news story elsewhere

ANOTHER HIGHLIGHT

of our emergency conference will be the presentation of the national charter to the first chapter to be organized and officially recognized in a relocation center—the Butte Chapter at Gila River, Arizona....Butte representatives will be Nobu Kawai and Ken Tashiro, formerly of Pasadena and Del Rey, respectively....a permanent office has been arranged at Gila for this chapter, as well as an executive secretary to be compensated by the project....plans for a 1943 membership and PACIFIC CITIZEN drive are already under consideration....chapters at Tule Lake, Poston and Heart Mountain are also almost ready for official recognition.

OUR THANKS

this week are tendered to Mr. Matsumura for his kind donation to the League....this gentleman formerly of the Washington Fuel Co. of Seattle, Washington, was on furlough from Minidoka, Idaho ... also to Mr. G. Nakashima of Ogden who handed us $5.00 to be sent to the Community Christmas Fund.

NATIONAL OFFICERS

Saburo Kido of Poston and Mike Masaoka of Washington will be among the advance guard to arrive in Salt Lake City for the emergency conference according to latest advices....national secretary Masaoka is due here Friday morning, November 13, while president Kido will arrive Saturday or early Sunday morning, the 14th....this office will no doubt be snowed under next week with the conference and accompanying rush of business, so our readers may again enjoy a treat in the form of a guest writer.

Nobu Kawai, The Volunteer

"WE ATTENDED THE CONVENTION"

"**W**hen I organized the Gila River chapter, I went to some of the JACL people I had known prior to the outbreak of war, who were supposed to have been big shots and so forth. And I asked them to help in organizing a chapter. And so many of them turned me down. They said, 'Nobe, I'll join, but I won't take an office. I'll just be a member in name only.'

"For the first time it occurred to me that there was a special quality—who were harmonious and peaceful. And soon as there was resistance, they faded out of the picture. They didn't have the moral courage to stand up for their convictions.

"For that reason I developed a lot of admiration for the people who had the guts to come out and express themselves. The one person or a couple of people that I admire is Harry Miyake from Santa Maria. He helped me very much. And Ken Tashiro. He and I ran the chapter.

"Oh, I don't know what our membership was. I imagine it was close to a hundred. We had a lot of members, but they weren't too active. But we kept in close contact with JACL headquarters. I was in constant communication with Sab Kido [in Poston] and Hito Okada [in Salt Lake].

"As officers of the Gila River chapter, we were invited to attend the convention in Salt Lake City during the war.

"So we attended the convention. And at that convention, we passed a resolution that the JACL would petition President Roosevelt for the reinstitution of

Selective Service for all Nisei. And we voted for that. And so we sent this telegram off to President Roosevelt. Of course, that received quite a bit of publicity."

NOW, THEREFORE, BE IT RESOLVED BY THE SPECIAL EMERGENCY MEET-ING OF THE JAPANESE AMERICAN CITIZENS LEAGUE, CONVENED IN SALT LAKE CITY, UTAH, THAT WE DO HEREBY REQUEST THE SELECTIVE SERVICE DIVISION OF THE WAR DEPARTMENT TO RECLASSIFY AMERI-CANS OF JAPANESE ANCESTRY ON THE SAME BASIS AS ALL OTHER AMERICANS

The WRA expected to be presented with a discussion of problems in the camps. They received a JACL plea to make the Nisei eligible for the draft so they might prove their loyalty on the battlefields of WWII. In drafting the plea, the Nisei at the camps, from which the JACL members came, had not been consulted. The plea did not represent a Nisei consensus of opinion. Nobu Kawai, its author, insists the JACL did not represent the Nisei.

The WRA and government agencies were under the impression that the JACL did represent the Nisei. The Tolan Committee, the army, Selective Service, and the WRA all described the JACL as being the representative of Japanese America. That's why they had sponsored the JACL national convention.

War Department Military Intelligence Division

MID 095 "Japanese American Citizens League," 1/4/43 (12/17/42)

Subject: Japanese American Citizens League, January 4, 1943

SUMMARY OF INFORMATION

The following information has been received which reflects the prevailing sentiment among delegates from relocation centers and free-zone chapters, as well as national officers, who attended the meeting of the Japanese-American Citizens League (JACL), held in Salt Lake City, November 17 to 23, 1942. The purpose of this meeting was to discuss the problems of the relocation centers, the matter of resettlement of evacuees, War Relocation Authority Policy, and JACL organization, problems and policy.

One of the outstanding problems at the present time is the fact that a sizeable criminal element, disloyal Japanese, and agitators are intermingled with the loyal groups, as reflected by reports from nearly all centers indicating that pro-Japanese agitators are spreading Jap propaganda in the centers and causing strikes, riots and other trouble; that gangsters terrorize loyal groups; and that the criminal element, including professional gamblers, operate quite openly in the centers. The opinion of the delegates concerning the cause for this condition is the failure of WRA officials to support the Japanese-American police and loyal Japanese-American officials in the relocation centers, and their refusal to severely penalize the trouble makers, plus the fact that the project directors and their assistants are largely social workers with no practical experience in government and policing. They know nothing about Japanese, and cannot discriminate between loyal and disloyal, thereby enabling the criminal and disloyal elements to intimidate the law-abiding and peaceable group and the internal police organization. Another difficulty is the lack of liaison other than the Administrative Staff between the internal police and the FBI or Military Police, and reports invariably leak back into the center about any informant, subjecting him to threats, intimidation and even beatings of himself and his family

• • •

The delegates at the JACL meeting unanimously passed a resolution advocating the application of selective service to Japanese Americans on the same basis as other citizens.

Regarding the loyalty of JACL members, it is reported that all members take an oath of allegiance to this country. The policy of the organization is completely loyal and in support of the war effort, although there may be some of the local chapter membership which is of questionable loyalty. The national officers seem to be an unusually competent group of men and appear to be loyal and patriotic. The JACL provides a valuable means of obtaining information regarding Japanese propaganda and activities in the centers and the most effective means of combating same.

Concerning the attitude of the JACL with reference to Negro organizations and Communists, it is stated that the organization refuses to affiliate with these elements.

It was reported by delegates that there is a strong element particularly the Kibei and pro-Japanese, who are opposing the JACL in the centers. The "Pacific Citizen," edited by Larry Tajiri and his wife, has been published in Salt Lake City for approximately six months. It depends on the JACL for financial support and its alleged purpose is to represent JACL to the general public and educate and supply information to Japanese-Americans. Its editorial policy is determined by whether or not subject matter is in the best interests of the people in the centers and of the war effort—if it is, the *Pacific Citizen* will support it.

It is informant's opinion that the national officials of the JACL are loyal and reliable individuals, such opinion being based on observance of these persons at this meeting.

If He Hollers Let Him Go

(A Novel)

by

CHESTER HIMES

Doubleday, Doran and Company

New York

1945

Maybe it had started then, I'm not sure, or maybe it wasn't until I'd seen them send the Japanese away that I'd noticed it. Little Riki Oyana singing "God Bless America" and going to Santa Anita with his parents next day. It was taking a man up by the roots and locking him up without a chance. Without a trial. Without a charge. Without even giving him a chance to say one word. It was thinking about if they ever did that to me, Robert Jones, Mrs. Jones's dark son, that started me to getting scared.

After that it was everything. It was the look in the white people's faces when I walked down the streets. It was that crazy, wild-eyed, unleashed hatred that the first Jap bomb on Pearl Harbor let loose in a flood. All that tight, crazy feeling of race as thick in the street as gas fumes. Every time I stepped outside I saw a challenge I had to accept or ignore. Every day I had to make one decision a thousand times: *Is it now? Is now the time?*

• • •

"Every time a colored man gets in the Army he's fighting against himself. Of course there's nothing else he can do. If he refuses to go they send him to the pen. But if he does go and take what they put on him, and then fight so he can keep on taking it, he's a cowardly son of a bitch."

Smitty had stopped his work to listen. "I wouldn't say that," he argued. "You can't call colored soldiers cowards man. They can't keep the Army from being like what it is, but hell, they ain't no cowards."

"Any man's a coward who won't die for what he believes.... As long as the Army is Jim Crowed a Negro who fights in it is fighting against himself.... You'll never get anything from these goddamn white people unless you fight them.... Isn't that right, Bob?"

"That's right," I said.

From the Files of
the Project Director

From the files of the project director, Ralph Merritt, at Manzanar Relocation Center in California, a copy of a JACL informant's report, dated December 16, 1942, includes:

> Well about three weeks ago the JACL had a emergency meeting and all of the big shots from Frisco (WRA OFFICIALS) and two representatives from each WRA center went to attend in Salt Lake City, Utah. Well one of our representatives, Fred Tayama stated something to this effect, "Change classification of the Nisei from FC to 1-A, because they are not aliens etc." Well it seemed like the Japanese population didn't like that statement or something or other that started at the convention.

• • •

Fred Tayama returned to Manzanar from the JACL convention, announced the passage of universal acceptance of Nobu Kawai's resolution embracing the draft, and was beaten up. Tayama named Harry Ueno as his assailant to project attorney Robert Throckmorton. Throckmorton wrote on the demonstration that followed.

WAR RELOCATION AUTHORITY
MANZANAR WAR RELOCATION AREA
Manzanar, California
In reply please refer to:
    OPA
January 2, 1943

MEMORANDOM TO: Mr. Ralph P. Merritt
                 Project Director
SUBJECT: Events Leading up to the Riot of December 6, 1942

In interviewing the twenty-two men who were detained as a result of the Manzanar incident of December 6, 1942, I have reached certain general conclusions....

The arrest of Harry Ueno, as a suspect in the Tayama case, was made by the Administration in good faith, as this man had been positively identified as an assailant by Fred Tayama and his wife.

... It was also decided that a larger meeting should be held at 1:00 P.M. in Block 22 further to discuss ways of bringing about Ueno's release.

The one o'clock meeting apparently went off according to plan. Inflammatory speeches were made insisting upon two lines of action: (1) the return of Harry Ueno; and (2) the removal from the center of certain "dogs" and stool pigeons and certain members of the Administrative staff....

Perhaps, the main significance of these comments is that they show that the primary reasons for the demonstration did not involve the question of loyalty or disloyalty or the fact that the anniversary of Pearl Harbor was at hand. The primary causes appear to be the (1) those which led the people to believe that Uyeno had been unjustly arrested; and (2) those which led them to hate Fred Tayama, other JACL leaders and certain members of the Administrative staff. There can be no mistake that the question of loyalty loomed large in the picture once the demonstration got under way.... However, it is clear to me that the demonstration as such was not planned until the ten o'clock meeting on Sunday morning, December 6, 1942.

Robert B. Throckmorton,
Project Attorney

Nobu Kawai,
The Volunteer

RETURN TO GILA

"So, when I returned to Gila, this Kibei organization, they were up in arms. They demanded to know why we had the right to send a telegram petitioning for reinstitution of the draft for the Nisei when we didn't represent all the Nisei.

"So I had to explain to them that we hadn't sent it in the name of the Nisei, but in the name of the JACL. And so they rather demanded that I come to their meeting and explain the actions of the convention to them.

"They invited me to this Kibei meeting. I said, 'Well, I won't speak in Japanese because my Japanese isn't that good. But I'll speak in English.'

"They said, 'That's all right, we'll have an interpreter there.'

"And so I was quite concerned whether this interpreter would interpret correctly what I say. So I asked Henry Miyake to go in there to monitor this interpreter."

The meeting is held in a mess hall. The Kibei attending are, "I imagine fifty or so."

Nobu Kawai says, "So I spoke, and I let the interpreter explain what I had to say. Then I explained to them this was a JACL move and we sent this petition in the name of the Japanese American Citizens League. And if it affects other Nisei, that isn't our fault. Our intention was to get the position of the JACL right before the U.S. government. And so anyway we got through that all right.

"Well, things were tense. It was after the beatings in other centers and so forth.

"In our block we had all the residents of Pasadena and people we knew. And so we were very much concerned. We went to sleep with baseball bats and hatchets under our beds, because we had heard about these attacks on JACL leaders in other camps."

Miye looks up from her knitting, "That's right! That's right! It was a very difficult time. In fact I was quite worried most of the time."

"Well, with her I feel sorry for her because it was on again and off again."

"Well, when you say on again off again, you better explain yourself," Miye says.

"Well, this on again off again thing, see. I was working in a camouflage factory in Gila, Arizona, when they had recruiters there for the 442nd Combat Team.

"And I got to thinking about it. Gee, I really owe it to myself and my family to volunteer for the army. Standing next to me was another fellow from Pasadena. And I said to him, 'You know, Jim, I think I ought to join the 442nd.'

"And he said, 'Yeah, I think so, too.'

"I said, 'Okay, let's go home for lunch, and tell our wives that we're going to join.'

"So I came home and told Miye. 'Miye, I'm going to join the 442nd.' And then I waited for Jim to come out of his barracks. He came down there and he said, 'You know, Ruby put her foot down. She won't let me join the army.'

"'Well, hell, Jim,' I said, 'Let's forget it.' So I told Miye, 'Well, Jim's not going so I guess I won't join either.' The more I thought why I shouldn't, the more it bothered me. I thought, 'Why should I not join just because Jim doesn't join?'

"And so I made up my mind that I was going to join. You know, I didn't care about Jim. I told her that I was going to join. So I went down to sign up. I came back and told her, 'I signed up!'

"I said, 'I'm going into the army. I think I'll go down to the administration office to see if I can move you up to Heart Mountain so you could be with your family.'"

THE FIRST CHRISTMAS IN CAMP: 1942
MANZANAR, CALIFORNIA

Ralph Merritt has taken over as commandant of Manzanar since the riots of December 6 and 7. As he writes his Christmas letter to his Aunt Luella, inside his house, all the children of Manzanar stand outside, on their side of the barbed wire, and sing him Christmas carols.

Manzanar, California   December 25, 1942

Dear Aunt Luella,

It is Christmas morning at Manzanar. The sun has not yet topped the Inyos, but its rays have turned the grey granite peaks of the Sierra to rose. Below is a white band of new snow. Still in the dark shadows are the rows of barracks that house our ten thousand Japanese evacuees.

Your father was the pioneer of Manzanar. He was the first white man to break the ground of this desert. He built his home where our barracks stand and here you were born. In those years following the Civil War there also were soldiers in Owens Valley to protect settlers from the Indians. This was the first time Manzanar faced the problems of race relationship. You and your brothers and sisters solved that problem by playing with Indian children. Your father solved it by becoming "the Captain" to every Indian in the Valley and the most honored man of his day among his Indian friends. Today Manzanar has again become the scene of a test of racial tolerance—the greatest test a democracy has ever met. We are face to face with the question of whether we can live in peace and security with American citizens of Japanese ancestry and Japanese who by virtue of our laws are non-citizens. To all of them we have pointed to American democracy as a better way of living. These people, ten thousand of them, are now held inside a barbed wire fence as a measure of national protection in this time of war.

The reality of this great drama is on my mind this Christmas morning because only thirty days ago the War Relocation Authority sent me here to Manzanar as Project Director with full administrative authority. It was like coming home to be back on the desert of Inyo that I have loved and once again to see the seven-mile shadow of Mt. Williamson. But Manzanar was a volcano about to erupt. I knew that too when I came. Evil work had been done by the slow boiling of many bitternesses. Some are old; some are as new as yesterday. These ten thousand people had no grudge in common. Many people were filled with many hates about many things—race hates, war hates, political hates, class hates such as those between Japanese born in America to whom Japan is a foreign country and Japanese born in American but educated in Japan who have become pro-Japanese and just the common kind of hates we all know too well.

On a Sunday morning not three weeks ago a mob gathered like the summer thunder storm that sweeps from the Sierra. As darkness came on mob violence grew and broke from the control of its leaders. As I walked in that mob at noon talking with people here and there and urging them to be calm and go home, I thought of many things. I thought of you and the happy ranch life here of years ago. I thought of the people now, in this Valley who now trusted me for their protection. I thought of our men overseas who might be more cruelly treated by Japan if tear gas failed to break up this mob. I thought of the innocent who might be killed while the guilty escaped if I had to turn to the military as a last resort. But after dark there was no other course. Soon there was the rattle of gun fire. Men fell in the blackness.

For days we lived under the military; no Japanese were seen outside the barracks; none came to work and sullen defiance hung over the camp. What would break the tension? How could these ten thousand people be led to want to work and play again? Could the real spirit of America be made to live among them?

Last Monday we buried our dead. At the Buddhist funeral held in the woods, beyond the Lacey Ranch, we mourned with their families the death of the two boys, innocent of wrong doing, the victims of the riot. The only soldier present stood at the head of one of the coffins—the brother of the dead boy. This soldier of Japanese ancestry was on active duty at a distant point, but the Army granted my request to bring him home to his family. The Buddhist Priest prayed that the lives of these young men would be a sacrifice for the sins of the all the camp. May their God and our God hear that prayer!

The next day the Japanese workers, four thousand men and women, were back at work. On Wednesday I suggested that the tragedy should not rob little children of Christmas trees and presents or young people of singing carols.

Last evening we visited our Children's Village with its sixty-five orphans. They sang "Jingle Bells" and "Away in a Manger" and we helped them open packages that were greeted with the usual shrieks of joy while Santa Claus with a Japanese accent shouted greetings to all. Before the door of our home in the barracks there was no mob but a hundred young people singing "O Come All Ye Faithful."

The star was overhead and the ragged crest of the Sierra was shining in the moonlight of Christmas Eve. Peace and Good Will had come to Manzanar.

So we greet this Christmas morning. Shall the problems of keeping this peace and good will be solved by the military, or by being overtrustful of this show of goodness, or is there some safe middle course through which the ideals of peace and good will can mingle with the realities of race tolerance? If there is an answer, it will be the corner stone upon which a future peace of the world will rest.

This story of your old home is my Christmas present to you.

Affectionately,
Ralph P. Merritt

CHRISTMAS AT HEART MOUNTAIN

by

FLOYD SCHMOE

On the windswept plateaus of northern Wyoming lies the state's newest and third largest city—the Heart Mountain Relocation Center. In long low tarpaper barracks, behind barbed-wire fences, and under the guns and searchlights of tall watchtowers live ten thousand Japanese Americans. Most of them came from the mild climate of southern California little used to and ill equipped for the rigors of winter in the north where the temperature sometimes reaches 40 degrees below zero.

There are more than four thousand children at Heart Mountain who had never seen a "white Christmas." This year they prayed for one.

When I went with them to their mess halls on Christmas night, the heavy pall of coal smoke lying like a grimey blanket over row upon row of dimly lit barracks reminded me of nothing so much as the mile long coke ovens of West Virginia. A cold wind was blowing but there was as yet no hint of snow. It had not been a white Christmas.

Programs varied in each of the large warehouse-like buildings which form the center and the only community gathering place of each of the thirty blocks making up the "city," but they all had one thing in common, it was the children's program.

At some parties there were speeches and singing, at others little plays and pantomimes, and at still others games and contests. Each messhall was decorated and each had a small Christmas tree—a special treat most of the centers did not have, except as they fashioned synthetic trees out of sage brush, greasewood and even pieces of packing crates, crepe paper and cardboard. New Years with its "omochi," and its "shime" would flavor strongly of the Orient and be for the adults who were of the Orient, but Christmas was thoroughly American and for the children who are American.

After the program, there were refreshments—dinner had been at four—and the master of ceremonies again took the floor. The big event of the day was at hand—Santa Claus was about to be announced.

He arrived by truck and his truck was full. Well wishing friends—most of them have never seen a Japanese in their lives—had sent in thousands of gifts and thousands of dimes and quarters with which to buy more. Santa Claus was authentic; a lot of padding, a painted face but an abundance of Christmas cheer and a real beard, a black Oriental beard. He meant well but he frightened the babies almost into hysterics. Obviously the small children had not been adequately prepared for Santa Claus.

There were stockings filled with oranges, nuts and candy for every boy and girl under fifteen. There were gaily wrapped gifts, at least three, for every one under 19, and enough left over so that every family had one extra. These gifts had been arriving for a month from individuals, Sunday school classes, young people's groups, mission societies, in every state in the union. More than 8,000 had arrived plus more than $2600 in cash. This happened in all the centers. At Minidoka more than 17,000 gifts accumulated and two weeks after Christmas the belated mails still poured them in.

For the small children, too young to be aware of the barbed wire and the guard towers and significance of it all, it was a wonderful Christmas, the best ever—but the gayety of their elders was strained. They were well aware of the fact that this year the spirit of the Prince of Peace did not rule in the hearts of all men. A year ago they had forseen this thing, now it was a bitter reality, next year it might be worse—it was not likely to be much better. For themselves they could stand it, but what about these children—you can't go on having Merry Christmases year after year in an internment camp.

For me however there was a ray of hope. This thing was going on in each of the ten Japanese relocations centers. Upwards of 70 thousand people all over the country had contributed to the happiness of those 50 thousand young American citizens with Japanese faces. Seventy thousand fellow Americans who two years ago had been unaware of the existence of these people had now shared a little bit in their well being. Sharing does something to people no matter who they are and I was sure they were seventy thousand hearts in America this Christmas night where a spot of warmth glowed a little brighter than it had a year ago.

Seventy thousand warm spots, I thought, may do something for America, it may kindle a fire. I prayed to Him who came that we might have peace that next year He may rule in the hearts of men that Christmas may be a real Christmas for these people, a real Christmas in a real home—an American home where people are free.

As we went "home" at nine o'clock snow as falling, the lighted windows looked brighter, shouts and laughter could be heard all over the camp. It was going to be a "White Christmas" after all.

(PC-2/4/43)

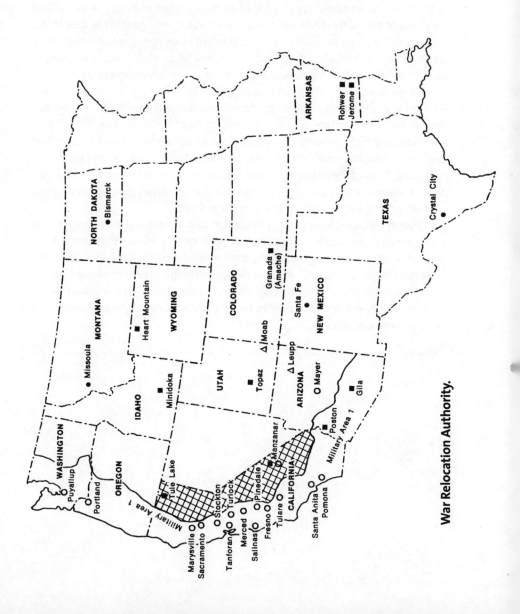

KEY

○ ASSEMBLY CENTERS
Puyallup, Wash.
Portland, Ore.
Marysville, Calif.
Sacramento, Calif.
Tanforan, Calif.
Stockton, Calif.
Turlock, Calif.
Merced, Calif.
Pinedale, Calif.
Salinas, Calif.
Fresno, Calif.
Tulare, Calif.
Santa Anita, Calif.
Pomona, Calif.
Mayer, Ariz.

■ RELOCATION CENTERS
Manzanar, Calif.
Tule Lake, Calif.
Poston, Ariz.
Gila, Ariz.
Minidoka, Ida.
Heart Mountain, Wyo.
Granada, Colo.
Topaz, Utah
Rohwer, Ark.
Jerome, Ark.

● JUSTICE DEPARTMENT
INTERNMENT CAMPS
Santa Fe, N. Mex.
Bismarck, N. Dak.
Crystal City, Tex.
Missoula, Mont.

△ CITIZEN ISOLATION CAMPS
Moab, Utah
Leupp, Ariz.

▨ Military Area 2 or
"Free Zone" until March 29, 1942

War Relocation Authority.

PART IV

Us and Them

Mike Masaoka:
The JACL vs. Japanese America

FEDERAL BUREAU OF INVESTIGATION

Origin Salt Lake City, Utah			File No. 100-4483
Made at	Date	Period	Made by
SALT LAKE CITY, UTAH	1/9/43	12/7,8,12,18	EDWARD J. KIRBY
		21/22/42	

Title	Character
SUBVERSIVE ACTIVITIES AT WAR RELOCATION	INTERNAL SECURITY-J

Poston representatives at recent J.A.C.L. conference which passed resolution urging support of Selective Service system on part of Japanese in U.S. forced by inmates of Poston to state that he did not represent all residents of Poston. Another Poston resident complains of pressure from pro-Axis groups of loyal Japanese.

DETAILS: At Salt Lake City, Utah

This is a joint report of the writer, Special Agent Blaney J. Burton, and special Agent George R. Blair.

Investigation in this case is predicated upon an interview with Confidential Informant SLC-167 and Confidential Informant T-1. These persons appeared at the Salt Lake Field Division and gave specific information on potential disturbances at Poston and Manzanar Relocation Centers.

• • •

Confidential Informant SLC-167 was one of the informant numbers assigned to Mike Masaru Masaoka. Agent Kirby explains that selected members of the JACL were named confidential informants to the FBI. Confidential Informant T-1 was Larry Tajiri, editor of the *Pacific Citizen*. He comes "highly recommended by SLC-167." Confidential Informant T-2 was Koji Ariyoshi: "He is member of the JACL and is designated as reliable by T-1 and SLC-167." Agent Kirby reports:

> Confidential Informant T-2 advised that certain Fascist advocates have been pushing the case relating to MINORU YASUII [sic] too strongly. He states that a great deal of money is being raised and that although he does not know, he does

not think that the money is being raised entirely with YASUII'S [sic] knowledge and consent. Ostensibly the purpose for which the money is raised is to bring YASUII'S [sic] case before the Supreme Court, however T-2 seems to think that the money is being raised probably for a bad purpose, perhaps for the purpose of propagandizing the various relocation centers. Informant states at the present time a great deal of propaganda relating to the YASUII [sic] case is being sent to the Tule Lake and Minidoka Relocation Centers. Informant states that as a matter of fact he believes that these people are trying to raise money in the name of YASUII [sic] without his knowledge and without saying exactly for what reason the funds are being solicited.

On November 25, 1942, the *Minidoka Irrigator* printed a letter from Minoru Yasui of Portland, Oregon, to George Tani of Oakland, California. They had never met. They knew each other from afar, only as members of the JACL. Yasui appealed to Tani from jail to raise money for his defense fund.

Well, I won my case for all good, loyal American citizens. Damn, I wish I were in a position to carry the fight further, but because of my personal citizenship status, I'm going to have my hands full. But even if I were to sacrifice my American citizenship which I have never and never will voluntarily relinquish, I'm glad to have established the fundamental citizenship rights of American citizens.

If the JACL doesn't carry on for me, all that I have endured thus far will have been in vain. George, rally the Nisei around and see if some definite steps cannot be taken to liberate the Nisei as a matter of right.

Agent Kirby reports that Confidential Informant T-3 is Joe Masaoka, "brother of SLC-167." T-5 is Hito Okada, "an officer of the JACL highly recommended by SLC-167 and T-1. Formerly an importer at Portland, Oregon. Believed to be reliable." Okada was the only member of the Portland JACL to be named a confidential informant. T-6 was Saburo Kido, "National President of the Japanese American Citizens' League." T-7 was T. G. Ishimaru, and T-8 was Susamu Togasaki. "Both T-7 and T-8 were delegates to the recent convention of the JACL in Salt Lake City and both were named in the statement, along with T-6, retracting the representation of anyone but themselves in the resolution pertaining to selective service classification 4C." Confidential Informant T-11 is SLC-167, Mike Masaoka, "National Secretary and Field Executive of JACL."

• • •

The inner circle of the JACL are private friends with the FBI. They don't represent the Japanese American people they said they did before the Tolan Committee, in 1942. Mike Masaoka no longer believed what he told the Tolan Committee: "We believe that the Japanese American Citizens League, as the only national organization established to serve the American citizens of Japanese ancestry, is in a position to actively lead the Japanese people residing in the United States." The government isn't mad about being lied to. Nobu Kawai at Gila, Fred Tayama at Manzanar, and Ishimaru and Togasaki at Poston, back from the JACL convention, all said the JACL represented no one but themselves. Did the WRA know of the JACL's abandonment of the Japanese Americans? Masaoka, the head of the JACL, shares a confidence with the head of the WRA:

Japanese American Citizens League
An All American Organization of American Citizens
National Headquarters

January 14, 1943

Mr. Dillon S. Myer, National Director
War Relocation Authority
Barr Building
Washington, D.C.

Dear Mr. Myer:

I must apologize for the tardiness of this confidential statement to you regarding the trouble in the centers. My excuse is (first) that I have been very ill and under a doctor's and a dentist's care for some time and (second) that I have attempted to obtain the thinking and collaboration of certain of our key people in the centers in order to give you a composite impression of our views. The enclosed report is one which combines our thinking as well as our recommendations, and I respectfully submit it to you for your consideration.

CONFIDENTIAL STATEMENT

In view of the fact that practically every person who has been beaten up in the centers is a member of our Japanese American Citizens League, many of our members have written suggesting that our organization create special gangs for the protection of our own membership!

Although the situation is well advanced in most of the centers, we believe that immediate action should be taken whereby, without warning or hearing, known agitators and troublemakers are moved out of the relocation centers and placed in special camps of their own.

The unanimous consensus of opinion is that the WRA ought to take immediate steps to segregate known agitators. Most of our chapter leaders have signified their willingness to name those whom they consider inimical to center welfare if their own names are not revealed.

Gordon Hirabayashi,
On Civil Disobedience

"TO WHOM IT MAY CONCERN"

"**W**ell, there were guys maybe a third of them were one or another type of draft violations. The others would be burglary. These were federal offenses." Gordon Hirabayashi describes life in the Federal Tank, in Seattle. He is a prisoner awaiting a decision from the Supreme Court. "Some of them were involved in murder, any kind of physical brutality and theft, anything up in Alaska."

Alaska was a federal territory, and Seattle was the closest Federal District Court.

"There were accusations of other kinds of threats, personal threats, bodily threats and so on. And just an array of normal types of crimes you could see on any docket in jail. They were on the federal ledger.

"There weren't the petty thieves and winos and that type. Although a few of them came up in connection with the draft. We used to talk between free periods, when we were by the windows, 'Aw! You petty guys!' We federal would put it on those state and county types.

"Well, at first I didn't know where I was going. For some reason, the lawyers and state senators didn't know. They said they had looked all day, before they located me. They visited camp, Puyallup, the day after I was picked up. I forget when, Saturday maybe.

"They had gone to Puyallup to visit friends. Then, in talking with my mother, Mary said she'd had a dream that I was tortured. Then she broke down and wept. The professor, her husband, couldn't stand that. He just said, 'Find him. Find him. Let her know where he's at.'

"So mom said, 'I spent all day to find out where you were.'

"Today on federal crime, the first place I'd check, is the Federal Tank and the U.S. Marshal to see if there's any action on the federal case. Where is he? But they went looking around. They didn't know what happened. After they located me, it was the third day, I was called out for a plea.

"And we had a lawyer, a young guy, John Dizeman from one of Seattle's leading firms. He was very interested. He was a friend of Art Barnett, the civil lawyer, looking after the legal part for the committee.

"Then, the next time I was with another lawyer. I didn't know what the reason was. I didn't quiz him too much. But later Art said, 'You know, at first you had this young fellow John Dizeman. Were you curious what happened to him?'

"I said, 'Yeah. How come they changed? Didn't work out?'

"And he said, 'Well, no. He's very interested and he wanted to continue, but Dave Beck, of the Teamsters labor union, came in and said, "We read in the paper where a guy from your firm is defending a Jap!"' We don't want anything to do with any firm that takes a stand like that.' He put the threat on them of withdrawing his business.

"So the senior called John in, and said, 'I don't personally object to it and I know you're interested in it, but you see, we are faced with this. We will have to withdraw.'

"And John, if he wasn't a struggling young lawyer, just starting off, he would have said, 'All right, the hell with it, I'm staying on.' He was deeply disappointed that he had to withdraw.

"Art Barnett went around to find a lawyer. He said it wasn't easy. They finally found this guy Frank Walters, who was a Republican, an American Legion member, and constitutional specialist. He was interested, and he did good work. He was not the most innovating type. Not an outstanding lawyer but with a good reputation with all those conservative organizations who was interested. That's how they got him.

"Barnett wasn't paid. But he consulted with Walters, and they checked with each other as they went. And periodically he called me down to the sheriff's office, out of the tank to tell me what the score is, and what's coming next. We had several skirmishes during the summer months. Plea was eight months, and some kind of procedure to drop the case.

"I had another one that I can't remember the term. But it refers to being accused on the grounds of race. And the judge threw that out. That was part of the original brief that went up to the Supreme Court from the Seattle scene. The big ACLU lawyers struck it out. They said, 'We don't want to deal with that sort of stuff.' And they struck it out.

"But Art Barnett remembers that one of the first questions that Associate Justice Jackson asked was, 'In this case, I would have thought that you would have raised race.' Art remembered Frank Walters turning around and looking at Art when that question came up. Because they wanted to put it in, but the senior lawyers, who knew about the Supreme Court said, 'We don't want to deal with that.'

"After the Supreme Court ruling came down in June . . . it must have been six weeks—maybe a month to six weeks . . . the FBI came to pick me up." Hirabayashi was out on bail at his parents' place, outside the military zone, in Wieser, Idaho. "And we went over to the U.S. District Attorney's office, in Spokane. He [U.S. District Attorney Connelly] said, 'Well, I guess you'll have to do your sentence now, since you can't go back to the road camp near Fort Lewis, since that's an excluded area. You might as well do it in the Federal Tank here [in Spokane].'

"And I said, 'Well, wait a minute, now. I got thirty days extra for an opportunity to do it outside [in the outdoors]. I hate to go back there and do thirty days extra.'

"He said, 'Well, I can't send you back there. We don't have money to send you down to the nearest other camp, which is Tucson, sixteen hundred miles.' And gee, I felt really stuck, you know.

"He said he didn't have the facility to send somebody that far to serve a sentence. The sentence was ninety days.

"You see, I had thirty days apiece consecutive. That's sixty. I asked the attorney if he could see if I could have ninety. I could serve it outside. I had a chance to serve it outside then. So when the judge [U.S. District Judge Lloyd L. Black] said, 'Does the prisoner have anything to say?'

"So the lawyer said, 'Your honor, I have a peculiar request. My client would like a little longer sentence. Fifteen days extra to each, to total ninety.'

"Nobody on the court—the judge, the district attorney, our attorney—had Supreme Court experience at the time. Nor were they sensitive to the restrictions they work under. And so they accepted it.

"The judge kind of laughed. And he said, 'Well, I can accommodate that. Well, why don't we simplify that. Why don't we say ninety days for both concurrently.'

"It sounded all right. It sounded like no difference, you know.

"And when it got to the Supreme Court, even though our whole thrust of the arguments, the hearings, was on the Exclusion Order. . . !" He's built to this climax, to the Exclusion Order, and drones on, "I have two counts against me. Count one, the Exclusion Order, count two, the curfew, for the same basic principle.

"When they got into their chambers for deliberations, the chief justice said this case, the Hirabayashi Case. There are two counts. They are concurrent. That means we need to take one and if that is upheld, we don't have to rule on the other, because he is already serving it."

The Supreme Court is off the hook, on the Hirabayashi and the Yasui cases. Hirabayashi sighs. His mistake. And *ex parte*, Yasui's mistake. Yasui has ridden the Hirabayashi case *ex parte*, having violated the same curfew order in Portland that Hirabayashi violated in Seattle.

Ruling on the Exclusion Order would involve consideration of the Military Orders, and congressional approval of the Military Orders affecting only Japanese American citizens had constitutional implications. Ruling on the curfew was a simple matter. Hirabayashi had violated the curfew.

"So you just decide the particular legal case and limited to that and nothing further. They said we rule on that. The guy has served his sentence so we don't need to rule on it. They don't do anything to rule on that."

The decision is delivered, and the District Court hands down the sentence; the prisoner, a Japanese American in WWII, thinks it would be nice to be on the road.

"I thought I would hitchhike. Well this is wartime. World War II. Total war!" Yes, a bad time for a Japanese American to be caught alone, isn't it? "Gas ration, and so on. Traffic was very slow," he drones on, deadpan. All Hirabayashi has for protection, from racist zealots, or zealous patriots passing in cars, is a letter from the U.S. Attorney, "To Whom It May Concern."

"It took me a couple of days to get down to Snake River Valley where my parents were. I stopped there and visited half a week. Then I left there and hitchhiked to Salt Lake City. It took another couple days—or three days. I usually slept just off the highway. This August, so I was warm. When I got to Salt Lake City, I looked up the *Pacific Citizen*. Larry Tajiri was the editor then. And I looked up some of my Seattle friends. I must have been there half a week."

It's 1943, America is in the war, his people are in camps because the JACL has convinced them the people in this state will kill them, riot against them, tear them limb from limb. JACL members in Utah, and every state he will visit, have written their state governors saying they are discouraging Japanese family and friends from moving to their states. They don't want the bad Japanese moving into their states and getting mixed up with the good Japanese. Better they all move together into the barbed wire reservations, out of sight, guarded by the army. Hirabayashi rides his thumb, sleeps by the roadside, eats in coffee shops in Washington, Idaho, Utah, unconcerned. America is not the nation the JACL cowers from.

"Then I hitchhiked down again to southern Utah. And traffic was terrible. I'll bet it's even slow now on that highway. It was steadily discouraging, and hot.

"I'm going through places, little burgs. One place I found it was the sheriff who picked me up. He said, 'Where are going?'

"I said, 'Oh, I'm going down to Tucson.'

"He said, 'Well, I'm going down about forty miles, and I'll give you a lift.'

"I rode with him and we talked. 'What are you doing. . . .' and so on.

"'I'm going over to serve a sentence. I'm out on bail, and here's a letter if you want to read it.'

"He stopped the car to read that letter. 'To Whom It May Concern.'

"He was a little upset. He wasn't sure what he should do.

"He let me off at my turn-off, and I continued on.

"When I got as far as Las Vegas, I gave in, and I picked up a bus for the last leg to Tucson. But it must have been nearly two weeks since I started, and I'm there. And when I reported to the FBI office, they said, 'Who are you?'

"I identified myself, and said, 'I'm here to serve my sentence.' I gave them my letter 'To Whom It May Concern.' He looked at it and said, 'We have no papers on you. We can't do anything for you.'

"I said, 'There must be something.' I said, 'I'll gladly turn around and go. But someday you're going to find those papers, and then I will have to interrupt and come back. I might as well get it over with.'

"He said, 'Well, this is midafternoon, why don't you go to an air-conditioned theater and come back about seven. We'll see what we can find out.'

"I told them Seattle should have my record. So should Spokane. This writer Connolly, the DA, should have it. And the Bureau of Prisons in Washington should have something or the Department of Justice.

"And when I came back, he'd heard from all of them. And somewheres in the bottom of the file, they had transferred the old files somewhere, since I hadn't shown up, they found that, too. So, they had all four things.

"So they said, 'Well, we're ready to take you up.' In the meantime I had gone to a movie and a restaurant.

"They took me to a federal road camp, prison camp, on Santa Catalina Mountains behind Tucson, on Recreation Hill.

"The road was about part way up the hill by the mountains. And it was about thirty miles from Tucson. We drove up there, and he parked me there. It's like a CCC camp, just like a highway road camp.

"And just for the heck it, I asked to be on the delivery crew, taking things, their lunch, ten miles up, to the top of the mountain. That is the recreation road. This was on federal land. And we are building a road.

"And I got on a softball team. One of the teams we played was the University of Arizona. But the university always traveled. We never traveled. We were always the home team.

"There were four or five types of prisoners there. Ones are regular prisoners you know, kidnappers, killers, thieves, and so on. Then, there was another category of Likurti Indians in that area. The Likurti Indians were a find. Then there was some whites. Some of them were conned into it. Because the Indians get money for informing, you know. In some cases they would set the guy up to give 'em something. They would say. 'Here is some money, go get me some liquor and leave it behind the billboard there and I'll pick it up.' They inform. And these federal liquor types, or Treasury Department, would be on the lookout and nab the guy while he's making the transaction. There is that type, and there are Indians with liquor. At that time it was a crime.

"There were Mexicans who waded across the river. There were conscientious objectors, and there were the draft violators. At that time they were picking up anybody that violated the draft regulations like change of address. You know, people aren't thinking about it. Most people, they get thirty or sixty days.

"Among the draft types there, Hopis from the old Arabi Reservation. And these guys are the Indians who claimed that they were a nation, an independent nation. 'We have a treaty with the U.S. and we are not boundable to their conscription. Besides, I don't want to go there. What am I fighting for, you know. I don't want to get in the paleface's fight.'

"So they refused. And they were there.

"We all wore their clothes, which is blue jeans and blue shirts. They had big white rocks on the perimeter—you are not supposed to go outside that range. But within that range you could roam around.

"At least two hours during the free period, a whistle would blow and you are supposed to stand where you could be counted. Visible, you know. And when that clears, another whistle would blow. And we could go about activities again.

"During the free period, the Indians had built a little hut for their own retreat. They had a hot stone pit for their steam bath. And they picked up some soapweed around there, and it's their soap. I didn't think it was soap.

"And the conscientious objectors, you know, these college types, they are sympathetic to the Indians, and they befriended them. They are trying like heck to get invited up there.

"In order to be up there with them you had to be on the ins a little bit. And nobody had succeeded. There I am the first week, about the third day, they befriend me. They say we're probably brothers. And one of them said the Hopis look quite a bit like Japanese. More than the Navajos who are quite angular and big nose—and he said, I've been stopped several times and accused of being Japanese.

"And he said, 'How do you say this word in Japanese? How do you say this word?'

"Well, some words have some similarity.

"You know, to the Hopis the sun is important. So they had a stone tablet. The sun is their symbol. You know they said, 'Your ancestor was the Rising Sun.' He said, 'There is a lot of connection.' I look quite a bit like them.

"So without any quality on my part, I get thrown in for the Exclusion Order and the curfew. Well, here it's just the opposite of discrimination. Without any quality on my part, they make a brother out of me. And then they invite me up there. So, I go up there, in friendship.

"I didn't mind the steam bath, but quality of the soap wasn't too good. They made soap from soapweed. I like commercial soap myself.

"They made a comfortable hut up there, and the guys say, 'Here we've been trying a month to get up there and you are just here, and you get invited up there.'

"Yeah! They treated me nicely, personally. The administration gave me job as one-man recreation crew. I just went around fixing home plate, fixing tennis practice place.

"They had an Indian affairs steward in the dining room in charge of the bakery section. And their baking was very good. And the bread was good. The pastries were very good, you know, compared to jail, which I remembered before. This was really first-class camp. He was with the Indian Service and worked with the Indian school in Oklahoma before. And his on-the-spot baking there was really very good. So, I just wrote the guy, instead of bitching, writing only when you're bitching, I thought I would give a compliment.

"I said this baking is really good from bread to pastries. I just wrote a little note. When I came through, the guy was waiting there to see which guy it was. He said, 'Are you Hirabayashi?'

"I said, 'Yeah.'

"He said, 'I got your letter.'

"I said, 'Well, we appreciate your baking.' That was about it.

"About that time, I was getting bored with the recreation all by myself all day. And so I asked him, when I next saw him. I said, 'Any chance to get on your crew? I want to work under you and learn.'

"And he said, 'Well, we just filled up our crew, and we don't have an opening now. Let me look into it.'

"And a day later, he stopped me and said, 'Hey, we have an opening. I worked something out.'

"I worked the bread crew. I really had to adapt when I got home to show my mother and my friends how to bake, you know, because they're used to baking things with always that smell of yeast in there. And it is just that they didn't go through sufficient full process, I guess. They used these small yeast. We'd be using about a pound of butter. We just throw one of those things in, you know. But I didn't know how to do a home batch. I was used to big institutional batch. Then, I got into pies and some cookies, finger rolls, and so on. In fact with all the experience that guy had, I contributed an idea.

"We were making finger roll pastries. You spread it out, put in some big sauce, and turn over here, and turn it over so it stays. When you wet it, it breaks when you're turning over the dough.

"Oh, he was showing me how to turn it. He could do it better than I could. I said, 'Why don't we wet this part and turn it.' It was small little thing. I was trying to get out of it being broken all the time. Just reverse the fold.

"He said, 'That's a good idea. Why didn't I think of that before?'

"And I got out just as I was getting into cakes. So I still don't make cakes.

"When I got out, I was carrying messages for friends of mine. I had one letter a guy was writing to his wife. I didn't think there was anything he couldn't put into his letter, but he asked me if I could (carry it). I taped it inside my socks.

"And just routinely this guy is saying, 'Take off your shoes.'

"He was just checking. If I was experienced I would have just taken it off and left it in the socks. What the hell! But I was trying to keep it.

"He said, 'What's that?'

"I said, 'It's a note I'm taking out to give to his wife.'

"Then they took my good time [Time off the sentence for good behavior]. They have statutory good time and work good time. They took away my work good time. If you're working they give three days a month. Nine days in three months.

"They checked me out of that prison routinely. But they didn't release me out at Tucson. At the bus station, they just took me to Pima County Jail. And I did nine days. Yeah, nine days in the general. I ran into guys who spoke no English, you know, just picked up crossing the river.

"In fact, even though I knew no Spanish and he knew no English, we could communicate some. I found out something about him. He needed some inquiries. I managed to get the jail guy to get somebody who spoke Spanish. They couldn't even ask that, you see.

"And they moved this guy out. I felt, gee, there's some value here. It was a crummy place, but the food was good compared to King County jail. They gave pretty good food.

"I remember one night I saw this huge shadow come down the wall. I got out of my bed and poked this guy and pointed. He looked and said, 'Ah! *La cucuracha.*' Cockroach—a giant cockroach! They're harmless, just like the little ones. But if you're not used to them, they look ominous.

"He took a wad of newspaper and just smacked it. After awhile they're just commonplace. Then, when I left, they gave me bus ticket back to Spokane.

"The first stop was Las Vegas, and it went through Needles, California—over the boundary." He'd crossed the line into Military Zone No. 1, the zone forbidden to all Japanese Americans. "I thought, Well I ought to tell the guy. Hey, I'm violating!

"But I don't want to be stopped out there, so I kept quiet. When I got home I checked the excluded area, Zone A. All of Tucson was excluded. I was in there, but I didn't get the extra thrill of knowing I was violating."

SHHH! HUSH! HUSH!

Headquarters Thirteenth Naval District
Seattle, Washington
Memorandum: March 10, 1943
From: District Intelligence Officer Thirteenth Naval District
To: The Director of Naval Intelligence
Subject: Japanese Evacuation and Relocation—in the Thirteenth Naval District (to March 10, 1943)
CONFIDENTIAL
CASE HISTORY
JAPANESE LOCATED IN STRATEGIC AREAS:
Prior to the outbreak of war between Japan and the United States an investigation had been conducted to ascertain the names and background information of all Japanese residing or being explored in areas of strategic importance. A periodic re-check was made in order that this information could be kept up-to-date.

—Japanese American Citizens League

• • •

When it became certain that evacuation of the Japanese was inevitable, the local chapters of the Japanese American Citizens League seemingly cooperated whole-heartedly with the designated evacuation authorities, offering the services of their members as translators and interpreters and in Seattle, Washington, loaning their office at 517 Main Street together with clerical and stenographic staff to the Provost Marshal and his staff and personnel of the Wartime Civil Control Authority.

With the knowledge and approval of the United States military authorities in charge of the evacuation, the Seattle Japanese American Citizens League prepared, along military lines, an organization known as the "Evacuee Administration Headquarters," that was to be in charge of the internal administration of the Puyallup Assembly, under the Caucasian staff of the Wartime Civil Control Administration.

• • •

While the Japanese American Citizens League group of Portland endeavored to coop-erate with the Wartime Civil Control Administration in a manner similar to that of the Seattle Japanese American Citizens League group at the Puyallup Center, their results were not so noticeable. In the first place, the Portland Japanese American Citizens League lacked the strong leadership that existed in the Seattle body, and secondly, fewer of the alien Japanese leaders from Portland were taken into custody by the Federal Bureau of Investigation. As a result there still remained among the Japanese at the North Portland Assembly Center many comparatively strong alien leaders—men to whom the Japanese American Citizens League members had, hitherto, turned for help and guidance—and were now more than a little hesitant to supercede.

Nisei—Lack of Unity

The lack of unity on the part of the Minidoka nisei has been in effect before the date of evacuation. It had its start at the time Minoru YASUI decided to make a test case of the constitutionality of the Curfew orders of the Western Defense Command and Fourth Army

• • •

Minoru YASUI was born at Hood River, Oregon, August 15, 1920. He graduated from the University of Oregon School of Law in 1939 and was admitted to the Oregon bar the same year. Completing the Reserve Officer's Training Corps course at the University, he was duly commissioned a Second Lieutenant in the United States Army reserves.

Through the influence of his father, YASUI secured an appointment on the staff of the Japanese Consulate in Chicago, Illinois. As a consequence of his duties as the Consulate, YASUI was registered with the United States Department of State as a propaganda agent of the Japanese Government.

• • •

On March 28, 1942 YASUI deliberately violated the curfew order of the Western Defense Command and then gave himself to the Portland police, stating it was his intention to test the constitutionality of the curfew order. His trial in Federal Court, Portland, Oregon, resulted in a verdict of guilty on November 16, 1942 and a sentence of one year in a Federal Road Camp and a fine of $5,300.

In so sentencing YASUI, Federal Judge James A. FEE ruled that the curfew and evacuation proclamation were not applicable to "American citizens." Judge FEE claimed that YASUI, through employment in the Japanese Consulate and registration with the State Department as propaganda agent of the Japanese government had elected, under dual citizenship status, to become a citizen of Japan. YASUI was found guilty, therefore by reason of being an enemy alien.

YASUI has appealed the citizenship ruling of Judge FEE, and a hearing was held February 19th in the district Court of Appeals, San Francisco, California. No decision has been announced to date.

• • •

Following the publicity in the Minidoka evacuee publication (The *Irrigator*) mentioned in the previous paragraphs, certain of YASUI's intimates got together and advertised a meeting for December 2, 1942.

This gathering was attended by some 300 persons who, as the *Irrigator* described them, "consider Judge FEE's decision as an "open wedge" in preserving the constitutional rights of the nisei and of reversing other court rulings that have held the evacuation and curfew proclamations are justified." A standing committee of ten "to see the YASUI case to the finish" was selected at this meeting, composed of:

[Minoru Yasui, is the most distinguished member the Portland JACL has. He was first to graduate from the University of Oregon Law School and is a Lieutenant in the Oregon State National Guard. George Tani is a lifetime member of the JACL from Oakland, California. He was brought into Minidoka to serve as the camp optometrist, after all the Portland optometrists refused to work for $19.00 a month.

All the names on this list of officers of the Civil Liberties League are also members of the JACL. Why that fact is neglected on this list suggests some rivalry between the Seattle and the Portland JACL, and might explain why Mike Masaoka reported Communists were on the Portland list—a malicious and false assertion.]

Dr. George TANI, optometrist of Oakland, California, and secretary of the self-government constitution committee,

Ronald Isamu SHIOZAKI, former Portland resident who was in the employ of a Japanese quasi-official firm in San Francisco at the outbreak of the war, and protegee of Clarence Edward OLIVER.

(See 13ND Case History of OLIVER dated January 13, 1943.)

Sue HADA, no available data.

George TAKIGAWA, former official of CIO affiliated Cannery Workers and Farm Laborers Union, Local #7. Radically inclined.

Richard Chihiro TAKEUCHI, former publisher of the *Great Northern Daily News*—a pro-Japan nisei who has applied for repatriation to Japan.

Florence TATEOKA, former paid secretary of the Japan Society of Seattle, and whose father, presently interned, was recipient of a wooden cup from the Japanese Foreign Office on the occasion of the 2600th anniversary celebration. Presently employed as instructor at the Navy Japanese Language School, University of Colorado, Boulder, Colorado.

Michael HAGIWARA, from Ketchikan, Alaska, who has a brother in the United States Army and a father in internment.

Milton MAEDA, a relative of YASUI, formerly employed on the Bonneville Dam Project.

Frank TORIBARA, an architect and trouble maker of a sort at the Puyallup Assembly Center.

Frank KINOMOTO, formerly employed by the Washington State Tax Commission.

This committee adopted the title "Civil Liberties League" and decided to contact the national Japanese American Citizens League for their official support of YASUI.

PROJECT ADMINISTRATION- War Relocation Authority Personnel.

It has been confidentially reported that both SANDOZ and TOWNSEND are Quakers. In addition, that SANDOZ and SCHAFFER are sociologists and that these two treat the project in the light of an experiment in sociology.

Both SANDOZ and TOWNSEND have permitted and encouraged Japanese folk dances, theatricals (*Shibai*) and other nationalist entertainment. They have assisted in the establishment of a library of Japanese literature, arranging for the Japanese books which had been confiscated from evacuees while at Puyallup Assembly Center being brought to Minidoka.

In has further been reported that while the project director, Harry L. STAFFORD, is a fine man, he spends most of his time playing golf and taking flying lessons, leaving the actual administrating in the hands of the various section heads. It is said that TOWNSEND and SANDOZ in particular have fostered discontent and urged disobedience to government orders. They have unquestionably contributed to the lowering of nisei morale at the project. It is confidentially reported that these two men have publicly, before nisei gatherings, stated that the entire program of curfew, contraband, evacuation and relocation, as far as the nisei are concerned, is unconstitutional, and that is all the result of "pressure groups," principally the California Joint Immigration Committee, the Sons of the Golden West, etc. and based entirely on racial and economic issues.

Outside influences and speakers, some of them known to be conscientious objectors and others with radical backgrounds who place "civil liberties" above all other considerations, have been invited to visit the project and address the evacuees.

Mrs. Mary FARQUHARSON, member of the American Civil Liberties Union, the Fellowship of Reconciliation, and former left wing Washington State Senator gave several lectures at Minidoka, at the invitation of TOWNSEND, January 31 and February 1, 1943. Mrs. FARQUHARSON's talks were largely devoted to the case of conscientious objector Gordon Kiyoshi HIRABAYASHI, Seattle nisei evacuation and curfew violator, whose appeal was heard in San Francisco Federal Court of appeals on February 19, 1943.

Floyd W. SCHMOE, a strict Quaker, Seattle committee secretary of the former "Keep America out of War," and identified with the Women's International League for Peace and Freedom, in his capacity of northwestern representative of the American Friends Service Committee and the Fellowship of Reconciliation, is permitted the freedom of the Center, with desk and stenographic assistance. SCHMOE has publicly criticized the entire evacuation program, has been most active in the defense of Gordon Kioyoshi HIRABAYASHI both at the Minidoka and Heart Mountain Relocation Centers and in Seattle. He has urged the nisei to support HIRABAYASHI morally and financially.

There has been no known instance where project authorities have invited any person to visit the Center to address the evacuees and give the government's side of the case.

• • •

HEART MOUNTAIN RELOCATION CENTER, CODY, WYOMING

During the period from September 31 to October 11, 1942, there were 986 persons transferred to this Center from the North Portland Assembly Center. In addition to those from Portland, there were 5,260 persons brought to the Heart Mountain Center from the Pomona Assembly Center, and 4,708 from the Santa Anita Assembly Center, both in California.

Project Administration—Personnel and Policy

The directory of the War Relocation Authority staff at the Heart Mountain Center, as of October 5, 1942, lists a total Caucasian personnel of 131. Sixty of this number are connected with the educational section. The key members of the staff include:

Christopher E. RACHFORD, Project Director
Douglas M. TODD, Superintendent, Community Enterprise
Guy ROBERTSON, Assistant Project Director
Philip W. BARBER, Chief, Community Services
Robert O. GRIFFIN, Chief, Internal Security

Internal Disorders

Chief of internal security GRIFFIN, soon after taking charge of the police force, discovered that liquor was being sold in the camp and that strong-arm tactics were being employed to assist in the rackets in which certain members of the police force were engaged. The police force of about 100 men was composed of about 60% nisei-kibei, 40% issei but all under the issei domination.

The acting chief of police was one "Rose" Ryozo MATSUI who had been raised from infancy by a Mr. De Vina, Metro-Goldwyn-Mayer cameraman in Hollywood. Until about six years ago MATSUI was unable to speak anything but English. During the past six years he acquired a thorough knowledge of Japanese. Prior to transfer to Heart Mountain, MATSUI (age about 35) had been assistant chief of police at the Pomona (California) Assembly Center.

Upon the failure of MATSUI to cooperate on a case under investigation, GRIFFIN asked for and received MATSUI's resignation as Chief of Police. Through coercion of MATSUI's lieutenants on the force the entire Japanese police force resigned.

The resignation of RACHFORD from the War Relocation Authority as of December 15th resulted in the elevation of Guy ROBERTSON to the directorship. One of the last acts of RACHFORD as Project Director was to reinstate MATSUI as Chief of Police and remove the suspension from his two chief aides, Captain of Police Ben OZEKI and Desk Sergeant Terry SENTACHI.

GRIFFIN is said to have been discharged and the direction of the internal security section is, temporarily at least, in charge of Mr. BARBER.

Kentaro Takatsui, Kibei-Nisei

WILL YOU VOLUNTEER FOR THE ARMY?
WILL YOU RENOUNCE JAPAN?

"**O**kay. This is a Chinese poem. A *Shigin*. It is called '*Kinshui jogai no saku*' 'At the Outer Fence of Kinshu Castle' by Maresuke Mubi. Remember, I was taught this about sixty years ago, in Japan.

Kinshuo-Jo

Sansen somoku utata koryo
The scenery of mountain and rivers looked desolate
Juri kaze was namagusashi shinsen jo
The wind there smells bloody, newly fought battle field
Shinsen unrou seibatsu susumazu
divine clouds won't help them conquer
Hito o katazu kinshu jogai
gives feelings of tension around the castle

"The samurai used to use that when they had a drinking party get together. Or a New Year's party. Something that has to be celebrated, with the samurai sitting there in a row, having sake.

"First thing they do is that somebody gets up, does shigin. When they do shigin, they do the *kembu* with the shigin. *Kembu* is a Chinese ideogram, it means 'sword dance.' *Ken* is 'sword,' *bu* is 'dance.' So they use the shigin at these drinking parties. Somebody does *shigin ginzuru*, chants the shigin, in front of the audience. Another samurai gets up and does the sword dance. Each movement has to match each word. That does not mean the shigin is militaristic. Because in the next verse the Kinshuo-jo about a student who leaves his home—he leaves home village to go out and study—but it also symbolizes a young man leaving his native village to seek his fortune in the city.

"So he leaves his home village, the word you know, home village, to go out and study. While he is pursuing his schooling, an unforeseen incident may come: accident or sickness, and he may have to die. The idea is that to die doesn't mean that you have to go back to your ancestral grave to die. That *kanji* is in there. Then he says, 'Unless I succeed in my studies, that is to graduate from the school that I go to. If I don't succeed, I will not return home, even if I die.' He says, 'There are graveyards wherever you go,' meaning that you can die in the mountains, bury your own bones, up in the mountains. That's what it means, those Chinese ideograms."

I think he means, "You don't need Japan to be Japanese." But as he gets to the meat of the story he wants to tell—a story inspired by "his Bible," Henry David Thoreau's essay *On Civil Disobedience*, an essay about disobeying a law to test its constitutionality—I'm confused.

He seems to be saying he was one of three thousand men who successfully resisted the Leave Clearance Registration Form [the WRA and Selective Service questionnaire] that contained Questions 27 and 28, the controversial loyalty questions. The WRA introduced the questionnaire at Tule Lake, to one block: Block 42.

I'm confused by his telling me the successful resistance to the questionnaire was led by a man whose name he refuses to give.

"The active Kibei leader who started this—I won't mention his name—well, he was one of the original leaders that started this thing. He's the one that came to me one day, and he says, 'You heard about this Block 42, and the thirty-five young boys taken in, taken to Alturas County jail.'

"They went to the WRA administration office. These young kids. Kids! And they said, 'You forced us into camp. We had no rights as citizens. And you demand that we answer the loyalty question so that you can draft us. We don't want none of that! Send us back to Japan!'

"Now people will say, right away, they will say, 'Ah, those guys, they're not Americans! They want to go back to Japan!'

"Look! When we were born, our father registered us with the Japanese Consulate, and we had Japanese citizenship. We had dual citizenship in those days.

"These Kibei renounced their citizenship, went back to Japan, lived there seven years or so, renounced their Japanese citizenship, and came back to America.

"Does this not prove that, when these young Nisei demanded to be expatriated to Japan, they didn't mean they wanted to go back to Japan! Even those

Kibei, raised in Japan, they wanted to come back here. It doesn't mean that they were disloyal! No!

"We had dual citizenship, in those days. People don't know this. I never see it emphasized in the *Rafu Shimpo*. The Japanese government never tried to draft us. We were Japanese citizens. They never called us 'God damned Jap,' or put us in prison and make us lose everything. And then the United States wanted draft us at Tule Lake. Ridiculous! That touched us. The kids were showing us the way. Made us cry and angry."

"That was the first block. The whole block was told—42 was told. That was the first one they picked on. They happened to pick on these northern California farmers. Most of them in that block were northern California farmers. And the Californians were very touchy about these things because they suffered a lot. Not like Washington state. In Washington state there wasn't that much prejudice, but the Issei from California, they were persecuted. So they were very touchy. Most of them came from the Sacramento Valley, north of Sacramento and that area. Small-time farmers.

"They picked on that block, and they told that block, 'Everybody in that block, seventeen years of age and older, come to the administration building and sign that Loyalty Oath. Or else a ten-thousand-dollar fine and twenty years in prison.' They didn't come. These boys didn't show up. I mean they didn't show up for registration."

They didn't sign the form. They didn't answer "Yes-Yes" or "No-No" to questions 27 and 28, or answer any question on the form. They didn't put their names on the form. They didn't touch the form.

"Thirty-five young boys got together, talked it over. I talked with them, many times.

"These thirty-five young boys were bravest among the bunch. They decided, 'Even if we get arrested, we don't care. Let's go to the administration and tell them that we are not going to register. We are not going to have anything to do with the Loyalty Questionnaire. Send us back to Japan.' This was their demand. Nothing happened that day, and they went back to their block.

"The next day, a whole army—this was described to me—this is hearsay—surrounded that block. Rifles, machine guns, and everything.

"We bachelors lived together. One, two, three—five of us bachelors lived together in that small cell there, in Block 4. The other side of the firebreak. So that's what touched our hearts and our minds. That's the reason I got mad. That's the reason Kibei got mad—put us to shame that seventeen-year-old kids were showing us the way. We got mad. That's how we started organizing, to fight this. You ask me, at my age, how come I didn't care if I spend twenty years in jail—that's my reason."

The leaders of the recalcitrant Kibei were cooks. And though most of the people in Tule Lake were from the Sacramento area, their leader was from Seattle.

"He was slightly shorter than me. He was one of the cooks. Kibei. From Seattle. He was probably a houseboy. Most Kibei were houseboys, cooks, you know. Cooking for the family, cleaning the house, all around you know. He wasn't physically strong. He got most of his education in Japan in his formative years.

"He got this idea of talking things over way back from the Japanese farming village. You see, Japanese farmers way back in the 1920s–1930s wanted rebuild a small bridge across a river, that's been washed away. All of those farmers get together and talk it over, you know. Have a little drink of sake. Homemade, you know, cheap stuff. They talk it over, arrive at consensus."

Both the WRA and the Selective Service, whose seals were on the form, threatened arrest and a fine for refusing to sign. It was a bluff. And the Kibei called that bluff. They expected to be arrested and to take the Application for Leave Clearance Form with its recruitment of volunteers for the army to court.

"This was the day after they were taken in, you see. The news got around. How the news got around is not through the newspaper. They had it hidden, and wanted to sweep it under the rug. Keep people ignorant so that somehow they could be cajoled into signing that statement.

"What spread the news so fast: Kibei cooks in the mess halls, and Kibei who drove the trucks delivering food from the warehouse to each of the mess halls. The cooks told the drivers, and the drivers told the cooks. That's how the message was spread around the camp so fast, because the food delivery truck driver was in sympathy with him. This was communication network.

"Oh, we had meetings all over the place. All over the place. We had meetings in the mess halls. All over the camp. The reason why the meetings were held in the mess halls is that most of the workers, the cooks in there, were Kibei. Ninety-nine percent of them were Kibei, because they used to be houseboys on the outside, you see, and they knew how to cook.

"They had signs written up in Japanese—mimeographed and pasted up in latrines all over camp. Oh yeah. These Kibei, boy! They were organized. Sharp! Everybody is concerned, because nobody wants to be drafted. There was not one woman at these meetings. All men."

The WRA came by night and took men away. The men thought they were under arrest. But they weren't under arrest by any law enforcement agency. They were taken by the WRA, with the FBI looking on, to smaller camps and kept secret. Kentaro Takatsui found himself "arrested" with a group of twenty-five.

"Within the twenty-five, there was really the mentors. And I was one of the mentors, but I don't want to brag about it. Four or five mentors. And then, about fifteen, but all of these fifteen were not leaders. I think about half of them were Block 42 boys. They were the ones that were arrested first. They were not the leaders.

"The ones that were picked up from among the 42 boys, they were the ones that first went to administration building demanding to be sent back to Japan. The reason they picked them up is because they were the oldest. They seemed to be the ones that conversant with the rest of the bunch. They knew each other because they all came from the Sacramento Valley. Farmers, you know. They were related, or friends.

"They couldn't come pick us up in the daytime. They were afraid it might start a riot. Someone knocked on cell door. 3:30 in the morning. 'Takatsui-san.' He knew how to say that in Japanese.

"The door was locked, so I opened the door, and there they were. Three hakujin wardens, and one of them was an FBI agent.

"I was taken to the administration building. Then, from the administration building, we were taken in civilian cars to Klamath Falls county jail—out of camp, up north about thirty miles.

"We were in Moab County Jail, and after Moab County Jail, to Leupp, Arizona. Leupp is a small isolation, small, you know, with barbed-wire fence and soldiers. Around sixty or seventy from all over. There are dissident leaders from all of the other nine camps. Inside that Leupp isolation camp, there was a jail! Ha! I was in that jail, with Harry Ueno with his Manzanar bunch. Ridiculous!

"When we came out of Klamath Falls County Jail—civilian jail—we went to what is called a CCC camp. [The former Civilian Conservation Corps.] There were a hundred something people there in that CCC camp. How they got there is because they wanted to follow us. They're the ones who refused to register. So they threw them in over there. But the reason they stopped doing that is because they realized that there's thousand something people that refused register. We went there before we were taken into the Tule Lake camp itself for the trial.

"There was a reason why they signed 'No-No.' It was because, during the registration drive, the project director came out and said, 'If you sign "No-No" you won't be picked up for the draft, neither will you be forced to go back to Japan, if you don't like that.' Something like that. Something along that line, because so many Kibei refused to register, because they wanted to follow our course of action." They wanted to go to court for refusing to sign the Application for Leave Clearance. They refused to register, thinking the WRA-printed threats of jail time and fines were genuine.

"Other people would say they were draft resisters, but we were not draft resisters. We were draft registration refusers. These other people who resisted and got arrested later was because they had signed the questionnaire. 'Yes-Yes.'

"Then they signed it. And then when the U.S. government wanted to draft them into the army because they signed 'Yes-Yes,' then they got put on trial.

Sure, you'd get put on trial, because you signed 'Yes-Yes' then refused to be drafted. That's natural.

"But in our case, we talked it over, we talked it over, we talked it over, and we decided that the best action was: don't sign anything, because once you sign anything, they got you. So for that reason, we decided to refuse to register." And they'd go to court for refusing to register. "We were a different group. It has never been mentioned before, and nobody knows about it, because none of us has ever surfaced."

The WRA kept the men secret, and saved embarrassment. That was good and bad for the three thousand, but meaningless to their people and the constitution. It took Takatsui and the leaders a long time to realize that nothing was happening.

"About seven of us were at Leupp. About half of us are gone already. And then I said that even after we were arrested that there were other leaders behind us that would carry on underground, which we did, after I came back to Tule Lake. Back to Tule Lake from Leupp, I found out they did a good job.

"The reason why I admitted . . . the reason why Kamiya admitted that 'Yeah we did this.' The reason for that is that we wanted the administration to think that they got the key man. Which I was not. Everybody pointed their fingers at me because it's a good idea to say, 'He's the leader,' because he himself would figure that he won't have to go twenty years in prison. 'He's the man!' Which I wasn't. Everybody did it to me. I was the fall guy!

"I know who the informant was in our group, but I don't want to mention his name. I don't really want to name names—but at the time, boy! We were so angry, that we said we were going to kill that S.O.B. But now, as I look back, he did us a favor. He did us a favor because if we had not been arrested, next day we would have this big—we had planned, you know—big parade. Get everybody together. We planned it on a weekend, so that everybody would not be working, you see. Then we were going to go up to the administration building—they were called *inu*—dog. That's not enough. Inu is more than that. Stool pigeon, double-crosser, informer, you know. And somebody might have been killed.

"About three thousand people remained in Tule Lake following our lead. And this was the largest group of any camp. We were the largest.

"And that's one of the reasons they made Tule Lake a 'disloyal' camp. They sent all the other 'No-No' people from the other nine camps to Tule Lake, because here are three thousand people who don't want to move out of here."

Joe Kurihara,
Veteran from Hawaii

Joe Kurihara was a Hawaiian-born Nisei, WWI vet, and author of a patriotic newspaper column. He joined the JACL thinking they were formed to fight the Evacuation and Internment; he discovered he was wrong and wrote:

> Truly it was my intention to fight this evacuation. On the night of my return to Los Angeles from San Diego was the second meeting which the Citizens Federation of Southern California (sponsored by JACL) held to discuss evacuation. I attend it with a firm determination to fight to the bitter end. I found the goose was already cooked. The Field Secretary of the JACL instead of reporting what actually transpired at a meeting they had had with General DeWitt just tried to intimidate the Nisei to comply with the evacuation by stories of threats he claimed to have received from various parts of the state.
>
> I felt sick at the result. They'd accomplished not a thing. All they did was to meet General DeWitt and be told what to do. These boys claiming to be the leaders of the Nisei were a bunch of spineless Americans. Here I decided to fight them and crush them in whatever camp I happened to find them. I vowed that they would never again be permitted to disgrace the name of the Nisei as long as I was about. (*The Spoilage*, Thomas & Nishimoto, 1969)

He was a fisherman, licensed navigator, and captain. He was a veteran and had proven his loyalty, according to the JACL standard of proving loyalty. Unlike the JACL, he was opposed to the Evacuation. When he evacuated to Manzanar Relocation Center, he spoke his mind against the JACL, against their All Camp Meeting of November 1942, against the evacuation of people from their homes and the order to draft the men. He was a natural leader.

Joe Kurihara gathered audiences of a thousand, or more, at Manzanar, against camp and against the JACL. After the Manzanar Riot of December 6 and 7, 1942, and the beating of JACL delegates to the JACL National Convention, Kurihara was removed to the now notorious Tule Lake, based on accusations that he was one of the masked men that beat up the JACL's Fred Tayama, and a leader of the riot. He was accused of leading a resistance movement at Tule Lake and was sent to Leupp.

At Tule Lake, he came under the sway of Dorothy Swaine Thomas, of the University of California's Japanese Evacuation Research Project, and provided information, including the above, about his life.

He wrote so passionately about his Americanism, and the errors of the government handling of the Evacuation, one wonders why he didn't take the issue to court. Instead, at Tule Lake, he gave up his U.S. citizenship.

He wrote to Miss Yoshiko Hosoi from an isolation camp in Leupp, Arizona, on July 5, 1942.

I, Joseph Y. Kurihara, one of the oldest members of the niseis Second Generation of Japanese Ancestry, do hereby take the liberty of expressing my views in respect to the treatment administered to the Niseis by the Government of the United States. Frankly speaking without prejudices, the Government of the United States has committed one of the greatest errors since the founding of this great nation, and without question the greatest injustice against one of its Citizens. May I ask what reparation the Government is considering to right the wrong? I believe the Government is fully aware of the error it has committed. Will it admit the wrong and compensate the Niseis for the injustice, or will it white-wash the fault of the Administration by pigeon-holing the issue? This inexcusable error and this discriminative injustice has caused the Niseis to change their mind.

The uninformed public may question and wonder as to who is responsible for the Niseis change of mind. If it is posted with the trend of events which took place since 1900, more so since the outbreak of the present war, it need not look back very far. Even myopics can readily see and point his accusing [sic] fingers at the guilty party or parties.

The denouncing phrase "Once a Jap always a Jap. The only good Jap is a dead Jap" has been repeatedly stated that today, even Japanese who strain their brains to converse in English may be heard uttering it with contempt.

Now why can't the Americans be just a little broadminded? Is it any fault of ours because we bear the features of the Japanese? Are we to be discriminated and condemned because we happened to be of Japanese blood without a fair trial? What is there that justifies the Americans to hate the Japanese so revoltingly? Is this hate that of today or yesterday, or even yesteryear? No! Personally, I know it is not that of today or yesterday or even yesteryear.

It is the hate of yesteryear of two score and ten years which sprouted immediately following the defeat of China, then know [sic] to the Western World as the "Sleeping Lion." It became greatly intensified in 1900 and double more so since the defeat of the Russian Bear (1905–06) which was then one of the greatest military powers of the world.

The pitied Japan has surprised the World thru the Victory over China and then she has paralyzed the world with fear thru the Victory over Russia. Her phenominal [sic] military successes have forced the World to grant her a just place among the families of nations.

Rising so rapidly from a Feudal State into one of the greatest of the first class powers has created suspicion and jealousy among those who professed friendship prior to their victories. Therefore, the intense persecution the Japanese have suffered for half a century has come not thru her untiring industries, but thru "Fear, Hatred, and Jealousy." This fear, hatred, and jealousy was characterized into a nightmare under the vicious title of "Yellow Peril."

This horrible dream of Yellow Peril was persistingly pounded into the minds of the Anglo-Saxon people at the slightest provocation, thereby indelibly imprinting in their mind, the hatred of the Japanese people. To soothe the fueling of hatred and jealousy, the insinuating word "Jap or Japs" came into birth and gained popularity most disgustingly since. Today many people use it as a common word to indicate the Japanese without the bitterness attached, but other than those who use it without malice, it commands the same ugly intentions embodied in it as was originally used. We Japanese know it and broad-minded as we are, we resent it. This word alone is responsible to a great extent, not speaking of the law prohibiting intermarriage in Pacific Coast States, for the non-assimilation of the Japanese with the Caucasians. Regardless of this unpleasant feeling many of us were true to this country at the outbreak of the War between Japan and the United States. I can state without exaggeration the majority of the Japanese-Americans were ready to bear arms and fight for the preservation of American Democracy.

We Japanese boys and girls were taught in Japanese Schools to be true to the country to which we owe our living. This the Japanese Government stresses by reminding us "*Kaku on.*" With such thought in mind I have willingly fought for this country to save Democracy in the first World War, and I was willing and ready to do my share in this war. This sincere desire to help prosecute this war to victory was demonstrated in my application for a position as a Navigator to Navigate the Bombers cross the Continent to New York from San Diego, and thence over the sea to England. This application was made sometime during the month of January at the Employment Department of the Consolidated Air Corporation. Much to my disappointment, I was very cleverly refused. Instead of informing me like a man to man, he avoided the painful issue by requesting me to come every day and see if there was an opening. Suspecting what he meant I asked him why was it necessary for me to call every day in person when others are being notified to report for work? The person in charge was unable to answer with the exception that if I wanted a job I just call and see if there is an opening.

It doesn't make sense when others have been and are being notified. I know of boys who applied for work, one as Navigator of a Bomber and the other as Radio Operator. They were notified to report for work. If they can be notified over the phone, why wasn't I?

Because I was a Jap. My credentials as master of ship, and the Certificate of Honorable Discharge from the United States Army were stated. But they were of no value. Instead a secret police was detailed after me as I left that office. The land lady also told me that two intelligence officers were investigating me and have gone thru my room. This gave me the first repulsive feeling which has taken root and grew with bitter experiences mounting from day to day.

Losing all hope of obtaining satisfactory work at San Diego, I then went to Terminal Island to see if the California Ship Building Company has anything along my profession. Here I was very gently told that I would not enjoy working if I was given a job. The fellow workmen will discriminate and make it very unpleasant. There were two Japanese boys working at the time who the Company thinks will be forced to quit through unjust discrimination by fellow workers. To make it easier for them, they were put on night shift. Though they were good welders and the Company did want to retain them, they finally left their work.

To my knowledge there were several Japanese-American Diesel Engineers operating out of San Diego on the Tuna Clippers. They were certified engineers with License. But they were flatly refused by the machinists Union of

America Federation of Labor solely thru discrimination. Such is the ways of even a labor Union where equal right and protection should have been tantamount.

Now, if it is not the hiring department, then it is the fellow workers and the labor union. May I ask are the Americans such narrow minded people? To me they do not seem so but somehow they must be. What could be the cause? I couldn't think of anything but the vicious propaganda that was mercilessly printed in all the leading chronicles of the Metropolis poisoning the minds and rerousing the animosities planted within their hearts during the past half a century.

General DeWitt, frightened beyond hope by the whirlwind successes of the Japanese military might and driven desperate by the hysterical cries of the office seeking petty politicians, has finally issued a proclamation, there by realising the Constitutional rights of the Japanese-American citizens. Probably we, the smallest of the minority group were not worthy of consideration. We were no-bodies. Our desire to serve and prove our loyalty was denied even by the Army. Able bodied Japanese boys were classed 4-D [sic]. Those in the Army were sent back into civilian life without an Honorable Discharge. In the face of these incontestable proofs to do our part we were classed unloyal.

Assembly Centers were erected at great expenses to the Government. Citizens and non-citizens alike, 110,000 of them were corralled like a bunch of sheep in godforsaken corrals and were made wards of the Government overnight. They were the most prosperous industrious, and law abiding residents of the country, but just because they happened to be Japs, they were thrown out of their homes as if they were mere chattles [sic]. After completely uprooting them economically and made them peniless [sic] and destitute, they were obliged to work for mere pittance of $16.00 A Month.

What he writes seems designed to rouse the Nisei reader to action. But what action?

After corralling us like a bunch of sheep in a hellish country, did the government treated us like citizens? NO! We were like aliens regardless of our rights. Yet when we are needed, we are told because you are citizens of the United States, you must do everything in your power to help defeat the Axis. To claim us as citizens of the United States after corralling us with aliens and treat us as aliens, is an insult to our intelligence.

He begs the question, U.S. citizenship and, alternatively, being treated as aliens:

Responsible government officials further tells us to be loyal, and to enjoy our rights as American citizens, we must be ready to die for the country we must show our loyalty. If such is the case, why are the veterans corralled like the rest of us in the camps? Have they not proven their loyalty already?

He seems to have described the JACL and the government's side of the question. His question marks highlight flaws in that point of view. Instead of urging his readers to band together, and find a sympathetic lawyer to present his case as citizen-veteran against the camps, he reacts personally. The JACL and the government acted against him out of spite, and he is "spited."

Now, who wouldn't be spited? I for one will not forgive. This Government of the United States as long as I live. I have sworn Severance of my allegiance to the Government of the United States and became 100 per cent pro-Japanese. I am today every proud of being a Japanese. There is nothing for any one of us to be ashamed of being a Jap. To be born a Jap is the greatest blessing God had bestowed upon us. To live as Jap is the greatest pride we can enjoy in life. And to die as Jap under the protection of the Japanese Flag which has weathered through many National storms without a defeat for 2,600 years is the greatest honor a man can ever hope to cherish. Such is my opinion today, and such will be my opinion tomorrow. Who made me so?

WAR RELOCATION AUTHORITY, APPLICATION FOR LEAVE CLEARANCE

WRA-126 Rev.

Budget Bureau No. 13-R022-43
Approval 1 Expires 7/31/43

WAR RELOCATON AUTHORITY
APPLICATION FOR LEAVE CLEARANCE
Relocation Center_____
Family No._____
Center Address_____

1. _____ _____ _____
   (Surname)   (English given name) (Japanese given name)
   (a) Alias _____

2. Names and ages of dependents you propose to take with you
   _____

3. Date of birth_____ place of birth_____

4. Citizenship_____

5. Last two addresses at which you lived 3 months or more (Exclude residence at relocation center and assembly center):
   _____ From_____ to_____
   _____ From_____ to_____

6. Sex_____ Height_____ Weight_____

7. Are you a registered voter?_____ Year first registered_____
   Where?_____ Party_____

8. Marital status_____ Citizenship of spouse_____
   Race of spouse_____

9. _____
   (Father's name) (Town or Ken) (State or Country) (Occupation)

10. _____
   (Mother's name) (Town or Ken) (State or Country) (Occupation)

In items 11 and 12, you need not list relatives other than your parents, your children, your brothers and sisters. For each person give name; relationship to you (such as father); citizenship; complete address; occupation.

11. Relatives in the United States (if in military service, indicate whether a selectee or volunteer):

349

(a) _____

    (Name)   (Relationship to you)   (Citizenship)

    _____

    (Complete address)   (Occupation)   (Volunteer or selectee)

(b) _____

    (Name)   (Relationship to you)   (Citizenship)

    _____

    (Complete address)   (Occupation)   (Volunteer or selectee)

(c) _____

    (Name)   (Relationship to you)   (Citizenship)

    _____

    (Complete address)   (Occupation)   (Volunteer or selectee)

(If additional space is necessary, attach sheets)

12. Relatives in Japan (see instruction above item 11):

    _____

    (Name)   (Relationship to you)   (Citizenship)

    _____

    (Complete address)   (Occupation)

    _____

    (Name)   (Relationship to you)   (Citizenship)

    _____

    (Complete address)   (Occupation)

13. Education

    Name   Place   Years of attendance

    _____   _____ From_____to_____

    (Kindergarten)

    _____   _____ From_____to_____

    (Grade School)

    _____   _____ From_____to_____

    (Japanese language school)

    _____   _____ From_____to_____

    (High School)

    _____   _____ From_____to_____

    (Junior college, college, or university)

    _____   _____ From_____to_____

    (Type of military training, such as R.O.T.C. or Gunji Kyoren)

                    (Where and when)

_____
(Other schooling)   (Years of attendance)

14. Foreign travel (give dates, where, how, for whom, with whom, and reasons therefore):

_____

_____

_____

15. Employment (give employers' names and kind of business, addresses, and dates from 1935 to date):

_____

_____

_____

16. Religion_____ Membership in religious groups_____

17. Membership in organizations (clubs, societies, associations, etc.). Give name, kind of organization, and dates of membership.

_____

18. Knowledge of foreign languages (put check mark (√) in proper squares):
    (a) Japanese   (b) Other_____(specify)

	Good	Fair	Poor		Good	Fair	Poor
Reading				Reading			
Writing				Writing			
Speaking				Speaking			

19. Sports and hobbies_____

_____

_____

20. List five references, other than relatives or former employers preferably persons resident in areas where you formerly resided, giving address, occupation, and number of years known:

_____
(Name)   (Complete address)   (Occupation)   (Years known)

_____

_____

_____

_____

_____

21. Have you ever been before an Alien Enemy Hearing Board? _____ _____

                                                                                   (Yes)   (No)

    If so, give date and disposition of case:

    (a) Have you ever been arrested or similarly detained?   _____ _____

                                                                                    (Yes)   (No)

    If so, state offense, date, court and disposition of case:

    (b) Have you ever been subjected to any disciplinary action since your evacuation?

____ ____

(Yes) (No)

    If so, state the circumstances and disposition of your case.

22. Give details on any foreign investments.

    (a) Accounts in foreign banks. Amount $_____

        Bank_____ Date account opened_____

    (b) Investments in foreign companies. Amount $_____

        Company_____ Date acquired_____

        Contents_____

23. List contributions you have made to any society, organization, or club:

Organization	Place	Amount	Date

24. List magazines and newspapers to which you have subscribed or have customarily read.

25. To the best of your knowledge, was your birth ever registered with any Japanese governmental agency for the purpose of establishing a claim to Japanese citizenship?

    (a) If so registered, have you applied for cancellation of such registration?

                                                                   (Yes or No)

When_____Where?_____

26. Have you ever applied for repatriation to Japan?_____

27. If the opportunity presents itself and you are found qualified, would you be willing to volunteer for the Army Nurse Corps or the WAAC?

28. Will you swear unqualified allegiance to the United States of America and forswear any form of allegiance or obedience to the Japanese emperor, or any other foreign government, power, or organization?

29. Have you ever worked for or volunteered your services to the Japanese or Spanish government?

_____ _____ If so, indicate which and give date:

(Yes) (No)

30. Have you ever registered any of your children with a Japanese or Spanish Consul? _____ _____ If so, give name and dates:

(Yes) (No)

Names	Dates	Names	Dates
_____	_____	_____	_____
_____	_____	_____	_____
_____	_____	_____	_____

31. Have you ever sent any of your children to Japan? _____ _____
If so give names and dates: (Yes) (No)

Names	Dates	Names	Dates
_____	_____	_____	_____
_____	_____	_____	_____
_____	_____	_____	_____
_____	_____	_____	_____
_____	_____	_____	_____
_____	_____	_____	_____

32. State any type of leave previously applied for, and indicate where leave clearance has previously been applied for, giving date and place of application.

33. If employment is desired, but no definite offer has been received, list the kinds of employment desired in order of preference:

First choice _____

Second choice _____

Third choice _____

(a) Will you take employment in any part of the United States?

_____ _____

(Yes) (No)

(b) Give location preference _____

_____

_____   _____

(Date)   (Signature)

_____

(Seal of Selective Service System)   Form Approved
                                       Budget Bureau No. 26-R645-43

(Local Board Date Stamp With Code)

353

STATEMENT OF UNITED STATES CITIZEN
OF JAPANESE ANCESTRY

1. _____ _____ _____
   (Surname)   (English given name)   (Japanese given name)
   (a) Alias _____
2. Local selective service board _____
   (Number)

   _____
   (City)   (County)   (State)
3. Date of birth _____ place of birth _____
4. Present address _____
   (Street)   (City)   (State)
5. Last two addresses at which you lived 3 months or more (Exclude residence
   at relocation center and assembly center):
   _____ From _____ to_____
   _____ From _____ to_____
6. Sex _____ Height _____ Weight _____
7. Are you a registered voter? _____ Year first registered _____
   Where? _____ Party _____
8. Marital status _____ Citizenship of wife _____
   Race of wife _____
9. _____
   (Father's name)   (Town or Ken)   (State or Country)   (Occupation)
10. _____
   (Mother's name)   (Town or Ken)   (State or country)   (Occupation)

In items 11 and 12, you need not list relatives other than your parents, your children,
your brothers and sisters. For each person give name; relationship to you (such as
father); citizenship; complete address; occupation.

11. Relatives in the United States (if in military service, indicate whether a
    selectee or volunteer):
    (a)_____
    (Name)   (Relationship to you)   (Citizenship)

    _____
    (Complete address)   (Occupation)   (Volunteer or selectee)
    (b)_____
    (Name)   (Relationship to you)   (Citizenship)

    _____
    (Complete address)   (Occupation)   (Volunteer or selectee)

354

(c)_____

| (Name) | (Relationship to you) | (Citizenship) |

_____

(Complete address)   (Occupation)   (Volunteer or selectee)

(If additional space is necessary, attach sheets)

12. Relatives in Japan (see instruction above item 11):

_____

(Name)   (Relationship to you)   (Citizenship)

_____

(Complete address)   (Occupation)

_____

(Name)   (Relationship to you)   (Citizenship)

_____

(Complete address)   (Occupation)

13. Education

Name	Place	Years of attendance

_____ _____ From_____to_____

(Kindergarten)

_____ _____ From_____to_____

(Grade School)

_____ _____ From_____to_____

(Japanese language school)

_____ _____ From_____to_____

(High School)

_____ _____ From_____to_____

(Junior college, college, or university)

_____ _____ From_____to_____

(Type of military training, such as R.O.T.C. or Gunji Kyoren)

(Where and when)

_____

(Other schooling)   (Years of attendance)

14. Foreign travel (give dates, where, how, for whom, with whom, and reasons therefore):

_____
_____

15. Employment (give employers' names and kind of business, addresses, and dates from 1935 to date):

_____
_____

355

16. Religion_____ Membership in religious groups_____
_____

17. Membership in organizations (clubs, societies, associations, etc.).
Give name, kind of organization, and dates of membership.
_____
_____

18. Knowledge of foreign languages (put check mark (√) in proper squares):
(a) Japanese   (b) Other_____(specify)

	Good	Fair	Poor			Good	Fair	Poor
Reading					Reading			
Writing					Writing			
Speaking					Speaking			

19. Sports and hobbies_____
_____
_____
_____

20. List five references, other than relatives or former employers preferably persons resident in areas where you formerly resided, giving address, occupation, and number of years known:
_____

(Name)	(Complete address)	(Occupation)	(Years known)

21. Have you ever been before an Alien Enemy Hearing Board? _____ _____
                                                         (Yes)   (No)
If so, give date and disposition of case:
(a) Have you ever been arrested or similarly detained?   _____ _____
                                                         (Yes)   (No)
If so, state offense, date, court and disposition of case:
(b) Have you ever been subjected to any disciplinary action since your evacuation?
____ _____ If so, state the circumstances and disposition of your case.
(Yes) (No)

22. Give details on any foreign investments.
(a) Accounts in foreign banks. Amount, $_____
Bank_____ Date account opened_____
(b) Investments in foreign companies. Amount, $_____
Company_____ Date acquired_____
Contents_____

23. List contributions you have made to any society, organization, or club:

Organization	Place	Amount	Date

24. List magazines and newspapers to which you have subscribed or have customarily read.

_____

_____

_____

_____

25. To the best of your knowledge, was your birth ever registered with any Japanese governmental agency for the purpose of establishing a claim to Japanese citizenship?

_____

(a) If so registered, have you applied for cancellation of such registration?

_____

(Yes or No)

When_____Where?_____

26. Have you ever applied for repatriation to Japan?_____

27. Are you willing to serve in the armed forces of the United States?

_____

28. Will you swear unqualified allegiance to the United States of America and faithfully defend the United States from any or all attack by foreign or domestic forces, and forswear any form of allegiance or obedience to the Japanese emperor, or any other foreign government, power, or organization?

_____   _____

(Date)   (Signature)

NOTE—Any person who knowingly and willfully falsifies or conceals material fact or makes a false or fraudulent statement or representation in any matter within the jurisdiction of any department or agency of the United States is liable to a fine of not more than $10,000 or 10 years' imprisonment, or both.

U.S. GOVERNMENT PRINTING OFFICE 16-236451

Frank Emi
and
Frank Inouye

February 7, 1943, in Hawaii, a call went out for 1,500 Japanese Americans for an all-volunteer combat unit. Ten thousand Japanese Hawaiians volunteered.

Pearl Harbor, the bull's-eye of the Japanese attack, and COMSINPAC Naval Headquarters were both located in Hawaii. All of Hawaii was under martial law. The Japanese of Hawaii were as free and as constrained as the non-Japanese residents of Hawaii. People were picked up and held under the same martial law that governed all of Hawaii. Most people, including Japanese Americans, stayed where they were and continued to live their lives, continued to work or not to work.

To volunteer for the army in Hawaii was the act of a free man. Volunteer or not, your family and friends were free. The only person affected by your choice was you. Your saying "Going off to fight is the only way I have to prove my loyalty" leaves it understood that the only loyalty you are proving is your own. That's honest. There was no JACL in Hawaii.

The situation on the mainland was different. The mainland was not attacked by Imperial Japanese forces. General John DeWitt, Commandant Western Defense Command, 4th Army, headquartered at San Francisco, said the army had information it could not reveal in detail (later proved to be false in the Hirabayashi, Yasui, Korematsu *Corum Nobis* decision in the Supreme Court) that the Japanese race posed a danger to America. And no martial law was declared. Instead, President Roosevelt gave the army the authority of Executive Order 9066, issued on February 29, 1942, to control, evacuate off the West Coast, and intern "All persons of Japanese ancestry" in the three West Coast states.

The JACL provided an illusion of Japanese American representation and cooperation. The truth is, the JACL did not represent Japanese American opinion, intentions, or civil rights. They did not consult with Japanese Americans. Their membership of approximately 1,800 existed as proxy organization for the whites, to deal with Japanese Americans.

After a year of isolation behind barbed wire, labeled 4-C, unfit for the draft because of race, the Japanese Americans were given the chance to earn their loyalty by volunteering for a segregated unit in the army.

Mike Masaoka was so sure of the popularity of the volunteer program for the 442nd Regimental Combat Team among white observers that he resigned his lofty position with the JACL and became the first Japanese American from the mainland to volunteer for the all-Nisei combat unit. He issued a JACL bulletin, dated February 4, 1943, and titled "Explanation of National Secretary's Volunteering." His bulletin was published in the *Pacific Citizen* the same day and was meant to rally the Nisei to volunteer in droves. The reality of camp was missing from Masaoka's singing patriotic zeal, the same way that British foreign occupation of India was missing from Gunga Din's passion to serve in a British uniform.

> I have volunteered for service in the Army of the United States, and specifically for the special combat team composed of loyal Japanese Americans which is now being organized by the War Department.
>
> As an American citizen, and particularly as American citizen of Japanese ancestry, I could do no less.
>
> I volunteered because I had to keep faith.
>
> I had to keep faith with "my" America. . . .
>
> I had to keep faith with the organization which has honored me. . . .
>
> I had to keep faith with my many friends, both Japanese and non-Japanese. They have expressed, time and time again, their confidence in me as a person and as an American. They expect, and rightfully so, that I am willing and eager to assume the same burdens and dangers as they themselves are called upon to assume. Many of my friends, most of my classmates, and even my former students are dressed in uniforms. I am embarrassed when I walk down the streets of any town or city, for my

"civies" [sic] are not only conspicuous but self-condemning in the "sea" of khaki around me. I often resent, but could do nothing about, those suspicious eyes marking me as a coward or a slacker. I know that I have presumed upon many of my non-Japanese friends whom I expected to protect me from the insinuating remarks of passers-by. I believe that I can now make them proud of their associations with me by wearing the uniform of the land we all love.

I had to keep faith with myself. . . .

He filled out and signed Form DSS 304A. Form 304A was the Selective Service version of the WRA Application for Leave Clearance form and contained questions 27 and 28, worded exactly like questions 27 and 28 on the WRA form.

Questions 27 and 28 were the "loyalty oath" questions.

The WRA and the JACL had convinced each other they were geniuses for making camp palatable to the internees. The sons would volunteer and save the people in camp, through their heroism. The public would realize they had been wrong to insist the Japanese Americans be herded together and isolated like rabid dogs. The Issei parents would display flags in their windows, for the boys in service. The 442nd would prove Japanese American loyalty, the WRA would be vindicated, and Japanese America would be freed. And the JACL would have control of Japanese America.

It didn't happen. Japanese Americans didn't fill out the forms as expected; they did not volunteer in droves. The total number of internee men eligible for induction from the nine camps was 19,963. Three thousand men were expected to volunteer for the all-Nisei segregated combat unit; later the number of men, to be provided by all nine mainland camps, was reduced to 1,500. A disappointing 805 Nisei volunteered. Thousands did not volunteer.

All internees were required to fill out and sign the Application for Leave Clearance that included the "loyalty oath," questions 27 and 28. Japanese Americans resented being thrust into camps, stripped of their rights, then asked to beg to join a segregated unit too suspect to have any Nisei officers. Their families and friends would remain in camps, held hostage by the government.

At Heart Mountain, Frank Emi's response to the questions is typical. "My first involvement in the resistance movement, if you will, began with the introduction of the so-called loyalty questionnaire. The questionnaire contained thirty questions. Two of the questions, number 27 and number 28, were controversial.

"'27. Are you willing to serve in the armed forces of the United States on combat duty wherever ordered?'

"If you answered 'Yes,' the implication was that you were volunteering for the army.

"Number 28 read '28. Will you swear unqualified allegiance to the United States of America and faithfully defend the United States from any or all attack by foreign or domestic forces [Up to this point no problem.] and forswear any form of allegiance or obedience to the Japanese emperor, to any other foreign government, power or organization?'

The wording of question 28 was similar to the JACL loyalty oath of 1942: "that I hereby renounce any other *allegiances which I may have knowingly or unknowingly* held in the past" [emphasis added].

One cannot unknowingly give their oath of allegiance, for to give an oath is to give one's word. One cannot unknowingly give their word. To unknowingly give your oath is simply ungrammatical. "Any form of allegiance or obedience" implies there is more than one form of allegiance that the swearer is aware of.

There was more than the subtleties of grammar at work in question 28. There was obvious linking of any answer with allegiance to the emperor of Japan. Many internees who had never been to Japan saw the question as a trap.

Notes Frank Emi, "If a Nisei answered 'Yes,' he or she was admitting a previously sworn allegiance to the emperor. And in the case of an Issei or first-generation immigrant, who were prevented from becoming citizens of this country because of racist naturalization laws at that time—if they answered 'Yes,' they would become persons without a country.

"After studying the questionnaire for some time with my younger brother Art, I finally came up with a response to the questions.

"Question 27: No, under no condition because of increasing discriminatory acts which were and are still aimed at Japanese Americans, but I will do my best in helping the war effort along other fields."

"Question 28: Under present conditions and circumstances, I am so confused that I am mentally incapable of answering sincerely.

"This is my feeling at the time.

"With the help of my brother, Art, we hand printed copies of my answer on sheets of paper and posted them on mess hall doors and other public places throughout the camp, with a notation that these were suggested answers to those two questions."

There were no free men at Heart Mountain, only inmates in a concentration camp. Heart Mountain's quota of men was 200. The call for volunteers had reams of publicity in the *Heart Mountain Sentinel,* run by the JACL's Bill Hosokawa and monitored by Reports Officer Vaughn Mechau. Guy Robertson, Project Director at Heart Mountain, threatened severe penalties against the Nisei under the Espionage Act: twenty years of imprisonment plus a $10,000 fine, or both, for not cooperating. Despite WRA pressure and threats, the Nisei were opposed to the army's volunteer effort. Only thirty-eight volunteered from Heart Mountain, nineteen of whom were eventually inducted. "The lowest number of volunteers of all the camps," notes Frank Inouye.

Credit for Heart Mountain's opposition to volunteering was claimed by Frank Inouye. Before the Evacuation he had been a twenty-four-year-old student at UCLA. At Heart Mountain, in February 1943, he went to a WRA–army meeting on the new Application for Leave Clearance form. The WRA hoped to ease the Nisei fears about questions 27 and 28.

Frank Inouye was a brooder, unsure of his feelings about being a Japanese American. He was an American because the country that surrounded him was America, and his education was American. He was Japanese because of his parents' upbringing, for which he was grateful and resentful at the same time. He was a good speaker, but he didn't have the words to explain why Americans should not treat him this way, until the questionnaire. He was moved to write a "manifesto" in response and went to the meeting to deliver it to all assembled.

Of the experience, he writes, "At the first Army–WRA meeting, the mess hall was jammed full of Nisei. Every seat was taken, and the aisles were also full of standees. There was a tension in the air that could be felt. I stood in one aisle clutching my 'manifesto' in one hand. After some introductory remarks, Lt. McDaniels recited the Army message. He stated that it was

> our mission . . . to return you to a normal way of life . . . its fundamental purpose is to put your situation on a plane which is consistent with the dignity of American citizenship. Not all Japanese-Americans are loyal to their government . . . [and] individuals who will not accept any obligation to the land which gives them their opportunity . . . are the disloyal ones.

"The refrain was always the same—be good American citizens, and someday, somehow, our rights will be restored. Only this time, the Nisei were being offered the opportunity of entering military service as volunteers in an all-Nisei unit, much as the Negroes had been offered the opportunity to enlist in all-black units during the Civil War. And everybody who read history knew what the casualty rates of those Jim Crow units were! So, here was a generous Uncle Sam offering its imprisoned charges a way to show our loyalty, by leaving behind our helpless and aged Issei parents," he writes with a sense of irony. "Never was there a word of apology for our being subjected to prisoner-of-war status, or for our loss of civil rights." So what does he want from the government? As he said, for all to hear his manifesto:

The means we have at hand, the plan is simple. We should, *we must demand now our true status in American life*. We still have time to discover whether we are being used as we have been used in the past, or if this time, the government is really extending to us the opportunity we need to prove once and for all our unswerving loyalty to America.

By our status, however, we should make clear that we mean the rights and privileges of full citizenship, not merely the handout of a tolerant society. We must demand that our name be cleared, and have it read to the world that there has never been a justification for our evacuation, and that we are fighting, not to redeem ourselves or to learn our names, but for what we have always believed in.

He's not just delivering a speech, he is organizing; but what is he organizing?

"Essentially, what I was proposing was a new, all-Nisei organization dedicated to combating the WRA's and the army's programs, and to give voice to the 'rank-and-file' citizens in camp, instead of leaving our fate and concerns in the hands of the JACL, which I regarded as a body of elitists out of touch with the typical Nisei.

"In the next few days, camp activities almost ground to a halt as each block began a process to elect Nisei representatives to the congress. Within days, these delegates assembled in the Block 22 recreation barrack. Following an election of officers, in which I was elected chairman, and Paul Nakadate secretary, we officially adopted the name Heart Mountain Congress of American Citizens. Its primary purpose was to obtain from the U.S. government an acknowledgment of the innocence of the Japanese Americans and their parents as a precondition to further registration and volunteering."

What he asks for is nothing. He is not asking that the government close the camps and return the people to their homes. He is not asking that the government return the parents and families of those who volunteer to their homes.

He is asking that the government remove the questionable parts of question 28 from the WRA form, before the Nisei fill it out and register. He's not asking for a change of anything except the JACL's wording of the loyalty oath. Still he boasts:

"Total submission and cooperation by the residents of Heart Mountain, long advocated by the Japanese-American Citizens League (JACL) and proclaimed by the WRA to be a 'happy' camp, were now revealed to be a lie."

And he claims credit for Heart Mountain's massive rejection of the volunteer program:

"The army had hoped that 1,500 volunteers would be enrolled from the ten camps. Heart Mountain's 'quota' was 200. But only thirty-eight volunteered from our camp; it was the lowest number of volunteers of all the camps. Had my message been delivered to the other camps, their totals would have been significantly less."

His new group, the Heart Mountain Congress of American Citizens, lasted a year, claimed success, and fizzled out, unnoticed and largely unknown by the people in Heart Mountain. They had asked for nothing. They had risked nothing. They were not willing to break camp rules and take the camps to court. They were not willing to break the laws against them walking out of camp without a pass, get arrested, and take the camps to court. They had no legal representation, because they didn't need it. What was the difference between their actions (or lack thereof) and the JACL's "total submission"? What were they organized for? In the end, nobody knew.

The other Frank, Frank Emi, who had plastered Heart Mountain with suggested answers to questions 27 and 28, was unaware of Frank Inouye and his organization of an alternative to the JACL.

The single accomplishment of the Congress of American Citizens may have been the emergence of Paul Nakadate as secretary. The congress died in January 1944. (Frank Inouye, relocated outside of camp shortly thereafter.) The Fair Play Committee declared itself in favor of creating "test cases" in February. Paul Nakadate was a member of the FPC's steering committee and often spoke for the FPC, though it was led by Kiyoshi Okamoto. Frank Inouye called the FPC "belligerent" and put quotation marks around "loyal" when writing about them, as if he was suspicious of their motives. The difference between Inouye's congress and the FPC was the difference between protest and resistance. The congress delicately complained. The FPC sought rules and laws to violate that would get them arrested, so they could take the camps to court. And in court, their guilt or innocence would be decided.

Nobu Kawai,
The Volunteer

"WITHOUT A WAR RECORD, I WOULDN'T HAVE A LEG TO STAND ON"

"I went to Heart Mountain and I got my wife settled. I talked to family and so forth. She had a younger brother, Ted. And he was very much interested in the reasons why I had volunteered. And so I sat down with him one evening and I reviewed the whole thing. And I told him that 'I feel that we definitely have to fight for our future.'

"'If we are going to return to the West Coast, we definitely have to go back and look for a better life than we had before the war.'

"And that one of main reasons for the evacuation was the scare tactics that the people used in saying the Japanese didn't know loyalty. They questioned our loyalty.

"And they weren't sure whether we would be loyal to the United States or Japan in the event of a war. And they peddled that propaganda so much that a lot of people began to get uneasy. And they said, 'Well if we don't know for sure whether they will be loyal to America, the safest thing is to evacuate them.' And that was the reason the evacuation eventually materialized.

"I felt that our biggest purpose was to prove our loyalty. The only way to prove our loyalty is to fight for our country.

"While I disagreed in the beginning with the concept of a segregated Nisei unit—I didn't believe in segregation—when it was explained to me, then I felt that that was probably the wisest thing to do. Just to go in as a Nisei unit.

"Any victories or any accomplishments that the Nisei make would reflect on the Nisei in general. And I was sold on it completely.

"And that is what I was explaining to this young fellow Ted. And I told him, 'When I go back to the West Coast, if I am fortunate to get back, I want to be able to stand on my feet and refute any arguments as far as disloyalty or questionable loyalty was concerned. Without a war record, I wouldn't have a leg to stand on.'

"That was the reason I was doing it. Not for myself but for the future of my children. I felt that it was very essential and that the Nisei show their loyalty and fight for the survival of the United States in the life and death struggle is this world war.

"And evidently I impressed him because the following day he volunteered for the 442nd Combat Team.

"When he told me he had volunteered, I was a little upset because I had told him, 'War is a very serious thing. Because you don't know for sure whether you are coming back. And I don't want to be put in a position where I had influenced you one way or the other. If it's your own decision, I really want to congratulate you. But if I in any way persuaded you to join the voluntary forces, I want you to rethink the whole thing.'

"He said, 'No, Nobe. It was my decision. I wanted to find out your reasons for volunteering.'

"'If that's the case Ted, I want you to explain that to your parents.' And see we had a family conference that night. I had him explain to his parents that I did not try to persuade him to join the army. That it was his own decision.

"And Teddy went. It got me mad. And so I went down to the administration and said, 'How come? I volunteered way before he did. He's going and I'm not going.'

"Well, they said, 'Just be calm. They'll be coming around to you.'

"So, I said, 'Okay.' I waited and waited and waited. They went to Camp Shelby. They went through basic training. They were almost ready to go overseas. And I went down there and just raised cain with them. 'I want to get into that thing. I volunteered because I wanted to be among the first to go ever. I don't want to go over there as a replacement. If I have to go as a replacement, I might as well take my chances with the Selective Service. Besides, I feel responsible for this kid. And if he's going over there, I want to be along side of him.'"

Min Yasui,
Resister Or Turncoat?

The Portland curfew resister, Minoru Yasui, lost in the Supreme Court. He was released from Multnomah County Jail, for time served, to Minidoka Relocation Center in southern Idaho. George Tani, the only active member of the Civil Liberties League, collected $3,000 for Yasui's defense from internees, soliciting apartment by apartment, block by block, while the other members of the league, Yasui's Portland friends, played cards rather than solicit their sections of camp. Tani surrendered the money to Yasui's cause, and then left camp for St. Paul, Minnesota, and service with Military Intelligence Division. The all-JACL Civil Liberties League disbanded after Masaoka accused them of being "Communistically formed."

Assimilation

ANOTHER WORD FOR RACIAL EXTINCTION?

T he *Pacific Citizen* was approved for free distribution to the Nisei soldiers of the 442nd by the FBI. The *Pacific Citizen* did not contradict or criticize the United States government. The *Chicago Defender*, a Negro newspaper, did criticize the selective application of the constitution and had war reporters following black units of the military. The *Chicago Defender* was not approved by the FBI.

In this editorial, the *Pacific Citizen* seems to say the racism whites visit on the colored minorities is the minorities' fault, for celebrating its difference from the majority.

THE PACIFIC CITIZEN
Official Publication of the
Japanese American Citizens League
May 13, 1943

END OF THE "CITIZEN"

For all Americans, including those of Japanese ancestry, we have always advocated complete absorption and assimilation with the economic and social life of this country. It therefore seems paradoxical that at the same time we must push such all-nisei projects as the Japanese American Citizens League and the *Pacific Citizen*.

We see, however, the time when the *Pacific Citizen,* having served its usefulness, disappears.

So long as the nisei are attacked upon a racial basis, so long must the *Pacific Citizen* continue. There will come a time, certainly, when an injury upon a nisei is an injury upon an individual citizen of this country. There will come a time when all the people of this country realize that an injustice to one of its citizens, nisei or any other, is an injustice to all. When that day comes, there will be no need for nisei newspapers.

The nisei press, like the Negro press, the Chinese press and the Italian press, reflects a social condition. It reflects an ingrown society whose bond is racial. Though that press depicts purely social activities, it indicates that we have not yet attained that ideal— the assimilation of all groups, blocs and peoples that constitute this country.

America cannot achieve her final growth until these ingrown social blocs have disappeared. The races that live side by side become the races that are pitted one against the other in the established technique of the Fascists, foreign or native.

When we have achieved one-ness with all the races of America, we shall have done away with the need for the minority press.

Ben Kuroki, Boy from Nebraska

MISSION OVER PLOESTI

Ben Kuroki, the only Nisei in the Army Air Corps, finally finds acceptance as an American and a sense of belonging in a B-24 named "The Red Ass."

"I was with the 93rd Bomb Group. And we were the first B-24 group to fight in England.

"So once you got on a combat crew, boy, everybody treated you differently. I mean it. . . . That was a great feeling. You really felt you belong, you know.

"And I was a top turret gunner when we flew the mission over the Ploesti oil refineries. And that one was my twenty-fourth mission." The 93rd Bomb Group was originally commanded by Colonel Edward J. Timberlake, "That's why they started calling us 'Ted's Traveling Circus.'" Because of his experience with B-24s, "Ted" Timberlake became the operational planner for the Ploesti mission and turned over command of the 93rd Bomb Group's thirty-nine aircraft to Lieutenant Colonel Addison Baker. The group was now called Baker's Traveling Circus.

Sunday morning, August 1, 1943, five bomber groups take off one after the other, 178 B-24 Liberators, each with a crew of approximately ten—1,725 Americans in all, and one RAF stowaway, take off from Bengazi, Libya, to bomb the oil cracking plants and refineries at Ploesti, Rumania. A round trip of twenty-seven hundred miles. Extra fuel tanks in the bomb bay. One thousand pound and 500 pound bombs and incendiaries. Four thousand pounds per B-24. Destruction, 311 tons of it, flying toward Ploesti.

The 367th Liberandos, and Kuroki's 93rd, Baker's Traveling Circus, found themselves flying toward Bucharest instead of Ploesti. They'd made a wrong turn. Radio silence was broken with calls of "Wrong turn!" That was just one mistake among many that plagued the Ploesti mission dubbed OPERATION TIDAL WAVE.

Thirteen hours later, he was back in Bengazi. Fifty planes and 500 men were lost. Kuroki and the other survivors were awarded the Distinguished Flying Cross.

This was Kuroki's twenty-fourth mission. One more and he could go home.

"I flew thirty missions in the B-24. It was only required to fly twenty-five, and I volunteered for five extra. Well, I just wanted to prove myself a little more—wanted to prove my loyalty as a Japanese American.

"Oh sure. It scared the hell out of me 'cause that was my twenty-fourth mission. But still kept on flying. You're still young, and I guess that's why they want young people in the service, 'cause you're all gung ho and you have no responsibilities and you have no family to worry about or anything like that." He and his family were from the inland state of Nebraska and weren't subject to the Evacuation and Internment in concentration camps.

"But, anyway after the thirtieth mission, I decided to come back while I was still in one piece."

Dr. Clifford Uyeda,
Traveler

"**I** thought everybody learned the same way. I remember sometimes I would look up somebody's telephone number, and I don't even think about it—days later, or weeks later, somebody says, 'Gee, what is that number?' And you know, I could always see that phone number. I could see it in the telephone book. I could always see it. I don't have to try to remember it. I just read it off again. I think that, for science, especially in chemistry, with all the signs and formulas that you have to write—in medical school, when someone would ask me about anatomy, I could always see that page. Page number, and then what I'd have to do is read it in my mind.

"I was the only person in my class that had to pay his way through medical school. All my classmates were in the Army Specialized Training Program, or the B12 program, and the government paid for everything.

"It was my medical school dean who said, 'Look, this program is coming on, so be sure that you apply.'

"So I applied to the navy.

"I got word from my dean's office that he was told that what the navy said was that they were not going to train anyone of Japanese ancestry at government expense. But he said, 'Don't worry. After all, there is the army. You are certain to be able to get in there.'

"I applied to the army, the headquarters in San Antonio. It took maybe a couple of months, then I got the identical answer from the army, saying the War

Department was not going to treat anybody of Japanese descent to an education. So I was not eligible to apply.

"Suddenly I got a call from the dean's office, saying that there is somebody here to see me. So I went, and there was this big man standing there. He said he was from the FBI. I thought that was strange. He told me to drop out of medical school and join the army. He said there was a group at Camp Shelby. The 442nd.

"That sort of got me mad. I told him, 'If you can convince my classmates to all drop out of medical school and go into the army, then I would go.'

"Then he told me that they were already in the service. As doctors. I told him I applied under the same program they did, and they didn't take me. Their way through school is paid for. I'm the only one paying his own way.

"He told me I should serve my country.

"It was a ridiculous thing he was saying. I finally told him I wasn't going to go. He left. Less than a month later, I got a notice to report for a physical. From the army.

"But the question was, what would I do if the order came? I had already made up my mind that if the order came, I would not go, whatever the cost. The order never came."

James Wong Howe,
American Cinematographer

"**Y**ou know, it's a funny thing. In my whole career, I have never made a Chinese or Oriental picture. At one time I wanted to, when I was under contract to MGM. They made *The Good Earth*.

"Now, I thought I would get that. But, what did they do? They gave it to Karl Freund, a German cameraman. I was a little disappointed. But, however, I don't think I could have made the film any better than Karl Freund made it, because he's a fine cameraman. And they put me on a Mexican picture called *Viva Villa!*

"Now, in my work, in photography, I always use lighting, what they call in painting 'the lost and found lines.' And the imaginary line. I light that same way. I go to art galleries. And I have a lot of art books. And I study the old masters, and see the way they paint, and they compose. And all these things together, then point of view, my observation has an influence.

"As far as inspiration goes. My work inspires me. And, of course, the story. I don't believe in falling in love with your own handiwork. I read. I'm really interested in the characters! In *Viva Villa!* the backgrounds are very hot and the faces were dark. In all the portraits. That was the nature of the story, of these peons that lived in Mexico. And the area where they lived.

"It was hard. Hot! And harsh! That showed you in what kind of conditions they were living. It was very difficult. Then they have the revolution and the war. And it made it, that the people never seem to have anything but suffering.

"The people say, 'Well, they probably get used to it,' but I don't think anyone gets used to suffering. But they just say, 'Well, that is the way it is,' 'n they have to exist 'n they get along 'n they try to do the best they can.

"And you find everything simplified. Because they don't have the thing that we have.

"Now, if you go into their home, we don't have the thing like I have here, now. They only would have the bare necessities. Necessities! You see?

"Just because I'm Chinese, to think that I could make a Chinese picture better than anyone else is, I think, more or less wrong. After all, I'm raised over in this country ever since I was five years old. I'm more American, really, than Chinese.

"You know," James Wong Howe says, "Being Chinese, you couldn't be naturalized. The only way you could be a citizen was to be born in this country. Or that your father was born in this country. You see?

"Since I wasn't born over here, I wasn't citizen 'til after the Second World War! When Roosevelt, President Roosevelt made all the changes. So during the war, I still had to register the draft! And did you know? I was drafted! Yeah!

"And I went up, took my physical. I had to line up. To get blood test.

"And they would get some blood, and they would put it in a little tube, and you write your name on this thing. Address it. Put a rubber band around it, and you throw it in a little basket!

"And I said, 'My god! They would lose this stuff. What keeps 'em from losing it?' And sure enough! They lost my blood!

"Time went on. I never was called. Until I got on a picture with Sam Goldwyn [*The North Star*, 1943, RKO-Goldwyn. D. Lewis Milestone. 105 min. Retitled: *Armored Attack*]. I think it was Sam Goldwyn. And they call me back to get more blood. They lost it. They said, 'Well, we can't send him down. He's on a film. If you want some blood, send your doctor down.'

"So they said, 'Well, the studio's got a doctor.' So they got a doctor, and he took more blood, you see?

"And when he sent it in, by the time that was processed, my birthdate had changed. And I got a year older. And I wasn't eligible for the draft! Free! So! Now! Then John Ford had a unit. Called the Ford Unit. And they worked under a General Donavan [William Joseph "Wild Bill" Donavan] And it was called O.S.S. Office of Strategic Service. And he wanted me to come and join with him, see?

"It's in the Navy. See? I said, 'I can't. How can I join?' I said, 'I'm not a citizen!'

"He said, 'Well! Tell ya what to do. We could fix that.'

"They wanted me. See? He said, 'We'll arrange it so you can join the Chinese army. Chiang Kai-shek's army. See? We'll arrange that. And they'll make you a major.' See, because in his unit, I had to be at least a lieutenant or something to do my work.

"And then he said, 'We could make you a lieutenant! You'll be a Chinese major, and then we'll borrow you and we'll make you a lieutenant! You'll work with us that way.'"

"So I said, 'You either take me this way or forget it!' You see?

"So they couldn't accept me because of not being a citizen. But I could join the Chinese army. You see? Then they could borrow me. Because China and United States were, you know, allies. They could borrow me then from the Chinese army. Now that's a ridiculous thing!

"Otherwise I'd probably been in the Ford Unit. It was a great unit. I would have liked to have been in it. Dangerous work! Because they sent you out, you know. Probably they were over in Burma and all through there. In the Pacific. I made war pictures like *Air Force*. But I didn't make any documentary war pictures. All these were in the studio. We went down to Tampa, Florida. The name of the picture was *Air Force*. We used Drew Field. And these are days that they just had the B-17s. *Air Force* was about a squadron of nine B-17s on a routine flight. To Hawaii. Honolulu. Just enough gas to go there. Fuel, but no ammunition. Halfway over or a little more they got the message over the radio that Pearl Harbor had been attacked.

"See? The situation is, you can't turn around 'n go back. There's no place to go. They had to land!

"So they finally land there. And the Japs chase them off. Well, we went down to Florida. Tampa. The runway was supposed to be built in the jungle. So they would camouflage.

"They thought they could build one of these runways in the jungles in Florida. But it was too soft. And it wouldn't hold. So, what we had to do then was to move the jungle over to the existing runways. We had people down there for a month moving trees and the jungle plantation over. See?

"So. One night we had a scene where the B-17s was coming in about a quarter to seven. Nine of them! Now! Remember, there's a war going on. And we could only keep 'em so long, they'd come in at a certain time and take off.

"Well, I had my lights and generators all set up. A waiting for them to come. Around about six o'clock, I said, 'I'd better turn on the lights. See if they're okay. Check 'em up.'

"Generator broke down! You see? It's six o'clock. And I went to the director, and I said, 'Look, Howard!' Howard Hawks. I said, 'Howard, the generator broke down. We got no lights.'

"He said, 'I can't worry about that.' He says, 'Jimmy, you're the photographer.' See?

"Well, fortunately, I had flares with me. So what I did was to take the mirrors out, the reflectors out of the backs of the lights, these big lights, mount 'em on a stand, and put the flares in front. So I used the flares for where the globes would be, you see?

"And I had my electrician wire all these flares up. There must've been about a dozen–fifteen of them. So he wired these flares all up. And, at quarter to seven! Here comes those B-17s. Beautiful sight! I had the light on the landing lights. So, I give the signal. He hit it, and all these flares lit up. And they flicker. And the smoke would drift through the camera lenses you know. And these B-17s cut down through this smoke and landed. The brakes squealing and the lights flashing. And they came out beautiful!

"And the flare and the flicker helped it. It was supposed to be a landing field. And the Japs had just hit it earlier. And there was a lot of wreckage around. So it worked out fine. Looked so good that the director, Hawks, said, 'Look, Jimmy,' he said. 'This is great. Finish the picture here with flares. Send the generator home!"

Frank Emi, Leader

"SAY, THIS GUY KNOWS
WHAT HE'S TALKING ABOUT"

"**O**h, the big meeting that was raised by the WRA—it was publicized in the *Sentinel*." The featured speaker was also from the *Sentinel*, Nobu Kawai, associate editor of the camp daily and a member of the JACL.

"It was held in one of these buildings that they use for church. Church building . . . about half the size of a full barrack," Frank Emi says.

"Nobu Kawai urged everybody to cooperate with the Loyalty Questionnaire. Nobu Kawai said that we should cooperate with the questions 27–28 registration." He pauses a beat, and says, "Cooperate" with a certain contempt, lowering his voice.

"And Okamoto stood up. He was a loner." This was Emi's encounter with Kiyoshi Okamoto, a soil test engineer from Hawaii.

"My picture is of an old, hard-bitten, rugged miner, a rugged individualist, he wore a goatee at the time. He had sort of a triangular face, more on the smallish size. Small features. He is very serious. Very seldom cracks a smile. Stern looking. He was a bachelor. He had glasses.

"And he said that what we had heard was Nobu Kawai's version of the constitution. And that he had read the constitution differently. The government had violated all of our constitutional rights, that we should think about this more before we go ahead and sign 'Yes-yes.'

"He would talk about the constitution, and how the government had abrogated all our rights, and how the government thought of us as 'Oriental monkeys.' He was very colorful.

"I think it was Dave Kawamoto and Sam Horino, and maybe Ben Wakaye, and we said, 'Say, this guy knows what he's talking about,' and we felt strongly about it ourselves, so we approached Okamoto and started talking to him. His speech was an inspiration to some of us who had similar feelings. During this period, he referred to himself as 'Fair Play Committee of One.' After that meeting, several of us got together with Okamoto and had a long talk."

Shisei Tsuneishi

"BLOCK HEAD"

"I was chosen as the block head of our block," Shisei Tsuneishi writes, in his ninety-third year, about camp forty years ago. "After serving for one year as the block head, I retired, and I took care of a Japanese Language Library." He works at the typewriter, typing his statement for the 1981 Bernstein Commission on the Wartime Relocation and Internment of Civilians, the so-called "Redress Commission."

"In 1943, there was so-called Loyalty Registration. We were subjected to answer many questions. It aroused a great dispute, particularly among Nisei. For me, as I was an alien enemy, there was no choice but to submit to the war policy of the U.S. But to Nisei, it was different, because they were American citizens.

"There were many super patriots who volunteered to serve in the army, in spite of the fact that their rights of citizenship had been ignored and confined within the barbed-wire fences. However, there were some Niseis who argued that they could not be loyal to the U.S. and serve the army, since the rights of citizenship have been actually taken away from them. They formed a group called 'Fair Play Committee' and started to have meetings at various mess halls, explaining their point of view. One day some of their leaders came to our block and asked me to serve as the emcee of the meeting they had planned to have at the mess hall in my block.

"I told them, 'Why don't you go to the present block head and ask about it?' The leader answered, 'We did, but he refused to take it. There is no one to ask,

380

and so we came to see you.' I hesitated a little, but finally I accepted it, for I have been sympathetic toward them." Reading his father's statement, Paul Tsuneishi learned his Issei father was not only aware of draft resistance at Heart Mountain, as it was happening, but that his father had opinions about it and had been involved.

"The gist of my talk at that Fair Play Committee meeting was as follows: Since I am an alien enemy, I am not in a position to express my opinions on the policy of the war of the U.S., but when I was young I went to the American schools for several years and learned about American history, as well as the constitution of U.S. I know why the colonists revolted against England. The Nisei also knows about them. I can understand why some of them refuse to be royal [sic] to U.S. and refuse to serve American army, while the rights of citizenship have been denied to them and put into the concentration camp without doing anything wrong." He wrote "royal" for "loyal." He was a poet. Was this slip of the tongue intentional as well as appropriate?

"Tonight, young people are going to speak what they have in their minds. I wish all of you please listen to what they say.

"At that time when I spoke at the meeting, three of my sons were already serving in American army. I was proud of it. At the same time, I justified some of the Niseis who refused to serve the army at that circumstance."

Forty years after camp, he uses the Heart Mountain Fair Play Committee to argue the case for redress. Paul is delighted. He is shocked. As he looks over his father's typewritten, signed, and dated statement, he discovers his father wasn't the dummy he thought he was, in a concentration camp.

In your New Year additionn [sic] of the SENTINTEL [sic] you had several poems which were very interesting. I have a poem here which I wish you would print in the SENTIN-TEL [sic]. This is how it goes.

THAT DAMNED FENCE

They've sunk in posts, deep into the ground
They've strung out wire, all the way around
With machine gun nest, just over there
And sentries and soldiers everywhere.
We're trapped like rats in a wire cage
To fret and fume with impotent rage
Yonder whispers the lure of the night
But that DAMNED FENCE in the floodlights glare
Awakens unrest in our nocturnal guest
And mockingly laughs with vicious jest.
With nowhere to go and nothing to do
We feel terrible, lonesome, and blue;
That DAMNED FENCE is driving us crazy,
Destroying our youth and making us lazy.
Imprisoned in here far a long, long time
WE know we're punished tho' we've committed no crime
Our thoughts are gloomy and enthusiasm damp.
To be locked up in a concentration camp.
Loyalty we know and Patriotism we feel,
To sacrifice our utmost was our ideal
To fight for our country, and die mayhap
Yet we're here because we happened to be a JAP.
WE all love life, and our country best
Our misfortune to be here in the West
To keep us penned behind that DAMNED FENCE
Is someone's notion of NATIONAL DEFENSE

—Anonymous

Frank Emi, Leader

"THAT'S WHEN I TOOK OVER"

"I seem to recall we contacted Kubota. He took judo. He was actually one of four judo instructors at the camp judo school, and a Zen man, a married Zen man, father of a daughter, and his wife had another child on the way. If it was a boy, he planned to name him "Gordon" for Gordon Hirabayashi. He had never met Gordon Hirabayashi, but like everyone in camp, he had read about his challenging the military curfew order and the exclusion all the way to the Supreme Court.

"He was a Japanese schoolteacher, and he spoke some English," Frank says, "so he might be a good man to translate our bulletins into Japanese. I think that's the way we got started with him. Then he became a very ardent supporter and said, 'If you guys get taken in with the FBI, I'll be right there with you. What you guys are,' he said, 'was *ippon* American. Upstanding American you know.' I thought it was pretty good sentiment on his part.

"He always used to tell us that over here he is a citizen of Japan. That he felt that the Nisei were wronged so badly, that's why he helped us from the beginning by interpreting all our bulletins in Japanese. And give speeches in Japanese, which Paul, or one of us would give in English. So, he was acting as a translator. When here an Issei who really didn't have anything to do with the draft would come out and stick his neck out and help us with everything he had."

The leaders of the Fair Play Committee were all Nisei, born in America, and American citizens. They were concerned that Kubota was a Japanese national, barred from citizenship. And as a noncitizen involved with American draft resistance, he risked a charge of sabotage, and the death penalty.

"So as far as Japan, he never mentioned that—No—we should be loyal to Japan or that Japan was going to win the war or anything like that—You know, he told us like this—'You are like Americans and they are treating you like dirt. What you are doing is a beautiful thing that you are fighting for your rights.'

"Among our leader group there was really none of us that were really in the process of getting arrested. We even had a family which made us 3-A, or over-age. The only ones in the process of being drafted were Ben Wakaye and Min Tamesa. That was it! Paul Nakadate was married. [Nakadate also had two brothers serving in the army.] So he wouldn't suffer the draft.

"He was the best educated one among us. He was a graduate from San Diego summer college. He was a good writer, speaker. He did most of the English speaking for us.

"In the beginning, Paul Nakadate was writing the press releases, but he was overamplifying some stuff that was not true. In one of the press releases, that he sent to James Omura, was about a big strike! We were going to recall Robertson! Stuff like that which was not true. And I thought that would reflect on our credibility. And that's when I took over.

"He sends releases about all the boys arrested for violating the draft at Heart Mountain to all the papers in the state and the *Rocky Shimpo*.

"The *Billings Gazette* sent a letter saying they reserved judgment on things like this, so they would wait until we go to court, and have our day in court, before they expressed an opinion on it. And I did get a letter from Edward Ennis's office. You know, the attorney general. To publicize our plight, the only thing I was sure of was James Omura.

"I felt so strongly that what the government was doing was absolutely wrong, you know, that they would take everything away from us, throw us in camp, and then treat us as if nothing happened—that we were subject to the draft, like anybody else on the outside. And I thought that was outrageous. If the public became aware of it, that might help our case.

"So, I just wrote letters to the editor. Letters to the newspapers. I didn't think of press releases, at the time. Just to publicize this one way or another."

ROCKY SHIMPO

February 16, 1944

Nisei America

KNOW THE FACTS

By JIMMIE OMURA

Let's Call a Spade a Spade

I am deeply disappointed at the failure of the Nisei editors to call a spade a spade. Hardly a voice has been raised in objection to the discriminatory features of the current reinstitution of selective service program among the Nisei. Instead, a chorus of hallelujahs greeted the War Department announcement.

Let us take a typical example from an editorial in the Minidoka *Irrigator* which was subsequently reprinted the *Pacific Citizen*. It said:

> The acceptance of the Nisei through the draft and his induction into the United States army through the normal channels undergone by any other John Doe American prove that America's faith in the Nisei has been fully restored.... We are now like other Americans whose services will be accepted by our country without discrimination....

There is nothing in the present program of drafting the Nisei that could give substance to such idealistic ravings. Discrimination continues as before. Faith in the Nisei has not been fully restored. Induction is not conducted through normal procedures. All these statements are false.

32- Question Draft Inquiry Sent Myer by Topaz Council

Redress of Grievances and Adjustments Prior to Military Induction under Proposal

Topaz, Utah, Feb. 19—First among the nine relocation centers to draft concrete questions indicating the desire of draft-age Nisei for a redress of grievances prior to their being inducted into service, the Topaz community council, acting through Project Director Charles F. Ernst, directed a 32-question inquiry to Dillon S. Myer, WRA national director, it was learned today.

Particular emphasis was placed on the discriminatory features of the program, the continued prohibition of Japanese from the west coast areas, application of the dependency allotment and veterans act, and the basis used in arriving at acceptability and non-acceptability of eligible Nisei.

Evacuees Warned against 'Lil Tokios'

Manzanar, Feb. 19—Caution to prospective relocatees not to resettle into areas where there are many residents of Japanese origin was voiced by Walter A. Heath, an official of the WRA.

"To protect the people already settled," Heath said, "the War Relocation Authority will not approve more leave to go into northern Colorado or northern Utah, including Denver and Salt Lake City."

He suggested that evacuees relocate in the east where there are not many Japanese.

Amache to Petition Draft Grievances

Lamar, Feb. 21—Protesting the reinstitution of selective service without reinstatement of the Nisei's civil rights, three meetings are held last week at Amache Relocation Center to discuss a petition of citizenship rights, James G. Lindley, project director, announced today.

The draft age Nisei at Amache are said to be contending that various restrictions on persons of Japanese ancestry be lifted before the Nisei are compelled to military induction.

Gloria Kubota,
Nisei and the Zen Man

"**A**ll of the husbands would kind of meet at our place. And somebody stole enough lumber to make a big table. They made the table right in the house, I think, otherwise it wouldn't come in. They made a big table. They made it big enough to put on a typewriter. Because we did all that work, you know.

"I took typing just one year. I wasn't very good, but I used to sneak in. I was trying to pluck at it. We were typing on that thing. And I was slow. I guess I was too slow, because, finally they got a better typist to come in and started typing the things."

"ONE FOR ALL AND ALL FOR ONE"

The Fair Play Committee was organized for the purpose of opposing all unfair practices that violate the Constitutional rights of the people as guaranteed and set forth in our United States Constitution regardless if such practices occur within our present concentration camp, the state, territory or Union. It has come strongly in recent weeks in regards to the discriminatory features of the new selective service program as it applies to the Japanese American nationals despite the loud and idealistic claims of nisei editors.

The Committee calls to your attention the Community Council of Topaz and Rowher which is genuinely interested in clarifying the draft issue to its people. WHAT HAS YOUR COMMUNITY COUNCIL DONE?...

...The Fair Play is out to give you that side which the Assistant Project Director and the JACL have not presented. The Fair Play does not believe with many writers, however, believes that they have the freedom and right to express their opinion. The Fair Play will fight for them for that right and privilege of expression despite the fact that some of the writers would want some people to shut up. In unfair practices of anti-groups they would like the Fair Players to shut up by employing moral intimidations via propaganda, the FBI, etc. Those methods do not obstruct the ideals of this group. In this instance we take Confucius' saying: Do not do unto others as you would not want others to do unto you.

AS OUR PUBLICATION IS LIMITED PLEASE PASS THIS COPY ON.

Hajiime "Jim" Akutsu, "No-No Boy"

1943, Hajiime "Jim" Akutsu became a "No-No" boy. He was not removed from Minidoka to Tule Lake because a sympathetic project director allowed him to stay at Minidoka to care for his mother, who was too ill to be moved.

With 1944 and the reinstitution of the draft for the Nisei from camp, the No-No boy of Minidoka received his notice to appear and became a draft resister. He walked across camp to test his idea for resistance on Min Yasui, a curfew resister from Portland, and a lawyer.

"I was looking for a leader, or somebody to work with. So, I told him that with Selective Service—reinstatement of volunteering and selective service that was coming up—I said, 'I had a way that I can beat this thing. That was to prove myself an alien. With my doing I hoped the government will reconsider my citizenship status.'

"Well his being an attorney, I thought maybe that I could get some clarification on a few things.

"He said, 'You'd better to take it easy.' In fact, he said, 'Forget about it.' And he said, 'What you should do is go along with the draft.'

"Min Yasui told me that I have a chance beat up or even get killed in federal penitentiary. And he said, 'There's lots of tough people there, and for what you're doing, they may harm you.'

"So, I just said, 'Thank you very much,' and that's it—left."

Akutsu and his like-minded friends, pointed to their original 4-C draft classification and said the government had declared them "enemy aliens," and as
enemy aliens, they were draft-proof. They knew this amounted to a renuncia-
tion of their U.S. citizenship. They asked for "repatriation" to Japan.

Akutsu was not acquainted with the people at other camps who thought
just like him. Why so many Nisei thought they could call the government's
bluff—"We're enemy aliens. Send us back to Japan"—and force the government
to respond with an apology, for having mistakenly put them into camps and
then mistreated them escapes me. But at camps Amache and Minidoka, there
were numbers of draft resisters basing their resistance on the government's
classification of internees as 4-C.

At most, an essential step was missing from their strategy: going to court,
to test the constitutionality of applying the draft law to internees.

James Omura,
Nisei Newsman

AT THE DENVER *ROCKY SHIMPO*

"And one of the things I noticed is that everyone was jumping on the people who were resisting. No one was offering any alternative. So I scratched around, anguished over it, and finally came up with the idea that if I throw out the constitutional theme, maybe they'd grab it. So that's what I did.

"In reading Okamoto's documents, I was attracted to the fact that he wanted to do it with a formal committee and that he wanted to take this case to the federal court. That he believed in fighting it on legal grounds. And I believed in doing it that way, too—not to break the law.

"I couldn't tell the people to organize, but in essence I was telling them to organize."

ROCKY SHIMPO

February 28, 1944

Nisei America

KNOW THE FACTS

By JIMMIE OMURA

Let Us Not Be Rash

THIS department has been queried as to our opinion in regard to the petition movement in war-born relocation centers. Our reply is simple.

We are in full sympathy with the general context of the petition forwarded to Washington by the Amache Community Council and the Topaz Citizens Committee. We do not necessarily agree on all the points raised, however.

Insofar as the movement itself is concerned, the Nisei are within their rights to petition the government for a redress of grievances. Beyond that, it would be treading on unsure footing. We must not forget that we are at war. This department does not encourage resistance to the draft.

It is reported that five at Amache and the thirty at Hunt are guilty of resisting the draft. There will probably be more before this matter is finished. We cannot conscientiously believe that by these sporadic actions anything concrete and fundamental can be achieved. Those who are resisting the draft are too few, too unorganized and basically unsound in their viewpoints.

EXPATRIATION is not the answer to our eventual redemption of democratic and constitutional rights. Unorganized draft resistance is not the proper method to pursue our grievances. Expressions and feelings of disloyalty, purely because democracy seems not to have worked in our particular case, are neither sound or conducive to a healthy regard of rights.

We agree that the constitution gives us certain inalienable and civil rights. We do not dispute the fact that such rights have been largely stripped and taken from us. We further agree that the government should restore a large part of those rights before asking us to contribute our lives to the welfare of the nation—to sacrifice our lives on the field of battle.

BUT those who have grown bitter with the evacuation must not forget that "eternal vigilance is the price of liberty." We have not been vigilant. We cannot condemn democracy for our present unhappy predicament. Democracy is not only a form of government, but it is also a spirit. If there is no spirit of democracy in our governmental leaders, we would not have democracy in action. Let us therefore not condemn democracy but the men who manipulate public affairs and the masses who sympathize and condone undemocratic ideals.

We should at all times stand firm on our God-given rights. We should let our voices be heard whenever an attempt is made to abridge such endowed privileges. But ours should not be an act of rashness or haste. We should think the matter through and in the ultimate end retain a proper regard for the implications and repercussions that in all probability would arise from our acts. There is no reason why we should not petition for a redress of grievances, but there is every reason why we should not resist the draft in the way it is being done now.

THE PACIFIC CITIZEN
January 8, 1944

NISEI USA
By LARRY TAJIRI

Nisei and the Films

The case for the Japanese Americans has been effectively presented in newspapers, magazines on the radio and through the means of special publications, but little used has been made to date of what is perhaps the most effective of all information media, the motion picture. The reasons for this, of course, are obvious. The high costs involved, and the apparent technological difficulties presented militate against the utilization of the motion picture screen in the fight for justice and fair play for this American minority group.

The eighty million Americans who are said to attend the movies weekly have seen such films as "Air Force," "Little Tokyo, U.S.A." and "Across the Pacific," which have pictured Japanese Americans as spies and saboteurs, although there is no official record of such disloyalty. It may be that the geographical location of Hollywood, in the midst of the sunkist racial hysteria of California, may have something to do with this attitude. For although hundreds of Japanese Americans today are fighting and dying in the armed forces of the United States, Hollywood prefers to picture them as bucktoothed, grinning saboteurs, and snarling disloyalists.

In the case of the film "Air Force," representations were made by various organizations and individuals regarding the film's inaccuracies in showing a fifth-column attack by Japanese Americans on the island of Maui in Hawaii, and in blaming the disaster on Hickam Field on Dec. 7 upon "local Japs" from Honolulu. All the horror rumors of the Japanese American sabotage on Dec. 7 in Hawaii were already disproved in official statements from the FBI, the War and Navy Departments and the Honolulu police at the time "Air Force" was being filmed. The story of the general buck-passing which ensued upon the presentation of protests regarding "Air Force" to the producers, the Warner Brothers (who, incidentally, have made some of the finest films of the war) makes a weird chronicle. It seemed that the Warner Brothers, the OWI and the War Department all disclaimed responsibility for the film's details. But despite the protests, no changes have been made in the film and it is still showing today throughout America.

DENVER POST

April 8, 1944

U.S. Arrests 17 More Heart Camp Japs

Seventeen more Japanese-Americans charged with refusing to report for preinduction physical examinations were arrested Thursday at the Heart Mountain internment camp by federal bureau of investigations agents and representatives of the United States marshal for Wyoming, the Denver FBI office announced.

The seventeen brought to a total of fifty-three the number of Japanese-Americans facing the identical charge in Wyoming. Twelve were arrested Wednesday, twelve others Tuesday, eleven March 25, and one was up March 26.

The newest group arrested will be arraigned Thursday before a United States commissioner at Cody, Wyo., and moved to jails in other towns. The dozen apprehended Wednesday pleaded not guilty, waived preliminary hearing, were unable to make $2,000 bond and were transferred to jail at Casper to await trial.

THE PACIFIC CITIZEN

Thursday, April 1, 1944

Official Publication of the

Japanese American Citizens League

LARRY TAJIRI—EDITOR

EDITORIALS:

Rocky Shimpo

If it is the function of a newspaper to inform and to counsel, then the *Rocky Shimpo*, a tri-weekly published in Denver, has, in the past two months, both misinformed and misguided. It must bear heavy responsibility for the fact that twelve, and possibly thirty Japanese Americans at the Heart Mountain center face prison terms for violation of selective service regulations. The English section of the *Rocky Shimpo* has editorially supported an attitude which would make a bargain-counter of loyalty, and it has magnified the protests of a small minority out of all proportion to their worth and influence.

394

The editorial function of a newspaper should remain the province of its editor, but when the irresponsible carrying out of this function approaches the thin edge of sedition and menaces the welfare of all Americans of Japanese ancestry, then it becomes the concern of all. It is difficult to believe that present editorial policy of the *Rocky Shimpo* is based on any naive belief that it will enhance the welfare of the Japanese American group. Already the adverse has been in effect. The *Rocky Shimpo* appears deliberately engaged in attempt to undo the positive services which Japanese Americans at war and producing for victory at home have contributed. The Hearst press, the Lechners and the Haanns could no more.

TIMELY TOPICS
By SABURO KIDO

Our copies of the *Rocky Shimpo* arrive about one week to ten days after publication. Consequently we are unable to keep up with the rantings of its misguided editor....

What we regret most is the fact that the Nisei in other centers seem to have been influenced by the misguided writings of the editor of the *Rocky Shimpo*. Today's local paper contained the Phoenix dispatch that the nine nisei from Poston who were charged with draft violations were sentenced to three years in jail. They gave the same reason as the Fair Play Committee members; that is, "they did not know if they were citizens or not."

The "fearless editor" of the Denver paper is sitting as a one man judge these days. The Minidoka *Irrigator* was reprimanded for not lambasting the draft. The *Heart Mountain Sentinel* is rivaling the JACL for Number One position for his venomous hatred. The Manzanar *Free Press*, under the caption of "A Disgrace to Nisei Journalism" gets a verbal spanking. And since the Gila *News Courier* wrote an editorial more or less in favor of cooperating with the JACL, it also may come under the displeasure of the almighty. We are gradually acquiring nice company on our side.

Err-Rocky Shimpo!

O n March 25, 1944, the anthropologists of the Community Analysis Section at Heart Mountain reported that the administration had banned meetings of the Fair Play Committee and that subscriptions to the *Rocky Shimpo* at Heart Mountain jumped from one thousand to twelve hundred. A sudden increase of two hundred. People who had been kids at Tule Lake, and paid no attention to the adults and their issues, do remember the voice of a man, regularly chanting in the streets between the barracks, "ERR-ROCKY SHIMPO! ERR-ROCKY SHIMPO!" and the rush of people toward the door to get their copy of *Rocky*.

FAIR PLAY COMMITTEE

"ONE FOR ALL AND ALL FOR ONE"

Saturday
March 4, 1944

We, the Nisei, have been complacent and too inarticulate to the unconstitutional acts that we're subjected to. If ever there was a time or cause for decisive action, IT IS NOW! We members of the FPC, are not afraid to go to war—we are not afraid to risk our lives for our country. We would gladly sacrifice our lives to protect and uphold the principles and ideals of our country as set forth in the Constitution and the Bill of Rights, for the inviolability depends on the freedom, liberty, justice and protection of all people including Japanese Americans and all other minority groups. But, have we been given such freedom, such liberty, such justice, such protection? No!

• • •

Thus, the members of the FPC unanimously decided at their last open meeting that until we are restored all our rights, all discriminatory features of the Selective Service abolished, and measures are taken to remedy the past injustices thru judicial pronouncement or Congressional act, we feel that the present program of drafting us from this concentration camp is unjust, unconstitutional, and against all principles of civilized usage, and therefore, WE MEMBERS OF THE FAIR PLAY COMMITTEE HEREBY REFUSE TO GO TO THE PHYSICAL EXAMINATION OR TO THE INDUCTION IF OR WHEN WE ARE CALLED IN ORDER TO CONTEST THE ISSUE.

Gloria Kubota,
Nisei and the Zen Man

They became the only organized resistance movement, in all the camps, when they declared their intent to refuse to appear for their physical examinations in order to get arrested and take the question to court, on March 4, 1944. The Fair Play Committee leaders asked to be arrested for encouraging others to resist the draft as a matter of right.

All but one of the leaders were born U.S. citizens. Most were married, or too old for the draft. Guntaro Kubota, as an Issei, an "enemy alien . . . ineligible for citizenship," was risking his life by being associated with the Fair Play Committee. Everything he did related to draft could be considered an act of war. As an enemy alien, he risked a death sentence.

Gloria Kubota says, "And so when my husband was asked to interpret what the Fair Play boys were saying. I thought, well, that's the only way they can make the money—raise the money. 'Cuz the Isseis have the money. The Niseis, they're young yet. They didn't have any money.

"And he said, 'Well, my wife is citizen. My children are citizens of this country. If I don't fight for them, who is going to?'"

And Grace adds, "There is one question they ask in this transcript. I was looking it over last night. His comment was, 'I was helping because I was a friendly enemy alien.'" She smiles.

Her mother says, "It was really cute how some of these old people followed him around. You know, and that's what they had to have was these Issei ladies to help raise the money for this trial.

"And there were thirty blocks in our Heart Mountain, you know, and it used to be cold, but he'd go all over, and they'd follow him around. Some people brought all the cash that they had, and they'd give it to him, you know."

THE PACIFIC CITIZEN
Official Publication of the
Japanese American Citizens League
Thursday, March 11, 1944

SGT. KUROKI MEETS UTAH'S GOVERNOR MAW

Expresses Appreciation For Stand Upholding Constitutional Rights

Speaking as a representative Japanese American who is doing his part in the nation's war effort, Tech. Sgt. Ben Kuroki, veteran of thirty heavy combat missions in Europe and North Africa, Tuesday met Herbert B. Maw, Governor of Utah, and thanked the latter for his stand upholding the constitutional rights of Americans of all ancestries.

He was also introduced on Wednesday evening at a meeting of the Salt Lake chapter of the JACL. Acknowledging the introduction by Prof. Elmer R. Smith, Sgt. Kuroki complimented the group for being members of the "one Japanese American organization which was fighting for the rights of Americans of Japanese ancestry."

Mits Koshiyama,
Fair Play Committee

A t the time the Fair Play Committee was organizing, Mits Koshiyama was a fun-loving seventeen-year-old kid from San Jose. Did he go to any of the meetings?

"Unfortunately, I didn't. But I read about it [in the *Rocky Shimpo*]. See, I was more interested in [being] with my buddies, go see the movies.

"My older brother [Howard] was interested. He later was drafted into the army. But he just went to listen. He says—one day he comes home, and he says, 'I put in $2. In for you, too. We're members of the Fair Play Committee.'"

Several men who'd received orders to appear for the physicals refused. They would have flunked their physicals and been free of the draft because of ulcers, heart conditions, or other ailments. They did not want to be free of the draft; they wanted to be counted as being against the concentration camps, in court.

Howard was drafted, and he served. He was interested in the Fair Play Committee's stand, but it was easier for him to go along with the tide.

"Not everyone in the family has to think the same you know," Mits Koshiyama says. "There's always one in every family, that's a little different. And that happened to be me."

Frank Emi, Leader

"YOU GOT A PASS?"

Frank Emi recalls the day he and Minoru Tamesa went out walking in camp. "We just went over there and started slowly out." March 29, 1944. A spring day. Nothing but dirt through the gate. Little square miniature white houses provided ventilation for the root cellars on the other side of the road that leads out of camp, down to the highway to Powell, on the left side, walk or drive thirteen miles; and the larger town of Cody, on the right side of the highway, walk or drive fifteen miles. Walking up to the gate, they faced the root cellars and the highway to the left; to the right lay Heart Mountain, spreading out wide and dark, looking down on camp.

"I remember the sentry said, 'You got to have a pass.'

"'Why?'

"'Well, that's the rule.'

"'No, you don't need a pass to come in and out. We're American citizens like you are. Why should we have a pass?'

"'Well, I'm going to have to stop you.'

"'We're going to leave. What are you going to do?'

"'We'll just have to put you in the guardhouse.'

"'Well. We're leaving.'" If they walked out, beyond the gate a few yards, across an imaginary line separating the "Military Zone" of the camp from America, would they be able to walk away?

"So they stopped us and put us in the guardhouse." The guard's only job was to keep detainees in camp, in camp. "We got good food though. The guardhouse food was better than in camp. It was some kind of roast."

GUY ROBERTSON, PROJECT DIRECTOR

Guy Robertson, according to the *Heart Mountain Sentinel*, "made his reputation as manager of the Peabody coal mines of Hudson and Grand Trunk Lodge and Transportation Company of Jackson Hole, Wyoming." He was born in Missouri, was fifty-two years old in 1942, and, according to the *Sentinel*, "He is constantly studying methods to improve and make the home more pleasant and habitable for Heart Mountain residents."

On March 30, 1944, Guy Robertson began a campaign to intimidate the Fair Play Committee out of existence and revive his camp's support of the draft. He summarily transferred to Tule Lake the founding leader of the committee, Kiyoshi Okamoto, and Isamo Horino, a member of the leadership who had walked out of camp; spent two days in Cody, a town fifteen miles away; and then walked back into camp in an attempt to create a test case challenging the WD-1 rules defining citizenship for the Japanese-Americans and the rule of camp.

Paul Nakadate was the leader of the Fair Play Committee after Kiyoshi Okamoto's removal to Tule Lake. Under interrogation he sounds more like the faculty advisor to a student debate club than a knowledgeable leader.

HEARING BOARD FOR LEAVE CLEARANCE
March 30, 1944

MEMBER OF LEAVE CLEARANCE BOARD: Guy Robertson, Project Director

Tom Horn, Acting Project Attorney

M. O. Anderson, Ass't Project Director

INTERVIEWEE: Paul Takeo Nakadate

1-4-D

Heart Mountain, Wyoming

USES# 22769

• • •

ROBERTSON: Did you have anything to do with the preparation of the three bulletins that were put out?

NAKADATE: No.

ROBERTSON: Did you agree with them?

NAKADATE: I disagreed on one point.

ROBERTSON: What was that?

NAKADATE: In order to contest this issue, it said something about refusing to go [draft]. I stated that this thing is an individual problem. It is for me.

ROBERTSON: What is the purpose of this—to hinder the workings of the Selective Service Act?

NAKADATE: No, I don't think so. I don't think they had anything to do with it.

ROBERTSON: When this bulletin came out plainly stating that, didn't the members all know about it and agree with it?

NAKADATE: No, that was brought to me afterwards.

ROBERTSON: Who put those out?

NAKADATE: I don't know, I'm only supposed to speak on the educational side and any grievances they want to bring up. On the other hand somebody else prints the bulletins, somebody else does this and I don't know what Okamoto does. That's why I say it isn't very democratic and isn't really fair play. Mr. Okamoto has been studying on this evacuation and I think he was driving at some evacuation problems, whether evacuation was justified or not. He seems to be connected with the Civil Liberties or something.

ROBERTSON: Does the organization have a counterpart in other centers?

NAKADATE: No.

• • •

ANDERSON: As far as you know, there is no responsible head or committee representing the Fair Play Committee?

NAKADATE: No. Well, Mr. Okamoto and the steering committee.

ANDERSON: When they signed those bulletins, "FAIR PLAY COMMITTEE," aren't you all bound to abide by the decision as set out by those bulletins?

NAKADATE: No. In fact, I don't know who wrote those articles.

ANDERSON: You have admitted you are a member of the Committee. The pamphlets come out as a committee. Don't you fear that as a member of the committee that they bind you to the views expressed?

NAKADATE: It is too late. Maybe so, but if I am over-ruled and they go ahead and do it, that's that.

ANDERSON: Have you taken any steps to resign?

NAKADATE: No. I feel in the long run it may be a Fair Play Committee. Some article in the *Sentinel* said it has always failed. One difficulty is that if I resign, maybe other people will resign and won't support it. If Okamoto resigns, he has followers. I don't believe in breaking up. A lot of people want to break up the JACL. I feel that if it isn't right, do something about it.

ANDERSON: But you are still a member?

NAKADATE: Yes.

ANDERSON: One of the pamphlets published by the Fair Play Committee makes the statement that members of the Fair Play Committee do hereby refuse to go to pre-induction physical examinations or to induction if and when called.

NAKADATE: Yes, I say that part I objected to.

ANDERSON: How do you justify your membership then? You state you are a member. This has been probably stated as the position of the Committee. How do you justify your continued membership, having obligated yourself to that viewpoint?

NAKADATE: I haven't obligated myself. If I don't like it I just don't like it. I say that I told them that I definitely didn't like that.

ANDERSON: Have you ever taken any steps heretofore to personally make known that you disagreed with that policy of the Fair Play Committee?

NAKADATE: Yes, I have spoken to Mr. Wakaye.

ANDERSON: Would you be willing to state in the *Sentinel* that you have stated that you disagree with that policy?

NAKADATE: Yes, I'll write you an article in regards to that.

ANDERSON: In other words, if you are asked and properly notified to appear for the pre-induction physical examination, will you go or refuse?

NAKADATE: That I don't know. I have to think that part over. That is my individual problem. I can't speak for anyone else's problem. No member should be bound by that and I think a lot of members have already reported for pre-induction physical. I can't say that all that don't go are members of the Fair Play Committee.

• • •

ROBERTSON: You are telling me now, no one will take responsibility for this Fair Play Committee bulletin.

NAKADATE: Only the writer can take that responsibility.

ROBERTSON: Then he has no authority to sign FAIR PLAY COMMITTEE on it.

NAKADATE: I guess so.

• • •

Frank Emi dismisses Nakadate's remarks as Nakadate's effort to confound and confuse Robertson and to protect Emi, the author of the "we will not go" bulletin, and to cover his ass.

Robertson and Anderson put Ben Wakaye, treasurer of the committee, through a "Hearing." Wakaye was an intellectual, a loner, shy and retiring, from San Francisco. Joining the Fair Play Committee, and becoming its treasurer, was unusual for him, as he was not a joiner and not a leader. His unusual act was a measure of his belief in the committee. Under questioning he does not do well. Robertson and Anderson lead him to declare, "I am sure up a creek."

From both Nakadate and Wakaye, Robertson gets the name of Frank Emi. The next day Robertson and a group of camp officials and the JACL's Nobu Kawai bring Frank Emi in for a Hearing. Also being heard is Minoru Tamesa, of Seattle. He is a member of the Fair Play Committee, and attempted to walk out of camp with Frank Emi.

The way Emi and Tamesa behave under hostile questioning is markedly different from Nakadate and Wakaye.

• • •

HEARING

FRANK EMI

March 31, 1944

10:30 A.M.

Project Directors Office

PRESENT: Guy Robertson, Project Director

M. O. Anderson, Assistant Project Director

M. L. Campbell, Chief of Internal Security

Donald T. Horn, Project Attorney

Lt. John H. Kellogg, Heart Mountain Military Police

Nobu Kawai, Sentinel Office

E. C. Gorman, Internal Security Officer

Frank Emi

Minoru Tamesa

Niro Abe

ROBERTSON: Which of you is Frank Emi?

EMI: I am.

ROBERTSON: Will you read the charge Mr. Horn?

HORN: (Addressing Emi) Do you have a copy of the complaint and of the warrant?

EMI: Yes.

HORN: It is alleged in this complaint that on the 29th day of March, 1944, you and Minoru Tamesa attempted to leave this Center, to pass through the gate, without a pass or permit or without any authority from the Project Director. That is the substance of the charge filed against you in this case. Do you want someone else to represent you?

EMI: Well . . . Mr. Campbell said the ones here would be witnesses. . . .

HORN: You understand the charges of the complaint; is that correct?

EMI: Yes.

HORN: Do you want to enter a plea of guilty or not guilty?

EMI: When you asked me if you want someone to represent me, do you mean someone here or some outside attorney?

HORN: Someone in here, or if you wish, you are entitled to some outside attorney.

EMI: Is this a hearing or a trial?

ROBERTSON: This will be a hearing for a WRA regulation. I will assess a penalty. If you are going to plead guilty, you don't need a representative. If you are going to plead something else, that is a different matter.

EMI: If this is going to be a, well, more or less of a trial, I would much rather have an outside attorney represent me. Just when he will come down I don't know.

ROBERTSON: You know we have to try these cases within forty-eight hours.

CAMPBELL: At the time I entered the guardhouse, I asked these gentlemen if they had passed through the gate without proper authority and they said they had.

ROBERTSON: You understand Frank, I am only trying you on a Project charge. You have violated a Project regulation. You know that. There isn't anything complicated about what I am going to do. If you can prove you had some....

EMI: Here is the reason I did that, Mr. Robertson. As far as guilty or not guilty I personally believe I am not guilty because I am an American citizen, and I wanted to find out how far my rights went. I wanted to find out how long I could be detained here against my will.

ROBERTSON: I understand that. You are supposed to obtain a pass before you can go through the gate. Lt. Kellogg is supposed to apprehend any one who goes through the gate without a pass. As to your rights, that will be taken care of later. If I can prove that you violated a Project regulation, it is up to me to assess a penalty, regardless of your rights in the matter.

EMI: In other words, Mr. Robertson, you imply that you have more power than is set forth in the constitutional bill of rights.

ROBERTSON: No, Frank, I have the power to do what I am doing.

EMI: Then I contend what you are doing is against the rights I have as a citizen of this country.

ROBERTSON: You have a perfect right to contest that at any time you want to. I would like Mr. Horn to outline the authority under which I am acting.

EMI: That is why I would like to have an outside attorney represent me.

HORN: This agency was established through an executive order issued by the president of the United States. And this executive order has delegated certain powers and authorities to the director of the War Relocation Authority. The director has delegated this power to Mr. Robertson; the power to enforce certain rules and regulations that are necessary for the proper administration of the project. In other words, you can't administer a project like this without necessary rules and regulations. I would like to ask you this....

ROBERTSON: Just a minute. You haven't explained that quite right. I don't make the rules. This is not one of my orders that has been violated. I want you to explain to him that he has violated 503 the Presidential order; that he has violated the military order and I am merely enforcing it. He has not violated the rules and regulations set up by the project director. Would you go into that just a little further?

HORN: I think that you are aware of the fact that this Project area is also a military area and has been established as such by the war department. And leaving the project without the proper authority is in violation of the regulations.

EMI: Just how far does the military have jurisdiction around this center? That is the jurisdiction over the outer boundaries of this project? All around the area? I would like to have Lt. Kellogg explain that if possible.

HORN: We'll take that up later.

ROBERTSON: We are trying to decide how to conduct this hearing.

HORN: The military police are in charge of the center gates and they are in charge of supervising the outer boundaries of this area. I would like to ask you this. Did you understand that you were not to leave the project without a pass or permit?

EMI: No. I thought as long as I am an American citizen I had the right to go where I pleased.

HORN: Have you ever been out of the center?

EMI: No.

HORN: Haven't you ever been out on short term, indefinite, seasonal or anything like that?

EMI: I was out on seasonal leave the first fall we were here.

HORN: Didn't you have a pass then?

EMI: I don't know. They fixed that all up for me. A farmer requested my services outside.

HORN: You have known as a matter of fact that you cannot leave this camp without a permit or pass though?

EMI: No, I don't.

HORN: How long have you been in the center?

EMI: About two years.

HORN: How old are you?

EMI: Twenty-eight.

HORN: You have a high school education?

EMI: Yes.

HORN: College education?

EMI: One year.

HORN: I would ask you one other question. You attempted to leave the area without a Project pass the 29th. Where were you going?

408

EMI: I had no particular place in mind.

HORN: Where were you going when you started out the gate?

EMI: Just outside.

HORN: And where were you going after you got to the outside?

EMI: No particular place.

HORN: You weren't intending to leave the area though?

EMI: No, I had no such intention. I just thought I would take a stroll.

HORN: Have you been in the habit of doing that?

EMI: No.

HORN: This is the first time?

EMI: Yes.

HORN: You have never left the project at any time without a pass?

EMI: No, that was the first time. Another thing that may have motivated me to stroll out there is the fact that Selective Service is now in—it is in effect have and now other American citizen so I didn't think there was any restriction.

HORN: Have you had a leave clearance hearing?

EMI: I had one from Mr. Carroll and he told me verbally that he had recommended me.

HORN: As far as you know, you don't have leave clearance?

EMI: I don't know.

HORN: You say you did have a leave clearance hearing?

EMI: Yes, I don't know just how it stands now.

ROBERTSON: For your information Frank, you haven't been cleared by the Joint Board in Washington yet.

EMI: I think at the hearing there was some question about my question 28 and I said that I was loyal and it was an unqualified "yes" and at that time I also said that until my citizen status and rights were clarified and restored I don't believe that legally or Constitutionally I had any obligation to enter the armed forces because of that present suppressed and unqualified citizenship status.

ROBERTSON: That is going into something else. Did you know that Lt. Kellogg stops everyone regardless of whether they are evacuee or not; me, any one of my forces. We all have passes that we have to show. It isn't merely if they have leave clearance; that means they have a pass and present it at the gate, both Caucasian and evacuee.

EMI: I have seen Caucasians come in with cars just wave at the guard and pass right through without stopping.

ROBERTSON: That is all true but I think in each instance the military police know that that person has a pass and they have examined it before. You will find that they all carry the same card that you carry when you go outside. That applies for everyone that goes outside the center. They all carry some kind of pass.

EMI: I don't know about these things because I never received one.

ROBERTSON: Did you intend to make a test case out of this?

EMI: I had no intentions of any kind. If . . . That depended on the outcome.

◆ ◆ ◆

ROBERTSON: I think I will decide this matter now then before it goes to trial. I think you have been held long enough, as punishment for the violation that has happened. I am perfectly willing to turn Frank loose into the area. You understand of course, Frank, that if you want to go out you will have to come to my office for a pass?

EMI: Will you give me that pass?

ROBERTSON: Not until you get leave clearance. I can't give you a pass without leave clearance.

EMI: Why have I been denied that leave clearance?

ROBERTSON: You haven't been denied that. The Joint Board just hasn't decided your case yet.

EMI: Under whose authority is the leave clearance board?

ROBERTSON: The WRA.

EMI: In other words if the legality of the leave clearance—

ROBERTSON: Just for your own information you can test the legality from the Project just as easily as you can from the jail. I believe you are on the stop list.

EMI: That's right.

ROBERTSON: We don't blame anyone for using the means at their command to rectify what they want but there are certain rules we have to abide by.

EMI: I would like to understand—Am I guilty in this case as far as you are concerned?

ROBERTSON: I think you are guilty.

EMI: I want you to remember, Mr. Robertson, that I haven't pleaded guilty.

ROBERTSON: We are not to trial over this matter because of your attitude. I thought a trial would be made out of this but as long as you have promised me to abide by the regulations there will be no need to make a trial out of it. You go out of the gate without proper authorization again and we will have to pick you up again.

EMI: I would like to know. . . . As far as my plea is concerned I was not guilty and if change it . . . that is up to you as far as the rest of it is concerned. In my opinion I think I am "not guilty."

KELLOGG: As a matter of regulations I don't think there is any question about it. I was down at the gate before they went out and I explained the rules we had to enforce and they said the reason they were going out was to get arrested and make a test case out of this. They knew they were breaking a rule and knew they were not supposed to go through.

EMI: Is there a law against going through?

ABE: Isn't the Constitution a little higher than the WRA law? If you were given orders to kill someone out here wouldn't you—wouldn't your conscience bother you? Would you obey that order just because it was on order?

ROBERTSON: I would enforce the law.

ABE: Any order you get from Washington, you would follow it?

ROBERTSON: Let me tell you something. I am an American citizen and I will obey the law and if I catch anyone not obeying law, I will punish them. The laws are enacted within the Constitution. These laws must be obeyed until they are declared unconstitutional. If I don't pick you up someone else will. A law is a law and know that. You have been in this country long enough to know that. If you want to appeal that the law is unconstitutional you must do that but you must obey the law while it is in effect until it is proven unconstitutional.

ABE: Don't you think it is unconstitutional?

ROBERTSON: I don't have the right to say.

ABE: If my citizenship is for the United States I think I should have a right to speak when it is right and when it is wrong. Doesn't your conscience ever hurt you? I am not for anyone like the WRA or JACL. I was brought up to respect the Constitution of the United States and the Bill of Rights and I was taught that if the United States calls for me to protect the Constitution of the United States I think I should go. I even have a wife and I am having a kid coming up. I think I should go. I am not kicking or anything. I am not fighting for the United States President or Secretary but I am fighting for the Constitutional rights. We are not bargaining with anyone. We are just fighting for our rights. You know just as well as I do. Doesn't your conscience ever bother you?

ROBERTSON: My conscience doesn't hurt me a bit when I enforce a law that is in effect. I am not a judge. We have nine judges, nine men that are supposed to be the highest tribunal in the land. They do not allow me to say whether it is constitutional or you to say so. It is up to that tribunal. They may nullify that law but until such time they say it is not a law, it is a law and every officer of the United States is to enforce it.

EMI: If you got a letter from Washington giving you an order would you enforce that rule and perform your duty regardless of whether you thought it right or wrong?

• • •

KAWAI: May I say a word Mr. Robertson?

ROBERTSON: Yes, Nobu?

KAWAI: I am here simply as a friend and have no interest other than as a friend of the party in this particular case and I am interested in it insofar as the civil liberties of the evacuees are concerned. I have discussed the implications of enforced detention in a relocation center as it applies to American citizens whether they have leave clearance or not. I believe evacuation has brought about a lot of questions which we feel should have a clarification by the Supreme Court. However, in contesting the legality of these particular rights which we feel are restricted, there are definite procedures to follow and I will support any sincere suit which is brought legally and in an American way, to contest the legality of our various restrictions. You, Frank, mention that we have a right, in your opinion, to return to the Pacific Coast area. I believe that right should be contested and I feel confident that in the near future a suit will be instituted but when it is instituted, it will be after the facts and legality are studied and I know that until we have a legal stand to ask for a decision on a particular case, we won't take action. It is true how regulations are not being enforced against the evacuees. I believe it is the constitutional right, I believe it is the American thing to do, to contest what, in our opinion, restricts the rights of an American Citizen. So what I say or whatever opinion I express I don't want the idea to get out or to go around camp that my opinion constitutes a stand on the policy of the Fair Play Committee because Frank is a member of that committee.

ROBERTSON: I think that statement is all right. I am not taking a stand against anyone.

. . .

ROBERTSON: Is your case about the same Tamesa?

TAMESA: As far as I am concerned, I am from Tule Lake and I didn't have any friends I can call on. All my friends are old people and they can't speak English.

ROBERTSON: You should know if you could go out without a pass.

TAMESA: That I don't know. I understood that those were the regulations as far as. . . . There is a doubt in my mind whether my personal feelings of your orders—I think they don't coincide with yours. We tried and were stopped and I respect Lt. Kellogg. I think he is doing his duty. He treated us very fairly and if he didn't do his duty I wouldn't respect him. I think it is the same in your case Mr. Robertson, you are following orders. What my beliefs are it is beside the point.

ROBERTSON: What mine are is beside the point too. Do you understand our attitude about the future?

TAMESA: I think there is not any future in going out and getting picked up every time.

ROBERTSON: As far as I am concerned and if it is alright with Lt. Kellogg, I will dismiss this case. You boys understand the case as well as I do. If you want to get the law repealed that is now in force, it is your right to contest it. If I didn't think the law was constitutional I would find out through the court and if they didn't think it was unconstitutional that is the final order. Until such time as they decide a law must be in enforce [sic].

EMI: What do you think about the evacuees being in here and as you know not having the right to travel freely and the fact that the Selective Service is applied to them now? Just what is your feeling about this? They don't have the right but must perform their duty or obligation.

ROBERTSON: That's the law Frank.

EMI: That sort of goes back to the thing that started the American Revolution doesn't it?

ROBERTSON: Something like that....

TAMESA: Could I express an opinion? Sometime ago I received a letter from the draft board that I was cleared by Naval Intelligence so I was okay for the Army. A few days ago I asked for a pass to Cody but was denied. That is one reason that I want to say...

HORN: Do you have a leave clearance?

TAMESA: No, I don't think so.

HORN: Did you have a leave clearance when you came here from Tule?

TAMESA: I was supposed to have been cleared. That's the way I understand it. I was denied a pass.

HORN: Who did you ask about getting a pass?

EMI: Whoever is in charge of that thing said you are on the stop list. Naval Intelligence can clear him but WRA has more power?

ROBERTSON: WRA can put anyone on the stop list. If you are on the stop list the case will come to review. That is why we have the joint board.

KAWAI: For the information of both Frank and Minoru will you outline to them what you outlined to me about the procedure of the joint board that they are doing this as fast as they can; that they will be through by the first of June and those who are segregated will be sent to Tule Lake and everyone remaining in the nine relocation centers will be eligible for leave?

TAMESA: I appreciate Mr. Kawai speaking in Frank's and my behalf but I don't know Mr. Kawai so.... I just received this letter from my draft board that Naval Intelligence has cleared me. I believe I only received it a week or so ago. In the meantime I don't believe I have broken any laws in the Center.

ROBERTSON: You did when you went through that gate without a pass.

TAMESA: Yes, but I am curious why I was put on the stop list.

ROBERTSON: I don't know this myself. In most every case the stop list is compiled by someone in Washington. You are put on the stop list for investigation and you have a hearing. It goes back to the board and they may put you on the stop list. The stop list means that you are not eligible for leave clearance and eventually they will be transferred to Tule Lake. They expect to finish this group of leave clearances by June 1st.

ABE: What is this Tule Lake? What does it represent?

ROBERTSON: It is where you are sent when you'd rather be loyal to Japan than to the United States, and are eventually sent back to Japan.

413

TAMESA: The point I was curious about was that this was a draft communication from the draft board and if at any time they said I was perfectly eligible for the Army and here I would be considered a very bad citizen and don't have the privilege of getting a pass and other matters....

ROBERTSON: Here is the idea on that. If you are on the stop list and if the Army calls you the Army is more powerful. Until they army calls you we have to enforce the stop list. When the Army calls you you must go or suffer the consequences. You can't get away from that. Until the Joint Board releases you from the stop list we have to apply the rule.

EMI: In my opinion I think that type of procedure is not very American. It does not conform to the democratic principles of this nation.

ROBERTSON: If you are on the stop list there is some reason for it. Are you sure that was Naval Intelligence? Wasn't it Army Intelligence?

TAMESA: How maybe it was. Yes, I think it was.

ROBERTSON: If they clear you and put you on the list for induction then I may clear you on the stop list.

TAMESA: I was curious about the thing. We have to follow the law.

EMI: One thing I would like to have clear in your mind Mr. Robertson. Any action that I have taken, it is not with the intent of disloyalty, it is purely from the standpoint that I consider myself a loyal American citizen.

ROBERTSON: I understand your loyalty. The only thing I think is that you proceeded the wrong way. I think that if you want to clarify it there is a legal channel open. An attorney would do you more good. You can't buck the law. If you want to test the legality of the law you should keep out of jail and have an attorney. If you follow the proper channel you will get farther.

TAMESA: I don't know about Frank but in my mind I was not sure if I was breaking the law until I was stopped. That was for my own satisfaction. I am sorry to have caused you trouble. They treated us very fairly down there so we have no kick coming on that.

ROBERTSON: I think we understand each other better now.

EMI: There is one last request I would like to make. Could I have a copy of this hearing?

ROBERTSON: I wasn't even going to have it transcribed but you may have a copy if you want it.

Fair Play Frank Emi
vs. JACL Nobu Kawai

Frank Emi of the Fair Play Committee and Nobu Kawai of the JACL and the associate editor of the *Heart Mountain Sentinel* were two of the best looking men in camp. Emi was known for his devotion to judo. Kawai had played football in junior college and was tall. Both were married, but that didn't stop the girls from whispering about them behind their hands, while flashing their eyes.

March 12, 1944, Kawai spoke at a meeting held at the Buddhist church, representing the JACL. His speech was designed to crush the Fair Play Committee's oddly negative influence on the restoration of the draft in the camps. The Fair Play Committee showed up with several members, and Frank Emi's little sister, each jotting down every word spoken by Nobu Kawai, so he would not be misquoted when the FPC members wrote their answers to the JACL.

One line stood out of Nobu Kawai's speech: "Let us remember that the majority can change the constitution and make this a dictatorship if they so desire."

Paul Nakadate, another handsome man and a leader of the Fair Play Committee, wrote in the *Sentinel*: "If in a democracy the majority rules and the minority has no chance but to show the public our loyalty by complying to the selective service program, I wish to inform our readers that is, in my opinion, a mistaken conception of democracy."

On March 18, 1944, the activities of the Fair Play Committee resulted in more, not fewer, refusals to appear for pre-induction physicals, and another *Sentinel* editorial directed against the Fair Play Committee, "Provocateurs." It accused the Fair Play Committee: "During this last week, in the hidden of boiler rooms and latrines, behind closed doors under the protection of darkness, leaders of the Fair Play Committee have fired with fanatical zeal the weaker members and departed far from their mimeographed statements which are purposely 'toned down' for public consumption."

"Provocateurs" goes on to warn of the majority that rules: "We know by past experiences that we never were accepted too readily even in our own communities or states. How will we be accepted after the war has much to do with our behavior now. Certainly these who impede the established procedures of the war effort are working a hardship on every person of Japanese ancestry.

"The United States Army does not need anyone of Japanese ancestry so much that a separate action would be taken on their behalf. The army, however, is giving loyal nisei the opportunity to prove that they are men among men and not whimpering weaklings who are afraid to prove themselves."

Frank Emi spoke up. . . .

HEART MOUNTAIN SENTINEL
March 25, 1944

To the Editors:

In defense of the FPC against the intimidations and slanderous editorials of the *Heart Mountain Sentinel,* the center's newspaper, I am writing this article.

I do not believe it is the policy of the Fair Play Committee to engage in any political disputes with individuals or any publications, but the editorial that appeared in the March 11 and March 18 issue of the *Heart Mountain Sentinel* was so un-American and unsound in the light of a democratic country, that I as member of the Fair Play Committee take this opportunity to try and straighten out some things for the benefit of the Sentinels editors.

The Sentinel editorial publicly announced that the FPC was being investigated and would soon be broken up on the rocks of law and reason. They hopefully look forward to such an event. The FPC would welcome such an investigation, for we are on the side of LAW and REASON. Furthermore, we are on the side of Justice, Humanity and Fair Play, but above all, we are on the side from which emanates justice, freedom, and liberty. The Constitution and the Bill of Rights of the United States.

The *Sentinel* editorial has now dropped down to the level of accusing the FPC of intimidating and threatening those who oppose the FPC, that the FPC leaders have tried to fire with fanatical zeal the weaker members in the latrines, behind closed doors, and under the protection of darkness. If the writers of this editorial can produce one single evidence of such a nature, I think the FPC would appreciate knowing of it. These editors who first tried intimidations and veiled threats against the FPC are now resorting to the usual smearing tactics to try and discredit and break up the FPC.

What manner of persons have we in the *Sentinel* editorial staff who express, who write such un-American, undemocratic, and bigoted words? Who are these people who would like to destroy anything that stands for justice, Constitutionalism, and humanity? Why would they like to intimidate, threaten, suppress, ridicule those who have the fortitude to stand up for justice, right-eousness, Constitutionalism, and for the very fundamentals which this nation was built upon?

What makes them try to present an artificial front, an apple-polished exterior to the public, while trying to stifle the truth of how we loyal American citizens of Japanese ancestry feel towards all the injustices, the discriminations, and the suppressing of our rights which are our rightful heritage? Is it because of selfish interests which exist in the hearts of certain individuals? Or is it because of certain designing motives of some persons, that they would carry on against anything or anyone that raises its voice for justice, equity, and perseverance of our constitutional rights?

Why do these editors want to blame the parents for the indecision of the nisei to respond to the present discriminatory program? These parents who have suffered untold hardships, who have suffered extreme self-denial, and who have made every kind of sacrifice for their children, who literally sweated blood so that they, the nisei may know what, may never experience insecurity, may receive the best in education, may hold respect of their fellow citizens.

These parents who although are ineligible for citizenship, nevertheless are loyal, upright examples of good citizens, who would never think of doing any-thing to jeopardize the future welfare of the children, who would gladly send their sons to the army with their blessing, if they, the niseis were treated like any other loyal American citizen. Why do they want to cast off their parents like an old discarded shoe, once they do not need their help any longer, just so they can further their own misconcepted and twisted ideas and motives.

Why these editors would shove the blame on the parents is beyond human comprehension. These persons must have parents, or at least had parents. They did not grow like weeds or animals. They did not grow up by themselves, nor received their education through their own efforts. Why they accuse the parents in such a cowardly way is beyond the imagination of any normal, intelligent person. The above questions, I would like to ask of our editors and the so called apple-polishing leaders of our community. Especially, of a former J.A.C.L. president of Pasadena and the present associate editor of our *Sentinel*, Mr.

Nobu Kawai, who spoke on Sunday, March 12, at the Heart Mountain Buddhist church.

Some members of the FPC who were present, took down in shorthand the text of his talk on Democracy, therefore the following quotes are entirely accurate. He said, quote, "The only true democracy is of one mind; the rule of the majority. If the minority raises the ire of the majority, the majority can rule. The majority can change the Constitution itself.

"The rights and privileges of the minority can be held up—cannot fight against democracy. I believe today that the Japanese are the minority and behind the eight ball. We have to use public relations to secure our future. Let us remember that the majority can change the Constitution and make this a dictatorship if they so desire. I am trying to put the right type of thinking into the minds of these persons." Unquote. Those are some of the highlights of his address.

Frank Emi
9-21-B

(To be continued in the April 1, 1944, issue)

HEART MOUNTAIN SENTINEL

April 1, 1944

To the Editor:

We would like Nobu Kawai to read the Constitution very carefully, especially the Preamble, also we would like to have him study the causes and underlying principles that motivated the American Revolution, the Declaration of Independence, the Boston Tea Party, and the Proclamation for the Emancipation of slavery, before making such a distorted misleading, disgraceful speech in front of intelligent people. If some high public official were to utter those same words to the American public, we dare not think of the consequences which would follow him. After all, we are still living in a democratic country.

What he says is, or would be, in complete harmony with the concepts of a Hitler or Stalin type of dictatorship government, but to apply such as interpretation to our democratic form of government is due, either to his inability to correctly interpret the Constitution, or his misconception of a free democratic country, or a gross refusal to believe in the instruments of our government, or to a stupid blunder on his part in making such public utterances. It seems like he made a mistake and the doctrines of Hitlerism instead of reading the Constitution of his own country.

The Constitution can be interpreted in many ways, but how long would his interpretation stand up in the eyes of the American public? It seems that he should not underestimate the intelligence of his fellow citizens, or at least spare them the insult of comparing theirs with the level of his own. Has JACLism again reared up its ugly head to spread its seeds of defeatism and bigotry through the *Sentinel* editorials? Stooging seems to be an accomplished profession of these JACL bigwigs.

Nevertheless, I believe the FPC respects his right to express his own opinions, whatever they are, but I think it is against the principles of this organization to let any such misconcepted ideas of Democracy and of our Constitution go by unopposed.

We nisei who are today fighting for justice and for the application of the real meaning of democracy as set forth in the Constitution by challenging the unconstitutional acts committed against us, a minority group will, if we are successful, emerge out of this present struggle of a right against wrong, of justice and democratic ideals against unconstitutional acts and discriminatory actions, with a great new faith in Democracy and the American way of life. We members of the FPC still believe, still have hope, that the Constitution of our country is not a mere scrap of paper. On that we are staking our all.

Those nisei who are responding to the present draft call under the present conditions may believe that they are doing the right thing. That is their belief and we respect them for it. But again there are many who are going because of fear. Fear of being thrown in jail, of being isolated in some concentration camp or some other form of punishment. Those people seem to have lost faith and hope in the principles and ideals of this country. They will go off to battle, and if they come back, they will still have the same feeling of mistrust, suspicion, lack of faith and confidence in the Constitution and the Bill of Rights that they had when they went off to war. Especially, if there are still some discriminations and injustices present when they come back.

On the other hand, we, who have made our decision to stay and fight to uphold our Constitution and for what it stands, for the future security of this Nation, and for the sake of other minorities as well as for the future of nisei will, if justice triumphs, be able to face the future unafraid, with a feeling of equality, with confidence, trust and faith in our country. We will be the staunchest defenders of these democratic ideals and principles. We will be a part of that mass of people who will never lose sight of the real and true meaning of Democracy.

If justice does not win out, then, whether we do our fighting here at home, or on foreign battlefields, the end result will be the same. The future of a democratic nation, the future of all minority people, and the future of ourselves is dark indeed.

The editors of the *Sentinel* said in today's issue, that we should be men among men and whimpering weaklings who are afraid to prove themselves. If these persons feel that what they say is right, that what they write is being loyal, why do they not volunteer their services to the combat unit? Why do they not back up their convictions with parallel action? To sit in an office and write bold words does not take courage. You do not have to be a man among men to utter such words behind an office desk. We members of the FPC sincerely believe that we doing the right thing as loyal American citizens if fighting for our rights and in trying to uphold our Constitution. We are backing up our convictions with our stand, regardless of the consequences. We have faith if our principles. We are ready to defend this faith, come what may.

We would like to ask one last question of the *Sentinel* editors and of the public. Who is the man? Who is the simpering weakling?

> The ideals of democracy have
> never been dream pictures but
> goals,
> The way toward our goals we
> will find only through our
> own exertions,
> Through tireless, patient and
> courageous exertions.
>
> Sigrid Undset
>
> Frank Emi
> 9-21-B

The following open letter is a reply by Associate Editor Nobu Kawai to charges made by Frank Emi in a letter to the editor. The concluding half of Emi's letter is printed above. —Ed. Note.

To Frank Emi and the FPC:

Because the welfare of the community overshadows the irrelevant considera-tion of personalities, I wish to answer your letter solely on the basis of the fun-damental issues in question.

I appreciate the sincerity of the Fair Play Committee in seeking the same ultimate end that the *Sentinel* and other nisei bodies have in view—justice and tolerance. We take issue, however with the means your committee employs in seeking that end.

The FPC points to forced evacuation, confinements, segregation in the army and other evidences of discrimination as an indication that our government looks upon us as secondary citizens. You advance the theory that selective service laws do not apply to nisei in view of such restriction of rights.

You reason further that acceptance of military service is tantamount to accepting such restriction of our rights and have declared that you will resist induction until our status as American citizens is clarified as protest to such discriminatory treatment.

The fallacy in your argument is your contention that a restriction of our rights means a loss of these rights. We don't lose any rights under the constitution until the constitution itself is changed.

We all feel evacuation and detention are unjust. The constitutionality of these issues are today pending decision before the Supreme Court.

If the Supreme Court rules the evacuation was constitutional, we will not have been deprived of any rights. We may then seek to avoid a repetition of any such injustice by constitutional amendment.

The fact that our rights have been restricted does not justify us to resist induction.

I believe you are sincere in your purpose. I trust there are none among you who seek only to avoid military service.

The constitution grants to American citizens all those rights embodied in the Bill of Rights. I believe those rights are for the enjoyment of loyal Americans. The moments a citizen violates the selective service laws and is convicted of draft evasion, he loses his claim to such rights.

While we are seeking justice and tolerance, it is important that we make a special effort to conduct ourselves as loyal Americans.

The use of selective service, at a time when our country is in a life and death struggle, as vehicle to attain our ends will be interpreted only as an act of disloyalty. It will destroy all the public relations we have worked so hard to build up.

While it is for the courts of law to decide the justification of your action, the damage you will have done to all nisei will outweigh any legal points you may win. You will be tearing down the very things you are trying to secure.

We can win the war, but lose the peace. So can we win our rights but lose public acceptance. There are no laws barring Negroes in major league baseball . . . yet, there are no Negroes playing in the major leagues. It is as important to win popular support as it is to fight for our rights.

The FPC no doubt feels it is justified in refusing induction. You feel your induction will be looked upon as a protest against intolerance and injustice. You regard yourselves as martyrs to the cause of the nisei. You feel the courts of law will uphold you.

If you are sincere in testing your case before the courts of our country, a few test cases by some of your leaders is sufficient. It is not necessary for large numbers to refuse induction.

My chief concern is for the young nisei who face the serious consequences of draft evasion and the stigma attached to it because they are led to believe they are doing the right thing.

I believe in the thousands of individuals and organizations who are working for our cause today. How long do think they would support us if we all refused to be inducted?

I believe in preserving all the good that our boys in the 100th battalion and the 442nd combat team have brought us by their sweat and blood.

When this war is won, the Ben Kurokis, fortified by their undeniable proof of loyalty through action, will plead our case for tolerance and justice before the bar of public opinion.

Let us never deny that we are anything but loyal American citizens. While we are fighting for our rights, let us conduct ourselves as good citizens so that no one can deny our claims to such rights.

Associate Editor
Nobu T. Kawai

P.S. It may be of interest to you that on March 12, 1943, I volunteered for combat duty with the 442nd Combat Team and today am ready to be inducted whenever called.

Saburo Kido, president of the JACL, issued Bulletin #10B, on April 13, 1944. It was public, a letter to James Omura, giving him advance notice of a letter from Roger Baldwin of the American Civil Liberties Union to Kiyoshi Okamoto, head of the Fair Play Committee. Kiyoshi Okamoto hadn't yet received the letter, but Saburo Kido had, and used it to demonstrate to James Omura his special relationship with the ACLU.

> Regarding your learned diagnosis of the position of the Fair Play Committee, a strange doubt runs through my mind. I know it is not right to question the opinion of a pundit of your caliber, but can it be possible that you are trying to pry into legal questions with a layman's smattering knowledge? I am just wondering because I have a copy of a letter written by Mr. Roger N. Baldwin, national director of the American Civil Liberties Union. You know and have heard about this organization, haven't you? In case you haven't, it is supposed to be the champion of civil rights in this country.
>
> For your future reference on this matter of legality of the draft as applied to the Nisei, will your permit me to quote from the letter sent to Mr. Okamoto? The ACLU's position may be wrong in your learned opinion, but at any rate here are the pertinent paragraphs. I have obtained permission to do so in advance so you need not worry.

Roger N. Baldwin's response to Okamoto seemed patronizing, contemptuous, and humiliating. He does not mention the Fair Play Committee or acknowledge Okamoto's leadership. Instead of sending his letter to Okamoto, he released it to the JACL, who published it as Bulletin #10B and in the *Pacific Citizen*; the *Heart Mountain Sentinel* published it on April 15, with headlines.

ACLU TAKES ISSUE WITH OKAMOTO

National Director States FPC Members Must Face Consequence of Evasion

The American Civil Liberties Union, an organization composed of many of the most liberal minds of the nation whose objectives include the defending of minority group rights, this week disagreed with the program devolved by Kiyoshi Okamoto, one of the organizers of the Fair Play Committee.

Although he did not mention the committee by name, Roger N. Baldwin, national director of the ACLU, with headquarters in New York, wrote to Okamoto outlining his observations and declared, "You fellows certainly have a strong moral case, but it is not helped by refusing to comply with the requirements of the draft act."

The leader of the Fair Play committee wrote to Baldwin before his transfer to Tule Lake. The text of Baldwin's letter as released by the New York office of the ACLU follows:

"In reply to your letter of March 28th, I have these observations to make:

"(1) The men who have refused to accept military draft are within their rights, but they of course must take the consequences. They doubtless have a strong moral case, but no legal case at all.

"(2) Men who counsel others to resist military service are not within their rights and must expect severe treatment, whatever justification they feel."

HEART MOUNTAIN SENTINEL

OMURA 'OUT' AS
SHIMPO EDITOR

James Omura was discharged as editor of the English section of the *Rocky Shimpo*, Denver tri-weekly vernacular newspaper, Wednesday night by the Alien Property Custodian according to an announcement this week by Thomas Morrisey, United States Attorney in Denver.

Gordon Hirabayashi,
On Civil Disobedience
"I GOT OFF AT SPOKANE"

"I got off at Spokane. And they were setting up my work situation. I just came out on bail to work for the Quakers in Spokane. I can't remember anybody by name. I just remember Floyd saying, 'Are you going to eat that again?' Several times, you know, even if it's dinner I'd take a couple of fried eggs. Somehow I miss 'em I guess. You know you kind of crave something. I had boiled eggs. Yeah, I had jail food. Prison is different. Prison food is like the army. Jail is terrible food.

"Well, fairly shortly after I got to Spokane, Floyd came through and said he was going to Heart Mountain and Minidoka.

"So I got a train ticket and I joined him at Billings, Montana. Then a train down to Heart Mountain, Wyoming. Then a train down to Minidoka, Idaho." In Minidoka and Heart Mountain, Floyd Schmoe and Gordon Hirabayashi talk up the American Friends Service Committee's assistance in relocating internees, outside of camp.

He receives Selective Service Form 304-A, "The Statement of United States Citizen of Japanese Ancestry," with questions 27 and 28, from his Draft Board in Seattle. Forbidden because of his race to travel to Seattle, he refuses the form, declaring it "is an outright violation of both the Christian and American principles of justice and democracy," in a letter, dated February 15, to U.S. Attorney Charles Dennis. Ironically, he will be returned to Seattle to face charges arising out of his refusal to fill out the form. Allen Pomeroy is the assistant U.S. Attorney, making the complaint and ordering Hirabayashi's arrest.

HOT OFF THE PRESS!

WEDDING BELLS AND JAIL CELLS

Jap Facing Trial Gets Permit to Wed Coed

Seattle, June 30—(A.P.) Gordon K. Hirabayashi, 24, Japanese-American who lost in the United States Supreme Court his fight against the army evacuation order for Japanese and Japanese-Americans and currently faces a new federal charge of failing to return a selective service form, obtained a marriage license application form in Spokane Thursday to wed an American girl.

The bride-to-be is Miss Esther Schmoe, 20, former University of Washington coed and daughter of Mr. and Mrs. Floyd Schmoe of Seattle.

Schmoe, who is northwest secretary of the American Friends Service committee, a Quaker social service agency, said:

"We haven't disapproved of the engagement. We have a great deal of admiration for this boy. If they are getting married now, it is their own affair, and they have our blessing."

In his difficulty with the selective service Hirabayashi protested that the form sent him involved racial discrimination.

WYOMING EAGLE

EDITOR JAP PAPER ARRESTED

DENVER, July 20—(U.P.)—FBI agents in Denver believe they have eliminated at least one of the causes behind Japanese-American violations of draft laws with the arrest of four Nisei....

Among those arrested today is the so-called "English Editor" of the *Rocky Shimpo*, a Japanese newspaper published in Denver. The editor, James Omura, is identified as the publisher of the pre-war *Current Life*, a Jap-American magazine published before Pearl Harbor in San Francisco.

Kiyoshi Okamoto
5604-D
Tulle [sic] Lake Segregation Camp
Newell, Calif.
July 2nd, 1944

To Fair Play Committee

By the way, the *Rocky Shimpo* is now controlled by the JACL.

You have no idea how the JACL is dispised [sic] by the common People of this town. No matter how Jimmie acts now, I will always respect the fact he was the only [one] who openly opposed them. (Jimmie, as I am given to understand, is very down-hearted . . . disappointed and disillusioned. Perhaps it is because I have failed in giving him proper support. OK)

Kiyoshi Okamoto

Frank Emi, Leader

LETTER TO A "NO-NO BOY"

JACL President Saburo Kido's Bulletin #10B falls into the hands of Frank Emi, with its predictions of gloom and doom for the members of the Fair Play Committee.

> There is another letter which was written to another Nisei draft evader in which Mr. Baldwin stated:
>
> "We are in receipt of your letter of April 2nd addressed to the Attorney General, stating your refusal to serve in the armed forces until the segregation of Japanese Americans is abolished.
>
> "The position you take is similar to that taken by several Negroes, all of when were prosecuted and sentenced. You have of course a moral case, but none in law, and you will have to take the consequences.
>
> "—Your conviction is a foregone conclusion."

And from another quarter, Frank Emi deals with a letter from a Minidoka "No-No" boy who tries to convince him that they are the same. Hajiime "Jim" Akutsu's letter mixes up grievances to be redressed in a court of law with newspaper gossip, congressional actions, and racist statements from the man in the street and gives each equal weight in his decision to ask for repatriation to Japan, without a day in court. He is obviously crazy, but he is also typical of the angry and confused Nisei in all the camps.

Jimmie H. Akutsu
5-4-F Hunt, Idaho
April 30, 1944
Fair Play Committee
Heart Mountain, Wyoming

Dear Sir:

As you will read by the time this letter reaches you there are six fellows from Minidoka who did not answer the call for induction on April 27, 1944. To these there are three more fellows who are out of the project and did not answer the call. Of the six fellows who did not answer the call, one happens to be my brother.

Since he is more or less taking the same stand as you people are, may I give you some of his reasons why he did not report for induction. In a very near future it will be my turn to follow him so can you please look into my or his case after I will be jailed.

First—He has been treated like a Japanese alien such as concentration or detention behind barbed-wire fence without a hearing or trial. His properties confiscated. His status changed to 4C without his acknowledgement and then back to 1A. Rights as citizen taken away as well as his freedom.

Then he has been told by Gen. DeWitt "Once a Jap always a Jap." American Legion "Issei, nessei [sic] deport them all." *New York Times* "Loyal or disloyal depart them all, because their skin is yellow." This [is] something we cannot change.

Second—therefore, this more or less proves him that he is a Japanese and will get deported. So he cannot and will not take up arms against that country he will be deported to. And so he feels no obligation to serve in the armed force of this country.

He was requested by the President and D. S. Myers to take the preinduction physical. This he did, otherwise he cannot make any appeal for reclassification. Within the 10 days after his exam he has the right to make an appeal. This he did, but the draft board does not follow out his right, he does not have to answer the call to induction. Just before his induction he wrote another letter to reclassify him to 4C. Finally the Jerome Board No. 1 answered him, mentioning repatriation, this again proved to him that he is a Japanese.

Have you noticed just a few months back some kind of a deportation bill went through the lower house by a big majority? The government is already making provision to deport the nseeei [sic] along with the issei after the war or before the war ends. You know as well as I that most of all of the nessei [sic] soldiers aren't coming back. How much nessei [sic] will there be after the war is really over?

And another thing, why do these fellows going in the army have to make out a indefinite leave paper plus lots of other passes? To me it looks like plain volunteering out of the centers, because the indefinite leave paper serves as a parol [sic] paper. To be paroled out of a jail during war means volunteering into the army. This isn't yet to me, Selective Service.

About last December the Portland *Oregonian* and Seattle paper had an issue saying to postpone the drafting of 900 fathers in state of Washington and replace them by taking 900 men out of Minidoka. At that time there were 980 men here at Minidoka of draft age. Some were single and others had four or five children. This meant taking better than 9 out of every 10 men here at Minidoka. Since hundreds have left camp, to make this quota they are branching to other centers. Do you think this is Selective Service, I most certainly think not, they are only Shanghaing [sic] us into a "Guinea Pig Outfit" since the first bunch that went over has already been tested and exhausted.

There is a question I'd like really to have cleared. Does a person who do not have a 1A classification be inducted into the army? Please answer me right away. Thank you I remain.

Sincerely yours,
Jimmie H. Akutsu

P.S. Are we under the jurisdiction of the International Law made at Geneva Conference? Also if we are put into a concentration camp for 6 months, does that make us a prisoners of war? Can you also answer these questions too.

Frank Emi
9-21-B
Heart Mountain
Wyo.

May 8, 1944

Mr. Jimmie H. Akutsu
5-4-F Hunt, Idaho

Dear Mr. Akutsu,

Your registered letter of April 30 arrived in Heart Mountain last week and I was asked to reply to you to the best of our knowledge.

The fifty-three boys from Heart Mountain who refused to go to their pre-induction physical are standing on the grounds that they are LOYAL AMER-ICAN CITIZENS and that they desire a clarification of their citizenship status and a restoration of their Constitutional rights before being inducted into the armed forces. Under no condition are they asking for expatriation or saying that they are disloyal to the United States. They have pleaded NOT GUILTY at their preliminary hearings and are expected to do so at their trial also. They are saying that they do not believe the draft law applies to them in their present suspended states in these concentration camps. That by reclassifying 4C, the Selective Service discriminated against them solely on the basis of race and ancestry. That drafting them out of these concentration camps is un-constitutional and against all principles of Democracy and civilized usage.

These boys are fighting for a principle as LOYAL AMERICAN CITIZENS. The real issue to them is not going to the army or not going to the army, but to fight for their Constitutional rights as loyal American citizens. They know what the consequences will be should they lose the case. Two, three, or four years in jail. But they feel that whether they win or lose the court case, they, as Americans of Japanese descent will at least have stood up as real Americans to fight for justice and the application of the true meaning of Democracy right here at home. That, briefly, is the feeling and the stand these boys have taken.

As to the chances of their winning their court case, there is about ten percent in their favor and about 90 percent against them and they all know it, but nevertheless they are fighting it out. That takes courage.

You mentioned that Gen. De Witt [sic] and the *New York Times* made some remarks about "once Jap, always a Jap" and "loyal or disloyal deport them all, because their skin is yellow." Naturally these kind of race-baiting statements would make anyone mad but don't ever let these things get you down and say that you are going to expatriate or say that you are not going into the army because you would rather go back to Japan. That would be a sad mistake for that is just what these kind of people want you to say. Besides, if you refuse to go to the Army and instead asked for expatriation, that would automatically make you guilty and I doubt whether you would even be given a trial.

You also asked whether a person who has not received their 1A classification can be inducted into the army. From the information that I have been able to gather from our attorney, it seems that they can induct you into the army no matter what classification you are in. Of course one can bring that irregularity up at the trial.

Frank Emi begs off dealing with the other questions and helping Akutsu with his case because of the complexities of dealing with the resistance at Heart Mountain. He does offer some good advice:

> If you could possibly retain an attorney it would be helpful, but unless you could get quite a number of people to back you up financially, it would be difficult.

And he closes with:

> Whatever you do in the future, I believe it would be wisest and most important to act as LOYAL AMERICAN CITIZENS and forget about expatriation and such. I believe it would benefit you more. Also, it might be of value if you would read over the Constitution of the United States, especially the Bill of Rights. That, essentially, is the basis of our stand.
>
> I hope you the best of luck and let us hope that everything will turn out for the best.
>
> > Sincerely yours,
> >
> > Frank Emi

Ben Kuroki,
Boy from Nebraska

A VISIT TO HEART MOUNTAIN

"I never did see the orders. They just came to my squadron and they told me, 'Kuroki, you gotta go to Heart Mountain.' And so I did. I was going to Heart Mountain, Minidoka, and Topaz. And I think there's been some misunderstanding about that. They never gave me any instructions. They just told me to go there. 'Course, I guess the directors or the people there had a general idea of what they wanted me to do. But that was some of the misunderstanding. JACL had nothing to do with me. They didn't tell me what to do. I was just told to go there, and so I just went to the camps, and whatever they had on their agenda, I did."

There were more Japanese Americans in Heart Mountain than Ben Kuroki had ever seen, up to that point, in his life. There were more Japanese Americans at this camp than in his entire home state of Nebraska.

"There were only four or five Japanese families within a fifty-mile radius of our home. We didn't see much of each other," Kuroki says. Nebraska was not Li'l Tokyo.

Heart Mountain was a town of ten thousand people—all of them Japanese and Japanese American—in the middle of nowhere.

He arrived, Monday, in a black car from camp, driven by a private in the army. "I was really quite shocked when I approached Heart Mountain and came up to the gate and saw these armed guards, and they were all wearing the same uniform I was wearing. And inside, behind the barbed were all these—my own people, so to speak. Most of them were American citizens. It was really quite a shock. I never did get over that."

He was greeted with a parade of Boy Scouts. There was a welcoming ceremony with camp dignitaries and parents of boys in the service, in front of a sign reading "Welcome Sgt. Ben Kuroki." His escort was Nobu Kawai, a JACL associate editor of the *Heart Mountain Sentinel.*

"It was at that time that Ben Kuroki visited the centers. So Ben and I appeared at several meetings and spoke. And it was at one of these meetings that the Fair Play Committee took issue with what I said," Nobu Kawai recalls.

Frank Emi, a leader of the Fair Play Committee, boycotted all the appearances of Ben Kuroki. "We heard that Ben Kuroki was coming. He himself was Nebraska boy, never knew anything about the camp, never was forced out of his home. I don't think he had, really, any business coming into these camps, trying to get as many people into the army as possible, to go into the military.

"So none of us went. Some of the resisters might have gone to listen to him, but none of us leaders were there."

"I was asked to speak, I guess, to this Fair Play Committee group," Ben Kuroki recalls. "And I'd been warned that they were quite militant and that they were concerned for my safety, so they were going to put on some extra guards."

Sgt. Ben Kuroki doesn't remember his escort, Nobu Kawai. But Nobu Kawai remembers they became great friends.

"This is a letter that I had written in reply to Frank Emi's letter to the editor. He had attacked me personally. And I felt that some kind of a reply was necessary. So I wrote to Frank Emi and the FPC: 'The fallacy in your argument is your contention that restrictions of your rights mean a loss of these rights.'"

The difference between a loss of his rights and a restriction of his rights made no sense; they were prisoners behind barbed wire with no freedom of movement, and no free exercise of their rights.

Ben Kuroki was unprepared for a whole community of people like him—men, women, and children—imprisoned behind barbed wire. And he wore the uniform of the guards, not the people. Kawai concludes his letter with:

When the war is won, the Ben Kurokis, fortified by their undeniable proof of loyalty through action, will plead our case of tolerance and justice before the bar of public opinion. Let us ever deny that we are anything but loyal American citizens. While we are fighting for our rights, let us conduct ourselves as good citizens so that no one can deny our claims to such rights.

Kawai adds, "I had p.s. there. Emi had mentioned that if we are so sincere about Selective Service then why is it that we don't join the army instead of sitting behind a desk in the office? I just had to put in this postscript: 'It may be of interest to you that on March 12, 1943, I volunteered for combat duty with the 442nd Combat Team and today am ready to be inducted whenever called.'

"I know that Ben Kuroki congratulated me. I got to know Ben quite well while he was in camp. His thinking and my thinking were pretty much parallel. He appreciated the stand that I took. And, of course, I appreciated the service that Ben had been to us and to the country. I admired his service record."

Kuroki remembers meeting a group he thought was the Fair Play Committee.

"I would say that everything was okay except at one time I made the statement that if they thought Japan was going to win the war, they were crazy. I said they were going to be bombed off the map. And I heard some booing and hissing. And that was probably the only real thing that stood out in my memory."

Between Monday and Saturday, he met a girl and asked her for a date. Dinner and a dance the night before he was to leave Heart Mountain and catch a bus to Minidoka. The girl was Kaoru Emi, the youngest sister of the Fair Play Committee's Frank Emi.

The next day Nobu Kawai thought it would be nice for a genuine hero to give the boys on the bus going to their pre-induction physicals a pep talk before they left camp.

Kuroki remembers, "He asked me to step in the bus. These young men were going into the service. So, I thought I'd go in and wish them good luck. I'm pretty sure I did, but the reception was cold. Nobody responded, so I just turned around, and just got off."

The day that Kuroki leaves, six men refuse to report for induction.

In Natrona County Jail, in Caspar, Wyoming, the resisters found themselves eating wild game. Moose, deer, tule elk. The jail provided the groceries, and the resisters did their own cooking. Not all the resisters enjoyed the rich diet. Jack Ishikawa was one of four brothers who had resisted the draft. He had a bleeding ulcer and eating was painful; he would have failed his pre-induction physical and wouldn't be affected by the draft. But he was opposing the draft on principle, with his brothers. He wanted to be heard. He wanted to go to trial.

In Laramie County Jail, in Cheyenne, they sing a song written by two men from Hawaii. The song is based on a Hawaiian worksong, "Hore Hore Bushi." Like the original worksong, "Song of Cheyenne" is rough, unsophisticated, manly, and oddly plaintive. The song was found, copied in Japanese, in the wallet of Mr. James Kado, a draft resister from Heart Mountain. From Heart Mountain, he has kept a series of three-inch-by-five-inch notebooks into which he had copied, by hand, the entire U.S. Constitution.

SONG OF CHEYENNE

By

Mr. Yanagisaki and Mr. Sumida

Aloha Cheyenne Kago-no-naka
To nanamey sunde-iru
Aloha Cheyenne, we're in the cage
Ten to seven of us live here
Hige-wa boboto haemasita
Dare-ga ichiban ngai-ko-to
Our beards have grown wildly
Who has the longest one?
Aloha, Waiomin, Larami Kauntie
Asa-wa hachiji-kara yoru-wa-kuji
Aloha, Wyoming, Laramie County
Eight in A.M. till nine in P.M.
Poker gaimu-ni bakuchi-bana
Neru-maeni-wa baka-bana-shi
Poker game we bet like hell
Before lights out we chat and chit chat

Aloha Harto-yama natsukashii
Itsu kaeru ka wakara-nai
Aloha Heart Mountain, we long for you
We don't know when we shall return
Mesu hoolu-no pooku sooseiji
Hara kudashi-nya kaka-te-yuku
Pork sausage in the mess hall
Gives us the diarrheic galloping trots
Aloha Harto-yama koi-no sora
Aloha Heart Mountain, I miss your sky

Min Yasui,
Resister or Turncoat?

In 1944, Minoru Yasui was a hero to many Nisei for having resisted the curfew and gone to the Supreme Court with Hirabayashi to test it in 1942. Mike Masaoka, spokesman for the JACL, had called Min Yasui "a self-styled martyr out to win headlines" in his "JACL Bulletin 142: Re: Test Cases." Yasui was also a member of the JACL. He replied with his own version of Masaoka's bulletin, answering Masaoka paragraph for paragraph. From jail, he also issued another bulletin, titled "Why We Should Support Test Cases." He says, "I strongly felt and still believe, that it is the duty of every American citizen to resist any infringement upon the basic principles of our nation. This is our duty as American citizens, as much as it is to fight and die on battlefields in defence of our nation."

In 1944, on behalf of the FBI and representing the JACL Denver office, Min Yasui and Mike Masaoka's brother, Joe Grant Masaoka, visited the resisters in jail and offered them dropped charges if they turned against their cause and agreed to testify against the leaders of the Fair Play Committee in the conspiracy trial.

They visited six men. Two of the men they visited were Yosh Kuromiya, the man who liked to sketch the mountain, and Ike Matsumoto, from the streets of Los Angeles, Li'l Tokyo.

Yosh Kuromiya,
Fair Play Committee

"**B**oth Min Yasui and Joe Grant Masaoka interviewed me. I was the fifth or the sixth one they took from a cell into this room, and there they were.

"Min Yasui challenged the government on the legality of the curfew law, by violating that law and were establishing a test case. I felt that we doing pretty much the same thing.

"I was rather confused as to where his position really was. I didn't know whether this was somebody I could trust or not. I had these mixed emotions about it. However, in the course of the interview it became apparent what his purpose was. And I lost respect for the person.

"There was no way that I would change my mind."

Ike Matsumoto,
Fair Play Committee

"Oh, yeah, he was saying we should change our minds 'cuz he heard that a lot of prisoners—not a lot of 'em—that one—was hit with a two-by-four. And when he said 'two-by-four' I figured, gee, that's a big stick. Nobody's gonna hit anybody with a two-by-four! So I figured this guy's giving me a lot of story.

"They said why don't I change my mind and go back to camp. And I said, gee, we been here this far, can't change our mind now!"

Not one of the Heart Mountain boys they interviewed accepted their offer.

James Omura,
Nisei Newsman

"MR. YASUI ISN'T IN YET"

In his secret report to the FBI, Yasui wrote: "Those who might want to change their minds, convinced of the error of their ways, would probably not be tolerated. For these separate and individual cells would allow considerable introspection and self-analysis. It would supplant individual decision for group pressure."

"Why that son of bitch!" James Omura said, on reading that line of Yasui's. "He is suggesting they be put into solitary confinement to break their will."

I took the Secret Report to the FBI out of his hands and reread the Yasui line. He was right.

"Well we always knew there was something wrong with him," Omura says. "Actually what made us very suspicious of him was that he came to the *Rocky Shimpo* to complain about the *Rocky Shimpo*'s emphasis on the Fair Play Committee.

"And I invited him, if he would write an objective article that we would give him just as much importance to that as anything else. Which he did, and which we published.

"Just before he left, I was holding the door open to the street, he turned around and he says, 'I'm going to see you go to prison, one way or another.'

"Over the weekend I thought about that. That bothered me a great deal. And on Monday, I came to work. I told the publisher, 'I think this man is an informant. And so we ought try to confirm it.'

"I didn't ask the publisher [Tetsuko Toda] to call the FBI. She volunteered. She knew an FBI agent. She made the call. And they told her that, 'Mr. Yasui isn't in yet. He's a little bit late this morning, and that we should try the marshal's office.'

"And when I called they told me that Yasui is very late this morning. It's possible that he sometimes goes to the FBI first before reporting in.

"I don't know what his third stop was. But I suspected it was to Naval Intelligence. His next stop was to the WRA, in the afternoon. So, I was very well aware that he was an informant."

Yosh Kuromiya,
Fair Play Committee

"Our attorney, Menin, suggested we try to thwart identification. Without identification we couldn't be tried. So, our attorney suggested we all get short haircuts and thus frustrate the prosecution's attempt to identify us. "That didn't sit well with me. Our purpose was to raise the issue."

Mits Koshiyama,
Fair Play Committee

"The federal prosecutor was rocking back and forth on his chair. And all of a sudden he just flipped over backwards, bang! He just fell out on the floor.

"Well, naturally, most of us young guys were in the front, so—ohh, we just laughed. It was so funny!

"And the old federal prosecutor got red faced and said, 'You won't be laughing when you hear the verdict!'

"When our lawyer Mr. Menin objected to what the federal prosecutor was saying, the federal prosecutor says, 'Your honor, if that lawyer doesn't sit down, I'll go over there and make him sit down.' And you know, Menin, he's pretty tough too. So he took off his coat, and he said, 'Your honor, let him try!'

"I thought he should have based our case on constitutional issues, because that's what we wanted."

The Sixty-Three Men
from Heart Mountain

The sixty-three Heart Mountain boys were represented by Samuel D. Menin of Denver and Clyde M. Watts of Cheyenne. The sixty-three decided against a jury trial. Carl Sackett, U.S. district attorney, was the prosecutor. T. Blake Kennedy was the judge. In his decision he said:

> While this case does not pass upon the legality of the removal; and the relocation of persons under the class here before the court, the opinion calls attention to the establishment by executive order of the War Relocation Authority and the right thereby afforded to effectuate a program for removal, relocation, maintenance and supervision of the persons under consideration. Our attention has not been called to any case in which the courts have construed the constitutionality of the removal and relocation of citizens of Japanese extraction, yet it would seem that the same logic which led to the conclusion that the curfew law did not violate their constitutional rights would justify a like conclusion in regard to removal and relocation.

In 1989, the U.S. Supreme Court struck down Hirabayashi and Yasui's violation of the military's curfew and Korematu's violation of the military's exclusion order on a writ of *corum nobis*. The Army had not only withheld evidence, they had lied. The Japanese Americans posed no threat to the United States. "Military necessity" was a sham.

The trial of the sixty-three ended on June 26, 1944. They were found guilty and sentenced to three years. The married men were sent to Leavenworth, Kansas. The single men did their time at McNeil Island, in Washington state.

Kozie Sakai

LETTER TO FRANK EMI

Kozie Sakai and his family operated the Sakai Store in Mountain View, California. His sisters ran the store and drove his custom-built Dodge truck from store to farm, taking orders and making deliveries. He was a regular visitor to the families around Mountain View, watching them grow their crops and expand their families and farms. With each delivery he gave many trading stamps, to encourage trade with his store. And for the kids he met, he had candies. The kids had grown up with him. Many of the kids were now resisters.

He would get a pass to leave camp on one pretext or another and visit the resisters in jail while they awaited trial; he was there during the trial, still the grocer of the Heart Mountain sixty-three. He ran errands for them and carried messages between camp and jail. After each visit to the boys in Cheyenne, Kozie would write Frank Emi a letter. At 11:30 P.M. on July 5, 1944, the day after the Fourth of July celebration, Kozie wrote:

Evening of July fifth.
Cowboy State.

Dear Frank,

Got to see the boys several minutes yesterday after noon in their downstairs cells. All are fine and impatiently waiting for their transfer to McNeils farm.

446

Imagine living in this congested condition for nearly a month. Folks and families should be very gratified that they are going to be moved soon. I know I shall be for the sake of the boys.

It's indescribable, as I've stated before. That is—there's nothing to describe. They actually brush each other's elbows in getting their exercise walk.

During these visits I collect all the boys' letters on a sly and mail them out.

Anything they need I jot it down and bring the following day. The boys worry about their folks who unnecessarily worry about them. So please, stress this point, Frank. It would be a good idea if folks back in camp would write an encouraging letter to their boy or husband the next time.

The boys are leaving here about nine o'clock Saturday night on a Union Pacific route that goes through Rawlins & Laramie. Through Pocatello, Oregon and Washington then hits North at some terminal for its destination.

The group that left for Leavenworth (Good heavens! they're there now.) were caged in, three guards including the driver on duty, and the bus had three or four nickel plated bars running on the outside windows. It was of grey color, with a wording U.S. Department of Justice written on the doors. There were several boxes on the inside rack presumably lunches for the boys. It even had a toilet inside the bus. But the bus itself wasn't so very conspicuous any passer by at a glance would just take it for some special car.

[Consider a man of obvious Japanese ancestry, alone in Cheyenne, Wyoming, where the newspapers say Nisei Fifth Columnists were tried and convicted—going from store to store asking for rope and large empty boxes—during WWII.]

Today I had an interesting and amusing incident.

I went into an ordinary corner hardware (half a block way from jail) and inquired for some ropes. He didn't have any, so I asked if I may buy some empty cartons, if he had any at all to spare.

He would not accept any money but asked what I was going to use it for.

I explained and said it was to pack the boys' belongings, who was to leave for jail soon.

He understood and then the fun began. He asked my name and were I was from. He said he was a German born in Austria. And that he was interrogated too of being a Nazi suspect. He told me he was proud to be a Nazi and gave me a Hitler salute (jokingly) saying "banzai!"

He didn't like Churchill and said so, in fact he didn't give a darn for a lot of these Americans.

But he sure had sympathy for us and said we were being mistreated. I didn't say very much and finally thanked him for the boxes and bid him goodbye. He opened the side door for me and gave his salute again, saying "Banzai!"

I went to his store again about four, five hours later. He remembered my name, saying, "Sakai, we'll know one of these days."

Goodbye,
Kozie.

Postmarked: Cheyenne, Wyoming. July 5th. 11:30PM 1944.

◆ ◆ ◆

Thirty-three unmarried men went to McNeil Island Federal Penitentiary, in Washington. Thirty married men were sent to Leavenworth, Kansas.

The resisters convicted and sentenced, the government now prepared for the trial of the leaders of the Fair Play Committee.

Gloria Kubota,
Nisei and the Zen Man

"**I** was pregnant with Gordon, ironing clothes in the laundry room. Someone from the FPC comes in and stuffs a pile of papers in my baskets of laundry. Then the FBI comes in and looks and talks, and I'm ironing clothes." She takes items out of the basket and irons. She takes her time ironing them, over and over as the FBI engages her in conversation. She doesn't want to expose the documents at the bottom of the basket. The FBI lingers and talks and talks. Finally they move on.

Ten days later Gordon is born.

"He said if we had a son, our son's name going to be Gordon. He said that's the kind of Japanese people should be. That's how we got the name Gordon.

"After I had Gordon, I brought him home from the hospital. The FBI came to check us up and to pick George up. They came and picked him up. And they started ransacking everything. And I had just brought home Gordon. He was about ten days old. Do you know I finally couldn't stand it. So I went to my mother's unit. When I went there, I got blind. I couldn't see for a whole day. And I was just all rattled up. And I'm so upset with everything. This crowd comes by to look at me, but I don't mind, I can't see then anyway."

Arthur Emi,
Little Brother

Kiyoshi Okamoto and Paul Nakadate were removed to the Tule Lake segregation camp. Frank Emi and Art Emi prepared to be arrested by dressing
up in their finest suits, and their families in their nicest clothes. They posed,
outdoors in the firebreak, for formal family portraits.

One morning, two FBI agents knocked on the door of Frank Emi's barracks
apartment and took him away in a car. Kiyoshi Okamoto, Paul Nakadate, and
Isamo Horino were all held at Tule Lake. Guntaro Kubota was in Cheyenne
County Jail. Minoru Tamesa and Ben Wakaye were doing time at McNeil Island
for draft evasion, as a result of the first trial. Now Frank Emi was gone to
Cheyenne.

Art Emi now represented the leadership of the Fair Play Committee, to the
people of Heart Mountain and the public.

"Well I fully expected to be arrested like the rest of them only they were picked
up first. And I told my wife, 'Okay, I'm ready to get whatever they do to me.'

"At that point, I wasn't picked up. And the other leaders were picked up.
There wasn't anyone that could take on the meetings, continue the meetings,
inform the parents what was going on, negotiate with the attorneys and then
keep the whole thing alive.

"So I was very fortunate to be in a position where I could help them
do that."

Frank Emi, Leader

"**W**e were charged with conspiracy to violate the Selective Service Act and counseling others to resist the draft. This was July 21, 1944.

"Indicted with us was Mr. James Omura, English-language editor of the *Rocky Shimpo*, based in Denver, Colorado. This we could not understand. We had never met Mr. Omura, and had never talked with him."

Omura retained his own attorneys (Sidney S. Jacobs and Lloyd C. Sampson) to keep his case separate from the Heart Mountain Fair Play Committee.

"We finally retained A. L. Wirin, a noted constitutional attorney for the Los Angeles ACLU, as private counsel. Mr. Wirin advised us that the chance of winning this case at district court level was pretty slim, and that our best chance was in the appellate court."

WYOMING TRIBUNE

October 3, 1944

NISEI WAR HERO HITS

JAPANESE-AMERICANS

WHO FIGHT THE DRAFT

"A stab in the back" is the way Sgt. Ben Kuroki characterizes the activities of Japanese-Americans who have been convicted on charges of conspiracy to violate the national selective service act.

A bemedaled veteran of 30 missions over Europe, the young soldier is of Japanese parentage. He said, in interview here:

"These men are Fascists in my estimation and no good to any country. They have torn down all the rest of us tried to do. I hope that these members of that Fair Play Committee won't form the opinion of America concerning all Japanese-Americans."

This intrepid young Nisei airman is the only Japanese-American to receive the Distinguished Flying Cross. He also wears the Air Medal with four Oak Leaf clusters, and has a cluster on his D.F.C., and a presidential unit citation.

He still hopes to get duty in the Pacific, and to add another campaign ribbon to the three he now wears.

(Wyo Tribune 10/3/44)

Nobu Kawai,
The Volunteer

"AM I IN, OR AM I OUT?"

"**I**n the meantime, my father got ill in Gila. And so I rushed down to Gila." From Heart Mountain.

While at Gila, "I went down to the draft board in Gila and jumped all over them. They were a crass bunch down there. And they said, 'Well, if you don't want to go in, you can withdraw your voluntary induction.'

"I said, 'Well the 442nd is about to go over. If I go in now, I won't have enough training. I would have to go over as a replacement. That's not my intention. It takes all the purpose in volunteering out of this thing. If that's what I'm going to be—a replacement, I'd rather not go and take my chances with Selective Service.

"And then I got a wire from Miye. 'Hey, your induction papers are in Cody, Wyoming.'

"I said, 'Whaaat?' And so I went to the draft board again and said, 'I can't go now, my Dad's funeral was pending.' So they postponed my induction. And we had the funeral.

"And then I went back to Heart Mountain. I said, 'Just where do I stand. Am I in, or am I out?'

"They said, 'We can't tell yet until we get word from your Pasadena draft board, your original draft board.'

"So I waited around and I waited around. And finally they sent me a reclassification. '4F.'

"I said, 'What does this mean?'

"They said it means, 'You're out.'

"And so I said, 'Now that I know that I'm not going into the army, you know the 442nd, let's relocate.' And so we went to Cincinnati, Ohio. And I took a job with McCall Publishing Company in Dayton, Ohio. And it was while we were in Dayton, Ohio, that we got a wire that Ted was killed in action. And so it was a short time he went over there, to France, that he was killed in action over there. And so I thought, gee, it was a good thing I had a talk with his parents and so forth."

HOT OFF THE PRESS!

THE PACIFIC CITIZEN

July 1, 1944

One Thousand Drafted from WRA Centers

More Than 3000 Called Up for Service From Relocation Camps

As of May 31, 1093 have been accepted out of 3,312 called. 139 have declined to report for pre-induction physicals.

Frank Emi, Leader

A SURPRISE WITNESS

"Our trial was held on 23 October 1944, in the Federal District Court in Cheyenne, Wyoming. During our trial, a surprise witness appeared in court.

"His name was Jack Nishimoto, a Nisei in his early forties. He lived near me at Heart Mountain.

"This Jack Nishimoto that testified against us in the trial, he went there and told lies. Barefaced lies! Like he said that if the government didn't agree with what we did, 'Frank Emi said that he would go back to Japan.' Yeah, he said that.

"He said, 'I heard Frank telling Dave Kawamoto in the latrine, don't go to the draft, the Fair Play Committee will take care of you.' That was the main thing. But that was stupid, because we came out in the open and said we're not going to the draft.

"We're going to contest the issue.

"And that thing about me advising Dave Kawamoto's mother that, 'Don't worry. We'll take care of him.' That never took place.

"So besides what actually happened, he did put in some outright lies. That really pissed me off."

WYOMING EAGLE

October 26, 1944

JAP-AMERICAN GI TESTIFIES AGAINST NISEI DEFENDANTS

Jack Nishimoto, one time resident of the Heart Mountain center, testified he had heard Frank Emi, one of the defendants, advising one of the young Nisei at the camp not to report when called for the draft. He had also told the court that the young Nisei's mother had been told by Emi "not to worry" that the Fair Play committee would "take care" of her son.

In a talk with Emi, after two boys at the camp had been arrested on charges of violation of the selective service act, Nishimoto said Emi had told him he advised the youths not to report for pre-induction physical examinations and to enter pleas of not guilty to the charges in court.

Harry Yoshida, a veteran of World War I and a former resident of the camp, testified he had attended some of the meetings of the FPC and that the men at the meeting were advised to "stay in a group" until their rights were clarified.

Frank Emi, Leader

"WHY WAS HE UP THERE?"

"We couldn't understand why he was up there," Frank Emi says of Jack Nishimoto's appearance in court. "The only thing we could surmise, the attorney said that they had nothing to tie me into the conspiracy, so they got him to testify. He was a friend of mine. I used to give him rides on my truck and things like that. But he was typical inu. One of these guys that's very Americanized. He's got features something like Gene Barry. That type of face."

WYOMING TRIBUNE

November 1, 1944

CASE TO BE GIVEN JURY

Closing Arguments in Trial Here of Eight Nisei

Wirin went to great lengths in his remarks on the Japanese relocation centers, which he said were concentration camps in the same sense as Germany's and Japan's prison camps. He said that the Nisei incarcerated there were in the same position as the Jews in the German camps.

The volatile attorney told the jury that the Tokyo radio, which reports any acts of race discrimination in this country to minorities all over the world, would broadcast their verdict in this case to the Africans who are on our side in this war, the Chinese who are fighting with us, the Hindus, and the Filipinos, with whom Japan would use it as a plea for cooperation. He said that this is not a local case, and that a "fair" verdict would help our soldiers in the Philippines.

Frank Emi, Leader

"WE LOST OUR CASE"

The case went the jury at 3:45 P.M. on November 2, 1944. The verdict was delivered at 9:30 P.M. On the morning of November 3, Judge Rice pronounced sentence.

"Just as Mr. Wirin had indicated, we lost our case," Frank Emi says. "Judge Eugene Rice sentenced the seven of us to four years at Leavenworth Federal Penitentiary. James Omura was acquitted. However, the court fight left him in bad financial shape. The JACL continued to harass him. This was a trial which never should have taken place for Jim."

James Omura,
Nisei Newsman

"VINDICATED AS A PERSON, VINDICATED IN MY PROFESSION"

The only Japanese American journalist supporting the Nisei right to petition for redress of grievances was out of print. From jail, James Omura wrote all the Nisei poets and writers he had encouraged and published in his newspapers and magazine before the war. He appealed to them for help in his defense. He received not one dime. Not one answer to his letters. The poets and writers were all publishing in the JACL *Pacific Citizen*, and the JACL controlled camp papers now.

Omura returned to the *Rocky Shimpo* briefly in 1947, but Japanese America did not respond to the lone critic of the JACL. The paper dropped him.

"When I was acquitted, I felt I was vindicated. Vindicated as a person. Vindicated in my profession."

WYOMING EAGLE

December 2, 1944

EAGLE COVERAGE OF NISEI TRIAL HERE APPLAUDED

The Wyoming Eagle was praised yesterday, by the only one of eight Japanese-Americans to be acquitted in a federal court conspiracy case held here last October, having upheld "the highest traditions in newspaper reporting" by the "very impartial treatment" of its coverage.

A letter from James M. Omura, former editor of the English section of the *Rocky Shimpo*, Denver Japanese-language newspaper, thanked the *Eagle* for its fair treatment of the case.

"The verdict of the jury in acquitting me leaves unimpaired the freedom of the press, one of the most important of our constitutional rights.

"It was also most refreshing to make the acquaintance of newspapers which uphold the best tradition of journalism. The *Eagle* and its companion publication, the *Wyoming Tribune*, covered the conspiracy trial in a very objective manner. The accounts of the trial were not racially prejudiced...."

James Omura,
Nisei Newsman

"IT WAS NO FUN"

"**I** returned to Denver and then tried to obtain work. I was hounded from one job after another. It took me three months to finally find a job.

"Actually I eventually went into landscape contracting. Because there I felt that I couldn't be molested or harassed by people who were against me."

His ostracism from the Japanese American community was so complete that even his admirers, including the resisters themselves, thought he was dead.

Actually, he was in Denver. Bowling used to be one of his favorite pastimes, but he gave it up. His eyes fill with tears and he becomes choked up, explaining why:

"Most of all it [the social ostracism by the Japanese Americans] was one of these subtle sort of things. You could feel it. You could feel the tenseness. I was in a bowling league, and I could feel the tenseness. It got so bad that I couldn't bowl any longer. It was no fun, I can tell you that."

463

White Bigot,
Where Are You?

The trial of sixty-three draft resisters in Cheyenne in June was the largest mass trial in Wyoming history. There were too many prisoners for any one jail. They were spread out among Laramie County Jail at Cheyenne; Albany County Jail at Laramie; Carbon County Jail at Rawlins; Wakshakie County Jail at Worland; Natrona County Jail in Caspar; and Park County Jail in Cody. If the United States was as full of Jap-hating bigots as the JACL said, now was the time for them to show themselves.

D-Day, June 6, 1944, was in the news with the Heart Mountain sixty-three, but there were no demonstrations. Every day the prisoners came and went, and the people of Cheyenne, Rawlins, and Laramie were unconcerned—no riots, no pickets, no protests. People regularly left camp, on a pass, for a day of shopping in Cody or Powell. There were signs in some shop windows that read "No Japs" in Cody, to the right and fifteen miles down the road from Heart Mountain and no signs in Powell, to the left and thirteen miles from Heart Mountain on the same road. No signs at all in Cheyenne.

July 4th came and went without riots, pickets, or protests at any of the jails or the camp. It wasn't that the people of Wyoming didn't know who was in town or what was happening. The sixty-three made "JAP!" headlines in the *Wyoming Eagle*, the *Wyoming Tribune* and the *Billings Gazette* every day.

Then came the July trial of the leaders. The JACL expected anti-Japanese sentiment to be spilling out of the mouths of hundreds of beady-eyed cowboys.

The army ordered Ben Kuroki to the trial to testify, but he was never called, because there was no crowd, no beady-eyed troublemakers, no lookie-loos. Where were the rabid white racists that made America unsafe for Japanese Americans? The JACL said they were all over the west, but Hirabayashi had been through Washington, Idaho, Utah, Arizona, and Nevada without encountering a single white racist. And for weeks, the newspapers of Wyoming had been all but advertising for racists to come to Cheyenne to party. And nothing.

On May 1, 1945, a group of seventeen more draft resisters from Heart Mountain were added to the list of those convicted of violating the draft by Judge T. Blake Kennedy, bringing the total to eighty. A. L. Wirin took over the defense of all of them, basing it on constitutional grounds.

Heart Mountain
Fair Play Committee

J ames Omura, of the *Rocky Shimpo*, was found not guilty. Kiyoshi Okamoto, Paul Nakadate, Isamu Horino, and Frank Emi were convicted of conspiracy to violate the Selective Service Act and sentenced to four years in Leavenworth. Minoru Tamesa and Ben Wakaye were convicted and sentenced to two years at Leavenworth, to be served concurrently with the three years they were serving for their failure to report for their pre-induction physicals. Guntaro Kubota was not counted as a member of the FPC, because of his non-U.S. citizenship, and was sentenced to two years.

Frank Emi says, "We filed an appeal to the Tenth Circuit Court of Appeals. Mr. Wirin requested bail for us, pending the decision of the Appellate Court. The judge refused, stating, 'You men are agitators, the camp will be better off without you.'"

In Leavenworth, "All of the conspiracy guys were in one cell. Horino and Nakadate. Tamesa and Wakaye. I think Toru Ino was with us, and this guy from Amache was with us. A guy named Kawasaki—Kawasaki was in our cell.

"I was on the top bunk, and Kubota was on the bottom bunk. And I think Okamoto was in one of the end bunks. He didn't communicate much with the rest of the group. He didn't engage in conversation with us. He was always on the aloof side. Oh, Harry Ikemoto was in our group, too, in that bunk. Ten to a cell." Five bunk beds. Upper bunk and lower bunk.

From Min Yasui's talks with six of the resisters had come stories of Japanese being beaten with two-by-fours by other prisoners inside the federal pen. Once the leaders of the Fair Play Committee arrived at Leavenworth, Frank Emi led them to stage a judo demonstration for inmates on "Sports Day." Frank Emi and the others let little Toru Ino throw them all. A little friendly mutual deterrence. The demonstration was effective. They had no problems with the other prisoners.

Grace Kubota Ybarra,
Daughter of Zen Man

"There's one absolutely memorable letter that we received that was a picture of my dad as he looked then.

"And he told us later that he and Frank Emi shared a cell together, and that Frank Emi drew that picture. It's something that's real important for us.

"Japanese was and always to the end of his life was his primary language. His English was absolutely horrible, and he writes this letter—and Frank Emi taught him, Frank Emi was not a very good teacher—because this is the letter:

"Dear Gloria and Makiko (My Japanese name),

"I am very sorry to Makiko. Last time I was send picture to Hitamaro. I know Maki want too, but I was very busy to draw picture. . . ."

The letter is written on lined paper. Most of it is filled with drawings in black and colored pencil, of blonde children playing with a beach ball and a bucket on the beach.

"Yeah, I remember the first time I saw him. I didn't think he was my father, because his cheeks were sunken in. And I remember him as a heavier-built, fuller-faced person. And for a long time in my child's mind, I thought that he was a substitute, that he wasn't my dad."

STARS AND STRIPES

Wednesday, August 1, 1945

B-29 GUNNER PLEASES MAMA, HELPS BUILD FIRE IN YOKOHAMA

By S/SGT. JOHN ADVENT

Stars and Stripes Correspondent

TINIAN—"I didn't think of it as my parents' birthplace—it's just another enemy country to me," said T/Sgt. Ben Kuroki, believed to be the first American of Japanese ancestry to bomb Japan.

The 27-year-old tail gunner from Hershey, Neb., flew 30 missions against Nazis before volunteering for combat in the Pacific.

During one of his 27 Pacific air-strikes, T/Sgt. Kuroki watched Yokohama, his mother's hometown, go up in smoke. Now he's anxious to bomb Kagoshima, because "dad will get a kick out of it. He was born there."

'We All Feel The Same'

"My father, mother, brothers and I all feel the same," he said. "We don't give a damn what happens to Japan or the Japanese. We are Americans."

Now with the 313th Bomb wing, Kuroki formerly was a B-24 gunner with Brig. Gen. Ted Timberlake's "Flying Circus" of the 8th Air Force.

Frank Emi, Leader

"THE PROUDEST THING I EVER DID"

"**I** can still remember a conversation I had with Guntaro one day, while we were sitting in our cell, at Leavenworth.

"He said, 'Emi, I'm really proud to be with you fellows. If I don't ever do anything else in my life, this will be the proudest thing I ever did because I had a part in your fight for a principle.' I will never forget his words."

On December 26, 1946, the Tenth Circuit Court of Appeals, sitting in Denver, reversed the convictions of all seven leaders on the grounds that the trial judge, Eugene Rice, failed to instruct the jury that the evacuees had a legal right to advise a refusal to comply with draftboard orders as a test case, in order to test the rights of persons of Japanese ancestry detained in relocation centers

Justice Bratton said, "one with innocent motives, who honestly believes a law is unconstitutional and therefore not obligatory, may well counsel that the law shall not be obeyed."

"We had finally won our battle," Frank Emi says.

Fair Play Committee Wins

Prior to their removal from their homes they had been law abiding and loyal citizens.

They deeply resented classification as undesirables. Most of them remained loyal to the United States and indicated a desire to remain in this country and to fight in its defense, provided their rights of citizenship were recognized.

For these, we have recommended pardons, in the belief that they will justify our confidence in their loyalty.

United States Amnesty Board

The convictions of the draft resistance leaders of the Fair Play Committee were reversed on appeal, on December 26, 1946.

The last man to walk out of McNeil Island was Jack Tono. He had lost his good time for remarks he made in prison. Fred Iriye died in a freak accident in the power-house the day before he was to be released. He threw a faulty switch and was electrocuted. His footprints were burned into the concrete floor.

In March of 1947, attorney A. L. Wirin went before the president's Amnesty Board and asked for a presidential pardon for all the 263 Nisei convicted of violating the draft from all the camps.

The draft resisters were granted a presidential pardon that recognized their cause on Christmas Eve of 1947. A year and day after the eight leaders of the Fair Play Committee won a reversal of their conviction, the eighty Heart Mountain resisters won a pardon and a restoration of their rights. Thanks to A. L. Wirin of Los Angeles, standing on the constitution they'd won.

The JACL made good on their prediction of social ostracism, which continues to this day.

Hajiime "Jim" Akutsu, "No-No Boy"

The round face wasn't smiling any more. It was thoughtful. The eyes confronted Ichiro with indecision which changed slowly to enlightenment and then to suspicion. He remembered. He knew.

The friendliness was gone as he said: "No-no boy, huh?"

Ichiro wanted to say yes. He wanted to return the look of despising hatred and say simply yes, but it was too much to say.

"Rotten bastard. Shit on you." Eto coughed up a mouthful of sputum and rolled his words around it: "Rotten, no-good bastard"

(—*No-No Boy*, John Okada)

"Ichiro" is another way of pronouncing "Hajiime," as in Hajiime "Jim" Akutsu, and it means "firstborn." John Okada, the author of the novel *No-No Boy*, was not himself a No-No boy. He was a veteran, with service in military intelligence in the Pacific. He chose very consciously to write about his friend Jim Akutsu, a No-No boy and draft resister from Seattle, as the Japanese American everyman.

When Okada died in 1971, his wife called the UCLA Japanese American Research Project and offered them a manuscript of her husband's unfinished novel on the Issei generation and his papers. The JACL's Joe Grant Masaoka, running the UCLA program, told her to burn the papers, sight unseen. He thought Okada was a No-No boy.

Joe Grant Masaoka was not a scholar. When he received a copy of Douglas Nelson's Masters thesis, "Heart Mountain," with chapters on the Fair Play

Committee, he made a show of physically ripping those chapters out, out, out. (But Nelson's book was published, with all chapters intact.)

Jim Akutsu returned to Seattle by train, like Ichiro, but unlike Ichiro, he says he was never spat on by a veteran. Turn off the tape recorder, and he says something else.

With the tape recorder off, he confirms that many incidents described in the novel were real.

"I believe my mother suffered because of the stand I took. Me, I'm pretty callous. If you're gonna do it, go ahead and try it. That's my attitude. So, never got into a fight. Nobody spit at me. Sure there was a lot of silent treatment. To me that doesn't hurt.

"She got ostracized. She got cut way from the Issei community. And the last thing that happened was, she was told not to come back to church.

"So she told me, 'I can't even go to church.'

"And it was shortly thereafter she took her life."

James Wong Howe,
American Cinematographer

"I HAVE A STORY. IT'S A BEAUTIFUL STORY."

"I made probably a hundred and fifty movies in my career. There's a lot of things I've done. Maybe there's a lotta things I haven't done yet. But I still like to get new approaches. Or used some of the old approaches and mix it becomes new," James Wong Howe says.

During the war, Chinese had to wear buttons, James Wong Howe says. The buttons read "I am a loyal Chinese American." He hated the buttons, but had to wear one. "Jimmy Cagney came on the set and laughed at me."

Kiyoshi Okamoto, the founder of the Fair Play Committee and leader of the organized draft resistance, was in the movies before the war, according to the *Wyoming Eagle* of October 28, 1944, not just any movie, but a movie starring James Cagney, photographed by James Wong Howe in 1939.

> The defendant Okamoto further stated that he had at one time worked in Hollywood as a movie actor and that he had taken a part in a picture which played in Cheyenne this week, "The Oklahoma Kid." He said he had played various other movie parts, usually portraying a Chinese.

It's too much to hope that Kiyoshi Okamoto, the resistance leader; James Wong Howe, the cinematographer who itches to make the great movie about camp; and James Cagney, the star, just happened to be working on *The Oklahoma Kid* when Cagney laughed at Wong Howe's "I am a Chinese" button. There were no buttons distinguishing between loyal yellow people and disloyal yellow people in 1939, when *The Oklahoma Kid* was shooting.

Several viewings of *The Oklahoma Kid* with Humphrey Bogart and James Cagney as western gunslingers on opposite sides of the law and with lots of crowd scenes in saloons and gambling halls have yielded not a glimpse of anyone in Chinese costume, or any costume that might be interpreted as Chinese, who might be Kiyoshi Okamoto.

James Wong Howe has not heard of any significant Nisei resistance in the camps, much less an organized resistance movement. But the story he wants to tell is a Japanese American story of camp.

"I have a story. It's very good. It's a beautiful story. I open with Santa Monica Beach. And you see a lot of people playing volleyball. I come in, and I see a Japanese. He's an Oriental. You don't know he's Japanese. But you know he's Oriental. And his girlfriend is playing amongst white kids, too. See? Suddenly the game's finished. They gotta go home. They'll be late. The sun is setting. So they go back. He and his girl, they're in love! You know, they're in love!

"They get in the car. And they're on their way home. And on their way home they notice people looking at 'em. Differently, you see? And some of the kids do that," Jimmy throws a violent gesture, "some do this," another violent gesture. "Suddenly they come home. The mother and father, 'It's terrible!' They're hysterical.

"'What happened?'

"'Don't you know? We all gotta go. Pack up and go to the camp.'

"They have to. And get so many hours. 'What are we gonna do with the property? We got the land. We got the vegetables. We gotta get rid of it.' See? Jesus Christ!

"Suddenly the newspaper people come! 'Will you hold this piece of pipe and take a picture? We gotta piece of pipe, we'll take it here.' It looks like a rifle.

"And they take a picture of the insecticide with that poison that goes through the spray can. And they publish these things. Big headlines in the newspaper. 'JAPS ARE GOING TO BOMB THIS COAST.' And 'You Gotta Be Careful of the Enemy!' and all that goddamned hysterical thing of the Hearst papers. See?

"See it's a beautiful love story between this boy and a girl.

"Suddenly. They have to go! See? And fit into Santa Anita. In the stable. And they're looking for each other. But finally he finds her. As he's looking for her, he sees many things. He sees a little kid pulling. About seven years old. 'Mama, mama! Take me back to America. Too many Japs here!' You see? See, she's never seen so many Japanese, and has been playing with white kids all the time. She's American! She's not Japanese! She's American! You see?"

The little Japanese girl crying to return to America first appears in Mike Masaoka's Final Report to the JACL, in 1944, and was possibly created by him.

"So suddenly! The boy and the girl, they get together. And they're out in the rain. And the lights going on quickly. And it's raining like hell. They set under a shelter. They say, 'Look, we better get married. If we don't, we'll be separated, we'll never find each other any more.' You see?

"Finally. They get shipped out to the camp. And they get married in this barn. In this stable. You see horses lived here before them.

"The younger group and the older group they have their own problem. The younger ones say, 'God dammit! We wanta prove what we are! We want to form a combat unit!'

"And the old ones say, 'Oh, you're crazy! You're *baka-na!*' And they start fighting amongst them.

"'What the hell do you wanta go and fight for them for? You're in here! They throw you in the can. You're American? What kind of American are you?'

"They have fights and killings. That's going on. See?"

Yes, James Wong Howe tells a story of camp that uneasily accommodates the JACL myth. But the cinematographer dreaming of being a filmmaker craves resistance, and where he knows of none, he creates it.

"You see, the place, it's hot! And the kids lying there. Some of 'em are crippled. They can't move. Now, they want a air conditioner. They want set it. So the officer. The American army officers they say, 'This is the wrong place.' They want take it to their office. And this woman she says, 'No! This belongs here! This belongs to these kids! Look at 'em!'

"And you see these kids lying there. And she wins! You see. She wins over these officers. With these stripes and everything. 'Cuz they want it. But through her got guts! I want show the women too all have guts, you see? They have more guts than the men! You see?" Jimmy Wong Howe says. The great eye of Hollywood realism interestingly sees the lack of resistance as an expression of Nisei emasculation. The JACL is the source of much of his story, but he doesn't mention them.

"It needs a screenplay. But I think it's a good story about what happens here in America. And I think the story should be told about during the war when they relocated these Japanese. They put 'em in the camps, you know. It's a good story because, look, you take American citizens of Japanese race thrown with the Japanese that are not citizens because of war situation. Hysteria! To get headlines for the newspapers and politics. They throw 'em into the camps. Freeze all their money. They have to sell their homes. Sacrifices. And go out and put into these prison camps." He introduces several lines from the JACL myth into his story: "And they fight amongst themselves to prove themselves. The Japanese American citizens, they formed together a regiment that later was allowed to go and fight, for the United States. Who had just put them in these camps. And they won more medals than any regiment in the Second World War. They were called the Four Hundred and Forty Second. And they made a movie about them that was called *Go for Broke!*" *Go for Broke!* was produced by Dore Schary and directed by Robert Pirosh. More importantly, Mike Masaoka and Larry Tajiri of the JACL were credited consultants on the film. "But it wasn't too good," James Wong Howe says of the movie.

"You see," he says, looking at me. The pupils of his large eyes adjust an F-stop, and he continues his thought.

"So that is a wonderful story. It's a human story. And it's a story about how people because of stress and something happening can lose their balance, lose their faculty of thinking. How they can handle a situation. And this happen to be handled very wrong. Why didn't they put the Germans in? There were just as many Germans that were here. That were dangerous. Or the Italians. Why did they select just the Japanese?

"Those questions got to be answered."

[Actually, the Justice Department did intern a number of Germans and Italians. Ten thousand Germans and a lesser number of Italians were held concentrated in separate camps at Crystal City, Texas, from 1942 to 1945. The Italians were designated "resident aliens" as opposed to the Japanese "enemy aliens." The army restricted the movements of 600,000 Italian "resident aliens" on the West Coast by requiring them to carry photo identity cards and obey certain rules. On the basis of individual hearings, 10,000 of the 600,000 were forced to "voluntarily relocate"; 1,500 were arrested for curfew, travel, and contraband violations; and 250 of these were sent to military camps for up to two years.]

"It sounds like a Fritz Lang movie to you." Yes, Fritz Lang. A crazy, popeyed, sniveling Peter Lorre, in the dock of a criminal's court held in a basement, stops the city, and cops and robbers both expose "justice" to be a shrieking bug-eyed farce that leaves the mothers of murdered children alone to cry. "It doesn't have to be a Fritz Lang movie. It can be any movie. I don't like to categorize it that way," James Wong Howe says. "I worked with Fritz Lang. We made a picture called *Hangmen Also Die* (1942, United Artists, D. Fritz Lang; script, Bertolt Brecht. 131 min.). He's a brilliant director. But I like the story for the story. You're a citizen? You're born here. You're a good citizen. You want to fight for the country. You see? And later on, when they put you in, you prove it by going out and fighting. See. But nevertheless, you've been hurt—damaged. Your family's been broken up. And your father's business. Had a thriving business. Had to get rid of it in forty-eight hours. The car. The home. Your girlfriend. Gets separated. You know? The children. They can't understand it. And they're put out there in this desert. Live in this shack. With a guard. Searchlights at night. Swinging around. You see? And there life goes on. Amongst these people. And they have their own problems.

"There's hatred among them there. The old ones. There are some old-timers that believed in the old Emperor. And they get 'em there, they don't understand the young ones, the American citizens. The ones that were born over here. See? So they have their problem."

Yes, but there's something missing. "I know the truth of it," the great cinematographer insists. "That damn thing could happen to the Chinese if there's a war. Still! They still have these camps. Now, I'm going to talk to Bob Wise. He's got a company. And he may be interested. I've talked to a lot of people. Americans. They're scared of it. All of them say, 'Oh, look, why bring an old sore up again?'

"I say, 'What the hell! You fellas do that all the time in the movies.'"

Appendixes

NUMBERS

There were no draft resisters from concentration camps at Gila River, Arizona, and Manzanar, California. From the remaining eight camps, the U.S. Department of Interior counts 315 draft resisters.

263 CONVICTED
28 RELEASED
6 DISMISSED
5 IN JAIL
4 OUT ON BOND
9 DRAFTED PRIOR TO INDICTMENT

On October 7, 1944, in Federal District Court, in Phoenix, Arizona, Judge David M. Ling fined the Poston (Colorado River) draft resisters one cent each and no jail term. The Poston resisters were represented by the same Abraham Lincoln Wirin who had represented the Fair Play Committee leaders. He paid the fines for all 112 with a dime out of his pocket, a dollar bill out of his wallet, and two pennies borrowed from his assistant.

From Heart Mountain, there were eighty-eight draft resisters; from Minidoka, Idaho, forty; from Granada, Colorado, thirty-five; and from Tule Lake, California, twenty-seven.

Judge Louis A. Goodman dismissed the indictments against twenty-seven draft resisters from Tule Lake, saying, "It is shocking to the conscience that an American citizen be confined on the ground of disloyalty and then, while so under duress and restraint be compelled to serve in the armed forces or be prosecuted for not yielding to such compulsion."

From Central Utah, there were nine draft resisters; from Rohwer, Arkansas, three; from Jerome, Arkansas, one.

Frank Emi was speaking at Cal State Los Angeles to a full auditorium. I sat in the back and swept my eyes over the crowd, and lost count at a thousand people.

"Are you Frank Chin?" a voice behind me asked. I was in no mood to be beaten up by a veteran or a patriotic Japanese American. I turned around and thought of answering, "No." But I didn't. I nodded. He leaned forward and asked in a low voice if I was the Frank Chin who'd been writing these things about the draft resisters. This was it. I sighed, and admitted I was.

"I wanta talk to you," the man said. Oh, oh, here it comes. "I was the only one to resist from Jerome," he said, and I perked up. "And I want to tell you, it wasn't worth it."

"I want to talk with you!" I said.

We went to a hallway and talked.

Joe Asa Yamakido was sent to Texarkana. He discovered he was the lone Japanese American resister from Jerome. He had expected more, from the response he had seen at the meetings. At Texarkana, he was jumped by the prisoners. "Luckily I kept on my feet. I didn't fall." And he kept his back to the wall. Like many Nisei, he knew judo. "If I'd fallen, I'd be dead." The guards got tired of watching and broke up the assault on Joe. He was naked, except for his socks. In the melee, they'd ripped his off clothes and torn them to shreds. Even his underwear. I could see how being the only resister and getting beaten up by the whole prison would have a dampening effect on his ideals. But I asked, "If this happened again, we go to war with Japan, the government sends you and your people off to camp, just like before, and then they draft you. Would you take the draft this time?"

"Same thing?" he asks.

"Yeah, same thing."

"Just like before?"

"Yeah," I said.

"I'd do the same thing. But it still wouldn't be worth it."

From all the camps, a total of 315 resisted the draft. Of these 263 were convicted. Twenty-eight were released without trial. Six cases were dismissed. Five resisted the draft from jail. Four were released on bond. Nine were drafted prior to indictment. (Figures are from the U.S. Department of Interior.)

Twelve from Hawaii resisted the draft.

Thirty-three thousand Nisei in the American armed forces in WWII.

Ten thousand volunteers from the Territory of Hawaii—under martial law. No camps.

Eight hundred and five volunteers from the mainland's nine concentration camps.

FROM PROCLAMATION 2762

GRANTING PARDON TO CERTAIN PERSONS CONVICTED OF VIOLATING THE SELECTIVE TRAINING AND SERVICE ACT OF 1940 AS AMENDED

KNOW, THEREFORE, I , HARRY S. TRUMAN, President of the United States of America, under and by virtue of the authority vested in me by Article II of the Constitution of the United States do hereby grant a full pardon to those persons convicted of violating the Selective Training and Service Act of 1940 as amended whose names are included in the list of names attached hereto and hereby made a part of this proclamation.

IN WITNESS WHEREOF, I have hereunto set my hand and caused the Seal of the United States of America to be affixed.

DONE at the City of Washington this 23rd day of December in the year of our Lord nineteen hundred and forty-seven, and of the Independence of the United States of America the one hundred and seventy second.

HARRY S. TRUMAN

By the President:
ROBERT A. LOVETT,
ACTING SECRETARY OF STATE

List of Names
Name, Date convicted and U.S. District Court

AKUTSU, Hitoshi Gene, October 2, 1944, Idaho. AKUTSU, Jim Hajiime, October 2, 1944, Idaho. AMATE, Atsushu Archie, October 8, 1945, Colorado. ASAI, Dix Takuro, October 31, 1944, Colorado. ASAI, Fred Teruro, October 31, 1944, Colorado. ETO, Yukio, July 9, 1945, Wyoming. FUJIHARA, Shiro, October 2, 1944, Idaho. FUJII, John Jiro, July 9, 1945, Wyoming. FUJII, Shigeru, May 26, 1944, Wyoming. FUJIMOTO, Albert Kenji, October 7, 1946, Arizona. FUJINAKA, Tatsuro George, February 21, 1945, Southern Idaho. FUJIOKA, Tom Tamotsu, October 7, 1946, Arizona. FUJIOKA, Yasuto, November 8, 1946. FUJITA, Hideo Frank, October 7, 1946. FUJIWARA, Hideyuki Henry, October 2, 1944, Idaho.

FUJIZAWA, Teruo, October 7, 1946, Arizona. FURUSAKI, Joseph, October 7, 1946, Arizona. GOISHI, Kazuto Jimmy, October 7, 1946, Arizona. HASHIMOTO, Masaru, March 27, 1944, Arizona. HATAKEDA, Jimmie Junichi, October 7, 1946, Arizona. HAYUMI, Yoshito Smith, October 2, 1944, Idaho. HIGUCHI, Matsuo, July 9, 1945, Wyoming. HINO, Bob Riyusho, October 2, 1945, Southern Idaho. HINO, Frank Shinichi, February 23, 1945, Southern Idaho. HIRABAYASHI, Gordon Kiyoshi, November 30, 1944, Eastern Washington. HIRABAYASHI, Henry Noboru, October 2, 1944, Idaho. HIRABAYASHI, Irvin Masanobu, November 4, 1944, Utah. HIRAI, Toro, October 7, 1946, Arizona. HIRAMOTO, Shizuto, October 7, 1946, Arizona. HIRATA, Tomoharu Henry, May 20, 1944, Eastern Arkansas. HIRAYAMA, Suzumu Harold, June 26, 1944, Wyoming. HIROSI, Kazuki, July 9, 1945, Wyoming. HIROSI, Kazuto, July 26, 1944, Wyoming. HIROSHIGE, Akira, June 26, 1944, Wyoming. HONDA, Seiichi, October 7, 1946, Arizona. HORA, Sadao, October 7, 1946, Arizona. HORI, Takeshi, June 26, 1944, Wyoming. HORINO, George Minoru, July 9, 1945, Wyoming. HOSHIZAKI, Takeshi, June 26, 1944, Wyoming. IDE, Takao Grant, June 26, 1944, Wyoming. IKEMIYA, Joe Yoshikazi, March 27, 1944, Arizona. IKEMIYA, Masaru Jim, March 27, 1944, Arizona. IKEMOTO, Harry Yoshikiaki, June 26, 1944, Wyoming. IMAI, Masefume, June 26, 1944, Wyoming. INABA, Hitoshi, October 31, 1944, Colorado. INO, Toru, June 26, 1944, Wyoming. (INOUE, Chozo, January 2, 1943, Hawaii*) INOUYE, George Washington, October 7, 1946, Arizona. IOKA, Harry Shuichi, October 31, 1944, Colorado. ISHIKAWA, George, June 26, 1944, Wyoming. ISHIKAWA, Kiyoshi, June 26, 1944, Wyoming. ISHIKAWA, Suetsugu, June 26, 1944, Wyoming. ISHIKAWA, Takeo, June 26, 1944, Wyoming. ISHIKAWA, Yoshimitsu, October 31, 1944, Colorado. ISHIMARU, Junichi, June 26, 1944, Wyoming. ISHIMARU, Yutaka, June 26, 1944, Wyoming. ISHIMOTO, George Kenichi, ISHIMOTO, Harry Kenji, October 8, 1945, Colorado. ISHIMOTO, Takao, October 8, 1945, Colorado. ISHIZAKI, Sam Isamu, June 26, 1944, Wyoming. ISOMURA, Iwaharu, October 28, 1944, Colorado. ITO, Hideo, June 30, 1944, Colorado. IZUNO, Masaichi, June 30, 1944, Colorado. KADO, James Yoshito, June 26, 1944, Wyoming. KAJIMURA, Hareo, September 25, 1944, Idaho. KAJIMURA, Tsutomu, October 2, 1944, Idaho. KAMINAKA, Joe, October 7, 1946, Arizona. KAMINAKA, Tamotsu, October 7, 1946, Arizona. KARIYA, Masahashi, October 7, 1946, Arizona. KARIYA, Yoneo, October 7, 1946, Arizona. KASAHARA, George Shigaki, December 29, 1944, Idaho. KASHIWAGI, Joe, October 31, 1944, Colorado. KATAYAMA, Shigeru, October 7, 1946, Arizona. KAWAHARA, Katsuyoshi, July 9, 1945, Wyoming. KAWAKAMI, Frank Masao, July 9, 1945, Wyoming. KAWAKI, Mosayuki, October 2, 1944, Idaho. KAWAMOTO, David Tetsutaro, June 26, 1944, Wyoming. KAWAMOTO, James Takako, April 1, 1946, Arizona. KAWAMOTO,

Kiyoshi, October 7, 1946, Arizona. KAWASAKI, Jimmie, October 28, 1944, Colorado. KAWASAKI, Jimmie, June 26, 1944, Wyoming. KAWASAKI, Thomas Tomeji, October 28, 1944, Colorado. KAWATO, Yukio, September 29, 1944, Idaho. KAYA, Larry Yoshio, October 7, 1946, Arizona. KENMOTSU, Shigeo, June 26, 1944, Wyoming. KIMURA, Frank Yoshimatsu, October 2, 1944, Iowa. (KIMURA, Frank Yoshimatsu, October 2, 1944, Iowa. KIMURA, Hideo, July 21, 1942, Hawaii.) KIMURA, Jim Tatsuya, June 26, 1944, Wyoming. KINOSHITA, Teruo, March 27, 1944, Arizona. KISHI, Masakiyo Michael, October 7, 1946, Arizona. KITASAKI, Kiyoshi, October 7, 1946, Arizona. KITAUCHI, Masaichi, October 7, 1946, Arizona. KITAYAMA, Kaoru, February 22, 1945, Idaho. KIYOMIZU, Shozo, September 29, 1944, Idaho. KODAMA, George Katsumi, February 21, 1945, Idaho. KODAMA, Lui Ikuo, October 7, 1946, Arizona. (KOFUKSADO, Mitsugi, October 17, 1942, Hawaii.) [KOGA, Dix. K. from JACL list published in PC January 3, 1948. No info about where sentenced] KOJIMA, Masao, October 7, 1946, Arizona. KOSHIYAMA, Mitsuru, June 26, 1944, Wyoming. KUBO, Tomeo, June 26, 1944, Wyoming. KUBO, Yoshi, October 30, 1944, Colorado. (KUJAWA, Anthony, July 20, 1944, Eastern New York.) KUMADA, Kazuo, June 26, 1944, Wyoming. KURAMOTO, Yutaka Ted, October 2, 1944, Idaho. KURANAGA, Heruyuki, October 7, 1944, Arizona. KURASAKI, George Noboru, June 26, 1944, Wyoming. KUROMIYA, Yoshito, June 26, 1944, Wyoming. KUROYE, Kenneth, October 7, 1946, Arizona. KUWADA, Makoto Jim, June 26, 1944, Wyoming. KUWHARA, John Takeshi, October 7, 1946, Arizona. MARUHASHI, Hutaka Frank, September 29, 1944, Idaho. MARUYAMA, Kenichi, October 7, 1946, Arizona. MARUYAMA, Shigeo, October 7, 1946, Arizona. MARUYAMA, Yukio, October 7, 1946, Arizona. MASUKAWA, Kitashi John, October 7, 1946, Arizona. MASUKAWA, Tsutomu Tom, October 7, 1946, Arizona. MATSUBA, George Kazuo, June 26, 1944, Wyoming. MATSUBARA, Sadao, October 7, 1946, Arizona. MATSUMOTO, Akira, June 26, 1944, Wyoming. MATSUMOTO, Minoru Corky, October 7, 1946, Arizona. MATSUMOTO, Teruo, July 9, 1945, Wyoming. MATSUMOTO, Toshimitsu, October 7, 1946, Arizona. MATSUSHITA, Kikuji, October 9, 1945, Wyoming. MATSUURA, Frank Morikazu, June 26, 1944, Wyoming. MATSUZAKI, Frank T., October 2, 1944, Idaho. MAYEKAWA, Masao, June 26, 1944, Wyoming. MINATANI, James Masaichi, June 26, 1944, Wyoming. MINATO, Kiyoashi, October 7, 1946, Arizona. MINOURA, Halley, June 26, 1944, Wyoming. MITSUOKA, Mitsuru, October 7, 1946, Arizona. MIYAHARA, Tamio Tom, June 26, 1944, Wyoming. MITAMURA, Koyochi, October 7, 1946, Arizona. MIYASAKI, James Goro, October 7, 1946, Arizona. MIYASAKI, Masanobu, October 7, 1946, Arizona. MIYASAKI, Thomas Shiro, October 7, 1946, Arizona. MORI, Hiroyoshi, October 7, 1946, Arizona. MORI, Shigeo, October 7, 1946, Arizona. MORI, Sutio Bill,

October 7, 1946, Arizona. MORIKAWA, Hiroshi, October 7, 1946, Arizona. MORITA, Ichiro, June 26, 1944, Wyoming. MOTONAGA, Ray Yoshio, June 26, 1944, Wyoming. MURATA, George Matsuji, October 7, 1946, Arizona. MURATA, Paul Seichi, October 7, 1946, Arizona. NAGAHARA, Masao, June 26, 1944, Wyoming. (NAGAKURA, Hiroshi Nakamura, January 18, 1943, Hawaii.) NAGA-SUGI, Hiroto, October 2, 1944, Idaho. NAGATA, Kunto, October 7, 1946, Arizona. (NAHA, Lewis Kooyouhema, August 12, 1943, Arizona.) Natto, Takashi, October 7, 1946, Arizona. NAKADA, Carl Koaru, June 26, 1944, Wyoming. NAK-AGAWA, George, September 29, 1944, Idaho. NAKAGAWA, George, April 28, 1945, Northern California. NAKAGUMA, Yoshitatusu, June 30, 1944, Colorado. NAKAHIRA, Satoru Joseph, November 18, 1944, Utah. (NAKAMURA, Jerry Masao, January 19, 1943, Hawaii.) NAKAMURA, Migaki, October 7, 1946, Arizona. NAMAMURI, Kazumi, October 7, 1946, Arizona. NAKASAKI, Kuzumi, October 7, 1946, Arizona. NAKASAKI, William Harumi, May 22, 1944, Arizona. NAKASHIKI, Kaiso Fred, October 7, 1946, Arizona. NAKASHIMA, Yoneo, October 7, 1946, Arizona. NAKASHINA, Isao, September 29, 1944, Idaho. NAKATSU, George, October 7, 1946, Arizona. NAKAYAMA, Iwao James, October 7, 1946, Arizona. NAKAYAMA, Masakaz, October 7, 1946, Arizona. NARUTO, Tochiharu Frank, January 19, 1945, Colorado. NIINO, George Schigehi, October 7, 1946, Arizona. NIMURA, Takanori, October 7, 1946, Arizona. NISHI, Itaro, October 7, 1946, Arizona. NISHIMURA, Robert Nubuo, October 7, 1946, Arizona. NOBUHIRO, Ben Tsutomu, October 7, 1946, Arizona. NOGUCHI, Tsutomu Ben, October 7, 1946, Arizona. NORIKANI, Joe Hajime, October 31, 1944, Colorado. NOSAKA, Kanichi, March 27, 1944, Arizona. NOZAWA, George Goro, July 9, 1945, Wyoming. NUMOTO, Saburo, October 2, 1944, Idaho. OGATA, Ben Tsutomi, March 2, 1944, Arizona. OGATA, Hisashi, October 7, 1946, Arizona. OKADA, Masao Ted, October 2, 1944, Idaho. OKAWA, Ichiro, June 26, 1944, Wyoming. (OKAZAKI, Kyoshi, July 6, 1942, Hawaii.) OKAZAKI, Satoru Fred, October 7, 1946, Arizona. OKI, Tadashi, June 26, 1944, Wyoming. OKI, Yoshio Tom, July 9, 1945, Wyoming. OKUMA, Toru Fred, July 9, 1945, Wyoming. OKU-MURA, Hideo, March 27, 1944, Arizona. OMORI, John Takashi, October 7, 1946, Arizona. OMOTO, Nubuo, September 29, 1944, Idaho. OMOTO, Roy Yasuo, October 2, 1944, Idaho. OTSU, Ninoru, March 27, 1944, Arizona. OYE, Hiromu, October 7, 1946, Arizona. OZAWA, Yoshikazu, October 7, 1946, Arizona. SAK-AGUCHI, Kunichika, October 2, 1944, Idaho. SAKAGUCHI, Sumio, October 2, 1944, Idaho. SAKAMOTO, Hisanari, October 7, 1946, Arizona. SAKAMOTO, Hisatoshi Harry, October 7, 1946, Arizona. SAKANIWA, Michio, October 7, 1946, Arizona. SAKATA, Tom Minoru, October 7, 1946, Arizona. SAKO, James Satoru, June 16, 1944, Wyoming. SAKO, Tomatsu Tom, July 9, 1945, Wyoming. SHI-BATA, Takeo, June 20, 1944, Eastern Arkansas. SHICEMASA, George Takeshi,

October 7, 1946, Arizona. (SHIMADA, Harry Masao, January 9, 1943, Hawaii.) SHIMANE, Chester Toru, June 26, 1944, Wyoming. SHIMANE, Fred Katsumi, June 26, 1944, Wyoming. SHIMANE, George Fujio, June 26, 1944, Wyoming. SHIMANE, Isamu, June 26, 1944, Wyoming. SHIMANE, Chester Toru, June 26, 1944, Wyoming. SHIMANE, Fred Katsumi, June 26, 1944. SHIMANE, George Fujio, June 26, 1944. SHIMIZU, Mineto, October 7, 1946, Arizona. SHIMIZU, Sunao Mike, October 7, 1946, Arizona. SHIMPO, Toshio Tom, October 7, 1946, Arizona. (SHINTA, Kengi, June 26, 1941, Wyoming. SHINTA, Kengi, June 26, 1941, Wyoming.) SHINZU, Osamu Sam, June 20, 1944, Eastern Arkansas. SUG-IHARA, George Jiro, January 25, 1946, Utah. SUGITA, Toyoji, July 9, 1945, Wyoming. SUKO, Shoji, October 23, 1944, Idaho. SUMI, Noboru, June 26, 1944, Wyoming. SUMI, Sachio Bill, June 26, 1944, Wyoming. SUMIDA, Ken Kenroku, June 26, 1944, Wyoming. SUMIDA, Robert Masahi, June 23, 1945, Montana. SUZUKI, Attushi, June 26, 1944, Wyoming. SUZUKI, Masayo, July 9, 1945, Wyoming. SUZUKI, Shizumi, July 9, 1945, Wyoming. TAGUMA, Norboru (Noboru), June 30, 1944, Colorado. TAYANAKA [spelled TAINAKA on JACL-PC list], Kenichi Ken, June 26, 1944, Wyoming. TAJII, Kingo, June 11, 1945, Arizona. TAKAHASHI, George Toshiharu, June 30, 1944, Colorado. TAKA-HASHI, Teruo Slim, October 7, 1946, Arizona. TAKAMOTO, George Shirhio, June 30, 1944, Colorado. TAKAMOTO, Yoshio, June 30, 1944, Colorado. TAKASAKI, Noboru, October 7, 1946, Arizona. TAKASHIMA, Mamoru, February 20, 1945, Idaho. TAKEGUMA, Hideichi, June 11, 1945, Arizona. TAKEUCHI, Hideo, October 30, 1944, Colorado. (TAMASHIRO, Masnobu, December 21, 1942, Hawaii. TAMASHIRO, Shunsho, October 24, 1942, Hawaii.) TAMESA, Minola (Minoru), June 26, 1944, Wyoming. TANABE, George Naoichi, June 26, 1944, Wyoming. TANABE, Shigeharu, October 7, 1946, Arizona. TANAHARA, Leo, October 7, 1946, Arizona. TANAKA, Leo Riniche, October 7, 1946, Arizona. TASHIRO, Frank Kiyoshi, September 29, 1944, Idaho. TONO, Jack Kiyoto, June 26, 1944, Wyoming. TSUNEDA, Ken, October 7, 1946, Arizona. TSUYUKI, Sumio, June 26, 1944, Wyoming. UYECHI, Joe Kejo, October 7, 1946, Arizona. UYEDA, George Susumu, June 26, 1944, Wyoming. UYEDA, James Tsutomu, July 9, 1945, Wyoming. UYEDA, Riyou, June 30, 1944, Colorado. UYEDA, Roy Masao, July 9, 1945, Wyoming. UYEMOTO, Terry Teruo, October 26, 1944, Wyoming. UYENURA, Torao, June 26, 1944, Colorado. UYENO, Shigero, June 26, 1944, Wyoming. WATANABE, Hirom, July 9, 1945, Wyoming. YAMADA, Fumio Bill, October 7, 1946, Arizona. YAMADA, Samuel, October 7, 1946, Arizona. YAMAKAWA, Toyoji, October 7, 1946, Arizona. YAMAKIDO, Joe Atsumi, October 24, 1944, Eastern Arkansas. YAMAMOTO, Yukio, October 7, 1946, Arizona. YAMAMOTO, Yutaka, October 7, 1946, Arizona. YAMAMURA, Masakazu, September 25, 1944, Idaho. YAMASAKI, Hedio Frank, September 29,

1944, Idaho. YAMASAKI, Junichi, October 7, 1946, Arizona. YAMAUCHI, Hiroshi, October 28, 1944, Colorado. (YAMAUCHI, Sosuki, December 27, 1944, Hawaii.) YAMAZUMI, George Katamori, July 13, 1944, Colorado. YAMAZUMI, George Katamori, July 13, 1944, Colorado. YANAGISAKO, Edward Hiromu, June 26, 1944, Wyoming. YANO, Ben, March 27, 1944, Arizona. YASUDA, Kentaro, October 2, 1944, Idaho. YASUDA, Minoru, October 7, 1946, Arizona. YENOKIDA, Susumu, June 30, 1944, Colorado. YENOKIDA, Tustomu Ben, October 28, 1944, Colorado. (YOKOYAMA, Harry Shoji, October 20, 1941, Hawaii.) YONEO, Domon, October 7, 1946, Arizona. YOSHIDA, George Maseo, June 26, 1944, Wyoming. YOSHIDA, Kei, July 9, 1945, Wyoming. YOSHIDA, Kenichiro Mike, November 4, 1944, Utah. YOSHIDA, Sakaye, November 4, 1944, Utah. YOSHIDA, Shingo, October 7, 1946, Arizona. YOSHIMURA, Fumio, October 7, 1946, Arizona. YOSHIMURA, John Yoshikiko, October 7, 1946, Arizona. YOSHIMURA, Niro Dick, September 30, 1944, Idaho. YUMEN, Ben Tsutomi, October 7, 1946, Arizona.

*Names in parentheses did not resist draft from camp.

AFTER THE WAR, WHAT HAPPENED TO THE JACL?

Mike M. Masaoka (October 15, 1915–1991), field secretary of the JACL and confidential informant to the FBI, became a Washington lobbyist representing the Japanese textile and other Japanese industries. His stand on redress was confused or purposefully confusing. He was for redress, but against money and individual payments. He was for special recognition of the Nisei who entered service in the armed forces from camp and against recognition or redress payments for camp draft resisters. He remains the most controversial figure of the JACL, even after his death. President Reagan signed redress into law in 1988. The redress bill didn't heed Masaoka's wishes, but did pay him tribute. The last tribute to Masaoka seems to be the quote from his "Nisei Creed" that adorns the Japanese American Memorial to Patriotism during WWII, in Washington, D.C.

Larry Tajiri (May 7, 1914–February 12, 1961), editor of the JACL *Pacific Citizen* and a confidential informant to the FBI, left the *Pacific Citizen* in 1953 and joined the *Denver Post* in 1954.

Bill Hosokawa (1915–), editor of the Heart Mountain *Rocky Shimpo*; obtained a job at the *Des Moines Register*, through a letter written on his behalf by Dillon Myer, head of the WRA, to Gardener Cowles, owner of the Cowles Newspapers. On January 9, 1987, Hosokawa wrote to Frank Chin: "I do not know what Dillon Myer wrote to Gardner Cowles about me. He never told me, and I have not seen copies of such letters. The idea that I in Iowa would, or could, continue to run a newspaper in Wyoming is ridiculous." The Myer letter to Cowles is in the WRA files of the National Archives, dated "Aug 26, 1943." Also in the Archives is a "REVIEW OF SOME SIGNIFICANT INFORMATION ORIGINATING IN AND RECEIVED BY DISTRICT INTELLIGENCE OFFICE, THIRTEENTH NAVAL DISTRICT–OCTOBER 1943":

> Following evacuation to the Heart Mountain (Wyoming) Relocation Center, HOSOKAWA founded a project newspaper, the *Heart Mountain Sentinel,* and acted as the editor-in-chief during the past year. Announcement has just been made of the release of HOSOKAWA from Heart Mountain to become the editorial copyreader of the *Des Moines* (Iowa) *Register.* Released with him were his nisei wife, Alice Miyake HOSOKAWA, his three year-old-sansei son, Michael, and his alien Japanese mother-in-law, Mrs. Tora MIYAKE, who is a parolee from internment. HOSOKAWA is to continue his editorials in the *Sentinel* and will not be replaced as editor-in-chief; Haruo IMURA, the present managing editor, is to assume the responsibility of carrying on that paper.

On September 15, 1978, his column in the *Pacific Citizen* was titled "'Redress' Campaign." He said:

> Many months ago I wrote that I thought JACL's proposal to seek "redress" from the United States government for injustices of the Evacuation was a bum idea. . . . First, the injustice and indignity of the Evacuation are not the sort of wrongs that can be compensated for with money.
> "Second, the redress campaign would be self-defeating in terms of a backlash against what we as a people have accomplished and what we hope to accomplish, and in dividing the Japanese American community even more widely than it is today.

From the *Des Moines Register*, Hosokawa moved to the *Denver Post*, in 1946, where he became editor of the editorial page. He retired in 1980. His books (all published by William Morrow) are *Nisei: The Quiet Americans*; *Thirty-Five Years in the Frying Pan*; and *JACL in Quest of Justice.* With Mike Masaoka he wrote *They Call Me Moses Masaoka* and *Old Man: Father of the Bullet Train.*

Nobu Kawai (March 21, 1907–) returned to his home and his old job at the creamery in Pasadena. He is living in retirement with his wife in the house they owned since before the war. In 1981, he wrote William Marutani, a former president of the JACL and a member of the congressionally appointed Bernstein Commission on the Wartime Relocation and Internment of Civilians. After showing his JACL and internee credentials, he wrote: "Whatever indignities we suffered or hardships we endured, I regard these as the price we paid for the advancements we now enjoy. For that reason, I can give no support to the petition for retribution now being pushed by some ill-advised activists."

Ben Kuroki (1917–   ) left the Army Air Corps with three Distinguished Flying Crosses and five Air Medals. He entered the University of Nebraska in 1947. He married a girl from Idaho; had two kids; and with money from his mother-in-law and his brother Fred, he bought a weekly newspaper in York, Nebraska, the *York Republican*. Being the publisher of a newspaper established him as "The first Japanese American ever in the weekly publishing business. I was a pioneer as a result." Things didn't work out as planned in York, but he got out with his "shirt intact" and moved to Blackfoot, Idaho, "about twelve miles from Pocatello" where he worked for (but did not own) a small daily paper, the *Blackfoot Bulletin*. The paper was sold within a couple of years, and the Kurokis moved back to Nebraska, where Ben worked at the *North Platte Daily Bulletin*. From there he moved to Williamston, Michigan, where he bought the *Williamston Enterprise*. He was celebrated as a war hero at the JACL convention in Detroit and wooed by the JACL. He remained polite but aloof from society. In 1965, the Kurokis moved to California so their daughters would have access to Japanese American society. Ben sold the *Williamston Enterprise* and took a job at the *Ventura Star-Free Press*, later becoming editor.

James Y. Sakamoto (March 22, 1903–December 3, 1955). His paper died at the beginning of WWII. After the war he returned to Seattle, with his wife. Crossing the street to work at the St. Vincent De Paul Society, on Fairview Avenue N. in Seattle, he was run down by a car. The driver claimed he could not see anyone in the street due to the early morning darkness. It was 6:50 in the morning. The driver was not held.

Minoru Yasui (1917–1988), the curfew violator judged guilty by the Supreme Court, in ex parte Hirabayashi, returned to the fold of the JACL. He authored "The Mothers' Petition" for the mothers, asking the government to please take their sons into the army from camp so they might prove their loyalty. Back in the good graces of the JACL, he ran the Denver office and clung to his status as a resister who knew what he was doing because he was a lawyer and publicly disparaged the draft resisters and the writer who dared support them, James Omura. In 1984, the Supreme Court judged that it had been fed false information by the U.S. Army, and reversed itself of Hirabayashi and Yasui ex parte Hirabayashi. Since the end of WWII, every Japanese American to achieve elective office, on the mainland, at any level of government—city, county, state, or national—has been a member of the JACL and has praised the JACL for their cooperation with the wartime policy of concentration camps and their stand against civil rights for Japanese Americans until they proved their loyalty. At this writing, in October of 2001, this support of every Japanese American in the president's cabinet, every Japanese American in Congress, every Japanese American every electoral office (on the mainland) still holds true.

Clifford Uyeda (January 14, 1917–). What holds true for the JACL does not hold true for Clifford Uyeda. His support of a pardon for "Tokyo Rose" and his criticism of the JACL in support of redressing the concentration camps marked him as uniquely his own man, and won him presidency of the JACL in 1978, as the "Redress President." After gaining a teaching fellowship at the Harvard School of Medicine, he was drafted into the U.S. Air Force and served in Korea 1951–1953. He had been separated from the society of his own people since 1936 and thought the atmosphere of prejudice that weighed on them might have lightened since WWII. He took a job as a pediatrician at Kaiser Permanente Medical Group. He is proud that he never joined the AMA. He led the effort of Japanese Americans to pardon Iva Toguri ("Tokyo Rose") and restore her U.S. citizenship. "The reinstatement of Iva Toguri's American citizenship in the mid-1970s is one the most satisfying events I can recall. Her plight symbolized the continued oppression of Japanese Americans, and I was proud to be of assistance in helping to further the cause of justice."

TO THE ISSEI?

Shosuke Sasaki (March 26, 1912–) worked in New York as a securities analyst and later moved back to Seattle and retired. While in New York he began a campaign against the word "Jap" as a foreshortening of "Japanese" and as a word suitable for polite society. He enlisted the help of the New York JACL in his campaign, begun in 1952, against dictionary and general newspaper usage. He and other Japanese Americans wrote scholarly letters pointing out the offensiveness of the term. "In 1952, such a letter sent to the president of Twentieth Century-Fox Film Corporation not only stopped Movietone News from calling the Japanese 'Japs', but resulted in the elimination of the word 'Jap' from all other motion picture productions of the company," wrote Sasaki in 1962, in "How to Attack the Newspaper Use of 'Jap'"–a booklet he published for the JACL. In the introduction, he wrote, "The fact that the newspaper use of 'Jap' has been practically stopped in every locality where adequately strong protests have been made indicates that the practice can be eliminated within a year or two throughout the United States." In the 1970s, he and "renegade" members of the Seattle JACL, inspired by Edison Uno of San Francisco, another "renegade," formed "the Seattle Group," dedicated to seeking redress for the concentration camps, specifically from congress rather than the courts. They wanted money, real redress, not publicity for the JACL and the 442nd that was the usual result of a JACL call for redress. Sasaki was the "Thinker" of the Seattle Group.

Uhachi Tamesa (December 22, 1883–January 11, 1988) established a $10,000 ($1,000 added in 1971) memorial scholarship fund in the name of his son Minoru Tamesa—one of the Heart Mountain Fair Play Committee that led the draft resistance at Heart Mountain—to be administered by the Seattle JACL. He was a friend of the resisters of Heart Mountain until his death.

TO THE KIBEI-NISEI?

Kentaro Takatsui (1915–April 20, 2001) was drafted in 1947 and went into the Army Military Intelligence Division and moved later to the Counter-intelligence Corps. His "resistance" at Tule Lake never appeared on his record. On paper, it's as if it never happened.

TO THE DRAFT RESISTERS?

Hajiime "Jim" Akutsu (January 25, 1920–September 23, 1998) drew the longest term, four years, among the 263 resisters sentenced to serve prison time. He prepared to be the only Japanese American left in McNeil Island by lifting weights and getting big, as he expected to be harassed by his fellow convicts. When he got out of McNeil Island, he was a short but big man. He got a job in an iron foundry. After work, he would go to the steam bath to sweat out the stuff and smells of the foundry. In the front of a surplus store, near the bathhouse, he saw John Okada, sitting on a table swinging his legs. "He doesn't even care about selling anything!" thought Akutsu. They became acquainted. Akutsu the No-No boy, draft resister, ex-con and Okada the war veteran, library science student, and would-be writer. They merged in Okada's only novel, *No-No Boy*.

Gordon Hirabayashi (1918–) moved to Canada to take a job teaching. Because he found teaching in Canada congenial, he became a Canadian citizen. Dale Minami led a team of attorneys—Don Tamaki, Lorraine Bannai, Karen Kai, Peter Irons, Dennis Hayashi, Mike Wong, and Russ Matsumoto—filing a writ of *error corum nobis* against the United States, at the U.S. Supreme Court. As a result, the guilty verdicts of Hirabayashi and Yasui ex parte Hirabayashi, as companion cases to Fred Korematsu, were reversed in 1984.

Tak Hoshizaki (October 3, 1925–) was released on Bastille Day, July 14, 1946, from McNeil Island Federal Penitentiary. He returned to Hollywood and a family-run gardening business. He earned a B.S. in 1951 and an M.S. in horticulture at UCLA in 1953. In between he married. In 1953, he was drafted. This time he went in as a free man. In 1960, he earned a Ph.D. in plant physiology and botanical sciences. He retired in 1989.

Dave Kawamoto (1918–1993) returned to Santa Clara and got a job at J.C. Penney in Mountain View. Later he took a job at the U.S. Postal Service. He met Toshiko Furuichi in 1947, at a girls' basketball game sponsored by the Mountain View Buddhist Church. "That night they had a dance. So I went, and I was dancing with one of the fellows that Dave knew, and then Dave cut in, and that's how I met him. All the girls were saying, 'How'd you meet him?' I said, 'We just met.' Then we started going to movies, and we went bowling. Those days that's the only activities there were. To go bowling. To go to movies. We had phone on the wall, and my father would answer, and Dave would ask for me, and I would go to answer the phone, and my father would say, 'Don't talk to him!' I say, 'Dad, I'm just talking to this guy.' My father would say, 'Hang up.' I say, 'Dad I can't do that. I'm just having a nice conversation.' Then he would inquire who I am talking to—very critical. My brothers could go out anytime do anything. But me, I couldn't do that. But when they met Dave, they were quite impressed. They didn't wince at all. You see, my father-in-law was very active in kendo. Martial arts. And they knew the Kawamotos were very active, and here was his son. . . . About six months before we were married, Dave asked me if I knew anything about, you know, resisters. And we discussed it. And I said, 'Well, people call them conscientious objectors, draft dodgers, and it doesn't bother me. Why should it?' I said, 'You're the individual. You did what you wanted to do.' He was surprised. I told my parents. They didn't object at all. My father said he had guts to stand up for his rights. My father was that way. He was very civic-minded, and very outgoing." The Kawamotos have three grown children. Dave died of a lung disease in December of 1993. He lived to see a measure of recognition and acceptance of the resisters when Donna Kato published an article in the *San Jose Mercury*'s *West* magazine. A few years later, San Jose State University president Robert Caret awarded Kawamoto a posthumous degree. Michi Weglyn, the activist-author of *Years of Infamy* had written and phoned Caret from New York, and explained that fifty-four years ago, the Evacuation had forced Dave to drop out of school before graduation. Caret responded by inviting Toshiko Kawamoto to attend the graduation ceremonies on May 25, 1996, accept the degree for Dave Kawamoto, and speak on his behalf.

Mits Koshiyama (August 7, 1924–) was notified during the Korean War that he might be drafted. He was ready to go, but was never called. Mits and his brother, who had been in the Military Intelligence Service during the war, ran a cut flower nursery together for twenty-four years. Mits finished his working years as a gardener for the Mountain View School District. He had three brothers, and they all served in the army during the war. In his family, there is no rift over the issue of camps and the service. He married in 1962 and has three children.

Yosh Kuromiya (April 1923–) gave up all ambitions of becoming a graphics illustrator and "like many of my Japanese friends" went into gardening. He married and had three children. In 1957, "After achieving a modicum of financial security," he studied landscape architecture at California Polytechnic College. Within two years he had a license to practice architecture. In 1968, he left the firm that he had been working for and started his own practice. He retired in 1995.

Ichiro "Ike" Matsumoto (August 3, 1923–). Ike, a taciturn and stubbornly committed resister, was sentenced to McNeil Island with his younger, more gregarious brother.

Teruo "Tayzo" Matsumoto (1926–). The Matsumoto brothers returned from McNeil Island, in Washington, to Torrance, California, and started a retail nursery. Tayzo was drafted into the army and served, then went on the inactive reserve list. He was called back to serve in Korea, with the 378th Combat Engineers.

Tom Oki (1919–), after McNeil Island, went to Los Angeles and worked as a gardener and attended Hemphill Diesel School. He worked as an engineer on fishing boats until 1956. He then worked at the American Fish Company and Young's Markets until his retirement.

TO THE HEART MOUNTAIN FAIR PLAY COMMITTEE?

Kiyoshi Okamoto (August 8, 1889–December 28, 1974). Art Emi was the last member of the Heart Mountain Fair Play Committee to see Kiyoshi Okamoto. He was different from the leader that had attracted attention and people to him in the concentration camp. "He was not what you would call a well-dressed man," said Art Emi. He saw him at gas station in California in a jeep that seemed outfitted for prospecting.

Paul Nakadate (August 18, 1914–June 1980) returned to Los Angeles, where he resumed selling insurance.

Arthur Emi (January 20, 1919–February 25, 1996) was never drafted, never arrested, and never served prison time, but always counted himself a member of the Heart Mountain Fair Play Committee.

Frank Emi (September 23, 1916–) was married before camp and had two children. He divorced after camp for reasons unrelated to his stand on the draft and camp. He returned to California from Leavenworth and took up gardening. He says he "liked taking tests" and, after passing the civil service examination, went to work for the U.S. Postal Service. After his retirement from the USPS, he passed another civil service examination and went to work for the State of California unemployment department. In 1982, he became a symbol of the efforts for redress conducted from camp to groups of Japanese Americans campaigning for redress. He joined one of these groups, the National Coalition for Redress/Reparations. He is a sixth-degree black belt in judo and teaches at the Hollywood Judo Dojo. He remarried and helps with his wife's *minyo odori* (folk dance) classes and performance.

Ben Wakaye (January 2, 1913–November 8, 1952) was an insurance salesman before the Evacuation. The draft classified him 4-F for health reasons. He joined the FPC because he wanted his convictions known. After his release from Leavenworth, he returned to San Francisco to live with his sister and maternal grandmother. He worked assisting his father with carpentry and then as a janitor. After a month in Stanford hospital, he died of kidney failure.

Minoru Tamesa (1906–1964) returned to Seattle and continued to fight for the Fair Play Committee, to get the Supreme Court to reverse the verdict of the lower court. A presidential pardon was one thing, but a reversal was the prize he sought. He died on April 11, 1964, of leukemia.

Guntaro Kubota (August 16, 1903–May 13, 1967). Grace Kubota Ybarra: "My father went to Leavenworth. He was there for sixteen months. He came back, and we were still out in Wyoming, and out of camps by then. We waited for him to come back. One of the very, very first things he and I did together was go to a movie. I'll never forget it. *Harvey Girls*–That's the movie. That had the song 'The Atchison Topeka and the Santa Fe.' And I remember that was most wonderful moment I ever spent. He came back and he was a very serious diabetic. And so he spent a lot of his time in the prison hospital. And one of the real delightful stories he tells us is he was a black belt in judo. And the fellow in the next bed was Mr. Pendergast." Boss Tom Pendergast was well known in Missouri for fixing elections for Democratic candidates. "My dad said, I will never forget this, 'When President Roosevelt died [and Truman assumed the presidency], Pendergast came up to me and he said, 'Kubota, I'll be leaving here in a few days.' My dad ignored that. He didn't really believe him. You know, he said, 'A few days later I saw a black limousine come with a younger woman and an older woman and they were both dressed in mink.' This is fantastic for us, you know. And he said Mr. Pendergast offered him, because my dad had instructed him in judo, invited him to come to Kansas City to be one of his heavies." He took the contractor's license test and became a landscape contractor. He drank and smoked, and he was diabetic. His good humor stayed with him as he had one leg amputated, and then the other, due to his diabetes.

James Omura (1912–1994). His acquittal of all charges was seen as a victory for freedom of the press. But the victory was bittersweet. The Japanese American press was closed to him. And Japanese society shunned him. He returned to writing for the *Rocky Shimpo* briefly, in 1947, but while his fire against the JACL blazed, it was out among the Japanese Americans. He went into landscape gardening, where he achieved great success in a specialized world not known to most people. He reemerged in Seattle at the hearings of the 1981 Bernstein Commission on the Wartime Relocation and Internment of Civilians. He took to researching the camps and the JACL for an autobiography. He died before he could finish it.

Index

Abe, Niro, 406, 411, 413
Abiko, Yas, 180
Adamic, Louis, 182
Advent, John, 468
Akutsu, Hajiime "Jim," 389–90,
    428–32, 472–73, 490
Akutsu (mother), 473
Allvine, Earl, 302
Anderson, M. O., 403–5
Anno (athlete), 117
Aoki, Helen, 178
Arnold, Edward, 176
Arnold (investigator), 277–78
Asther, Nils, 119

Baldwin, Roger N., 423–24
Barber, Philip W., 336
Barker, Reginald, 15
Barnett, Art, 325–26
Barrow, George, 37
Beck, Dave, 325
Bender (investigator), 277, 280–81
Bendetsen, Karl Robin, 219–21, 240–41
Benkei (samurai), 25–26
Biddle, Frank, 205
Biscailluz, Eugene, 186
Bishop, Walter, 302

Black, Lloyd L., 326
Blair, George R., 321
Blood, Henry H., 187
Borah (senator), 272
Bowron (mayor), 280
Bratton (justice), 470
Briggs, Mary, 252
Bryan, Alfred, 46
Burton, Blaney J., 321

Caddigan, Jack, 108
Cagney, Jimmy, 474–75
Campbell, M. L., 406–7
Capra, Frank, 119, 222
Carey, Harry, 209
Carpenter (FBI agent), 284
Carr, William C., 248, 250
Chin, Brian B., 196–98
Chino, Franklin, 183, 187
Costello, John M., 233
Courtney, Alan, 302
Cowles, Gardener, 486
Crane, W. E., 119
Crawford, Claude, 186

Davis, Clyde Brion, 129–30
DeMille, Cecil B., 15

DeWitt, John L., 197–98, 220, 244, 343, 358, 429
Dillinger, John, 261
Dizeman, John, 325
Donovan, William Joseph, 375
Drake, Charles, 209
Du Bois, W. E. B., 236–38

Eaton, Edith, 18
Eaton, Winifred, 17–18
Edward VIII, king of Great Britain, 215
Egan, Larson, 214–15
Egan, Raymond B., 98
Egan (sheriff), 214
Eisenhower, Milton, 226–30, 264
Emerson, Faye, 209
Emi, Arthur, 163–65, 168, 170–71, 361, 450, 492
Emi, Frank Seishi, 72–74, 163–66, 168–71, 203, 358–64, 378–79, 383–84, 402, 405–22, 428–32, 434, 446–48, 450–51, 456–58, 460, 466–68, 470, 480, 492–93
Emi, Hisako Alice, 72, 74, 95, 164–65
Emi, Kaoru, 72–74, 163–65, 169, 435
Emi, Tsune, 163–66, 168–69
Ennis, Edward, 384
Ernst, Charles F., 385

Farquharson, Mary, 335
Fee, James A., 300, 333–34
Fischer, Fred, 33
Fisher, Ann, 157
Fisher, Galen, 303
Fisher, Ham, 257–58
Folland, William H., 187
Ford, John, 375
Freund, Karl, 374
Fujii, John, 128
Fujioka, Shiro, 151
Fujita, Toyo, 15–16
Furiya, George, 183
Furuichi, Toshiko, 491
Furutani, Brownie, 118, 128

Garfield, John, 209
Gens, Jacob, 233

Gibson, Ed, 36–37
Gibson, Matilda, 36
Gillette, Guy, 184
Goldwyn, Sam, 375
Goodman, Louis A., 480
Gorman, E. C., 406
Griffin, Robert O., 336

Hada, Sue, 334
Hagiwara, Michael, 334
Harvison, John, 248–49
Hata, Hisao, 178, 186
Hauff, Wilhelm, 37–39
Hawks, Howard, 209, 376–77
Hayakawa, Sessue, 14–16, 109–10, 119
Heath, Walter A., 386
Heidt, Horace, 152
Himes, Chester, 309
Hirabayashi, Gordon, 76–83, 96, 134, 154–62, 225, 271–76, 324–31, 335, 383, 425–26, 445, 490
Hirabayashi, James, 76–77, 80–83, 134, 155–56, 271–72, 276
Hirabayashi, Paul, 154
Hirabayashi, Rhoda, 160–61, 273
Hirakawa, Joe, 135
Hirano, Bob, 178
Hoover, Herbert, 263
Horino, Isamo "Sam," 379, 403, 450, 466
Horn, Donald T., 406–9, 413
Horn, Tom, 403
Hoshi, Stas, 134
Hoshide, Harry, 128
Hoshizaki, Tak, 490–91
Hosoi, Yoshiko, 344
Hosokawa, William "Bill," 53, 109, 242, 257–58, 269–70, 294–95, 361, 486–87
Howe, James Wong, 209, 374–77, 474–78

Ikemoto, Harry, 466
Iki, Bob, 180
Imai, Blossom, 109–10
Imai, Frances, 109–10
Imura, Haruo, 128, 487
Inada, Lawson, 218, 244, 247

Inagaki, George, 229–30, 240, 248, 303
Ince, Thomas, 15
Ino, Toru, 466–67
Inouye, Frank, 358–64
Iriye, Fred, 471
Irwin, Wallace, 68–69
Ishida, Dixie, 187
Ishida, Teiko, 303–4
Ishikawa, Jack, 436
Ishimaru, T. G., 251, 322–23
Ito, Chuzaburo, 86
Ito, Kenji, 292
Ito, Tokogoro, 109

Jacobs, Sidney S., 451
James, Burton, Mr. & Mrs., 132, 135
Jeffra, Harry, 185
Jenkins, Ab, 187
Jung, Alan, 120

Kado, James, 436
Kahn, Gus, 75
Kanai, Lincoln, 243, 245
Kanazawa, Tomiko, 183
Katsu, Fumi, 180
Katsuno, Peter, 155
Kaufman, J. J., 149
Kawai, Aki, 253
Kawai, Harry, 253
Kawai, Hiro, 253
Kawai, Miye, 54–57, 151–53, 239–41,
    247, 313, 453
Kawai, Nobu, 53–60, 151–53, 239–41,
    247–50, 253–54, 304–6, 312–13,
    323, 365–66, 378, 406, 411–12,
    415–22, 434–35, 453–54, 487–88
Kawai, Toichiro, 54–55
Kawakami, Iwao, 105–6, 125, 128
Kawamoto, Dave, 213, 379, 456, 491
Kawasaki (prisoner), 466
Kaye, Sammy, 208
Kellogg, John H., 406, 410
Kennedy, Arthur, 209
Kennedy, T. Blake, 445, 465
Kido, Saburo, 107, 188, 240, 248, 284,
    304–5, 322, 395, 423, 428
Kido, Saburo, Mrs., 185

Kimberly (colonel), 186
King, MacKenzie, 186
King, William H., 187
Kinomoto, Frank, 334
Kirby, Edward J., 321–22
Kitano, Mary, 179
Koga, Dixie, 128
Koga, Tats, 303
Koike, Hizi, 133
Kondo, Carl, 177
Kono, Bill, 119–20
Koshiyama, Howard, 401
Koshiyama, Mits, 401, 444, 491–92
Kubota, Gloria, 214–15, 387, 398–99, 449
Kubota, Gordon, 398, 449
Kubota, Grace. See Ybarra, Grace Kubota
Kubota, Guntaro, 214–15, 383–84,
    398–99, 450, 466, 468, 470, 493
Kurata, Ruth, 127, 179
Kurihara, Joe, 343–48
Kuroki, Ben, 206, 212, 370–71, 400,
    433–35, 452, 465, 468, 488
Kuroki, Cecile, 187
Kuromiya, Yosh, 299, 439, 443, 492
Kyne, Peter B., 84–85, 121

Lang, Fritz, 477
Lange, Arthur, 46
Lean, David, 16
Lehmkuhl, Jack, 197–98
Lewis (general), 259–60
Lida, Lillian, 183
Lindley, James G., 386
Ling, David M., 479
Lortel, Lucille, 109
Lovett, Robert A., 481

Maeda, Milton, 334
Markus, Aron, 248
Masaoka, Joe Grant, 202, 322, 438–39,
    472–73
Masaoka, Mike Masaru, 183, 186–88, 206,
    219–41, 243–44, 246, 248, 303–4,
    321–23, 359–60, 438, 477, 486
Masatomi, Emile, 93
Masuda, Tom, 292
Matsuda, Chiyoko, 183

Matsui, Ryozo "Rose," 336
Matsumoto, Ichiro "Ike," 204, 297–98, 440, 492
Matsumoto, Ken, 186, 229–30, 240
Matsumoto, Teruo "Tayzo," 492
Matsumura (donor), 304
Matsuyama (police trainer), 284
Matthews, J. B., 234
Maw, Herbert B., 187, 222, 400
Maxwell, Dora, 303
McCarthy, Joe, 33
McDaniels (lieutenant), 362
Mechau, Vaughn, 361
Menin, Samuel D., 443–45
Merriman, Lee, 59, 248
Merritt, Ralph, 310, 314–15
Mifune, Toshiro, 8
Miller, Glenn, 302
Miller (doctor), 162
Milliken, Dr. & Mrs., 249
Minamato no Yoshitsune, 25–26
Minami, Sam, 277
Mittwer, Frederick, Mrs., 177
Miyake, Harry, 305, 312
Momotaro, 61–62
Mori, Toshia, 119–20
Mori, Toshio, 182, 190–92
Morimoto, Lucille, 177
Morrisey, Thomas, 424
Mubi, Maresuke, 337
Mukaeda, Katsuma, 120
Mundt (investigator), 234
Murase, Kenny, 177–80, 183
Murphy, Yuji, 30, 92
Musser, Burton W., Mrs., 187
Myer, Dillon S., 303, 323, 385, 429, 486–87

Naganori, Asano, 10
Nakadate, Paul Takeo, 363–64, 384, 403–6, 415, 450, 466, 492
Nakaji, Y., 186
Nakamoto, George, 118, 127
Nakamura, Nisaidayu, 133
Nakamura, Toshiro, 93
Nakamura, Tura, 133

Nakashima, G., 304
Namura, Gongoro, 120
Nelson, Bat, 185
Nelson, Douglas, 472–73
Nichols, Dudley, 209
Nishimoto, Jack, 456–58
Nishitani, Misao Marietta Sadie, 110
Nogi, Maresuke, 47–49
Noguchi, Ayako, 179–80
Noguchi, Isamu, 243
Nunome, Kanjii, 187

O'Brien, Bob, 303
Okada, Hito, 240, 248, 303, 305, 322
Okada, John, 95, 472, 490
Okamoto, Kiyoshi, 364, 378–79, 391, 403, 423–24, 427, 450, 466, 474–75, 492
Okazakai, Bob, 177
Oki, Tom, 174–75, 199–201, 492
Okuda, Ken, 272
Okuma, Caryl F., 217
Okuma, Fumi, 176
Oland, Warner, 109
Oliver, Clarence Edward, 334
Oliver, Nellie Grace, 169
Omura, James, 11–12, 63–67, 95, 103–4, 115–16, 118–21, 124–28, 131, 135, 176, 184–85, 192, 216–18, 223, 232, 242–45, 277, 283–85, 385–86, 391–93, 424, 426, 441–42, 451, 460–63, 466, 494
Osato, Sono, 183
Otani, Curtis, 128
Ottennelmer, Albert, 132
Oyama, Joe, 177
Oyama, Molly, 177

Palmer, William Fleet, 252
Pendergast, Tom, 493
Perry (commodore), 27–28
Pirosh, Robert, 477
Pomeroy, Allen, 425

Rachford, Christopher E., 300, 336
Raymond, Harry, 75
Reagan, Ronald, 486

Reid, Don, 208
Rice, Eugene, 460, 470
Ridgely, John, 209
Ring, Eleanor, 273, 276
Ringle, K. D., 186, 255–56, 278
Roberts, Olive, 89–90
Robertson, Guy, 336, 361, 403–14
Roosevelt, Franklin Delano, 207, 272, 286, 493
Rundquist, George E., 303

Sackett, Carl, 445
Sakaguchi, Chico, 179
Sakai, Kozie, 214, 446–48
Sakamoto, James Y., 94, 109–10, 112–13, 115–16, 134, 150, 172, 185, 240, 259, 277, 293, 488
Sampson, Lloyd C., 451
Sandoz (director), 335
Sano, Lillian, 187
Saroyan, William, 180, 189
Sasaki, Shosuke, 5–10, 34–37, 50–52, 95, 288–93, 489–90
Sasaki (athlete), 117
Satow, Mas, 240
Schary, Dore, 477
Schmoe, Esther, 273, 426
Schmoe, Floyd W., 273, 316–17, 335, 425–26
Schonher, John, 198
Shimano, Eddie, 180
Shinoda, Joseph, 277–78
Shiozaki, Ronald Isamu, 334
Shiroma, Joho, 128
Slocum, Tokie, 277–78, 280–81, 283
Smith, Ben, 271
Smith, Elmer R., 400
Smith, Frank Herron, 231
Sone, Monica, 95
Sparkman (investigator), 231
Spivak, John L., 137–39
Stafford, Harry L., 335
Stanley (lieutenant commander), 278
Stanwyck, Barbara, 119
Stimson, Henry, 220
Stockton, Edward A., 195, 198

Story, Chick, 108
Stratton-Porter, Gene, 121–24
Sugahara, Kay, 200
Suiyama, Franklyn, 127
Sumida (composer), 436–37
Suski, Louise, 118, 282
Sutton, judge, 265
Suyemoto, Toyo, 181, 184
Suzuki, George, 183

Tajiri, Lawrence "Larry," 118–20, 125, 127–28, 240, 243–45, 248, 295–96, 303, 308, 321, 393–94, 477, 486
Tajiri, Vince, 180
Tajitsu, Kazuko, 183
Takada, Ichitaro, 92
Takahashi, Johnny, 169
Takaike, Nobe, 288
Takata, Ichitaro, 93
Takatsui, Kentaro, 21, 24–32, 40–41, 44–45, 47–48, 337–42, 490
Takeda, Bean, 178
Takeno, Roy, 178
Takeuchi, Dick, 127
Takeuchi, Richard Chihiro, 334
Takeuchi, Seiran, 93
Takigawa, George, 334
Tamesa, Kay, 88–91
Tamesa, Kimio, 92
Tamesa, Minoru, 402, 406, 412–14, 450, 466, 493
Tamesa, Uhachi, 86–92, 96–97, 490
Tanaka, Hitoshi, 185
Tanaka, Togo, 178, 183, 186, 188, 202, 277
Tani, George, 322, 334
Tashiro, Art, 177
Tashiro, Ken, 118, 304–5
Tateoka, Florence, 334
Tayama, Fred, 240, 251–52, 277, 310, 323, 344
Tennyson, Alfred, 71
Terazawa (salesman), 157
Thomas, Clayton, 13
Thomas, Dorothy Swaine, 344

Thomas, Elbert D., 187–88, 222
Thoreau, Henry David, 22–23, 338
Throckmorton, Robert, 310–11
Timberlake, Edward J., 370, 468
Tobias, George, 209
Toda, Tetsuko, 442
Todd, Douglas M., 336
Togasaki, Susamu, 322–23
Togo (admiral), 47–48, 93
Toguri, Iva, 489
Tolan, John, 12, 230, 232
Tono, Jack, 471
Toribara, Frank, 334
Townsend, George, 261–68, 335
Townsend, Lemond, 262
Truman, Harry S, 481
Tsuchiya, Scotty, 303
Tsuchiya, Tak, 158–59
Tsukamoto, Jiro, 259–60
Tsukamoto, Walter T., 172
Tsuneishi, Paul, 49, 71, 150, 169, 174,
    201, 381
Tsuneishi, Shisei, 70, 380–81
Tsuneishi, Warren, 178

Uchimura, Kanzo, 76–77
Ueno, Harry, 310–11, 341
Undset, Sigrid, 420
Ushiwakamaru, 25–26
Uyeda, Clifford, 49, 136, 150, 173,
    372–73, 489

Voorhees, Charles B., 249
Voorhees, Jerry, 249

Wada, Yori, 180
Wakaye, Ben, 379, 405–6, 450, 466, 493

Wallis, Hal B., 209
Walters, Frank, 325–26
Wampus, George, 119
Watanabe, Hide, 169
Watanna, Onoto, 17–18
Watts, Clyde M., 445
Weicher, Theodor, 4
Welles, Orson, 153
Wells, Jack, 46
Whiting, Richard A., 98
Williams, Frederick Vincent, 186
Wirin, Abraham Lincoln, 451, 459–60,
    465–66, 471, 479
Wirin, Al, 303
Wolf, Edgar Allan, 109
Wong, Anna May, 109, 119
Wood (colonel), 263–65

Yamakido, Joe Asa, 480
Yamamoto, Hisaye, 179
Yamamoto, Toshi, 266
Yamasaki, Tomomasa, 178–79
Yanagisaki (composer), 436–37
Yanai, Lily, 179
Yasuda, Harry, 128, 176
Yasui, Minoru, 225, 300–301, 322, 327,
    333–34, 367, 389, 438–39, 441, 445,
    467, 488–89
Ybarra, Grace Kubota, 214–15, 398,
    468, 493
Yeto, Genjiro, 17
Yonemura, Hitoshi, 183
Yoshida, Harry, 457
Yoshida, Masao, 183
Young, Gig, 209
Young Togo, 184–85
Yuranosuke, Oishi, 8–10

About the Author

Frank Chin was born in California in 1940, to a Chinese immigrant father and a fourth-generation Chinatown mother. He received his BA in English, from the University of California at Santa Barbara, in February of 1966. He is the author of two plays, *The Chickencoop Chinaman* (1972) and *The Year of the Dragon* (1974). He is also the author of a collection of short fiction, *The Chinaman Pacific and Frisco R.R. Co.* (1988); two novels, *Donald Duk* (1991) and *Gunga Din Highway* (1994); and a book of essays, *Bulletproof Buddhists* (1998). He wrote the critical essays in and coedited two studies of Asian American writing with Jeffrey Chan, Lawson Inada, and Shawn Wong: *Aiieeeee! An Anthology of Asian American Writers* (1974) and *The Big Aiieeeee! An Anthology of Chinese American and Japanese American Literature* (1991).